AUSTRALIAN RELIGIOUS THOUGHT

AUSTRALIAN RELIGIOUS THOUGHT

WAYNE HUDSON

© Copyright 2016 Wayne Hudson
All rights reserved. Apart from any uses permitted by Australia's Copyright Act 1968, no part of this book may be reproduced by any process without prior written permission from the copyright owners. Inquiries should be directed to the publisher.

Monash University Publishing
Matheson Library and Information Services Building
40 Exhibition Walk
Monash University
Clayton, Victoria 3800, Australia
www.publishing.monash.edu

Monash University Publishing brings to the world publications which advance the best traditions of humane and enlightened thought.

Monash University Publishing titles pass through a rigorous process of independent peer review.

www.publishing.monash.edu/books/art-9781922235763.html

Series: Monash Studies in Australian Society

Design: Les Thomas

Cover image: Arthur Boyd. *The mining town (Casting the money lenders from the temple)* c.1946
Oil and tempera on composition board
87.4 x 109.4 cm
National Gallery of Australia, Canberra
Purchased 1974
Reproduced with permission of Bundanon Trust

National Library of Australia Cataloguing-in-Publication entry

Creator:	Hudson, Wayne, author.
Title:	Australian religious thought / Wayne Hudson.
ISBN:	9781922235763 (paperback)
Subjects:	Religious thought--Australia.
	Theology--Australia--History.
Dewey Number:	210.1

Printed in Australia by Griffin Press an Accredited ISO AS/NZS 14001:2004 Environmental Management System printer.

The paper this book is printed on is certified against the Forest Stewardship Council ® Standards. Griffin Press holds FSC chain of custody certification SGS-COC-005088. FSC promotes environmentally responsible, socially beneficial and economically viable management of the world's forests.

CONTENTS

Acknowledgements vii
Preface viii
Introduction ix

Chapter I
Shapes of Disbelief 1

Chapter II
Sacral Secularity 61

Chapter III
Religious Liberalism 93

Chapter IV
Religious Thought and Philosophy 132

Chapter V
Theology in Development 170

Chapter VI
Postsecular Consciousness 197

Conclusion: Refiguring the National Imaginary 235
Index 239

For Charles and Raphael

ACKNOWLEDGEMENTS

I wish to thank the Australian Research Council for supporting early research in this field and the Australian Centre for Christianity and Culture, Charles Sturt University, Canberra, for providing me with ideal research facilities. I am also indebted to Ross Chambers for his invaluable assistance over many years. Some of the issues raised in this volume go back to inspiration I received at the University of Sydney from the late Crawford Miller. I would also like to acknowledge the generous support given to me at a crucial stage of my career by Ian O'Connor, the Vice Chancellor of Griffith University. My gratitude goes to Richard Ely for his detailed critical comments and to my research assistants, Robin Trotter and Eilidh St. John. I have also benefited from the help of Alan Atkinson, Frank Bongiorno, James Charlton, Scott Cowdell, James Franklin, Regina Ganter, John Gascoigne, Michael Gladwin, James Haire, Ian Hunter, Thorwald Lorenzen, Ann McGrath, Stuart Macintyre, Gregory Melleuish, Jill Roe and Ray Williamson, who read draft text. My grateful thanks to the librarians at the National Library of Australia and to the editorial staff at Monash University Publishing, Rachel Salmond and Joanne Mullins. Above all, I wish to thank Catherine Hudson for her judicious suggestions.

PREFACE

This volume has its genesis in research I have pursued in British intellectual history and German philosophy, much of it focusing on the interfaces between religion, heterodoxy, and social reform. My early work was on the German Jewish philosopher Ernst Bloch. Later I contributed to debates about utopianism, republicanism, civil society and citizenship. Recently I have written extensively about deism and atheism in the English Enlightenment. In the early 2000s when I was working on the concept of religious citizenship I became aware that religious thought was not a major theme in Australian history. Before long I was collecting material of many different kinds and sensing that I might have the beginnings of a book. Initial reactions, however, were not all favourable, and some historians were reluctant to concede that there was significant religious thought in Australia. When I first mentioned the book to a publisher, the amused reply was that such a book would be a short one. I soon realised, however, that it would be impossible to write a one-volume survey of Australian religious thought, so I decided to concentrate on specific themes in Australian intellectual history rather than to write a social history of ideas dealing with religious thought more generally.

As the work took shape, I received substantial help from readers of early drafts. Their questions forced me to rethink my concepts and to recognise the many things that I could not hope to cover, such as Christian writings designed for church-going publics. My colleague Stuart Macintyre posed the most challenging question; he wanted me to make better sense of how the patterns in Australia compared with those in other settler societies. I am not sure that I have been able to address his question in the way it deserves. Nevertheless, I have, I hope, brought together a substantial body of research and interpreted some of it in innovative ways.

INTRODUCTION

No-one denies that there was religious thought in Australia. Nonetheless, the weight of historical opinion has probably inclined to the view that Australian religious thought was not of great importance. This volume seeks to qualify this verdict. It shows that there has been more religious thought than most historians have assumed – in terms of quantity and range, and in terms of substance and significance. That this fact has been little noted has to do with divisions that have shaped our history.

Religion in Australian History

No adequate account of European settlement in Australia can ignore the role of religion in shaping Australian attitudes and institutions.[1] Religion cannot be said to have determined the main features of Australian life, but without it the history of the nation would have been different.[2] Moreover, the older tendency to discuss religion as a sub-category, of interest only to minorities, is misleading. Religion was involved in the formation and workings of major national institutions. It was also of relevance to large numbers of Australians who were not particularly or conventionally religious. There was no strongly entrenched separation of church and state in Australia,[3] as is clear from the use of religious oaths, services for the legal profession and regular prayers before sessions of parliament. In early New South Wales the Church of England was part of the civil administration; in 1825 the leading Anglican clergyman was given a position in the Legislative Council and the Executive Council second only to the Governor.[4]

As Richard Ely rightly insists, transportation itself had its religio-moral economy, realised in, for example, Governor Arthur's mixture of Benthamite

---

1   A. Atkinson, "Reinventing Religion in Nineteenth Century Australia" (unpublished manuscript, paper given to the Heretics, 11 October 2007), 1, referred to in D. Stoneman, "The Church Act: The Expansion of Christianity or the Imposition of Moral Enlightenment" (PhD diss., University of New England, 2012), 6.
2   See J. D. Bollen, *Protestantism and Social Reform in New South Wales 1890–1910* (Melbourne: Melbourne University Press, 1928), 1.
3   M. Maddox, *God under Howard: The Rise of the Religious Right in Australian Politics* (Sydney: Allen and Unwin, 2005).
4   B. Fletcher, "The Anglican Ascendancy, 1788–1835," in *Anglicanism in Australia: A History*, ed. B. Kaye et al. (Carlton: Melbourne University Press, 2002), 7–20 and R. Border, *Church and State in Australia 1788–1872: A Constitutional Study of the Church of England in Australia* (London: S.P.C.K, 1962).

penology and evangelical reformism in Tasmania.⁵ The civil role of the Church of England in the early colony was substantial and, when allied to elements of enlightenment and common law, contributed to the formation of major institutions and voluntary organisations.⁶ Evangelical Christianity was an influence on New South Wales' fifth governor, Lachlan Macquarie, having been an element of the culture of New South Wales from the presence of the first chaplain of the prison colony, Richard Johnson (ca 1756–1827). Protestant Christianity influenced conceptions of economics and property⁷ and churchmen played a significant part in public life in colonial Australia.⁸

Nor was the importance of religion confined to the servants of empire. By 1820 Catholic priests in New South Wales were paid by the government and, in 1834, allowance was made for the role of a Catholic Bishop, sixteen years before the Catholic hierarchy was acknowledged in England. Governor Bourke's Church Act of 1836 gave equal official recognition to the Anglican, Catholic, Presbyterian and Wesleyan Methodist churches and provided grants for the establishment of church buildings and for stipends for clergy of all four denominations.⁹ A Protestant version of Christian culture shaped many

---

5   R. Ely, "Pains and Penalties: The Religio-Moral Economy of Transportation to New South Wales and Van Diemen's Land," in *Re-Visioning Australian Colonial Christianity: New Essays in the Australian Christian Experience, 1788–1900*, ed. M. Hutchinson and E. Campion (Sydney: Centre for the Study of Australian Christianity, 1994), ch. 3; A. G. L. Shaw, *Sir George Arthur, Bart, 1784–1854: Superintendent of British Honduras, Lieutenant-Governor of Van Diemen's Land and of Upper Canada, Governor of Bombay Presidency* (Carlton, Vic.: Melbourne University Press, 1980).

6   Early Anglicanism in Australia took the form of church establishment. The first bishop, William Broughton (1788–1853), a Caroline churchman who later developed Tractarian sympathies, emphasised that church and state were mutually dependent. Nonetheless, the Anglican ascendancy in New South Wales came to an end when the Church Act of 1836 gave financial assistance to denominations equally. Despite this, the Anglican Christian Social Union was claiming as late as 1898 that Christian law had the ultimate right to rule social practice in Australia; see Bollen, *Protestantism and Social Reform in New South Wales 1890–1910*, 89, and Fletcher, "The Anglican Ascendancy, 1788–1835".

7   M. Lake, "'Such Spiritual Acres': Protestantism, the Land and the Colonisation of Australia, 1788–1850" (PhD diss., University of Sydney, 2008); A. O'Brien, "Religion," in T*he Cambridge History of Australia, Vol. 1 Indigenous and Colonial Australia*, ed. A. Bashford and S. Macintyre (Melbourne: Cambridge University Press, 2013), ch. 17.

8   See M. Gladwin, *Anglican Clergy in Australia, 1788–1850: Building a British World* (London: Royal Historical Society, 2015).

9   P. Curthoys, "State Support for Churches 1836–1860," in *Anglicanism in Australia: A History*, ch. 2; see also the discussion in Chapter II of this book and J. Woolmington (ed.), *Religion in Early Australia: The Problem of Church and State* (Stanmore, NSW: Cassell Australia, 1976).

INTRODUCTION

aspects of civil order in the Australian colonies until at least the 1860s.[10] Christians were notably active in politics and in women's organisations, such as the Women's Suffrage League, the Women's Christian Temperance Union and the Young Women's Christian Association. Primitive Methodists and Bible Christians were leading advocates of social reform towards the end of the nineteenth century, providing many of the founding members of the first Parliamentary Labor Party,[11] while nonconformists contributed to the establishment of civil liberties in South Australia. Presbyterians and Congregationalists also accepted a Christian duty to improve society and took part in education and political life.[12]

Likewise, there was a long-standing relationship between the Catholic Church and the Australian labour movement.[13] Catholic conceptions of natural law had an influence on the Australian approach to industrial relations.[14] Religion also played a major role in conservative politics, and most conservative Prime Ministers were Protestants. Moreover, despite suggestions that religion does not figure prominently in Australian life, in the early twenty-first century two religious political parties, the Democratic Labor Party and the Family First Party, are represented in the Australian federal

---

10   G. P. Shaw, "'Beyond Discipline?' The Historical Context of Theological Thought in Australia," *St Mark's Review* 133 (1988): 14–20 and "Judaeo-Christianity and the Mid-Nineteenth Century Colonial Civil Order," in *Re-Visioning Australian Colonial Christianity*, 29–39; Kaye et al., *Anglicanism in Australia*.

11   R. D. Linder, "The Methodist Love Affair with the Australian Labor Party, 1891–1929," *Lucas* 23/24 (1998): 35–61; P. O'Farrell, "The History of the New South Wales Labour Movement 1880–1910: A Religious Interpretation," *Journal of Religious History* 2 (1962): 133–51.

12   For Presbyterians, see M. D. Prentis, "The Presbyterian Ministry in Australia 1822–1900: Recruitment and Composition," *Journal of Religious History* 13 (1984): 46–55, and *The Scots in Australia* (Sydney: UNSW Press, 2008); R. S. Ward, *The Bush Still Burns: The Presbyterian and Reformed Faith in Australia, 1788–1988* (Wantirna, Vic.: R. S. Ward, 1989); M. Wood, *Presbyterians in Colonial Victoria* (North Melbourne: Australian Scholarly Publishing, 2008); M. Hutchinson, *Iron in Our Blood: A History of the Presbyterian Church in NSW, 1788–2001* (Sydney: Ferguson Publications, 2001). For Methodists, see D. Wright and E. Clancy, *The Methodists: A History of Methodism in New South Wales* (Sydney: Allen and Unwin, 1993). For Congregationalists, see G. Lindsay Lockley, *Congregationalism in Australia*, ed. Bruce Upham (Melbourne: Uniting Church Press, 2001) and G. Nadel, *Australia's Colonial Culture: Ideas, Men and Institutions in Mid-Nineteenth Century Eastern Australia* (Melbourne: F. W. Cheshire, 1957), 250–2.

13   M. Hogan, *The Sectarian Strand: Religion in Australian History* (Ringwood: Penguin Books, 1987), 170–205; J. Brett, "The Sectarian Foundations of Australian Liberalism," *The Sydney Papers* 14, no. 3 (2002): 160, 168–75; R. Rivett, *Australian Citizen Herbert Brookes 1867–1963* (Carlton, Vic.: Melbourne University Press, 1965).

14   M. Hogan, *Australian Catholics: The Australian Social Justice Tradition* (Melbourne: Collins Dove, 1993).

parliament, as are smaller parties in state governments. The religious right plays a significant role through parliamentary groups such as the Lyons Forum and the Australian Christian Lobby.

Nor is it accurate to depict Australians as indifferent to religious concerns. Aboriginal people in Australia have remained focused on the sacred, and religion was crucial to European social identity in nineteenth-century Australia, even if there was sometimes a certain reserve about public declaration of personal religious belief in a society in which beliefs were often not exchanged across religious boundaries in social contexts.[15] Most nineteenth-century Australians understood Christianity in terms coloured by the ethnic derivation (English, Scots, Irish, Welsh, Italian, German). Moreover, a considerable public, at least in the major cities, had an interest in nineteenth-century religious controversies.[16] Religious questions were extensively covered by the colonial press and sermons were a significant part of the literature of the colonies.[17] Despite their distance from Europe, Australians had access to a surprising range of sources through the mechanics institutes and schools of arts, church book societies, lending libraries and literary societies, the Workers' Educational Association, communist and anarchist bookshops, and various spiritualist and theosophical outlets.

It is also important not to accept, without question, the notion of an irreverent national temper. Those who questioned religion often only did so in limited domains and frequently conformed to religious customs at weddings and funerals. Likewise, those who questioned religion were not necessarily outside it or free of religious concerns. Granted that there is some empirical basis for the references to laconic speech and sardonic irony, there was considerable diversity in practice. As Stuart Piggin argues,[18]

---

15 For the Australian tendency to avoid public profession of belief in secular contexts, see W. Hudson, "Cultural Undergrounds and Civic Identity," in *Creating Australia: Changing Australian History*, ed. W. Hudson and G. Bolton (Sydney: Allen and Unwin, 1997), ch. 17. For the overlap between Anglicanism and common law involving the appointment of clergy as magistrates, see A. Sharp, "Samuel Marsden's Civility: The Transposition of Anglican Civil Authority to Australasia," in *Law and Politics in British Colonial Thought: Transpositions of Empire*, ed. S. Dorsett and I. Hunter (New York: Palgrave Macmillan, 2010), 129–48.

16 W. Philips, *Defending 'A Christian Country': Churchmen and Society in New South Wales in the 1880s and After* (St. Lucia: University of Queensland Press, 1981).

17 K. Inglis, "Speechmaking in Australian History" (Allan Martin Lecture, presented at ANU, Canberra, 2007), and *St Mark's Review* 230 (2014).

18 S. Piggin, *Spirit of a Nation: The Story of Australia's Christian Heritage* (Sydney: Strand Publishing, 2004). Piggin draws attention to the presence of both pan-Anglican and pan-evangelical tendencies within Australian Anglicanism. His work is an important correction to the older historiography.

accounts of nineteenth-century Australia as a godless society are overstated, and evangelical Christianity decisively shaped the nation, its values and institutions, although it did so in interaction with other Christian, social utilitarian and secularist tendencies. Similarly, those who assert that religion leaves few traces in the lives of Australians do not adequately register Catholic, Mormon, Jewish or Muslim male experience, just as large numbers of women have been religious for much of our history.[19] The extent of Australian sectarianism also undermines the idea that Australians did not take religion seriously; sectarianism arguably intensified following the publication of the papal *Ne Temere* decree of 1908, which declared marriages performed by Protestant ministers or civil celebrants invalid,[20] and again after the Catholic rejection of conscription in 1916.

Religion then was a basic element in Australian society, even if sometimes carried lightly. Thousands of churches were built and tens of thousands of men and women gave their lives to religious concerns, often at personal cost, not only in cities but also in country towns. In the same way, it is important to qualify any dualism between religion and Enlightenment. The Enlightenment had a crucial role in shaping the nature of colonial science and the widespread belief in the possibility and desirability of improvement, as John Gascoigne has argued.[21] However, for many Australian colonists Enlightenment was part of religion, and true religion was understood as a means to Enlightenment, with the result that Christian attitudes and Enlightenment projects were often intertwined.

To be fair, it is true that the diversity of Australian Protestantism has sometimes made it difficult to appreciate the range and depth of Christian contributions to the national life. There were four groups of Methodists; the Presbyterians were divided between those who followed the Church of Scotland and those who turned to one of the Scottish free churches; and the Baptists were divided in the nineteenth century between those who followed the evangelical preacher Charles Spurgeon in England in rejecting historical criticism and religious liberalism and those who were committed

---

19 A. O'Brien, *God's Willing Workers: Women and Religion in Australia* (Sydney: UNSW Press, 2005).
20 See P. Ayres, *Prince of the Church: Patrick Francis Moran, 1830–1911* (Carlton, Vic.: Miegunyah Press, 2007), 251–2.
21 J. Gascoigne, with P. Curthoys, *The Enlightenment and the Origins of European Australia* (Port Melbourne: Cambridge University Press, 2002), 39, and J. Gascoigne, "Introduction: Religion and Empire, An Historiographical Perspective", *Journal of Religious History* 32 (2008): 159–78.

to union without creed.²² The connection between religion and social reform has not, of course, gone unnoticed. Catholic historians have chronicled the struggles of the Irish in Australia.²³ The whole issue of Protestantism and the state has been revisited many times, and Anglican relations with the state are also much studied. Social engagements by conservative, moderate and radical Christians are well documented. Christians were behind many reform movements in the nineteenth century; W. H. Gresham of the Land Tenure Reform league was not alone in characterising his concerns as 'applied Christianity'. Christians of many varieties worked for Aboriginal welfare, whether Catholics and Anglo-Catholics in Western Australia, South Australian Lutherans or Tasmanian Evangelicals.²⁴ Protestants often combined religious individualism and support for capitalism with social innovations to build up the Kingdom of God, including schools, improving societies of all kinds, banks, libraries and homes for the blind and the aged.²⁵

It is also important to remember that until 1960 Australia was a nominally Christian country, with as many as forty per cent of the population affiliated with the Church of England. The establishment of the colonies in the eighteenth and nineteenth centuries and their Federation in 1901 were often seen in providential, indeed explicitly Christian, terms.²⁶ Nation-building in Australia was not divorced from Christian attempts to build the Kingdom of God and the churches had major, albeit historically variable, roles in the provision of education, health care and welfare. They also provided prison and army chaplains and conducted weddings and funerals.²⁷ For practical purposes, Christianity was the national religion and an integral part of

---

22 For analysis of the differences between Particular and Union Baptists and the status of Calvinism, see M. Chavura, "Calvinism and the Spurgeonic Tradition among the Baptists of New South Wales: The Downgrade Controversy," in *Re-Visioning Australian Colonial Christianity*, ch. 5. For a general history, see K. Manley, *From Woolloomooloo to 'Eternity': A History of Australian Baptists* (Milton Keynes: Paternoster, 2006).
23 For a traditionalist Catholic interpretation, see T. L. Suttor, *Hierarchy and Democracy in Australia 1788–1870: The Formation of Australian Catholicism* (Carlton, Vic.: Melbourne University Press, 1965), ch. 7.
24 Henry Reynolds draws attention to key examples such as George Augustus Robertson and the Reverend John Gribble; see *This Whispering in Our Hearts* (Sydney: Allen and Unwin, 1998), especially ch. 7.
25 I. Breward, "Protestantism in Australia, New Zealand and Oceania to the Present Day," in *The Blackwell Companion to Protestantism*, ed. A. E. McGrath and D. C. Marks (Oxford: Blackwell, 2004), ch. 23.
26 R. S. M. Withycombe, "Australian Anglicans and Imperial Identity, 1900–1914," *Journal of Religious History* 25 (2001): 286–305.
27 P. Jalland, *Australian Ways of Death: A Social and Cultural History 1840–1918* (Melbourne: Oxford University Press, 2002).

Australian education, medicine, welfare and law, as well as an instrument for the governance of Indigenous Australians.[28] Moreover, large numbers of Australians took their spirituality from confessional traditions.[29] The churches were also social critics of national policy in areas such as employment, welfare and education. In Australia, as elsewhere, the Bible was regularly invoked to condemn unjust arrangements.[30] Hilary Carey is right to emphasise the importance of imperial support for religion and the degree to which support for a Protestant establishment was replaced over time by pride of race and faith associated with colonial imperialism.[31] Nonetheless, Protestantism was a large part of Australian political identity until well into the twentieth century, and Biblical language shaped parts of the discourse.[32] Religious organisations often supplemented the dominance of practical, the utilitarian and the technical perspectives on Australian public life,[33] while making major contributions to the social weal.[34]

In Australia there was sometimes no rigid divide between the religious and the secular. Whereas Americans take the separation of church and state for granted, Australians have largely accepted government help for religious institutions and, despite the shift away from state-funded religious education in the 1870s, they have made extensive use of church schools and hospitals.

---

28 J. Mitchell, *In Good Faith? Governing Indigenous Australia through God, Charity and Empire, 1825–1855* (Canberra: ANU E Press, 2011).
29 K. Massam, *Sacred Threads: Catholic Spirituality in Australia 1922–1962* (Sydney: University of New South Wales Press, 1996), 1–2.
30 See G. Maddox, *Religion and the Rise of Democracy* (London: Routledge, 1996). Maddox's emphasis on the link between Christianity and social radicalism influenced many of his students.
31 H. Carey, "Religion and Identity," in *Australia's Empire*, ed. D. Schreuder and S. Ward (Oxford: Oxford University Press, 2008), ch 5. Carey suggests that religion was essential to the business of Empire and that religion was an imperial undertaking for most British settlers. See also B. Fletcher, "Anglicanism and Nationalism in Australia 1901–1962," *Journal of Religious History* 23 (1999): 215–33; and A. Atkinson, *The Europeans in Australia: A History*. Vol. 2, Democracy (Melbourne: Oxford University Press, 2004), ch. 9.
32 R. Boer, *Last Stop Before Antarctica: The Bible and Postcolonialism in Australia*, 2nd ed. (Leiden: Brill, 2008).
33 For a discussion of this issue, see G. Melleuish, *The Power of Ideas: Essays on Australian Politics and History* (North Melbourne: Australian Scholarly Publishing, 2009), ch. 2.
34 Here the very substantial work of Catholic religious orders, especially in rural areas, should be noted; see A. Doyle, *The Story of the Marist Brothers in Australia 1872–1972* (Drummoyne, NSW: E. J. Dwyer for the Marist Brothers of the Schools, 1972); P. Kneipp, *This Land of Promise: The Ursuline Order in Australia, 1882–1982* (Armidale, NSW: University of New England, 1982); M. R. MacGinley, *A Dynamic of Hope: Institutes of Women Religious in Australia*, 2nd ed. (Darlinghurst, NSW: Crossing Press, 2002) and *Ancient Tradition, New World: Dominican Sisters in Eastern Australia 1867–1958* (Strathfield, NSW: St Pauls Publications, 2009).

Indeed, Australia is unusual in international terms in that a high percentage of all services are delivered through church agencies.[35] Again, around a third of Australian children are in religious schools. There is also a limited Christian presence in the tertiary sector through church-based university colleges, Christian student associations and one major Catholic University plus a small extension of the American University of Notre Dame.

Of course, the 'irreligious Australia' narrative has some basis in fact. Some of those who came as convicts, many of whom were hostile to the role the clergy played as moral police, were irreligious,[36] even if previous historiography characterising many of the lower classes as 'practical atheists' needs qualification.[37] Bush writing in Australia was also prone to anti-clericalism and many were inclined to suspect the moral uplift of the parson, even if the overall picture was more complex.[38] Reports that most colonists were not religious were made from time to time in New South Wales.[39] Some social strata were influenced by indifference to the Christian religion or by natural religion, which could, depending on the context, be either an ally of Christianity or a substitute for it. In nineteenth-century Australia various deist and pantheist ideas circulated beneath the surface[40] and arguments advanced by deists such as John Toland and Matthew Tindal were discussed.[41]

---

35 J. Murphy, "Church and State in the History of Australian Welfare," in *Church and State in Old and New Worlds*, ed. H. M. Carey and J. Gascoigne (Leiden: Brill, 2011), 261–85.
36 B. Smith, *Australia's Birthstain: The Startling Legacy of the Convict Era* (Crows Nest, NSW: Allen and Unwin, 2008).
37 A. M. Grocott, *Convicts, Clergymen and Churches: Attitudes of Convicts and Ex-convicts towards the Churches and Clergy in New South Wales from 1788 to 1851* (Sydney: Sydney University Press, 1980), 104.
38 For a fine discussion, see H. M. Carey, "Bushmen and Bush Parsons: The Shaping of a Rural Myth: The 2010 Russel Ward Annual Lecture University of New England, 15 April 2010," *Journal of Australian Colonial History* 13 (2011): 1–26, especially p. 3. See also M. Lake, "Protestant Christianity and the Colonial Environment: Australia as a Wilderness in the 1830s and 1840s," *Journal of Australian Colonial History* 11 (2009): 21–44.
39 According to *The New South Wales Magazine* (1 December 1833, 298), most colonists had no interest in religious controversies and considered all religions the same. However, this much cited report was not based on Australia-wide evidence and probably refers to specific strata in the colony. The fact that the pages of the Sydney weekly journal, *The Atlas*, were dominated by the Puseyite controversy in Anglicanism from 1844 to 1848 suggests that Australians were interested in religious disputes, especially if these disputes had political implications.
40 See the missionary reports in *Historical Records of New South Wales*, 1796–1799, vol. 3: 707–14. I owe this reference to Stephen Chavura.
41 P. L. Gregory, "Popular Religion in New South Wales and Van Diemen's Land from 1788 to the 1850s" (PhD diss., University of New England, 1997), 292, 375.

Heterodox forms of religious activity, including several forms of astrology, were found.[42]

Criticism of religion and the churches was not muted. Both the *Bulletin* in the late nineteenth century and the Communist press in the twentieth century argued that religion was pathological, a view also embraced by many psychiatrists. There were also recurrent bursts of criticism of theism and religion from scientists, as well as attacks on the churches for their oppressive attitudes to sexuality.[43] Criticism of religion, however, served to keep religion central to a range of debates.

The Neglect of Religious Thought

Given the considerable influence of religion on the history of Australia, why has religious thought been comparatively neglected by historians, especially when an extensive scholarly literature has been devoted to it in particular cases or with regard to specific issues? Historians have not left religious thought out of accounts to which it is relevant, but they have not often dealt with it in its own terms and have also tended to avoid detailed discussion of philosophical and theological ideas. Important work has been done on the influence of religious thought on Australian political thought and on wider cultural trends,[44] but sustained discussion has been relatively scarce. There have been political and cultural reasons for this.

The notion that eighteenth-century Australia was an irreligious society proved popular in the middle decades of the twentieth century, partly because some believed that Australian distinctiveness could be explained in part by reference to an anticlerical and godless convict past. National historians such as Russel Ward, Brian Fitzpatrick, Ian Turner, Lloyd Churchward, Robin Gollan and Geoffrey Serle were often critical of religion and it is

---

42 M. Perkins, "'An Era of Great Doubt to Some in Sydney': Almanacs and Astrological Belief in Colonial Australia," *Journal of Religious History* 17 (1993): 465–74.
43 D. Marr, *The High Price of Heaven* (St Leonards: Allen and Unwin, 1999).
44 For the influence on political thought, see especially the works of Gregory Melleuish, including inter alia G. Melleuish, *Cultural Liberalism in Australia: A Study in Intellectual and Cultural History* (Oakleigh, Vic.: Cambridge University Press, 1995), "Conceptions of the Sacred in Australian Political Thought," *Political Theory Newsletter*, 5 (1993), 39–51 and "Liberal Intellectuals and Early Twentieth Century Australia: Restoring the Religious Dimension," *Australian Journal of Politics and History*, 35, 1 (1989) 1–12, and now studies by Marnie Hughes-Warrington, Ian Tregenza and Stephen Chavura. For wider cultural trends, see the scholarship of Alan Atkinson, Frank Bongiorno, Hilary Carey, Manning Clark, James Franklin, Alfred Gabay, John Gascoigne, David Hilliard, Bruce Kaye, Stuart Macintyre, Jill Roe, Penny Russell, George Shaw, Barry Smith, and many others.

not unfair to see a link between the exclusion of religion from left-wing historiography and the tendency of nationalist historians to endorse a secularist confession.[45] A shared anti-imperialist sensibility and a desire to celebrate the newness of Australian culture led them to exclude religious intellectual life from the national narrative.[46] Of course, the stances of individual historians were often more complex. Russel Ward (1914–1995), for example, despite his difficult relationship with his Methodist headmaster father, was not insensitive to religion and had personal visionary experience of Jesus Christ.[47] Nonetheless, it was Ward's portrayal of an anti-religious bushman that was taken up. His admission that he dealt with the 'typical' and not the 'average' Australian was not.[48] There was also a connection between sympathy for the Communist Party and a tendency to downplay religion. Moreover, ironically, the idea that Australia was a radically secular country was sometimes put forward by Catholic historians, partly because they interpreted Protestant conceptions of the secular as non-religious.[49]

The relative neglect of religious thought in secular historiography may have been due in part to the predominance of confessional approaches in the writing of Australian religious history. Most of those who wrote about religion in Australia were personally religious and many of them wrote within confessional frameworks. With exceptions, Catholics wrote about Catholics, Anglicans about Anglicans, and Presbyterians about Presbyterians.[50] There were relatively few overviews and the larger story was not told.[51] Not all Australian historians, of course, neglected the importance of religious

---

45 For a fine contextualisation of Fitzpatrick's marginal position among historians, see S. Macintyre and S. Fitzpatrick (eds), *Against the Grain: Brian Fitzpatrick and Manning Clark in Australian History and Politics* (Carlton, Vic.: Melbourne University Publishing, 2007).
46 J. McCalman, *Journeyings: The Biography of a Middle-Class Generation 1920–1990* (Carlton, Vic.: Melbourne University Press, 1995).
47 For Ward's religious background and its effect on his historiography, see R. Ward, *A Radical Life: The Autobiography of Russel Ward* (South Melbourne: Macmillan, 1988), especially p. 107.
48 R. Ward, *The Australian Legend*, 2nd ed. (Melbourne: Oxford University Press, 1965), 8.
49 See Suttor, *Hierarchy and Democracy in Australia 1788–1870*.
50 For examples of confessionally-oriented historiography, see inter alia J. G. Murtagh, *Australia: The Catholic Chapter* (Melbourne: Polding Press, 1969); P. O'Farrell, *The Catholic Church and Community in Australia: An Australian History*, 3rd rev. ed., (Kensington: University of New South Wales Press, 1992); Ward, *The Bush Still Burns*; Wood, *Presbyterians in Colonial Victoria*; Hutchinson, *Iron in Our Blood*; Wright and Clancy, *The Methodists*; and J. D. Bollen, *Australian Baptists: A Religious Minority* (London: Baptist Historical Society, 1975).
51 J. Hirst, *Sense & Nonsense in Australian History* (Melbourne: Black Inc. Agenda, 2009), 18.

thought. Indeed, Manning Clark (1915–1991) in his six-volume *History of Australia* made conflicts between different worldviews and styles of belief central to the national story. Clark interpreted Australian history in terms of a clash between Catholic Christendom, Calvinism, and the Enlightenment. After Clark's death, however, younger historians, sensitive to issues of race, gender and power, turned away from history written in terms of religious worldviews. Large numbers of Australian historians, especially in the second half of the twentieth century, believed that religion was a barrier to social progress and not among the things that mattered. When historians returned to religion as a factor in Australian history, they were inspired largely by international developments, including developments suggesting that secularisation might not be inevitable – at least not everywhere or in the immediate future.

Scope

This volume attempts to make a larger place for religious thought in Australian historical writing. Drawing on my own research and the work of other scholars, my task is to alert the reader to the wealth of materials available. To do so, I draw attention to the ideas of a wide range of intellectuals, using 'intellectual' in the French sense of one who generates text. I use the term 'religious thought' to refer both to forms of thought falling within religion in an organisational sense and forms of thought outside religion in an organisational sense which involve sacral perspectives in part indebted to it. In both cases, the relationship to religion in an organisational sense is crucial.[52] Such usage is clearly historical, not analytical, but it catches how Europeans tended to construct 'the religious' in Australia. I do not open the gates so wide as to include all kinds of spiritual thought and I do not identify 'the religious' exclusively with 'the sacred', or assume that 'the sacred' is always religious. The relationship between 'the religious' and 'the sacred' has been fluid and ambiguous in Australia. Many Australian intellectuals have not found the sacred in religion; and some have found it outside religion altogether.

A contextual understanding of 'religion' and 'religious' avoids over-precise definitions that preempt the field that needs to be explored. I do not deny that it is possible to offer more encompassing definitions of religion, based,

---

52 For a comparable approach, see G. Bouma, "Defining Religion and Spirituality" in *The Encyclopedia of Religion in Australia*, ed. J. Jupp (Port Melbourne, Vic.: Cambridge University Press, 2009), 22–27, especially 23–4.

for example, on specific constructions of the self, or that a case can be made for criticising the term 'religion' itself. Much of the recent scholarly literature in religious studies has done this.[53] However, while it is true that European constructions of 'religion' have limited applications to other parts of the world and, arguably, had little application in classical times even in Europe, they have considerable application to European settlement in Australia. My approach attempts, however, to take account of the fact that not all religious thinkers accepted conventional religious beliefs and also of the fact that intellectuals critical of religious beliefs sometimes adopted confessional stances.

In the same way, I am wary of the Eurocentrism associated with some uses of the term 'Aboriginal religion'. This is a complex and sensitive area. I discuss some of the problems associated with European Australians' interpretations of Aboriginal law in Chapter V. Nonetheless, I do not deal with Aboriginal sacred thought and am keenly aware that I cannot do justice to Aboriginal Christianity, which receives some attention in Chapter V. My treatment of Christianity is also limited in certain respects. I do not play down its importance or hide the fact that most of the intellectuals discussed in the book were Christians. Nor do I ignore the contributions of churchmen to many different areas or seek to diminish the extent to which Anglican, Catholic, Lutheran and Calvinist traditions are central to the Australian story. I also allow for contributions made by Evangelicals to social reform and educational practice. My focus, however, is on *contributions to religious thought* rather than confessional developments, which would rightly figure more prominently in a work by a social, cultural or church historian. Hence, handbooks of the beliefs of denominations, works of popular apologetics and statements by bishops or church leaders and the like are not my primary concern. I do not, however, underestimate the role of the churches in making theological, philosophical and cultural materials available, both to intellectuals and to Australians generally, through educational institutions, publishing houses, seminaries, Bible colleges and religious libraries. And I deal with Christian theology at length, arguing for its significance in a range of contexts.

---

53 See T. Asad, "Anthropological Conceptions of Religion: Reflections on Geertz," *Man* 18 (1983): 237–59, and *Genealogies of Religion: Discipline and Reasons of Power in Christianity and Islam* (Baltimore and London: Johns Hopkins University Press, 1993); T. Fitzgerald, *The Ideology of Religious Studies* (Oxford: Oxford University Press, 2003); R. M. McCutcheon, *Manufacturing Religion: The Discourse on Sui Generis Religion and the Politics of Nostalgia* (Oxford: Oxford University Press, 2003); and B. Nongbri, *Before Religion: A History of a Modern Concept* (New Haven: Yale University Press, 2013).

INTRODUCTION

I should also emphasise that this volume is written from the standpoint of *intellectual history*. A range of different methodological approaches can be adopted in studying religious thought, ranging from biographical and textual studies of the religious thought of thinkers to a social history of religious ideas. Here I adopt a biographical and textual studies approach, while noting to some extent transactions between biographical, socio-political and structural constraints. Consistent with this, most of my sources are published writings. I do not deal with archival sources, music, architecture, art, film, television, forms of social action, or instructional texts. I am not writing a cultural history of the Australian imaginary. I do use examples from literary texts where their status as religious thought is self-evident, but I make no attempt to do justice to religious influences or manifestations of the sacred in literature more generally. I mention no plays and barely deal with novels.

My use of the term 'Australian' is also flexible, since much of the thought at issue was not for the most part 'Australian' in an exclusivist sense. Large parts of it came from somewhere else and did not change completely when individuals got off the boat. Until Federation, and indeed long afterwards, many were born elsewhere and their effective contexts might be one colony and/or the English-speaking world as a whole. Religious thought in Australia was often transnational. For much of the time Australian intellectuals responded and contributed to international developments in Britain, Europe and the United States, but also to developments in Asia, the Pacific and Africa,[54] and this was also sometimes the case when their religious thought took nationalist or localist forms. The Empire was a very important context for religious thought, but there were also interactions with South African, Latin American and Israeli religious thought. Australian religious thinkers knew about intellectuals elsewhere and read their works. Moreover, as Marilyn Lake has argued, they were often

---

54   Interconnections between Empire and religion are now much studied and it is argued that several empires competed in the nineteenth century; see H. M. Carey (ed.), *Empires of Religion* (Basingstoke: Palgrave Macmillan, 2008) and *God's Empire: Religion and Colonialism in the British World, c.1801–1908* (Cambridge: Cambridge University Press, 2011). For multiple empires, see P. Cunich, "Archbishop Vaughan and the Empires of Religion in Colonial New South Wales", in *Empires of Religion*, 137–60, and A. Cunningham, T*he Rome Connection: Australia, Ireland and the Empire 1865–1885* (Darlinghurst, NSW: Crossing Press, 2002); see also A. O'Brien, "Saving the 'Empty North': Religion and Empire in Australia" in *Empires of Religion*, 177–96; and R. Strong, *Anglicanism and the British Empire c.1700–1850* (Oxford: Oxford University Press, 2007).

agents in their own right, and not only passive recipients.[55] Likewise, Australian thinking about religion was by no means just thinking about Australia alone. Australian missionaries, for example, were active in Africa, India, China, Vietnam, Japan, Korea, the Philippines, Tonga, Fiji and New Guinea,[56] and their activities in the longer term had an impact on Australia's understanding of its place in the world, as the history of Australian-led inter-church meetings in the Asia–Pacific region shows.[57]

Within these limitations, and drawing on the ideas of the German Jewish philosopher Ernst Bloch,[58] I find religious thought in the irreligious as well as in the pious – not only in the works of philosophers and theologians, but also in the writings of political thinkers, novelists and poets. I also pursue patterns across standard confessional and ideological lines, on the assumption that individuals have multiple identities and that their views often do not reduce to traditional labels such as 'theist' or 'atheist', 'believer' or 'unbeliever', 'Catholic' or 'Protestant', even though the use of such labels is sometimes essential.

Finally, this volume does not purport to be a comprehensive history that covers everything. It is selective, and explores only *six themes*, each of which is discussed primarily in one chapter, although, obviously, the themes selected often have a secondary presence in other chapters. It does so by offering *soundings*, in the naval sense of attempts to determine where materials are to be found. The themes are not presented in strict chronological order, although an attempt is made to convey broad movements of thought over time. Obviously there are decisions involved in discussing under one theme particular intellectuals who could be discussed under others. In several cases, in the case of Catherine Spence, for example, an intellectual could appear under various headings. My decisions are meant to highlight what has not received sufficient emphasis and to show familiar material in another light, but other presentations are obviously possible. These themes offer only partial vistas on a vast field.

---

55 See A. Curthoys and M. Lake (eds), *Connected Worlds: History in Transnational Perspective* (Canberra: ANU E Press, 2005).
56 There are many resources for the study of Australian Christian missionaries. For a less well-known case, see J. Brown, *Witnessing Grace: Presbyterian Missionaries in Korea* (Seoul: Presbyterian Church of Korea, 2009).
57 F. Engel, *Christians in Australia*. Vol. 2, Times of Change 1918–1978 (Melbourne: Joint Board of Christian Education, 1993), ch. 7.
58 W. Hudson, *The Marxist Philosophy of Ernst Bloch* (London: Macmillan, 1982); see also W. Hudson, "Bloch and a Philosophy of the Proterior," in *Ernst Bloch and the Privatization of Hope*, ed. P. Thompson and S. Žižek (Raleigh: Duke University Press, 2013), ch. 1.

Introduction

I now introduce the six themes discussed in the book. One theme is *the extent of disbelief*, a term used here in a technical sense, but one which may have the capacity to throw new light on some of the material. Australian historians have often associated criticism of Christianity in Australia with *unbelief*. They have also written about religious thought in terms of religious thinkers versus secularists. My discussion reveals more crossed trajectories. It draws a pragmatic distinction between *unbelief*, or an inability to positively accept religious tenets even when there is some desire to do so, and *disbelief*, or a positive conviction that various religious tenets are false and irrational, sometimes allied to an unsympathetic comportment towards those beliefs and those who entertain them. It then hypothesises that disbelief was not uncommon in Australia and that strains of disbelief were often found among religious and irreligious thinkers alike, whereas unbelief was a less common position until the late twentieth century. There is a danger here of conceiving of these patterns as partitional boundaries, which they often were not in Australia. My discussion of disbelief opens up fresh perspectives. It deals not only with well-known forms of heterodoxy, but also with less obvious cases of disbelief associated with esoteric perspectives and with disbelief found among thinkers with confessional commitments. It offers a new optic, but is by no means the whole story.

Another theme is what I term *sacral secularity*, or the tendency to associate the secular with sacral characteristics, while acknowledging its relative autonomy from ecclesiastical control. Sacral secularity is a neglected feature of Australian religious thought, even though it arguably contributed significantly to Australian political and social arrangements. In much of the historiography the non-religious character of Australian secularism has been taken for granted. This is misleading in several respects. Between 1788 and 1900 many Australians were critical of organised religion, depending on the church or denomination at issue, but they were not necessarily hostile to the sacral, and some of them relocated it in less clerical domains. Moreover, sacral secularity also played a part in debates about educational reform in the nineteenth century and in the emergence of public theology discourse after 1920.

Yet another theme is *religious liberalism*. Religious liberalism was concerned to modernise and reform religious beliefs and practices. My discussion focuses on prominent religious liberals. It suggests that religious liberalism was not confined to the reinterpretation of traditional religious beliefs. It also went to the valorisation of everyday life and a wide range of social concerns, often summed up as what true or modern Christianity required. I draw attention to the quality and seriousness of liberal religious thought, to its transnational character and to its associations with social reform.

A further theme is *the extent to which traditions of philosophy impacted on religious thought* in Australia. My discussion emphasises the philosophical capital available to religious thinkers in Australia, depending on their social backgrounds and access to education. While some traditions of philosophy provided support for religious claims, others posed challenges to them. Australian religious thought was shaped by traditions of both sorts.

Another theme is *the development of theology in Australia*. Theology in Australia has a rich and complex history, but one which has received relatively little scholarly attention. My discussion draws attention to the quantity of theology written in Australia, the quality of theological research and debate, and the gradual emergence of independent theology, as confidence grew and as more attention was paid to local contexts and Australia's Asia–Pacific geography.

Finally, I discuss the emergence of what I term *'postsecular consciousness'*. My discussion ranges from the presence of sacral naturalism in nineteenth- and early twentieth-century poets to writers influenced by vitalism and process philosophy; writers who sought to ground the sacral in the sciences; writers who attempted to recover a spiritual concept of place; and writers who found the sacred in the context of environmental philosophy or psychoanalysis. I conclude with a sketch of the rise of 'transcultural eclecticism', which may call forth another religious thought altogether.

Obviously no-one can be equally expert in all these areas, or across all the sources. This book then is not the complete history of Australian religious thought that may eventually be needed. I hope, however, to establish that Australian religious thought has been more interesting and more significant than many writers have assumed.

Chapter I

SHAPES OF DISBELIEF

A critical attitude to Christianity has not been uncommon in Australia. Historians, however, have been inclined to associate criticism of Christianity with *unbelief*. Their approach is not without justification, but it does not always draw out the peculiarities of the Australian, as opposed to the British or American, context and, arguably, does not always capture the porous inter-weavings of different strands in the thought of individual thinkers.

In this chapter I aim to undermine the standard view that Australian intellectuals can be easily classified as believers or unbelievers, religionists or secularists. The standard view is arguably too schematic. It gives the issue of belief a justifiable primacy because this issue often shaped the responses of individual intellectuals, especially before 1960. In Australia, however, believing in religious doctrines was not always as central as in some other countries, while a critical or irreverent attitude to religious beliefs, whether those of one's own childhood or those of others, was not uncommon. To promote a more complex hermeneutic in this chapter I draw a largely pragmatic distinction between *unbelief*, or an inability to positively accept religious tenets, even when there is some desire to do so,[1] and *disbelief*, or a positive conviction that various religious tenets are false and irrational, often allied to an unsympathetic comportment towards those beliefs and those who entertain them.[2] Whereas unbelief is commonly found in individuals nostalgic for the values and coherence that religious beliefs once provided and often associated with a certain sadness, disbelief is often associated with certainty about what is false.

---

1   G. Szczesny, *The Future of Unbelief*, trans. E. B. Garside (New York: George Braziller, 1961).
2   For studies of disbelief in seventeenth- and eighteenth-century England, see my *The English Deists: Studies in Early Enlightenment* (London: Pickering and Chatto, 2009), a major reinterpretation of deism and the English deists, and my *Enlightenment and Modernity: The English Deists and Reform* (London: Pickering and Chatto, 2009). See also W. Hudson, D. Lucci and J. R. Wigglesworth (eds.) *Atheism and Deism Revalued: Heterodox Religious Identities in Britain, 1650–1800* (London: Ashgate, 2014).

Obviously the terms 'disbelief' and 'unbelief' are ideal constructions, not precise descriptions. They are also more enlightening in some cases than others. Further, sharp distinctions between belief, disbelief and unbelief cannot always be drawn. Particular individuals have their own patterns and sometimes migrate, not very consistently, between unbelief and disbelief. Not infrequently they hold a range of different views at the same time. Again, particular individuals could disbelieve in some things and not others: in Christianity, but not in God; in the supernatural, but not in natural mysteries; in religion, but not in morality. My use of the term 'disbelief' does not displace the complexity or the ambivalence of much of the evidence, just as my emphasis on disbelief builds on, but does not replace, earlier scholarship.[3] Nor do I imply that religious thought is reducible to questions of belief. I do not deny that some religious traditions emphasise religious experience or ungrounded faith, rather than belief in doctrines. Nor do I deny that some forms of heterodoxy can be construed as secular confessions. Again, I am only discussing disbelief in the thought of intellectuals, not Australian culture more generally, and my discussion mainly focuses on the nineteenth century and the first half of the twentieth. I also do not deal in depth with the question of why disbelief was prominent among Australian intellectuals, although the prevalence of sectarianism in Australia was probably a factor.

Allowing for these qualifications, this chapter deploys the optic of disbelief to offer fresh perspectives and as a stimulus to further research. Strains of disbelief, I contend, can be found in the religious thought of intellectuals in Australia across multiple sites and contexts.[4] Nonetheless, disbelief was not a natural kind and varied in different periods and from place to place. At times disbelief had something religious about it and mostly was neither as propositional as it was in France nor as fierce as it was in Latin America.[5] It also often differed from the more strident disbelief found at significant conjunctures in the United States.[6] Many Australians who experienced disbelief

---

3   See, for example, F. B. Smith, *Religion and Freethought in Melbourne 1870 to 1890* (M.A. diss., University of Melbourne, 1960) and T. Frame, *Losing My Religion: Unbelief in Australia* (Sydney: University of New South Wales Press, 2009), ch. 2. Tom Frame casts his discussion in terms of unbelief in 'theistic religion'.
4   For an argument about negativity as a major theme in Australian poetry, see P. Kane, *Australian Poetry: Romanticism and Negativity* (Cambridge: Cambridge University Press, 1996). Cf R. Border, *Church and State in Australia 1788–1872 A Constitutional Study of the Church of England in Australia* (London: S.P.C.K., 1962).
5   For the darker strains of French disbelief, see P. Klossowski, *Sade: My Neighbor*, trans. A. Lingis (Evanston, IL: Northwestern University Press, 1991).
6   H. M. Morais, *Deism in Eighteenth-Century America* (New York: Columbia University Press, 1934). For some of the origins of these differences, see J. Butler, *Awash in a Sea*

were respectful of personal faith in Jesus Christ, provided it was not used to impose beliefs contrary to reason on others. This partly reflected the milder forms of Christianity found in Australia, as compared with, say, Spain or Russia.

Disbelief in Australia might imply a negative stance towards various religious beliefs and practices, but hostility to institutional religion did not necessarily imply a lack of concern for spiritual values.[7] Again, many of those who regarded a range of religious tenets as false possessed a personal faith of their own and were believers in some contexts and disbelievers in others. In Australia disbelief was sometimes disbelief in 'churchism', or the religion of the clergy. It was rarely associated with hostility to ethical values. There was also little sense that disbelief itself could be the basis for social life, despite the existence of societies devoted to propagating freethinking and humanism. Many Australians argued for a religion without creed or ceremonies, and, in contrast to the United States, there were few deist chapels.[8] In some cases disbelief was a matter of disbelief in the religion of one's childhood. In other cases belief in the religion of one's childhood was compatible with disbelief in the religious beliefs of others. Disbelief and belief then were not necessarily incompatible. Disbelief could be part of confessional religion, just as disbelief in one or more religious doctrines was often compatible with an untroubled belief in immediate experience.[9]

My discussion in this chapter begins with the rise of doubt in the eighteenth and nineteenth centuries and continues with the presence of elements

---

    of Faith: Christianizing the American People (Cambridge, Mass: Harvard University Press, 1990). Butler argues that American religion was shaped by 'Enthusiasm' in the eighteenth century rather than by the Calvinism of the Puritans.

7   Theologians have long recognised that atheists may be morally authentic, that honest agnosticism may be a contemporary experience of God, that faith in the sense of an inner compartment or horizon is more important than belief in a creedal sense and that the refusal of belief is different from the repudiation of inadequate objectifications of it.

8   For the contrasting American patterns, see J. Turner, *Without God, Without Creed: The Origins of Unbelief in America* (Baltimore and London: Johns Hopkins University Press, 1985).

9   Many Australian poets have explored spirituality beyond belief, sometimes signalling the possibility of a future recovery of spiritual experience; see, for example, Charles Harpur's "The Silence of Faith", the Tasmanian poet Vivian Smith's ruminations in "A Room in Mosman", Fay Zwicky's combination of irreverence with spiritual restraint in "Mrs Noah Speaks", Alan Wearne's "St Bartholomew Remembers Jesus Christ as an Athlete", Lesbia Harford's "I am no Mystic" and Peter Porter's "The Unlucky Christ"; see also Dennis Haskell *Listening At Night* (Sydney: Angus & Robertson, 1984) and, more generally, Toby Davidson's excellent study, *Christian Mysticism and Australian Poetry* (Amherst, NY: Cambria Press, 2013).

of disbelief in agnosticism, freethought, secularism and atheism. I then turn to the less obvious terrains of esoteric discernments and confessional verdicts – that is, cases where the presence of disbelief is not so intuitive or socially predictable. I do not, of course, suggest that agnosticism, freethought, secularism and atheism can be reduced to disbelief. Indeed, these trends often involved forms of scepticism, which could undermine the certainties of disbelief as much as the certainties of religious faith. At other times heterodoxy could itself amount to a confessional belief, and a heterodox person could be as certain in their beliefs as a Christian. Disbelief, I suggest, was in the mix, but the thought of a particular intellectual was rarely reducible to it.

Objections to Christianity were widely discussed in nineteenth century Australia as reports of theological, philosophical and scientific developments in Europe and the United States poured into the colonies, including of the challenges to the historical reliability of the Bible posed by German higher criticism, especially as found in the works of liberal theologians such as David Strauss (1808–1874) and F. C. Baur (1792–1860). Mrs Humphry Ward's novel *Robert Elsmere* (1888), which contained detailed discussion of 'higher criticism' and its influence on Christian belief, was widely read in Australia. From the 1860s on, doubts about the historicity of the Bible were raised in educated circles and there were debates among defenders and critics of Darwin, Huxley and Spencer. *Essays and Reviews*, published in 1860 by leading English liberal theologians, included an essay in which the influential liberal Anglican divine and Master of Balliol College, Oxford, Benjamin Jowett (1817–1893) accepted the need for historical critical approaches to the Scriptures. For many, the shift from implicit faith in the historical reliability of the Bible to a critical attitude towards the reliability of the Scriptures proved unsettling.

In Adelaide, the Chief Justice of South Australia, Richard Davies Hanson (1805–1876), later Chancellor of the University of Adelaide, questioned the authority of the Bible and embraced Darwinism in his paper on 'The Relation between Science and Theology', delivered to the Philosophical Society in 1864.[10] In 1869 Hanson published a life of Jesus as a purely human figure.[11] In 1867 E. W. Cole (1832–1918), the owner of the Bourke Street

---

[10] Included in R. D. Hanson, *Laws in Nature: Four Papers read before the Adelaide Philosophical Society* (Adelaide: Adelaide Philosophical Society, 1864). Hanson published further radical religious views in *The Jesus of History* (London: Williams and Norgate, 1869) and *The Apostle Paul and the Preaching of Christianity in the Primitive Church* (London: Williams and Norgate, 1875).

[11] Hanson, *The Jesus of History*; for discussion, see D. Hilliard, "Strong's Liberal Contemporaries: Adelaide, 1870–1914" (paper presented at the Strong Symposium, University of South Australia, 7 July 2006).

Book Arcade, published a naturalistic account of the origins of Christianity that appealed neither to the divine nor to miracles.[12] Historical criticism threatened to undermine older assumptions, although it was often unclear whether the outcome was unbelief, let alone disbelief.

Developments in the contemporary sciences also made an impact on the credibility of Christianity, although works of Christian apologetics appealing to the general sense of providence in nature continued to appear for decades. Scientists were often better disposed towards religion and more theologically literate than a modern reader might suspect, partly because many of them were clergymen.[13] Even when it became clear that Christianity faced serious challenges from the emergence of Darwinism, many still took a providential harmony for granted and concentrated on how the new perspectives could be integrated into such a framework. Thus William Edward Hearn (1826–1888), the first Professor of Modern History and Literature, Political Economy and Logic at the University of Melbourne, did not hesitate to apply Darwinian ideas to the evolution and organisation of economic society. His *Plutology, or the Theory of the Efforts to Satisfy Human Wants* (1864), the first large scale work of economic theory written in Australia, was praised by leading British economists such as William Jevons and Alfred Marshall. Hearn argued that societies, like other organisms, evolved towards multiplicity. Nonetheless, his conclusions were not sceptical.[14] A prominent layman of the Church of

---

12 E. W. Cole, *The Real Place in History of Jesus and Paul*, 2 vols (Melbourne: E. W. Cole, 1866–68). Cole also dealt with the challenge of comparative religion in *Religions of the World* (Melbourne: E. W. Cole, 1866) and the historicity of the Old Testament in *An Essay on the Deluge* (Melbourne: E. W. Cole, 1870). Subsequently Cole's bookshop was boycotted. Cole saw himself as living in an age of transition in which creeds that had passed as current for centuries were being questioned. In Britain the key arguments emerged much earlier. The first atheist publication, for example, was an *Answer to Dr Priestley's Letters to a Philosophical Unbeliever* (London: Matthew Turner and William Hammon, 1782).

13 A. M. Moyal, *Scientists in Nineteenth Century Australia: A Documentary History* (Melbourne: Cassell, 1976). This pattern was well established by the early nineteenth century. The Reverend William Buckland, for example, merged theology and geology in works such as *Vindiciae Geologicae*; or, the *Connexion of Geology with Religion Explained* (Oxford: Oxford University Press, 1820); *Reliquiae Diluvianae* (London: J. Murray, 1823); and *Geology and Mineralogy Considered with Reference to Natural Theology* (London: William Pickering, 1836).

14 See J. A. La Nauze, "Hearn on Natural Religion: An Unpublished Manuscript," *Historical Studies: Australia and New Zealand* 12 (1965): 119–22. Apart from the impact on Hearn's social and economic thought, Darwinism was taken up by some members of the group around the periodical *Quadrilateral* in Hobart. Unitarians, socialists and advocates of racial discrimination all sought support from Darwin's theories. For discussion, see T. Frame, *Evolution in the Antipodes: Charles Darwin and Australia* (Sydney: UNSW Press, 2009), ch. 6.

England, he wrote a book entitled *Essay on Natural Religion*, in which he marshalled early nineteenth-century science to show that there was evidence for 'an all wise Creator and Governor of the Universe'.[15] Others, such as Professor Sir Frederick McCoy (1817–1899), rejected Darwinism altogether. Later in the century some evangelicals, including the leading colonial scientist cleric the Reverend William Branwhite Clarke (1798–1878), claimed that Darwin's theory provided further evidence for the truth of Christianity.[16] Christian responses to Darwin varied quite considerably, then, and disbelief emerged in different timeframes on different issues.

Doubt and uncertainty manifested more clearly in Melbourne in the 1870s, as Christian intellectuals attempted to come to terms with the challenges posed by the agnosticism of the British philosopher Herbert Spencer (1820–1903) and with the findings of British and German cultural anthropology. There was also considerable interest in the humanised version of Christianity popularised by Matthew Arnold. The need to rethink the Bible in more historical terms was not, however, evident to most churchgoers and Sunday Schools boomed. Most Protestant churchmen were convinced that the narratives found in the Bible were descriptions of events that really happened. Gradually, however, the standard Christian apologetics came to be questioned in intellectual circles. Much of this apologetics went back to the seventeenth and eighteenth centuries – to the cosmological argument restated by Locke in his *Essay Concerning Human Understanding* (1690); to Bishop Butler's argument for revelation based on the analogy of the obscurity of nature in his classic work *Analogy of Religion, Natural and Revealed* (1736); and to Paley's *View of the Evidences of Christianity* (1794). In stages some Melburnians became aware that matters were not simple. Both scientific challenges and the Biblical criticism produced by the Anglican bishop John Colenso (1814–1883), who dismissed key Old Testament texts as post-exilic forgeries, were widely noted.[17] There were also challenges to Christianity from the side of comparative religion. The eminent South Australian, B. T. Finniss (1807–1893), for example, wrote several articles in the *Melbourne Review*, attempting to show that all

---

15 La Nauze, "Hearn on Natural Religion".
16 A. Mozley, "Evolution and the Climate of Opinion in Australia 1840–76," *Victorian Studies* 10 (1967): 425–26, and D. N. Livingstone, *Darwin's Forgotten Defenders: The Encounter between Evangelical Theology and Evolutionary Thought* (Grand Rapids, MI: Eerdmans, 1987). For religious response to the Darwinian challenge more generally, see Frame, *Evolution in the Antipodes*, ch. 7. Later evangelical responses to Darwin were sometimes influenced by trends at Princeton Seminary in the United States.
17 For detail of Christian responses to evolution and Higher Criticism, see W. Phillips, "The Defence of Christian Belief in Australia, 1875–1914: The Responses to Evolution and Higher Criticism," *Journal of Religious History* 9 (1977): 402–23.

of Christ's teaching in the New Testament existed in older Hebrew, Hindu, Buddhist and Greek writings and in Egyptian inscriptions.[18]

For some minds such criticism provided a basis for disbelief. Freethinkers, often from evangelical Protestant backgrounds, held forth in theatres on Sunday nights in Melbourne. They argued that the Bible was full of contradictions and incompatible with science. Such speakers also attacked the immorality of the Old Testament and doctrines such as the atonement and eternal punishments. In the 1880s radical clubs appeared in Melbourne and, in the new critical climate, religious questions were discussed with sophistication and earnestness in the *Melbourne Review* and the *Victorian Review*. In the context of a public deeply interested in such matters, a debate about the validity of miracles took place in the pages of the *Victorian Review* in 1879. This debate was between the journalist and novelist Marcus Clarke (1846–1881)[19] and the scholarly Anglican Bishop of Melbourne, James Moorhouse (1862–1915), a leading figure in the colony.[20]

In an essay covering biblical criticism, comparative religion and metaphysics,[21] Clarke argued that Christianity was moribund and that the advance of science had led people to abandon belief in the miraculous.[22] It was as useless, Clarke insisted, to attempt to prove revelation by appealing to events in direct opposition to all known experience as to demand a complete reversal of human experience and its expression in natural law.[23]

---

18 See B. T. Finniss, "Religion and Science," *Melbourne Review* 5 (1880): 394–417; see also Hokor (H. K. Rusden), *The Person*, Character, and Teaching of Jesus: A Lay Sermon Read to the Sunday Free Discussion Society, Turn Verein Hall, Melbourne, October 6, 1872 (Melbourne, H. Thomas, 1872); G. Walters, "Some Aspects of Religious Thought in Melbourne," *Melbourne Review* 37 (January 1885): 2–15.

19 For biographical details, see M. Wilding (ed.), *Marcus Clarke* (Melbourne and New York: Oxford University Press, 1977) and *Wild Bleak Bohemia: Marcus Clarke, Adam Lindsay Gordon and Henry Kendall* (North Melbourne: Australian Scholarly Publishing, 2014).

20 Moorhouse was eminent before he arrived in Victoria, his sermons having been well received at Cambridge University; see his *Some Modern Difficulties Respecting the Facts of Nature and Revelation* (Cambridge: Macmillan, 1861). For a fine study of Moorhouse, see M. Sturrock, *Bishop of Magnetic Power: James Moorhouse in Melbourne, 1876–1886* (Melbourne: Australian Scholarly Publishing, 2005).

21 M. Clarke, "Civilization Without Delusion," *Victorian Review* 1, no. 1 (1879): 65–75.

22 Two thousand copies of the *Victorian Review* containing Clarke's article and the Bishop's reply were sold in three days. Moorhouse did not believe that human prayers could change God's plans or purposes. For excellent context, see J. Roe, "Challenge and Response: Religious Life in Melbourne, 1876–1886," *Journal of Religious History* 5 (1968): 149–66.

23 M. Clarke, "A Letter to His Lordship, The Anglican Bishop of Melbourne," *Melbourne Review* 5, no. 17 (1880): 103–12. In 1882 and the following years Bishop Moorhouse gave three courses of lectures on recent findings in Biblical research in which he admitted that he did not believe in eternal punishments.

These arguments had been in circulation since the deist controversy in the eighteenth century and were familiar to some educated clergy, as well as to readers of the Scottish philosopher David Hume.[24] Clarke was deeply influenced by deist arguments and planned to write a book in the style of the English deists Matthew Tindal or John Toland, entitled *Priestcraft and the People*. He assumed that Christianity had been shown to be based on untruths and depended on miraculous narratives that belonged to an earlier age. Nonetheless, Clarke himself was not entirely free from religious hopes, although he held that the elevation of the race was the only religion now possible for mankind. He looked forward, however, in the coming century to the prospect of a civilisation without an active and general delusion.

In his reply to Clarke, Moorhouse conceded that articles of faith might need to change in the light of increasing knowledge. A liberal Christian thinker in the tradition of the British theologians F. D. Maurice (1805–1872) and Benjamin Jowett (1817–1893), Moorhouse recognised that the Scriptures were not infallible and needed to be interpreted in light both of scientific discoveries and the latest Biblical scholarship. Here, he drew on the scholarship of his friends J. S. Lightfoot (1828–1889) and B. F. Westcott 1825–1901), Anglican scholars at Cambridge who had responded to the challenges posed by historical criticism.[25] Moorhouse went on to publish a series of books explicating such principles. Happy to accept a theory of the atonement that emphasised that Christ had given up divine powers and capacities in becoming human, he left a remarkable text reinterpreting Christianity in terms of the German philosopher Schopenhauer's philosophy of will.[26] Moorhouse was an outstanding Anglican public intellectual in Australia. His practice of addressing the wider public as members of a Christian society was memorialised after his death in the Moorhouse Lectures, some of which were of a high standard.[27] Despite his scholarly efforts, however, some of the

---

24 The Sydney weekly, *The Atlas*, reprinted a major defence of miracles from *The Edinburgh Review* in 1845.
25 Moorhouse's religion ultimately rested on personal mystical experience and he assured listeners that God communicates as readily to people now as when he wrestled with Jacob; see J. Moorhouse, *Jacob: Three Sermons Preached before the University of Cambridge in Lent 1870* (London: Macmillan, 1870). His expositions of the Bible were very popular and thousands attended his annual lectures in Melbourne.
26 See E. C. Rickards, *Bishop Moorhouse of Melbourne and Manchester* (London: 1920), Appendix II.
27 For an interpretation of their significance and content, see T. Frame, *A House Divided? The Quest for Unity Within Anglicanism* (Brunswick East, Vic.: Acorn Press, 2010), ch. 12.

public remained persuaded that traditional Christian doctrines, including the atonement and hell fire punishments, were unreasonable.[28]

Clarke, on the other hand, became more radical as the years passed. Clarke's objections to Christianity were moral as well as intellectual and, over time, he found that these objections went to the goodness of the universe and not only to specifically Christian claims. In his great novel, *For the Term of His Natural Life* (1874), serialised in 1870–1872, Clarke problematised the optimism of the Enlightenment, with its faith in reason and its arguments alleging that design could be discovered in the natural world. In his novel Clarke explicitly attacked official religion and false notions of God, while exploring a world pervaded by injustice and fate.

The same mixture of intellectual and moral considerations motivated others in Melbourne to develop unorthodox liberal theologies. Dublin-born barrister and respected Anglican layman, Justice George Higinbotham (1826–1892), for example, addressed a Scots Church Literary Association meeting on 'Science and Religion' in 1883, in which he made a plea for a rational creed that honest men could believe. The laity in all professedly Christian countries, he claimed, evinced a growing and profound distrust of church systems of religious and moral belief. Like the German poet and dramatist Gotthold Ephraim Lessing (1729–1781), whose religious ideas were discussed in intellectual circles in Melbourne, Higinbotham drew a contrast between the Christianity of the churches and the religion of Jesus. The Christian creeds, he suggested, had been the most dangerous and insidious enemies of the religion of Christ.[29] Higinbotham rejected belief in the supernatural and in miracles and suggested that only the Unitarian church, which rejected the doctrine of the Trinity, preserved the idea of the unity of God in a credible form.[30]

Higinbotham was convinced that there was a fundamental difference between the discoveries of modern science and the teachings of the churches. He believed that the clergy were self-interested and aggravated useless differences, so that real reform could only come from the laity.[31] Personally pious, Higinbotham was not outside Christianity, as he himself understood

---

28　T. Suttor, "The Criticism of Religious Certitude in Australia, 1875–1900," *Journal of Religious History* 1 (1960): 26–39.

29　G. Higinbotham, *Science and Religion or The Relations of Modern Science with the Christian Churches: A Lecture* (Melbourne: Samuel Mullen, 1883), 17.

30　Higinbotham, *Science and Religion*, 20; see also E. E. Morris, *A Memoir of George Higinbotham: An Australian Politician and Chief Justice of Victoria* (London: Macmillan, 1895).

31　Higinbotham, *Science and Religion*, 22.

it, but his views implied an alternative conception of the nature of both religion and the church. In his radicalism, he agreed with the suggestion made by the British Unitarian leader James Martineau (1805–1900) that the idea of God would have to go into retirement for a season. In place of traditional religious dogma, a reformed church, free from creeds, was needed – a church in which laymen of all kinds could unite:

> The expulsion of the idea of God from the human mind, even for a short time, by the act of man himself, must lead to perplexity, doubt, and weakness of thought, and to disorganised and unregulated action in the life of the individual and of society. But the Unitarian theist, and I think he alone, can watch and wait the course of events not only without despair, but with serenity and confidence. He possesses the most ancient faith of the world, a faith as old as the time when the human mind had, for the first time, evolved in it a dim consciousness of itself, and of the universal presence, power, and goodness of a mind infinitely greater than itself … Man will survive the temporary withdrawal of his highest ideal. It will be better for the race, the theist knows, that religion should disappear from the world for a time than that men should do dishonour to themselves and grievous wrong to their children by conspiring to perpetuate the subjection of the human mind to partial, untrue, and conflicting systems of religious thought.[32]

For Higinbotham, these were *matters of citizenship* and the laity needed to achieve self-government in religion as well as politics. The bad behaviour of the churches forced every thinking layman, he declared, 'to set out alone and unaided on the perilous path of inquiry'.[33] These were principles with political and social implications. Higinbotham did not doubt, however, that a form of religion was necessary for civilisation. This religion should be based on the evidence for God in nature and on the life of Jesus of Nazareth, without the imposition of dogmas, which tended to impede the practice of religion in the true sense. Indeed, there should be an end to all compulsory subscription to creeds, he argued.[34]

---

32 G. Higinbotham et al., *Addresses Delivered in Connection with the Opening of the New Unitarian Church, Grey Street, East Melbourne* (Melbourne: George Robertson, 1887), 10.
33 Higinbotham, *Science and Religion*, 15.
34 Higinbotham, *Science and Religion*, 24; see also G. M. Dow, *George Higinbotham: Church and State* (Melbourne: Pitman, 1964).

Higinbotham's call for the abolition of creeds struck a chord with some of his contemporaries,[35] including those aware of the problems raised by the study of comparative religion, an issue featured in articles in the *Melbourne Review*. He equivocated, however, between residual Christianity and a secular spiritualism, which saw the experimental discipline and discoveries of the natural sciences as a new basis for ethical conduct. In response to Higinbotham's lecture, Bishop Moorhouse admitted that parts of the Scriptures were cruel. He also conceded that there were conflicts between the Bible and recent scientific discoveries. Other critics of Christianity went further. Thus, Judge Hartley Williams (1842–1929), a rationalist influenced by the American Unitarian Theodore Parker (1810–1860), argued in *Religion Without Superstition* (1885) that the doctrines of popular Christianity, such as the Trinity, the divinity of Jesus and the Atonement, were crude superstitions that disfigured and obscured true religion.[36] Williams opposed dogmas and creeds, while acknowledging a form of pure theism, which he took to be 'a scientific fact'.[37]

As the cases of Higinbotham and Williams suggest, criticism of Christianity in Melbourne was heavily laced with anticlericalism and laicist utopias of a future world in which there would be no priests. Many Christian responses to such objections to Christianity relied on traditional apologetics and recycled old arguments for the 'evidences' of Christianity and miracles.[38] Theological interpretations of design in nature were popular,[39] as they had been in the late eighteenth and early nineteenth century, when Charles Wilton (1795–1859) promoted natural theology through his *Australian Quarterly Journal of Theology, Literature and Science* (1828–1829), along with arguments building on older traditions of physico-theology imported from Britain.

There were also attempts to defend Christianity in more philosophical terms. A Wesleyan, the Reverend John Blacket (1856–1935), who may have been influenced by the philosopher William Mitchell (1861–1962) at the

---

35 See, for example, the pamphlet published by Justice Hartley Williams, *Religion Without Superstition* (Melbourne: George Robertson, 1885).
36 Hartley Williams, *Religion Without Superstition*, ch. 5.
37 Williams, *Religion Without Superstition*, xxiv.
38 See, for example, J. Moorhouse, *The Bishop of Melbourne in Reply to Judge Williams, on Religion Without Superstition* (Melbourne: M. L. Hutchinson, 1885); R. B. Vaughan, *Arguments for Christianity Delivered in St. Mary's Pro-Cathedral* (Sydney: Edward F. Flanagan, 1879) and *Science and Religion: Lectures on the Reasonableness of Christianity and the Shallowness of Unbelief* (Baltimore: Baltimore Publishing Co., 1879); and Z. Barry, *Christian Free-thought Sermons* (Sydney: Lee & Ross, 1876) and *Christian Dogma, Unaffected by the Common Hostile Criticism* (Sydney: Joseph Cook & Company, 1884).
39 See Gascoigne, with Curthoys, *The Enlightenment and the Origins of European Australia*.

University of Adelaide, developed a Kantian philosophical theology in answer to unbelievers in such works as *Theistic Essays for Thoughtful Men and Women* (1891) and *Not Left Without Witnesses* (1905). According to Blacket, religious beliefs were 'regulative' postulates required for practical life, not matters of empirical fact. Nonetheless, criticism of the Scriptures went to the religious regulation of daily life, and Protestant churchmen were quick to defend the institution of marriage and strict Sunday observance against laxity. Not everyone, however, was convinced that changes in contemporary thought amounted to infidelity, and many of those who doubted the truth of historical Christianity accepted a civic version of Christianity and the project of 'a Protestant nation', especially in the context of imperial concerns.[40]

Disbelief in Agnosticism, Freethought, Secularism and Atheism

Agnosticism in Australia was associated with educated groups and refined consciences. As in Britain, agnostics yearned for what the British philosopher Herbert Spencer dubbed 'the great unknowable', while holding that it was immoral to believe what could not be demonstrated. In some cases they also struggled to develop a naturalism that was not dependent on theism or design.[41] Largely imported from England, where the Anglican philosophical theologian Henry Mansel (1820–1871) had insisted on the limits of knowledge but still sought to develop a natural theology based on science and evolution, agnosticism was often a more religious outlook than some historians suggest. Agnostics in Australia were also often less histrionic about the ebb of religious belief than doubters in England, such as Matthew Arnold (1822–1888) or Alfred Lord Tennyson (1809–1892), whom they often read.[42] Agnostics experienced disbelief in specific aspects of 'churchism', while inhabiting a range of ambiguous spaces. Most agnosticism in Australia involved perplexity, as traditional versions of Christianity declined in credibility, and those affected by agnosticism often changed their views back and forth on particular issues over time.

Ada Cambridge (1844–1926), for example, poet, novelist and wife of an Anglican clergyman, struggled with religious doubt and ethical anxieties

---

40   See Schreuder and Ward, *Australia's Empire*, chs 1, 8 and 6.
41   See J. Ward, *Naturalism and Agnosticism* (London: Adam and Charles Black, 1899).
42   For transitional doubt among British intellectuals, see Basil Willey's classic study, *More Nineteenth Century Studies: A Group of Honest Doubters* (London: Chatto and Windus, 1956).

in Melbourne. Cambridge underwent a religious crisis when she became aware of the Higher Criticism of the Bible, including David Strauss' *Life of Jesus* (1835), which dismissed the miraculous elements in Jesus' biography as mythical. She was also influenced by the high ethical concerns of the American Transcendentalist Henry David Thoreau (1817–1862). In due course she became hostile to organised religion and concerned that religious duties not take precedence over earthly joys.[43] In her novel *A Marked Man* (1890) she promoted frank discussion of sexual and social ethics and encouraged the critique of religious practices. In *The Three Miss Kings*, serialised in *The Australasian* between 23 June and 15 December 1883, she explored the religious dilemmas of Elizabeth King, a conservative woman who comes in contact with Kingscote Yelverton, a humanitarian free thinker. Yelverton did not believe in religious creeds, held that all religions were the same, and maintained that the Bible should be read in the light of reason and science. Under Yelverton's influence, Elizabeth distinguished between religion and churchism and resolved to follow her own inner light:

> Your Church creed ... is just the garment of religion ... they are all little systems that have their day and cease to be – that change and change as the fashion of the world changes. But the spirit of man – the indestructible intelligence that makes him apprehend the mystery of his existence and of the great Power that surrounds it – which in the early stages makes him cringe and fear, and later on to love and trust – that is the *body*. That is religion, as I take it. It is in the nature of man, and not to be given or taken away. Only the more freely we let that inner voice speak and guide us, the better we are, and the better we make the world and help things on. That's my creed, Elizabeth. You confuse things ... when you confound religion and churchism together, as if they were identical. I have given up churchism, in your sense, because, though I have hunted the churches through and through, one after another, I have found in them no adequate equipment for the work of my life. The world has gone on, and they have not gone on. The world

---

43 See A. Tate, *Ada Cambridge Her Life and Work 1844–1926* (Carlton, Vic.: Melbourne University Press, 1991), and for pathbreaking criticism and interpretation, see T. Davidson, "Ada Cambridge: Pioneer of Australian Mystical Poetry", *Antipodes* 24 (2010): 27–34, and *Christian Mysticism and Australian Poetry*, ch. 2

has discovered breechloaders, so to speak, and they go to the field with the old blunderbusses of centuries ago.[44]

Belief in the existence of God was all that mattered, and religion was a living thing, independent of creeds. Cambridge herself largely agreed with Yelverton's advice to Elizabeth:

> If you only honestly believe what you *do* believe, and follow the truth as it reveals itself to you, no matter in what shape, and no matter where it leads you, you will be all right. Be only sincere with yourself, and don't pretend – don't, whatever you do, pretend to *anything*. Surely that is the best religion, whether it enables you to keep within church walls or drives you out into the wilderness. Doesn't it stand to reason? We can only do our best, Elizabeth, and leave it.[45]

A related message was implicit in Cambridge's idealisation of the bush service conducted by the squatter in 'Burrawannah':

> It was a sermon without any capital O's, of course, or the sentimental platitudes generally associated therewith, and it was a sermon which did not exhort those 'anxious inquirers' to do what, under the common conditions of human nature, was impossible, on pain of being lost for ever. Only a few words of help and encouragement, from one who had himself felt the want of them in the incomprehensible difficulties and struggles of an aspiring life – a few words of evident, earnest truth, which required no graces of rhetoric to commend them, and which in 10 minutes stored their simple hearts with comfort and their simple heads with as much food for thought as they could hold.[46]

In the poem "Sic vos non vobis", which appeared in *The Australasian* in April 1883, she saw herself as breaking away from narrow binding creeds and outward forms. In the end there was:

> No martyr's crown but this –
> That ye were not afraid to take
> A lonely way for Conscience' sake.[47]

Only by abjuring the comfortable creeds could our small spark of good be kept alive:

---

44 A. Cambridge, *The Three Miss Kings* (London: Heinemann, 1891), 188.
45 Cambridge, *The Three Miss Kings*, 189.
46 A. Cambridge, "Up The Murray," *The Australasian* (22 May 1875): 646.
47 A. Cambridge, *The Australasian* (14 April 1883): 455.

> Religion, genius, instinct, fancy, thought,
> All to one narrow mould and fashion brought,
> One middle level of all commonplace.
> Break out, my honest brother, brave and strong,
> Thou that dost keep a living conscience still!
> Give thy true thought to unconventioned speech!
> Sink not dear Self in the one-liveried throng,
> But sprout and spread like growing tree at will,
> And thine own individual stature reach.[48]

This stoical creed involved relating to the subject as autonomous and self-reliant, a sermonical second person, driven by inner conscience rather than external constraints. It was austere and demanding:

> Nay, ask me not. I would not dare pretend
> To constant passion and a life-long trust.
> They will desert thee, if indeed they must.
> How can we guess what Destiny will send –
> Smiles of fair fortune, or black storms to rend
> What even now is shaken by a gust?
> The fire will burn, or it will die in dust.
> We cannot tell until the final end.
> And never vow was forged that could confine
> Aught but the body of the thing whereon
> Its pledge was stamped. The inner soul divine,
> That thinks of going, is already gone.
> When faith and love need bolts upon the door,
> Faith is not faith, and love abides no more.[49]

Cambridge's religion was a form of radical individualism, and her poetry was arguably a form of worship. She passed from youthful piety to agnostic doubt and had a mystical last phase in which she explored her relationship to that which has no shape or name.[50] In *Unspoken Thoughts* (1887), a text subsequently withdrawn or repressed, Cambridge spoke of the loss of old certainties and of being afloat on a shoreless sea. She still clung, however, to what the soul itself perceived as truth, in contrast to the external codes

---

48   A. Cambridge, "Individuality," *Unspoken Thoughts* (London: Kegan Paul, Trench, 1887), 119.
49   A. Cambridge, "Vows," in *The Oxford Book of Australian Religious Verse*, ed. K. Hart (Melbourne, Oxford University Press, 1994), 26.
50   Cf Davidson, *Christian Mysticism and Australian Poetry*, ch 2.

of any religious system. In her last collection of poems *The Hand in the Dark* (1913) and her late essays *The Lonely Seas*, she was distant from Christian orthodoxy, but open to a mysticism of experience:

> My soul was out on the Lonely Seas, with the One Who knows All; and never did the official religion, with its complicated dogmas and impossible demands, seem more purely official, more unreal, and out of place.[51]

Cambridge's stance was exceptional, but was to become less uncommon after her death.

The novelist Henry Handel Richardson (1870–1946) was more definite in her agnosticism, and she explored its viability in novels which were not nostalgic for any form of religious belief. Influenced by popular interpretations of Nietzsche and by the works of Danish writers such as Danish philosopher and theologian Søren Kierkegaard (1813–1855) and literary critic Georg Brandes (1842–1927), in her masterpiece *The Fortunes of Richard Mahony* (1930) Richardson took up the conflict between science and religion in terms of Mahony's quest for meaning.[52] In *Maurice Guest* (1908) she analysed the fortunes of a group of Nietzschean 'free spirits' and explored contemporary ideas about gender and sexuality. These ideas included the version of androgyny promoted by the Swedish philosopher scientist and mystic Emanuel Swedenborg (1688–1772) and the theories of how women were harmed by erotic relationships with men proposed by the Viennese sexologist Otto Weininger (1880–1903). At this stage of her life, Richardson was attracted by Nietzsche's atheism and his call for a transvaluation of all values.[53] She saw little value in Christianity as a positive creed.

This does not mean, however, that Richardson paid no attention to the sacred and the mysterious.[54] For many years Richardson was in the shadow of her father Walter, who was both a rationalist enemy of 'the citadel of orthodox superstition' and a leading spiritualist in Victoria. Richardson senior embraced the Higher Criticism and defended many classic deist

---

51   A. Cambridge, "The Lonely Seas", *Atlantic Monthly* 108 (July 1911): 98.
52   M. Ackland, *Henry Handel Richardson: A Life* (Melbourne: Cambridge University Press, 2004), ch. 2, 58.
53   Ackland, *Henry Handel Richardson*, 47.
54   Dorothy Green questioned A. D. Hope's reading of Richardson as Nietzschean and argued that she in fact developed a highly critical examination of Nietzsche's views; see D. Green, *Ulysses Bound: Henry Handel Richardson and Her Fiction* (Canberra: Australian National University Press, 1973); see also J. Fletcher et al., *Between Two Worlds: 'Loss of Faith' and Late Nineteenth Century Australian Literature Essays: by Vincent Buckley* (Sydney: Wentworth Books, 1979).

positions. The fact that he had lost his faith in the authority of the Bible and became something of a freethinker did not mean, however, that he found himself in a secular universe. On the contrary, Richardson senior believed that spiritualism was the original religion of humanity and was convinced that there was empirical evidence for a world of spirits.[55] Spiritualism, he believed, was sapping the foundations of ecclesiastical Christianity and could be the basis for a new Catholic faith friendly towards social reform.[56] In *Ultima Thule* (1929) his daughter analysed the mental illness of a figure resembling her father and implied that such religious concerns were unhealthy. Despite her reservations about organised religion, however, Richardson passed in due course from active disbelief in immortality and religion to a moderate spiritualism, based on direct experience.[57] Agnostics then could be spiritualists as well. They could also achieve religious depths that they could not translate into literal terms.

Freethought in Australia was less definite than agnosticism and encompassed a wide range of views. Moreover, as in Britain, there were differences between social strata. For many of its adherents, freethought was about liberating oneself from superstition and living a more autonomous moral life.[58] Thus, according to the 'Bushman's Bible' in the *Bulletin*, the Old Testament was full of monstrous tales, the decision to end human life was an individual right, and divorce should be allowed by mutual consent.[59] In Sydney, under the editorship of John Feltham Archibald (1856–1916), the *Bulletin* attacked organised religion as fancy and superstition which gave rise to bigotry and intolerance.[60] Nonetheless, although they were mostly disbelievers, freethinkers found it difficult to emancipate themselves from religion entirely. Even that fierce critic of institutional Christianity, Alfred George Stephens (1865–1933), of 'Red Page' in the *Bulletin* fame, noted that the loss of religion might be something to regret, even though he personally

---

55 A. Gabay, *Messages From Beyond: Spiritualism and Spirits in Melbourne's Golden Age, 1870–1890* (Melbourne: Melbourne University Press, 2001), 3. Richardson's father was the first President of the Victorian Association of Progressive Spiritualists and obsessed with issues in Biblical criticism.
56 Gabay, *Messages From Beyond*, 66–7.
57 Ackland, *Henry Handel Richardson*, 239.
58 Smith, *Religion and Freethought in Melbourne 1870 to 1890*.
59 See *The Bulletin*, 4 July 1891, 7; 26 November 1891, 7; 6 September 1891, 7, 37; 26 September 1891, 6; 29 October 1892, 6; 25 March 1893, 4; 17 February 1894, 7; 16 June 1894, 4; 14 July 1894, 6; 12 October 1895, 7.
60 For Archibald, see Sylvia Lawson's fine study, *The Archibald Paradox: A Strange Case of Authorship* (Sydney: Allen Lane, 1983).

expected that religions would eventually disappear as human beings found a rational stick to replace the irrational crutch:

> For even the clerical party is forced to admit that every year religion and religious observances have less hold upon Australia, and exercise less influence upon the development of the national character. Our fathers brought with them the religious habit as they brought other habits of elder nations in older lands. And upon religion, as upon everything else, the spirit of Australia – that undefined, indefinable resultant of earth, and air, and conditions of climate and life – has seized; modifying, altering, increasing, or altogether destroying. In the case of religious belief the tendency is clearly to destruction – partly, no doubt, because with the spread of mental enlightenment the tendency is everywhere to decay of faith in outworn creeds; but partly also, it seems, because the Australian environment is unfavourable to the growth of religion, and because there is in the developing Australian character a sceptical and utilitarian spirit that values the present hour and refuses to sacrifice the present for any visionary future lacking a rational guarantee.[61]

Nonetheless, he was sober about what followed from this:

> We have lost religion, and we have not yet adapted ourselves to the loss. Like a drunkard suddenly deprived of his dram, we are ill at ease, unready for emergencies. Whether religion did or did not do more harm than good is a profitless question. The religious stage was one stage in human evolution, as natural as the irreligious stage that is superseding it. Religion gave to all men what they were in their day and generation fitted to receive.[62]

Rationalism then could be a combative form of cultural politics with confessional characteristics.

There is also evidence that anti-religious interpretations of the philosophy of Nietzsche encouraged some Australians towards disbelief, although the patterns were complex, with both unbelief and new belief part of the mix. Nietzscheanism was an influence primarily on writers and artists rather than on philosophers, although John McKellar Stewart (1878–1953) lectured on Nietzsche at the University of Melbourne in 1915, and the

---

61 "A Word for Australia," in A. G. Stephens, *The Red Pagan* (Sydney: The Bulletin Newspaper Company, 1904), 153.
62 Stephens, *The Red Pagan*, 155.

Queensland poet philosopher William Baylebridge drew extensively on Nietzsche in his paraphilosophy.[63] Nietzsche offered Australian thinkers a critique of Christianity and an alternative moral vision. There were several Nietzscheanisms in Australia, each coloured by local cultural struggles and concerns. Often it was the possibility of a radical individualism, unfettered by moral inhibition, that appealed to Australians.

Once they had given up Christianity, both the poet and scholar Christopher Brennan in Sydney and the novelist Henry Handel Richardson in London derived a version of heroic individualism from Nietzsche. Sydney-born novelist Christina Stead (1902–1983) was inspired by the text of *Thus Spake Zarathustra*,[64] extracts from which were published in *The Bulletin* as early as 1900, while the artist Norman Lindsay (1879–1969) asserted a virulent paganism against a decadent and out-worn Christianity. Norman Lindsay also illustrated the translation of *The Antichrist* by Queensland writer and activist P.R. Stephensen (1901–1965) and strongly endorsed what he understood to be Nietzsche's bid for cultural freedom. Synthesising his own elitist ideas with those of Nietzsche, Lindsay contended that Christianity had been substantially undermined:

> Wherever the clarity of Nietzsche's vision rested, it penetrated all that is tawdry and pretentious in the structure of human morality behind which mankind muddles an aimless course between his primitive fear of cold, hunger and darkness, and the retribution of his own tribal laws. To the tottering fabric of Christianity he delivered a gigantic blow, from which there is no recovery for that debased creed.[65]

Lindsay detested Jesus of Nazareth,[66] represented Christianity as a form of decadence, and used his art to attack Christian morality:

> Apart from the drivelling incomprehensibility of God sacrificing his only begotten son on my account, I intuitively rejected the story of Calvary for its maudlin appeal to pity – self-pity, the most degraded of all emotions. Aspiration of the spirit in me rejected Jesus as the symbol which

---

63 For discussion of Baylebridge, see Chapter VI in this book.
64 R. Baker, "Christina Stead: The Nietzsche Connection," *Meridian* 2 (October 1983): 116–20.
65 N. Lindsay, *Creative Effort: An Essay in Affirmation* (Sydney: Art in Australia, 1920), 11.
66 N. Lindsay, *My Mask: For What Little I Know of the Man Behind it: An Autobiography* (Sydney: Angus and Robertson, 1970), 39.

debased all dignity in the human ego; a symbol which implied that suffering was a virtue and that "the poor, the base, the wicked and the dull" were God's chosen people.[67]

Prayer was fear, he alleged, the admission of weakness, and mature belief required atheism:

> All belief in life begins by denying a belief in God. For God is the emblem of man's irresponsibility, his childishness, his cowardice. It represents his desire to shelve the problem of Life, to thrust the burden of it from his own shoulders.[68]

Similarly, Lindsay attacked 'Faith' and insisted that no genuine intellect had ever accepted 'a creed'. At the same time, he promoted and defended 'Belief' as part of an ethos of 'creative effort':

> Belief at its highest is the effect of understanding, of conviction by scepticism. But Faith exists by repudiating inquiry, by wilful ignorance, by submission to any will but one's own.[69]

Lindsay also included various contemporary challenges to the credibility of Christianity in his novel *Red Heap* (1930) and was clearly out to undermine belief in Christianity where and when he could.

Nonetheless, as in other instances, Lindsay's enthusiasm for Nietzsche did not terminate in an entirely secular outlook. On the contrary, Lindsay endorsed his own form of cosmic parareligion, for which this life was a training for something else and the tensions of life pointed to cosmic dimensions of human existence. 'There is no understanding of, nor meaning for earthly Life, unless it can be accepted as a probation, a test, a breeding ground for effort,' he wrote.[70] Consistent with this, he accepted a form of 'Futurity', and insisted that 'Life' was indestructible.[71] Nor did his revolt against the notion of an external divine being imply that reality was without purpose. On the contrary, the later Lindsay was convinced that chance did not dictate the salient events of any life dominated by an obsession to achieve a definite objective.[72] There was a pattern at work in events, if not a theodicy of a traditional kind. Lindsay's mixture of cosmic

---

67 Lindsay, *My Mask*, 40.
68 Lindsay, *Creative Effort*, 66.
69 Lindsay, *Creative Effort*, 68.
70 Lindsay, *Creative Effort*, 43.
71 Lindsay, *Creative Effort*, 16–17.
72 Lindsay, *My Mask*, 121.

parareligion and paganism was a major influence on the Sydney bohemian scene.⁷³

Clearly the lines between unbelief and disbelief were often ambiguous and disbelief could go with new beliefs. In some cases, freethinkers and spiritualists sat side by side (spiritualists were divided between those who were anti-Christian and those who were not). This convergence was found, for example, in the Lyceum Movement, founded by the spiritualist Andrew Jackson Davis (1826–1891) in Melbourne, in the *Harbinger of Light: A Monthly Journal Devoted to Zoistic Science, Free Thought, Spiritualism and the Harmony of Philosophy*, and in popular freethought lectures.⁷⁴ The same themes were taken up by the Freethought Association, established in Brisbane in 1875. Although freethought continued to flare up in radical publications, it was difficult to sustain in the long term and, as in Britain, tended to turn towards positively minded ethical humanism and programs for ethical improvement.⁷⁵

Whereas agnosticism and freethought were attitudes adopted towards religious belief, non-religious secularism in Australia was more directed to the role of religion in public life. Explicit secularism was largely an import from Britain,⁷⁶ with the migration of two major British secularists, Charles Southwell (1814–1860), who had edited the world's first atheistic newspaper, the *Oracle of Reason*, and Joseph Symes (1841–1906). The friend of the well-known British atheist Charles Bradlaugh (1833–1891), Symes, who arrived in Victoria in 1884, regarded the idea of God as physically and logically impossible and was a bitter enemy of Christianity. Elected President of the Victorian Branch of the Australasian Secular Association, he became notorious for associating the rites and emblems of Christianity with phallic

---

73   Lindsay was not alone in producing such amalgams. The poet Hugh McCrae filled the bush with naked gods; see his "The Deathless Gods," *The Lone Hand* 5, no. 28 (1909): 429. Norman Lindsay's son Jack Lindsay also wrote a vitalistic study of Nietzsche, *Dionysos: Nietzsche Contra Nietzsche: An Essay in Lyrical Philosophy* (London: Fanfrolico Press, 1928).
74   See Gabay, *Messages from Beyond*, chs 2 and 5.
75   See S. Budd, *Varieties of Unbelief: Atheists and Agnostics in English Society 1850–1960* (London: Heinemann, 1977): 106–12.
76   For British secularism see F. B. Smith, "The Atheist Mission: 1840–1900," in *Ideas and Institutions of Victorian Britain*, ed. R. Robson (London: Bell, 1967); W. S. Smith, *The London Heretics 1870–1914* (London: Constable, 1967); E. Royle, *Victorian Infidels: The Origins of the British Secularist Movement 1791–1866* (Manchester: Manchester University Press, 1974) and *Radicals, Secularists and Republicans: Popular Freethought in Britain 1866–1915* (Manchester: Manchester University Press, 1980). Leading British freethinkers influenced by Paine, such as Charles Southwell, George Jacob Holyoake (1817–1906), George Foote (1850–1915), and the Devil's chaplain, Robert Taylor (1784–1855) were well-known in the colonies. For the British background, see Royle, *Victorian Infidels and Radicals, Secularists and Republicans*.

sex symbols. He helped to establish a secular press in Melbourne with *The Liberator: A Weekly Radical and Freethought Paper*. Nonetheless, although Symes could not bear the hypocrisy of theists and attempted to come to terms with Darwin's harsh universe, his outlook involved a moral protest against that universe, not an affirmation of it:

> (Nature) is producing more beings than can live upon the earth. The result is a fight, a battle for life; and the strongest, the one with a good constitution can survive, while the others go to death. This being so, what kind of being is your god? ... is this design? ... this infinite god, he is infinitely immoral. The universe is a gigantic crime. (Applause)[77]

Not all secularists were as rabid as Symes. Many were former clergy, or the children of clergy. Similarly, many members of the Australasian Secular Association, founded on 17 July 1882, were from nonconformist backgrounds. Many secularists were critical of authority in general and progressive in their politics.[78] In Australia, as in England, there were tensions among secularists between those who despised all religion and those who tended to a form of secular religion aiming at moral improvement. Likewise, there were splits between those who tried to avoid offending Christian opinion and those closer to the atheist Charles Bradlaugh in England, who sought to offend whenever possible. The mix of religion and disbelief in secularist thought could also be complex.[79] Secularists were preoccupied with criticising religion and with their attempts to eliminate religious oaths in courts of law and other ecclesiastical residues. Mostly they were better at expressing their disbelief in religion than at articulating their positive views. Indeed, they often used Biblical language, especially the psalms and

---

77   J. Symes, *The Liberator* (3 August 1884), as quoted in F. B. Smith, "Joseph Symes and the Australasian Secular Association," *Labour History* 5 (November 1963): 32; see also J. Symes, *Ancient and Modern Phallic or Sex Worship* (Melbourne: J Symes, 1887); D. M. Berry and J. Symes, *First Debate Between Rev D. M. Berry and Joseph Symes: Is it Rational to Believe that Jesus Rose from the Dead?* (Melbourne: Liberator, 1884).
78   See R. Dahlitz, *Secular Who's Who: A Biographical Directory of Freethinkers, Secularists, Rationalists, Humanists, and Others Involved in Australia's Secular Movement from 1850 Onwards* (Balwyn, Vic.: R. Dahlitz, 1994).
79   N. Sinnott, *Joseph Symes: The "Flower of Atheism"* (Lidcombe, NSW: Atheist Society of Australia, 1977) and J. Skurrie and N. Sinnott, *Joseph Scurrie's Freethought Reminiscences* (Lidcombe, NSW: Atheist Society of Australia, 1977); see also Smith, "The Atheist Mission: 1840–1900" and "Joseph Symes and the Australasian Secular Association," *Labour History* 5 (1963): 26–47. Cf. H.M. Carey, "Secularism Versus Christianity in Australian History" in *Secularisation: New Historical Perspectives*, ed. C. Hartney (Cambridge: Cambridge Scholars Publishing, 2014), ch 2.

the prophets, to express secularism itself, and some of them set up para-church groups.

The Irish-born lawyer and parliamentarian Henry Bournes Higgins (1851–1929), for example, was among those who promoted the guarantee of religious freedom in section 116 of the Australian Constitution, which provided that no religion should be established and no laws be allowed to interfere with religious freedom. Higgins made concrete suggestions as to how religion could be managed in the Commonwealth and he contributed to the natural law or fairness element in Australian industrial relations.[80] Originally a Methodist, Higgins became sceptical under the influence of the agnosticism of the poet Robert Browning (1812–1899) and became convinced in stages that religion was untrue. Another prominent lawyer, Sir John Latham (1877–1964), Chief Justice of the High Court of Australia from 1935 to 1952, was a leading atheist and an early member of the Rationalist Society. Latham arranged the Australian tour of British freethinker Joseph McCabe (1867–1955), organised a rationalist society in Melbourne, campaigned for rational social arrangements, and believed that human beings would be virtuous if they were not infected with the poison of religion. He was an active opponent of religious education in state schools.

Atheism in Australia involved a greater degree of certainty than agnosticism or some forms of freethought. To be an atheist it was necessary to resolve matters others left unresolved. In Australia atheism often amounted to the conviction that there were no supernatural beings – a kind of cleaning up of the world picture, rather than a world picture in its own right. Many atheists regarded the truth of atheism as obvious and, until the late twentieth century, scientists, high school teachers and autodidacts became atheists without generating original arguments of any great depth. Some of the most interesting atheists were anarchists. The Melbourne Anarchist Club, founded as an offshoot of the Australasian Secularist Association in 1886 with British philosopher Herbert Spencer (1820–1903) as its spiritual father, combined disbelief with faith in social and moral progress. Melbourne anarchists believed that social evolution had reached the point where it was possible to escape from the chains of ecclesiastical and political bondage and to understand the natural laws of society instead. Australian anarchists were divided, however, on ethical questions and prone to sectarianism. They were involved in arguments about tactics and the merits of various European anarchist movements. Anarchists also intended to have

---

80   J. Rickard, *H. B. Higgins: The Rebel as Judge* (Sydney: Allen and Unwin, 1984).

an almost religious belief in the equality of all human beings. Although they might disbelieve in God, they were still in some sense committed to sacrality. However, they did not produce major intellectual texts until the middle of the twentieth century, when they became more open to feminist and green perspectives.[81]

A more substantial atheist tradition emerged in stages in university departments from the 1930s onwards. This atheism made substantive criticism of arguments for theism and opposed irreligious intrusions into science and philosophy. It was inclined to combative disbelief, not only in God and Christianity, but also in religion of any sort. Here the atheist Scottish Australian philosopher John Anderson (1893–1962) was a major influence. Anderson, who took up the Chair of Philosophy at the University of Sydney in 1927, brought his own uncompromising version of Scottish philosophy to Australia, including a form of realist metaphysics, a form of the doctrine of univocity, according to which there was one kind of truth, one kind of being, and one kind of knowledge, and his own version of traditional syllogistic logic. Anderson was a naturalist metaphysician with no peer in Australia in his lifetime. His philosophical views were complex and involved a form of radical pluralism. For Anderson there were no ultimate units in reality but only complex entities constantly in flux and all possibilities and dispositions were unreal.[82] Consistent with this ontological severity, nothing existed outside of space-time and there was no consciousness, although Anderson accepted the reality of generals, relations and feelings.[83]

Anderson published little in his lifetime and his amalgam of empiricism and realism gained only moderate attention outside Australia. Within Australia, however, Anderson's philosophy was a major force and seemed to some to dispose of religious illusions altogether. Anderson was a militant champion of disbelief. He was certain that religious claims were false and gave arguments for his views. Anderson rejected religion as irrational and subjectivist and dismissed contemporary attempts to relate religion to religious language and religious experience. He also adopted a literal account of meaning, which seemed to leave little room for religious propositions of any kind. Anderson rejected the traditional proofs of the existence of God, especially the argument from design, and characterised any notion of God

---

81 S. Merrifield, "The Melbourne Anarchist Club 1886–1891," *Bulletin of the Australian Society for the Study of Labour History* 3 (1962): 32–43.
82 J. Anderson, *Studies in Empirical Philosophy* (Sydney: Angus and Robertson, 1934).
83 See J. Anderson, "Mind as Feeling," in *Studies in Empirical Philosophy*, 68–78.

as a supernatural being as a logical impossibility.[84] His philosophy excluded the supernatural and, indeed, any non-natural realm. He persuaded many of his followers to disbelieve in religion of any kind and to accept that there was no meaning or purpose to human life. Indeed, he implied that such a stance was part of the intellectual and moral advance that philosophy made possible. In addition, Anderson drew anti-religious practical consequences from his theoretical positions. He attacked Christianity on both ethical and logical grounds, denouncing Christian conceptions of good and evil as servile slave morality. He also advocated sexual as well as intellectual freedom and campaigned vigorously for 'no religion in education'.[85]

Anderson, however, owed more to religious thought than he cared to admit and greatly enjoyed combative contests with theologians before student audiences. As his critics noted, there was something of the Calvinist clergyman about him and he became a cult figure for his disciples. Moreover, his philosophical views were not as far from the religious metaphysics of the period as he suggested. Indeed, he drew on the metaphysics developed by the Australian Jewish philosopher Samuel Alexander (1859–1938), for which everything was made up of space-time, despite the fact that this system was explicitly designed to support theological claims.[86] Likewise, his classical realism could, arguably, be developed in a religious direction, as could his insistence on an ontological logic, an ontological conception of categories and the need to base ethics on the good as a natural quality found in the world – all theses associated with medieval Christian philosophy. This was not, however, the side of his thought that impacted on religious thought in Australia.

As a tough-minded intellectual creed, Andersonianism made no concessions to what human beings wished to believe. It gave anti-religion considerable intellectual respectability in Sydney, especially in legal, medical and educational circles, and inspired the Freethought Society that formed around Anderson.[87] Moreover, Anderson's tendency to argue that religion was nonsense was accentuated among his followers. They included the

---

84   A. J. Baker, *Australian Realism: The Systematic Philosophy of John Anderson* (Cambridge: Cambridge University Press, 1986), 118–20.
85   See J. Anderson, "Address," in *Religion in Education: Five Addresses Delivered Before the New Education Fellowship (N.S.W.)* (Sydney: New Education Fellowship, 1943), 25–32.
86   Anderson attended Alexander's Gifford Lectures in Glasgow in 1916–18. For general studies, see B. Kennedy, *A Passion to Oppose: John Anderson, Philosopher* (Carlton South: Melbourne University Press, 1995); A. J. Baker, *Anderson's Social Philosophy* (Sydney: Angus and Robertson, 1979), 112–29, and *Australian Realism*.
87   J. Franklin, *Corrupting the Youth: A History of Philosophy in Australia* (Paddington, NSW: Macleay Press, 2003), 35.

distinguished historian of philosophy John Passmore (1914–2004), the social philosopher Percy Partridge (1910–1988), and the philosopher of ethics John L. Mackie (1917–1981). Mackie argued in *The Miracle of Theism: Arguments For and Against the Existence of God* (1982) that there were no good arguments for the existence of God. In *Ethics: Inventing Right and Wrong* (1977) he proposed that ethical judgements were arbitrary, and not true or false. Both claims were destructive of popular Christianity. The case against Christian ethics was subsequently continued in the work of distinguished Australian philosopher Peter Singer (b.1946), who developed a rationalist version of utilitarianism that allowed him to attack the sanctity of human life and to justify infanticide. Singer claimed that naturalism plus rationalism eliminated the taboos of religious consciousness, and resulted in a more advanced ethical outlook, especially in the context of animal rights.[88] Singer's views were answered by Christian thinkers, but any impression that Christian ethical claims were self-evident was eroded.[89]

Esoteric Discernments

Disbelief might, of course, be expected in the context of agnosticism, free-thought, secularism, anarchism and atheism. In Australia, however, disbelief was also found in what I will call 'esoteric discernments', specifically in the religious thought of intellectuals involved in spiritualism, theosophy and gnosticism, understood widely as approaches to spirituality based on enhancing natural faculties. In each case, a critical attitude to popular Christianity went with a less critical attitude to immediate spiritual experience, with the result that rationalistic stances and credulity were often found in the same persons.

In the nineteenth century spiritualism provided an experience-based alternative to religious belief, and some spiritualists took up the cause in a decidedly rationalistic spirit.[90] Indeed, they frequently held that Christianity was false. Thomas Walker (1858–1932), for example, graduated from being a spiritualist lecturer and medium to being the founder of the Australasian Secular Association. Many spiritualists sought 'scientific' explanations of

---

88 P. Singer, *Animal Liberation: A New Ethics for our Treatment of Animals* (New York: Random House, 1975), and Chapter IV of this book.
89 For example, G. Preece (ed.), *Rethinking Peter Singer: A Christian Critique* (Downers Grove: InterVarsity Press, 2002).
90 Melbourne produced the only strong spiritualist and secularist associations in Australia, although a Freethought Association was set up in Brisbane in July 1875; see Gabay, *Messages From Beyond*, ch. 2

spirit and believed that immortality could be demonstrated in terms of the laws of material forces. Human beings, they inferred, had allowed themselves to be misled by superstition instead of studying the laws of the Creator. Thus, belief in encounters with the dead was, for spiritualists, compatible with disbelief in popular religious claims, and some of them were freethinkers. A related enthusiasm for phrenology was often allied to disbelief, and there were sometimes overlaps between phrenological and deist concerns.[91] Finally, spiritualism had a millenarian side, based on a sense that the present age was one of transition in which people would gradually emancipate themselves from traditional beliefs. It was also associated in Melbourne with social reform.

A mixture of disbelief and credulity was found, for example, in Alfred Deakin (1856–1919), Australia's second Prime Minister, Barrister-at-Law, and sometime President of the Spiritualist Association. Deakin combined elements of disbelief in institutional religion with multiple quests for enchantment[92] and spiritual experience, as a description of what may have been an out of body experience makes clear:[93]

> Was I waking or dreaming when just at the seaside at the close of the year and in the early dawn it seemed as if I had died or my spirit had been set free and soared up somewhere in the illimitable where there was a sense without sight of myriads of spiritual beings bright and free lofty and rejoicing and beyond them an intense white radiance spreading down billions of leagues from the Lord and Soul of all beheld only as a heaven of unquenchable living light into which or before which I floated like a dark atom of earthy substance into the infinite blaze of Divine Glory [sic].[94]

---

91 See D. de Giustino, *Conquest of Mind Phrenology and Victorian Social Thought* (London: Croom Helm, 1975), chapters 1 and 6 on phrenology as rational religion, and P. L. Gregory, "Popular Religion in NSW and Van Diemen's Land from 1788 to the 1850s" (PhD diss., University of New England, 1994).

92 Deakin has been the subject of a learned biography by J. A. La Nauze, *Alfred Deakin: A Biography*, 2 vols (Carlton, Vic.: Melbourne University Press, 1965) and an excellent study by John Rickard, *A Family Romance: The Deakins At Home* (Carlton South, Vic.: Melbourne University Press, 1996). Apart from the books Deakin published in his lifetime, his unpublished papers run to thousands of pages. For an outstanding study of Deakin's mysticism, see A. Gabay, *The Mystic Life of Alfred Deakin* (Cambridge: Cambridge University Press, 1992) and D. Hilliard, "Intellectual Life in the Diocese of Melbourne," in *Melbourne Anglicans: The Diocese of Melbourne 1847–1977*, ed. B. Porter (Melbourne: Mitre Books, 1997), 27–48.

93 For discussion of Deakin's 'narratives' which may have sometimes been fictive but not fictional, see Gabay, *The Mystic Life*, ch 6.

94 A. Deakin, "Clues," 4:622 (17 February 1894), *Alfred Deakin Papers*, Series 3, National Library of Australia, MS1540/3/287; A.Gabay, *The Mystic Life*, p. 128. See A. Gabay,

The young Deakin was a convinced spiritualist, who regarded spiritualism as a new revelation for moderns. A medium himself, he attended séances and claimed divine guidance for his early work, *A New Pilgrim's Progress Purporting to be Given by John Bunyan Through an Impressional Writing Medium* (1877).[95] Convinced that scientific alternatives to the religion of the churches were possible, in his spiritualist phase Deakin developed various parareligious substitutes for the rituals of the church, as exemplified in the handbook he prepared for the Spiritualist Sunday Schools in about 1877 when he was President of the Victorian Association of Spiritualists, which listed new 'Beatitudes':

> *Conductor.*— Blessed are the faithful;
> *Children.* — For they shall dwell in the confidence of men and of angels.
> *Conductor.* — Blessed are the dutiful;
> *Leaders.* — For they shall find the peace which cannot be bought or sold.
> *Conductor.*— Blessed are the punctual;
> *Children.*—For they have learned the lesson which stars and planets teach
>   They are students of God.
> *Conductor.*— Blessed are the orderly;
> *Leaders.*— For theirs is the first law of progress,
> *Conductor.*— Blessed are the innocent;
> *Children.*— For they shall have peace of conscience,
> *Conductor.*— Blessed are the pure in heart;
> *Leaders.*— For they shall see God.
> *Conductor.*— Blessed are the faithful, the dutiful, the punctual, the
>   orderly, the innocent, the pure in heart;
> *All.*— For theirs is the republic of heaven.[96]

Deakin maintained that what was now called the Christian religion was not absent from the beginning of the human race. In the same spirit, Deakin believed that Christianity was wider than the churches. Indeed, he proposed

---

"Alfred Deakin and Swedenborg: The Australian Experience," *Journal of Religious History* 16 (1990): 74–90; D. Hilliard, "Emanuel Swedenborg and the New Church in Australia," *Journal of the South Australian Historical Society* 16 (1988): 70–86.

95 A. Deakin, *A New Pilgrim's Progress* (Melbourne: Terry, 1877), written through the hand of a private medium in the city of Melbourne, professedly by the spirit of John Bunyan.

96 A. Deakin (ed.) *The Lyceum Leader, Compiled from the Lyceum Guide for the Melbourne Progressive Lyceum by the Conductor* (Melbourne: E. Purton & Co., 1877), 5. Jill Roe has drawn attention to the importance of both religious and parareligious attitudes in Australia in "A Tale of Religion in Two Cities," *Meanjin* 40 (1981): 52–3.

his own syncretist system, which combined Jesus and Buddha as spiritual teachers with aspects of the thought of transcendentally minded thinkers such as James Martineau in Britain and Ralph Waldo Emerson (1803–1882) in the United States.

In due course Deakin joined the Theosophical Society. Like other spiritual seekers of the period, he conceived of God in non-anthropomorphic terms as the 'Supreme Self'. As he wrote in 1889 to his long-time correspondent, Harvard philosopher Josiah Royce,

> Your crowning and closing conception of the Logos suffering with us, in us, and *as* us, was the first solution of the problem of evil at which I leaped in my youth, and I have never recognised for years any other possible Deity than that Supreme Self to which you point.[97]

In his search for a religion compatible with a scientific outlook Deakin integrated an immanent mysticism with the evolutionary theories of Spencer and Darwin, on the assumption that properly carried out scientific inquiries would identify the relevant spiritual processes in human psychology.

Here he drew on the psychological theology developed by the Swedish philosopher, scientist and clairvoyant, Emanuel Swedenborg, including his doctrine of divine influx, his ethics of unselfed love and his moral theology or doctrine of 'uses', which conferred theological depth on the simplest activities of ordinary life. For Deakin, who followed contemporary psychology closely, including the work of William James (1842–1910) at Harvard, revelation could be both psychological and genuine. Accordingly, Deakin made sense of his own mystical experiences in terms of messages from the unconscious and sought to explain prophecy in terms of peak experiences occurring through subliminal channels. In *The Gospel of Islam* (1897) he reinterpreted the revelation received by the prophet Mahomet in these terms. In the same way, Deakin also looked forward to a convergence of East and West and identified with esoteric Buddhism, devoting three chapters to it in his *Temple and Tomb in India* (1893). Deakin had no problem, however, with the Christianity of Jesus and in the 1890s he joined Charles Strong's progressive Australian Church.

Deakin was the leading social liberal in Victoria and his religious moralism set the pattern for a major strand of Australian liberalism after him. He claimed to be guided by providence in daily life, especially in his work for

---

97 W. Murdoch, *Alfred Deakin: A Sketch* (London: Constable, 1923), 129.

federation.⁹⁸ Deeply committed to a moral conception of the state derived from British Idealism and to the view that government should empower people to be active citizens, Deakin believed that the aims of human life should not be reduced to those of commerce.⁹⁹ His religious opinions were not orthodox, but his political and social views were, in some respects, religious.

Disbelief in traditional religious beliefs could also be combined with openness to mystical concerns of a less enthusiastic type. The Scottish newspaper owner and Victorian magnate, David Syme (1827–1908), for example, thought himself out of traditional religion, while retaining an interest in mysticism as a field of research. It is harder to place him in relation to either disbelief or unbelief, although he rejected his father's Calvinism, including the doctrines of original sin, predestination and eternal punishment. Syme studied theology for two years at a liberal academy at Kilmarnock in Scotland, before travelling in Germany, where he encountered a range of exciting philosophical ideas.¹⁰⁰ He attended classes at the University of Heidelberg in 1849, where he became more interested in Hegelianism than in theology.¹⁰¹ In due course, he brought his enthusiasm for German philosophical and social ideas to Melbourne. Over time, Syme moved away from formal religion, but not from the social idealism associated with German Protestantism. Unlike most Melburnians, he was critical of British political, social and economic institutions, and indeed of the whole legacy of what he termed 'the hegemonic ideas of 1688'. His economic thought had no theological dimension and, unlike many who favoured free trade, he did not assume that a beneficent providence ensured harmony between self-interest and the common good. He also retained a Calvinist emphasis on human selfishness and harsh real world conditions.¹⁰² Syme sympathised with German conceptions of an ethical state embedded in a civil economy. He was also abreast of radical thought in Britain, including Chartism, through his brother Ebenezer, who was a

---

98 Gabay, *The Mystic Life of Alfred Deakin*, 120.
99 See J. Brett, *Australian Liberals and the Moral Middle Class: From Alfred Deakin to John Howard* (Melbourne: Cambridge University Press, 2003). For context, see S. Macintyre, *A Colonial Liberalism: The Lost World of Three Victorian Visionaries* (Melbourne: Oxford University Press, 1991).
100 D. Veitch, *David Syme: The Quiet Revolutionary* (Flemington: David Syme Foundation, 2001), ch. 7.
101 Veitch, *David Syme*, chs 7 and 30.
102 For religious influences on Syme's political and economic thought, see G. Melleuish, "David Syme, Charles H. Pearson and the Democratic Ideal in Australia", *Australian Journal of Political Science*, 44, 2 (2009) 213–228, especially 216–219.

friend both of the novelist George Eliot (1819–1880) and of the leading British secularist George Holyoake.[103]

From the intellectual depth of his family origins and his extensive reading, David Syme emerged as a citizen with substantive views on philosophy and science, as well as politics. Syme set out his complex political and economic ideas in his *Outline of An Industrial Science* (1876). He also supported women's suffrage and many movements for improvement and reform in Melbourne. His emancipation from confessional religion did not imply, however, a disinterest in spiritual matters; Syme shared Deakin's interest in spiritualism. He also had his own scientific interests and wrote a significant critique of Darwin entitled *On the Modification of Organisms* (1891). After weighing various standpoints and engaging with a wide range of authors, such as John Stuart Mill, William James and James Martineau, Syme concluded in his most extensive philosophical work, *The Soul, A Study and An Argument* (1903), that life was constituted by the integrating formative energy of a primordial mind.[104] Likewise, religious sentiments were the inevitable products of the cosmos and belief in immortality was instinctual:

> We are inclined to the opinion that the universality of the belief in a future life is due to the operation of instinct, which, as Hume held, is independent of all the laboured deductions of the understanding. The instinct of self-preservation is the Will to live, and is limitless as regards time. It projects itself beyond the present life into a new world. And the instinct survives in spite of the apparently overwhelming evidence against it. It is stronger than reason, more powerful than the evidences of sense …
>
> I have endeavoured to show that it is the mind that organises and actuates the body, and not the body that organises and actuates the mind. This organising power of the mind is manifested in organism modifications generally, more especially in the reparative processes, previously described. It is quite conceivable, therefore, that the mind may act, and be acted upon, directly without the intervention of the bodily structure.[105]

There was, however, no room in Syme's universe for either supernatural mysteries or public cult and, under his editorship, the Melbourne *Age* opposed

---

103 Veitch, *David Syme*, chs 4, 5 and 9.
104 D. Syme, *The Soul: A Study and An Argument* (London: Macmillan, 1903), 29.
105 Syme, *The Soul*, 190, 203.

church interference in secular affairs. Nonetheless, although he was anti-Catholic, Syme was a cultural Protestant and less actively hostile to the churches than the politician Henry Parkes (1815–1896) and his *Empire* newspaper in New South Wales.

Another form of esoteric discernment was associated with gnostic strands found in elite circles in Sydney,[106] where a refined form of Hellenism sometimes included respect for the Greek mystery religions. The first Professor of Greek at the University of Sydney, Charles Badham (1813–1884), a leading Plato scholar, allied the cultural religion of Classicism with mystical interests and a free-minded Christianity.[107] In a related spirit, his colleague, Mungo MacCallum (1854–1942), who shared Badham's enthusiasm for classics, used a psychological spiritualism to interpret magical themes.[108]

The poet and comparative literature scholar Christopher Brennan (1870–1932) developed related spiritual psychological interests. Born a Catholic and educated at the University of Sydney where he studied under the philosopher Francis Anderson, Brennan was abreast of contemporary philosophical developments in France and Germany, as well as in Britain and the United States. He studied in Berlin from 1892 to 1894 and taught German and Comparative Literature at the University of Sydney from 1909. Brennan lost his faith around 1890, when he read the agnostic British philosopher Herbert Spencer.[109] After his years in Berlin he regarded religious doctrines as unworthy of the human being. Nevertheless, Brennan's disbelief led him towards spiritual experiences. He became involved with the British Society for Psychical Research and sometimes attended Sydney's theosophical Liberal Catholic Church.

Brennan disbelieved in dogmas, but not in mysteries, and he attempted to integrate transcendence and disbelief in a rational outlook by means of a Symbolist philosophical aesthetic, drawing on the work of the French poet Mallarmé (1842–1898).[110] Brennan interpreted Symbolism in neo-mystical

---

106 Gregory Melleuish has explored the role played in the nineteenth century by the University of Sydney as a religious centre charged with upholding the values of civic humanism and tempering the negative effects of the growth of commerce and democracy. See his comprehensive study, *Cultural Liberalism*.

107 See C. Badham, *Speeches and Lectures Delivered in Australia* (Sydney: William Dymock, 1890) and G. Melleuish, *Cultural Liberalism*, 62–6.

108 Mungo MacCallum, *Tennyson's Idylls of the King and Arthurian Story from the XVIth Century* (Glasgow: Maclehose, 1894). MacCallum became Vice-Chancellor and then Chancellor of the University of Sydney. Melleuish, *Cultural Liberalism*, 83–5.

109 C. J. Brennan, "Farewell, the Pleasant Harbourage of Faith," in *The Oxford Book of Australian Religious Verse*, 19.

110 Cf G. Melleuish, *Cultural Liberalism*, 97–101.

terms, as if it was a religion. He developed complex philosophical views and, under the influence of Herbert Spencer, identified Kant's 'thing in itself' with unknowable ultimate reality, of which mind and matter were manifestations. In the same spirit, he rejected any absolute distinction between subject and object. Brennan's transcendentalist outlook was compatible with a remarkable cultural mysticism. Granted that knower and known were inseparable, poetry, according to Brennan, had a transcendental and indeed a quasi-religious mission because it was able to link the discursive mind with the transcendental self, as rational reflection alone was unable to do:

> Between our discursive mind and our true self there may be a gulf, but also a means of communication – the sea of the subconscious ... The self no longer remains suspended in air as a logical phantasm – and idealism itself has often turned to pessimism in despair of being able to bring it into vital connection with this imperfect yet real life – it has now become something dynamic ... The transcendental self in us is not something abstract but a concrete reality: only, its full potency is not yet manifested, it is yet in process of development. The mind, like the material world, is going through an evolution. It is by coming to know the world that we come to know ourselves ...[111]

Brennan set out his philosophical aesthetics in *Towards the Source* (1897) and *Poems* (1913), claiming that the French literary movement known as Symbolism made possible a non-religious form of religion. According to Brennan, Symbolism was the contemporary medium for communication with the transcendent that overcame the dualism between the imperfect and the transcendental self.[112] Brennan's interpretation of Symbolism was influenced by German Romanticism, particularly by philosopher and poet Friedrich Hölderlin (1770–1843). It was a form of anthropological idealism, although Brennan also allowed for faith in 'the Unknowable'. Brennan contrasted 'facts' acquired in a direct and intuitive fashion with discursive reason's grasp of an 'Idea'.[113] He represented human beings as caught in a structure of practical action in which their thinking was shaped by their interests, although he did not deny the role of orientations derived from transcendental ideas.

---

111 C. J. Brennan, "Symbolism in Nineteenth Century Literature" (six lectures given June–July, 1904), Lecture II "The Facts of Poetry," in *The Prose of Christopher Brennan*, ed. A. R. Chisholm and J. J. Quinn (Sydney: Angus and Robertson, 1962), 80–81.
112 Brennan, "Symbolism in Nineteenth Century Literature," 48–173.
113 C. J. Brennan, *Fact and Idea, Read before the Australasian Association for the Advancement of Science, January 1898* (Sydney: Government Printer, 1899).

By 1901 Brennan was combining the ideas of the pragmatist philosophers F. C. Schiller (1759–1805) and William James and advocating his own form of constructive philosophy, from which a distinctive philosophy of religion could be built. Brennan proposed a marriage of pragmatism, for which Ideas were responses to human needs and did not provide unmediated access to the real with a spiritual evolutionism indebted to paganism and Gnosticism. The result was a modernist transformation of gnosis that envisaged a restoration of the humanity driven from Eden.[114] Brennan saw harmony as the goal of the evolutionary process, but access to the real required the engagement of the whole self. It could not be achieved by discursive reason. To go beyond the abstract sciences and attain self-consciousness the human being had to take into himself both the inside and the outside of the world until the whole potency of the self was realised. Human beings moved forward by means of experiments that proved less or more adequate ways to achieve harmony.[115] Brennan's modernist remake of gnosticism was continued by some members of his circle, but had little impact on the wider society.

Disbelief in institutional religion was also compatible with an involvement with the movement known as theosophy. The term 'theosophy' is used for various philosophical movements of differing cultural value. Historians mostly use the term more narrowly to characterise esoteric movements that claim that it is possible to attain spiritual knowledge by developing latent higher powers or spiritual senses. Traditions of this sort were taken seriously during the Renaissance and afterwards, especially in Germany, Sweden and Russia. The movement that called itself 'Theosophy' in nineteenth-century Britain, was not, however, a cultural tradition of this kind, but a syncretic Orientalism associated with Madame Blavatsky (1831–1891), Colonel Olcott (1832–1902) and Annie Besant (1847–1933). This form of Theosophy was influential in nineteenth- and early twentieth-century Australia and promulgated by visiting speakers who claimed occult powers and/or to have received letters from mysterious 'Ascended Masters'.[116]

---

114 C. J. Brennan, "The Wanderer," in *The Verse of Christopher Brennan* (Sydney: Angus and Robertson, 1960), 157, and "Farewell, the Pleasant Harbourage of Faith" in *The Oxford Book of Australian Religious Verse, 19.* See also Davidson, *Christian Mysticism and Australian Poetry*, 22–26. A mixture of gnostic and Romantic themes was also found in the works of another leading Sydney intellectual, John Le Gay Brereton (1827–1886). See G. Melleuish, *Cultural Liberalism*, 95–101.

115 Here I draw upon Gregory Melleuish's perceptive discussions. See G. Melleuish, *Cultural Liberalism*, 97–101. and "Liberal Intellectuals in Early Twentieth Century Australia:Restoring the Religious Dimension", 4–5.

116 On theosophy in Australia, see Jill Roe's masterful study, *Beyond Belief: Theosophy in Australia, 1879–1939* (Kensington: New South Wales University Press, 1986).

Despite its exotic features, Theosophy was attractive to many intellectuals in Australia because it offered spiritual experience as an alternative to faith. Theosophy opened new horizons in many different areas. It made intellectuals in Australia more aware of the great spiritual traditions and languages of Asia, while leaving spiritual searchers free to think and believe whatever they liked. Theosophists insisted that Theosophy was not a religion or a dogma or a sect, but a matter of free judgement. Like Ernest Scott (1867–1939), later Professor of History at the University of Melbourne,[117] they could be both rationalist and credulous, albeit in different parts of their minds.

The success of Theosophy in Sydney owed much to the fact that it had a resident spiritual teacher and clairvoyant in Charles Webster Leadbeater (1847–1934), who had been a high-church Anglican curate and lived in Australia from 1914 until 1929. Leadbeater remains a controversial figure, but he was arguably more substantial than his critics suggest. Intellectually capable, he had studied with Madame Blavatsky and worked with Annie Besant on an occult chemistry. He had personally received letters from Ascended Masters and had travelled widely in India, Burma and Ceylon.[118] In Ceylon he had subscribed to Buddhism and the ideal of pan-Buddhist unity, and promoted educational and other progressive causes in the theosophical manner. Initiated with the help of the Ascended Master Kathumi, Leadbeater claimed to be able to see thought forms, occult bodies, planes and the spiritual forces released by Christian sacraments, including eucharistic rites.[119] He was also active in mystical masonry and may have engaged in sexual and well as ritual magic.[120] In Australia he became controversial for his radical sexual teaching and because of reports that he engaged in sexual activities with young boys. In his many publications Leadbeater drew on his clairvoyance to make extraordinary claims; for example, he wrote an occult history of Java, in which he insisted that a new sub-race was emerging in Australia and New Zealand.[121]

---

117 Scott married Annie Besant's daughter and edited *The Austral Theosophist* briefly, although later he became disillusioned.
118 See C. W. Leadbeater, *Thought Forms* (London: Theosophical Publishing, 1901) and *Occult Chemistry: A Series of Observations on the Chemical Elements* (Adyar, Madras: Office of the Theosophist, 1908), both with Annie Besant. See also *Man Visible and Invisible* (London: Theosophical Publishing House, 1902) and *The Christian Gnosis* (Sydney: St Alban Press, 1983). For his life, see G. Tillett, *The Elder Brother: A Biography of Charles Webster Leadbeater* (London: Routledge & Kegan Paul, 1982).
119 C. W. Leadbeater, *The Science of Sacraments: An Occult and Clairvoyant Study of the Christian Eucharist* (Sydney: St. Alban Press, 1920).
120 G. Tillett, *The Elder Brother*, 87.
121 C. W. Leadbeater, *The Occult History of Java* (Madras: Theosophical Publishing House, 1951) and *Australia and New Zealand as the Home of a New Sub-Race* (Sydney: Theosophical Society in Australia, 1915).

Leadbeater attempted to develop a rational aesthetic form of esoteric Christianity. In this he collaborated with J. I. Wedgwood (1883–1951), a consecrated bishop of the Old Catholic Church, to revise the Old Catholic Liturgy and set up the Liberal Catholic Church, offering a cocktail of traditional liturgy, radical freedom of belief and esoteric magic. Leadbeater's version of Christianity was based on Ascended Masters and the manifestation of Lord Maitreya, rather than on Jesus Christ. It relied on clairvoyant vision and spiritual experience, rather than faith. Accordingly, the teachings of his Liberal Catholic Church were unorthodox, despite its use of traditionalist forms. According to the Liberal Catholic Church all religions awere revelations from God, and the Jews had no monopoly on religious truth. No-one needed to be converted from another religion, and Buddhism, Hinduism and Christianity could all be combined. There was, to be fair, a new ethical religious vision in all this, and Liberal Catholics discerned before most other Christians that religion would have a new function in the world that was now emerging. Leadbeater was the prophet of this transformation. He was a major cultural figure in Sydney, promoting theosophical approaches to colour, music and ritual. He also played a leading role in the detection of Krishnamurti as the Maitreya Buddha and in the building of the Star Amphitheatre at Sydney's Balmoral Beach, where Christ was expected to appear. With his energy behind it, the Sydney Theosophical Lodge became the largest in the world.[122]

Theosophy in Sydney was a form of spiritual naturalism, for which esoteric phenomena of various kinds occurred in and not outside a law governed universe. It was highly critical of popular religion, while offering direct access to the spiritual world. Seeking to combine the spiritual, science and art, like spiritualism, it claimed a scientific status. Theosophists were cultural and social progressives and were involved in causes such as animal welfare, town planning and vegetarianism. They also developed a cultural centre at The Manor, Clifton Gardens in Sydney and influenced new developments in the arts.[123]

Theosophy was a major influence on Australian feminist writers, making it possible for them to manage their disbelief without abandoning enchantment. In colonial Queensland novelist Rosa Praed (1851–1935), for example, combined disbelief in orthodox religion with a ready belief in

---

[122] For esoteric trends generally, see N. Drury and G. Tillett, *Other Temples, Other Gods: The Occult in Australia* (Sydney: Methuen, 1980).

[123] See J. McFarlane, *Concerning the Spiritual The Influence of the Theosophy Society on Australian Artists 1890–1934* (Melbourne: Australian Scholarly Publishing, 2012).

the revelations of her partner, psychic medium Nancy Harward, with whom she wrote novels, some with occult themes. Through Nancy, Praed made contact with two superphysical entities, 'F.' and 'K.' and came to identify her experiences at séances with the life of a woman in ancient Rome. She also explored esoteric Buddhism in two novels, *As a Watch in the Night* (1901) and *Nyria* (1904), without moderating her hostility to Christianity.[124] This again suggests that some intellectuals rejected traditional Christianity because it failed to provide spiritual experiences and not just because they thought that its claims were incredible and without scientific support.

Another form of theosophy, the movement known as Anthroposophy, was influential in Australia, although it is harder to relate to disbelief. Based on the spiritual teachings of the Austrian philosopher and scientist, Rudolf Steiner (1861–1925), Anthroposophy flourished among some poets, painters and architects. Unlike Blavatsky, Steiner embraced an esoteric form of Christianity. He also made contributions to European modernism through his reconstruction of Goethe's aesthetics and his architecture. In addition, he founded a well-known form of alternative education in the Waldorf Schools, as well as the biodynamic agriculture movement. Australians showed considerable interest in his philosophical ideas and some wrote studies of his philosophy.[125] Steiner's innovations in the arts had an impact not only on teachers, but on artists and architects, including Marion Mahony Griffin (1871–1961)[126] and, through her, Walter Burley Griffin (1876–1937) and the design of Canberra. Anthroposophists were often critical of the teachings of the churches, but tended to believe a good deal of what Steiner said.

After the Second World War, modernist forms of gnosticism emerged in Australia – forms in which openness to direct spiritual experiences did

---

124 For Praed's theosophy, see K. Ferres, "Rosa Praed and Spiritualism," *Australian Cultural History* 23 (2004): 7–23, and C. Roderick, *In Mortal Bondage: The Strange Life of Rosa Praed* (Sydney: Angus and Robertson, 1948).

125 A. Anderson, *Dramatic Anthroposophy: Identification and Contextualization of Primary Features of Rudolf Steiner's "Anthroposophy", as Expressed in His "Mystery Drama", Die Pforte der Einweihung (The Portal of Initiation)* (Otago: University of Otago, German Department, 2005) and H. Ginges, "The Act of Knowing: Rudolf Steiner and the Neo-Kantian Tradition" (PhD diss., University of Western Sydney, 2012).

126 J. Roe, "The Magical World of Marion Mahony Griffin: Culture and Community in Castlecrag in the Interwar Years," in *Minorities: Cultural Diversity in Sydney*, ed. S. Fitzgerald and G. Wotherspoon (Sydney: State Library of NSW Press, 1995), 82–102.

not imply esoteric cosmological commitments of the type associated with Theosophy and Anthroposophy. Modernist gnostics interpreted mystical and esoteric writers allegorically or in psychological terms. The religious thought of Nobel Prize-winning novelist Patrick White (1912–1990) can perhaps be understood against this background. White combined an inner sense of divine reality with an aesthetic rejection of conventional Christianity. After 1959 his religious thought was characterised by a critical attitude towards the churches. White was a modernist and an enthusiast for the sublime in religion as well as in art. He held that it was possible to apprehend the nonmundane in the immanence of daily life. For a time he attended Anglican churches, including Christ Church St Laurence in Sydney, with Manoly Lascaris, his Greek Orthodox partner, only to find that churches destroyed the mystery of God.[127] The mature White conceded, however, that he hated what he loved:[128]

> What do I believe? I am accused of not making it explicit. How to be explicit about a grandeur too overwhelming to express, a daily wrestling match with an opponent whose limbs never become material, a struggle from which the sweat and blood are scattered on the pages of anything the serious writer writes? A belief contained less in what is said than in the silences. In patterns on water. A gust of wind. A flower opening. I hesitate to add a child, because a child can grow into a monster, a destroyer. Am I a destroyer? this face in the glass which has spent a lifetime searching for what it believes, but can never prove to be, the truth. A face consumed by wondering whether truth can be the worst destroyer of all.[129]

He was clear, however, that those who rejected religion often adhered to an unprofessed faith:

> I suppose what I am increasingly intent on trying to do in my books is to give professed unbelievers glimpses of their own unprofessed faith. I believe most people have a religious faith, but are afraid that by admitting it they will forfeit their right to be considered intellectuals. This is particularly common in Australia where the intellectual is a comparatively recent phenomenon. It is easier for me to make

---

127 P. White, *Patrick White: Letters*, ed. David Marr (London: Jonathan Cape, 1994), 19, and *Patrick White: Selected Writings*, ed. A. Lawson (St. Lucia: University of Queensland Press, 1994).
128 P. White, *Flaws in the Glass: A Self-Portrait* (London: J. Cape, 1981), 146.
129 White, *Flaws in the Glass*, 70.

these admissions, because I am not an intellectual, only a doubtful Australian, and in many other ways beyond the pale. The churches defeat their own aims, I feel, through the banality of their approach, and by rejecting so much that is sordid and shocking which can still be related to religious experience. This is what I am trying to do, perhaps more than before in *The Vivisector* which is coming out this year.[130]

He also may have had some belief in immortality, without coming closer to institutional religion. White mercilessly ridiculed institutional religion in his novels and plays, while attributing mystical enlightenment to misfits and eccentrics and celebrating an Australian civil religion of struggle and failure. His disbelief, however, did not exclude an apophatic mysticism of ordinary life – a mysticism that implied that human knowledge of the sacred was always imperfect and not something on the basis of which positive statements could be made:

I feel that in my own life anything I have done of possible worth has happened in spite of my gross, worldly self. I have been no more than the vessel used to convey ideas above my intellectual capacities. When people praise passages I have written, more often than not I can genuinely say, 'Did I write that?' I don't think this is due to my having a bad memory, because I have almost total recall of trivialities. I see it as evidence of the part the supernatural plays in lives that would otherwise remain earthbound.[131]

This dialectic of apophaticism and immanence gave his best novels extraordinary power. In *Riders in the Chariot* (1961) White studied the spiritual journeys of four outsiders and transposed the crucifixion to outback Australia, as if to imply wondrous monstrous events occurred in hidden lives. White described himself at various times as a lapsed Anglican egotist, an agnostic pantheist, and an occultist existentialist, although none of these labels captured his exploration of the mystical in the ordinary or his implicit

---

130 Letter to Clem Semmler, 10 May 1970, in *Patrick White Letters*, 362–63. For more positive readings, see L. McCredden, *Luminous Moments: The Contemporary Sacred* (Hindmarsh, SA: ATF Press, 2010), ch. 3, and "Splintering and Coalescing: Language and the Sacred in Patrick White's Novels," in *Patrick White Centenary: The Legacy of a Prodigal Son*, ed. B. B. Ashcroft and C. vanden Driesen (Newcastle upon Tyne: Cambridge Scholars Publishing, 2014), 43–62; see also M. Giffin, *Patrick White and the Religious Imagination: Arthur's Dream* (Lewiston: Edward Mellon Press, 1999).
131 P. White, *Patrick White Speaks* (Sydney: Primavera Press, 1989), 125–6.

claim that magic realism could sometimes access truth unobtainable by other means.

There was also a strand of disbelief to be found among feminists with an interest in Christian Science, an American mind religion with modernist gnostic features. Christian Scientists derove their religion from Mary Baker Eddy, an American healer who wrote a textbook *Science and Health with Key to the Scriptures* in 1875. Christian Science offered its adherents a sophisticated metaphysical interpretation of Christianity, as well as a daily regimen believed to protect against sickness and disease. Feminists with an interest in Christian Science often moved away from organised religion without writing at length against particular Christian doctrines, even though they rejected the creeds of mainstream churches. Here it is useful to consider the far from straightforward case of novelist Miles Franklin (1879–1954).[132] As a young woman Franklin was fiercely critical of the anthropomorphic God promoted by the churches:

> Before I was ten I became critical of the anthropomorphic God as interpreted in the churches. I did not warm to One thus revealed as the semblance of a bullying and mean old man who must have all his own way, be praised all the time and for attributes which were deplorable in us.[133]

Nonetheless, although Franklin was militantly anticlerical in *My Brilliant Career* (1901) and said to be 'of no religion', she retained a severe sense of the difficulty of religious questions:

> My dissatisfaction with God was shelved for the moment, but it was the early symptom of a questioning mind, that heaviest of handicaps in the struggle for worldly success or mental complacency … a mind dependent on its own search for God and open to the discovery that it takes a greater mind to find God than it does to lose him, a mind with austere, demanding, lonely standard that calls for fortitude, and fortitude is a great absentee.[134]

---

132 For Franklin's complex personal path, see J. Roe and M. Bettison (eds), *A Gregarious Culture: Topical Writings of Miles Franklin* (St Lucia: University of Queensland Press, 2001) and J. Roe, ed., *My Congenials: Miles Franklin and Friends in Letters* (Pymble: Angus & Robertson, 2010), *Stella Miles Franklin: A Biography* (Pymble: Harper Collins, 2008) and *Her Brilliant Career: The Life of Stella Miles Franklin* (Cambridge: Harvard University Press, 2009).
133 M. Franklin, *Childhood at Brindabella: My First Ten Years* (Sydney: Angus and Robertson, 1963), 109.
134 Franklin, *Childhood at Brindabella*, 114.

Franklin corresponded with leading radicals of the period such as novelist Joseph Furphy (1843–1912) and feminists Rose Scott (1847–1925) and Vida Goldstein (1869–1949). She also associated from time to time with Melbourne adherents of Christian Science and probably took part in Christian Science activities with some of her Australian friends during her nine years in the United States.

Christian Science played a significant role in the development of Australian feminism, partly because it promoted the independence and self-government of women,[135] and partly because it seemed an avant-garde movement that allowed women to see themselves at the front of world thought. Christian Scientists used Christian language, but in a metaphysical sense. They could combine contempt for popular religion with claims about a reality transcending the senses. Australia's leading suffragette, Vida Goldstein, veered towards such views. Goldstein came from a wealthy Polish Jewish family and founded the Women's Peace Army in Melbourne in 1915. Through her contact with a leading progressive Melbourne churchman, the Reverend Charles Strong (1844–1942), she became interested in land, penal and social reform. Goldstein was convinced that rationalism and mysticism could be fused. Her religion was the liberation of women and she envisaged her work for the cause as a sacred obligation to other women. When Goldstein realised that her attempt to develop a women's political movement independent of political parties was a failure, she turned to Christian Science and worked as a Christian Science practitioner for the last twenty years of her life, serving as the second leader of the First Church of Christ, Scientist in St. Kilda Road, Melbourne.[136] While still ridiculing popular religion, she now turned to metaphysical prayer as the most realistic way to respond to the outbreak of world war, and fought for the right of Christian Scientists to rely on prayer as their only means of healing.[137] Disbelief in popular religion, then, could lead

---

135   Jill Roe has pioneered the exploration of this theme in her "Testimonies from the Field: The Coming of Christian Science to Australia, c1890–1910," *Journal of Religious History* 22 (1998): 304–19. There was already evidence that metaphysical religion could facilitate a move from a transcendent deity to an immanent divine in the Australian reception of New Thought; see the New Thought novel by Veni Cooper-Mathieson, A *Marriage of Souls: A Metaphysical Novel* (Perth: Truth Seeker Publishing Company, 1914), 147.
136   L. M. Henderson, *The Goldstein Story* (North Melbourne: Stockland Press, 1973) and J. M. Bomford, *That Dangerous and Persuasive Woman: Vida Goldstein* (Carlton, Vic.: Melbourne University Press, 1993).
137   The writer Kylie Tennant (1912–1988) was raised in Christian Science, but developed her own independent ideas. Her fine play, *Tether A Dragon*, suggests that she was sympathetic to Deakin, if less inclined to dabble in occult mysteries herself.

intellectuals to more philosophical and complex forms of belief rather than away from religion altogether. Instances involving Christian Scientists could be matched with instances involving New Thought, another mind religion imported from the United States.[138]

Disbelief then needs to be understood in terms of the complexes in which it was embedded. Many intellectuals sympathetic to esoteric concerns were looking for a more spiritual understanding of reality than the churches were able to provide. Some were influenced by European and Australian forms of Romanticism. Intellectuals of this sort were far removed from the tight-lipped pragmatists of the older stereotypes.

Confessional Verdicts

Disbelief could also be found in what might be called the 'confessional verdicts' passed by religious intellectuals on religion in general, on the religion of others, or on secular society. In the nineteenth and twentieth centuries a form of disbelief played a role in many varieties of confessional religion, although this confessional disbelief became perhaps less general and often more moderated in tone and comportment after 1960. I conclude this chapter by noting a few such cases of confessional disbelief.

Until late in the twentieth century many Australians disbelieved in religions other than their own. In a culture with only a limited sense of the incommensurability of cultural traditions, it was not uncommon for Protestants to despise Catholics for their worship of saints, Catholics to sneer at Protestants for their high-mindedness, and Jews to look down on Christians as people who lacked tradition. In a context in which sympathies were often proximate rather than all-embracing, some Christians could be unremitting rationalists in particular domains. Evangelical Anglicans, for example, often displayed a rationalist disbelief in the hostility they directed towards the church of Rome; among these people was T. C. Hammond (1877–1961), Principal of Moore College in Sydney,[139] who delighted in exposing Roman Catholic 'mistakes'.[140] Anglo-Catholics, on the other hand, frequently directed their disbelief at those they perceived to be their

---

138 See F. Bongiorno, "A Short History of New Thought in Australia, 1890–1914," *Australian Cultural History* 23 (2004): 25–42.
139 Evangelical Christianity was an influence on the early governors and in the Colonial Office in Britain. It has continued to be a more significant influence than some historians suggest; see S. Piggin, *Evangelical Christianity in Australia: Spirit, Word and World* (Melbourne: Oxford University Press, 1996), 28–31.
140 For discussion see ch IV.

cultural and social inferiors.[141] Something like this was present perhaps in novelist Martin Boyd (1893–1972), who studied at St. John's Theological College at Morpeth in New South Wales as a young man and later joined for a time a monastic community seeking to revive the Franciscan order in the Church of England. Like the hero of his novel *Loved Gods* (1925), Boyd was taken both with the aesthetic appeal of religion and with the alternative social and cultural vision it implied. Nonetheless, he remained concerned that Christianity might not have a basis in real life, especially sexual life, and was received into the Roman Catholic Church only on his deathbed.

A number of Anglican women, on the other hand, found that religion provided a residue of meaning, even after disbelief had evacuated positive religious doctrines from their minds. Poet Gwen Harwood (1920–1995), for example, who had been a novice in an Anglican Franciscan convent in Brisbane, frequently used religious language in her later poetry, which included esoteric compositions, even though she was convinced at times that human beings could not understand being or death:

> During *Magnificat*
> an urchin stopped to write
> on the church wall. He chalked
> his message: GOD IS MAD.
> I say amen to that.[142]

---

141 The Anglican Catholic tradition in Australian Anglicanism included an Anglo-Catholic minority and a larger group who were influenced by prayer-book Catholicism; see B. Porter (ed.), *Colonial Tractarians: The Oxford Movement in Australia* (Melbourne: Joint Board of Christian Education, 1989); A. Cooper, "Newman: The Oxford Movement: Australia" in *Shadows and Images: The Papers of the Newman Centenary Symposium, Sydney, August 1979*, ed. B. J. Lawrence Cross (Melbourne: Polding Press, 1981); L. C. Rodd, *John Hope of Christ Church: A Sydney Church Era* (Sydney: Alpha Books, 1972); C. Holden, "Awful Happenings on the Hill": *E. S. Hughes and Melbourne Anglo-Catholicism before the War* (Melbourne: St. Peter's, 1992); and D. Hilliard, "Anglo-Catholicism in the Religious Ecology in Melbourne," in *Anglo-Catholicism in Melbourne: Papers to Mark the 150th Anniversary of St Peter's Eastern Hill 1846–1996*, ed. C. Holden (Parkville: University of Melbourne, 1967), 169–87, and "The Transformation of South Australian Anglicanism, c1880–1930", *Journal of Religious History* 14 (1986), 38–56. For a late twentieth-century example of confessional disbelief on the part of Anglican clergy, see the criticisms made by the Anglo-Catholic theologian and Archbishop of Perth, Peter Carnley (b. 1937) of the theology of Anglican evangelicals in his "Introduction to the *Colloquium*" and "T.C. Hammond and the Roots of 'Sydney Arianism'," *St. Mark's Review* 198 (2005): 3–10.

142 G. Harwood, "Dust to Dust," in *Selected Poems* (Sydney: Angus and Robertson, 1975), 76.

Disbelief was also important for some Catholic intellectuals. Thus the outstanding poet Francis Webb (1925–1973) combined mystical piety and disbelief in poetry of exceptional beauty. Born in Adelaide and educated by the Christian Brothers, Webb explored alternatives to Christianity, but became disillusioned with Norman Lindsay and Douglas Stewart's cult of heroic self-assertion. Instead, he identified in stages with a Franciscan emphasis on the ordinary and with the dialectical model of the sacred fool, declaring:

> But I have taken the little, obscure way
> In the dim, shouting vortex; I have taken
> A fool's power in his cap and bells[143]

In major works such as *A Drum for Ben Boyd* (1948), *Leichhardt in Theatre* (1952), *Birthday* (1953), *Socrates and Other Poems* (1961) and *The Ghost of the Cock: Poems* (1964), Webb celebrated disbelief in idealised images of saints and heroes and turned to immanence in the form of the 'thisness' of things, a major concept in the thought of the Franciscan philosopher, Duns Scotus (1266–1308). For Webb, faith implied a radical critique of secular beliefs, as well as the liberation of the body and the oppressed senses, even though the interaction between religion and experience was always vexed. As he wrote in "The Canticle", 'I sing as that maker directs. May I speak only as a man'.[144] Here, as elsewhere, Webb combined a Thomist sense of the presence of God in all things with an Ignatian emphasis on access through the definite.[145] For Webb, a critical attitude towards superficial or inflated stances could lead over into an apprehension of a mystical reality.

Later Catholic intellectuals also evidenced elements of disbelief within fideistic frameworks, and the pattern extended into the twenty-first century as Catholic intellectuals experienced doubts that others had come to much earlier. Melbourne poet and critic Vincent Buckley (1925–1988), for example, was more independent minded than some of his public stances might suggest. Cambridge-educated and involved with the struggle for civil rights in Ireland, Buckley belonged to the Catholic Left as a young man and wrote for the Melbourne papers *The Catholic Worker* and *Prospect*. The young Buckley was a religious humanist influenced by the French philosopher of

---

143 F. Webb, "Cap and Bells." in *Collected Poems*, ed. T. Davidson (Crawley: UWA Publishing, 2011), 17.
144 F. Webb, "The Canticle," in *Birthday* (Adelaide, 1953).
145 See B. Ashworth, *The Gimbals of Unease: The Poetry of Francis Webb* (Nedlands: Centre for Studies in Australian Literature, University of Western Australia, 1996), 29–58; see also Davidson, *Christian Mysticism and Australian Poetry*, ch. 4.

personalism Emmanuel Mounier (1905–1950) and the neo-Thomist philosopher Jacques Maritain (1882–1973). He defined religion as the impulse to establish the sense of the human being's life and human relationships as being bonded with forces in the universe, which have their correlations in his own psychic life.[146] As a literary critic, Buckley valued poetry that sought to create a new sense of God and to redefine His action in the world.[147]

Over time Buckley stopped believing that religion was the means of expanding humanism and, when the Catholic Church changed after the Second Vatican Council, he became a religious independent for whom poetry continued the work of religion for post-confessional people. The later Buckley retained a sense of the mystery at work in the universe:

> I have never really had any *idea* of God because I tend to think visually. I would prefer to say that the universe is alive and, as Mircea Eliade would say, 'the universe speaks to us' and that the power of its life is God. I have always taken this approach to the question.[148]

Convinced that certain facilities of the psyche had been impaired by modernity, he accepted the need for a shift from the transcendent to the immanent, although he continued to believe in an inconceivable immortality:

> I have always been puzzled by the question of immortality, but I am convinced that there is some form in which people preserve their individual identities eternally. The actual state, of course, is quite inconceivable to me.[149]

The Catholic poet James McAuley (1917–1976) also combined religious faith with elements of disbelief. A distinguished performer in many fields, the young McAuley was a freethinker, influenced by John Anderson (introduced earlier in this chapter). Later he sympathised with gnosticism and other forms of mysticism. For some years he played the organ at the Liberal Catholic Church and studied the works of Traditionalist writers such as Ananda Coomaraswamy (1877–1947) and René Guénon (1886–1951), an

---

146 V. Buckley, *Poetry and the Sacred* (London: Chatto and Windus, 1968), 11.
147 J. Tulip, "Religious Models in Modern Australian Poetry," in *Toward Theology in an Australian Context*, ed. V. C. Hayes (Bedford Park, SA: ASSR, 1975), 59–68; see also V. Buckley (ed.), *The Incarnation in the University: Studies in the University Apostolate* (London: Geoffrey Chapman, 1957) and *Notions of the Sacred* (Melbourne: University Catholic Federation of Australia, 1968).
148 V. Buckley, *The Bulletin* 92, no. 4695 (1970): 41.
149 Buckley, *The Bulletin*: 41.

interest he shared with Buddhist poet Harold Stewart (1916–1995), with whom he perpetrated the Ern Malley hoax in an attempt to discredit modernism in Australian poetry.

Despite his enthusiasm for French Symbolism and the work of Christopher Brennan, McAuley came to disbelieve in modern social and cultural life. In the 1940s he took an interest in cultural developments in New Guinea and became convinced that Durkheimian communalism, based on meaning publicly produced, offered an alternative to Western secularism, a sentiment reinforced by his friendship with Alain Marie Guynot de Boismenu (1870–1953), a Missionary of the Sacred Heart. Subsequently McAuley converted to Catholicism as a communal form of life sustained by a realist metaphysics. Drawing on the works of Jacques Maritain, for whom acts of knowledge were determined by reality,[150] McAuley became convinced that social arrangements should be based on the natural metaphysics of the human mind, just as sexual norms had to be derived from the pre-existing ontological order rather than from the whims of human beings.[151] In 1959 McAuley articulated his disbelief in modern secular humanism in an important collection of essays, *The End of Modernity*, in which, following the writings of the American-Austrian political philosopher Eric Voegelin (1901–1985), he conceived of the loss of the Greco-Christian tradition as a cultural disaster and construed modernity as a continuation of gnosticism in a more negative sense.[152]

After the Second Vatican Council, McAuley, like other traditionalist Catholics, found it hard to control his inner disbelief in modernist forms of Catholicism. Confronted by the uncertainties of Biblical scholarship, he retreated to a minimal creed. He did not return to secular humanism, but there was a note of resignation in his acceptance of a world in which the good were likely to fail and in which ironic displacements were to be expected. Hence the theme of "Captain Quirós", a poem he began in the 1950s and completed in 1964, was failure, checked by a remnant of faith and love. In his personal life McAuley moved closer to Romanticism and celebrated the beauty of the Tasmanian landscape in what later would be called a postsecular spirit.

---

150   J. McAuley, "On Being an Intellectual," *Quadrant* 4, no. 1 (1959/1960): 23–31.
151   This was also the philosophical basis for McAuley's right-wing politics. He was the editor of *Quadrant* from 1956 to 1963 and actively campaigned for the largely Catholic Democratic Labor Party. He justified his strong support for B. A. Santamaria's movement on the ground that organisational struggles did not cease to be critically important because intellectuals had distaste for them.
152   See Davidson, *Christian Mysticism and Australian Poetry*, 26–33.

There is a related strain of disbelief in the poetry of McAuley's fellow convert, Les Murray (b. 1938). From a Free Presbyterian background in which a rigid strict form of Calvinism was taken for granted, Murray invokes a theology of the plain and ordinary ('the ordinary mail of the other world'), while defending the need to maintain the high Christian civilisation of Western Europe and some form of 'wholespeak'.[153] Murray disbelieves in discursive rationalism. For him poetry is 'the only whole thinking' and religions are 'poems'.[154] God is in the world, he declares, as poetry is in the poem. This incarnational side of Murray's thought is balanced, however, by deep-seated disbelief. Murray disbelieves in optimistic anthropologies and in himself as the sole author of his life. He is convinced that the apparent lack of meaning in the universe is a consequence of the defects of human beings, not of the universe:

> Everything except language
> knows the meaning of existence.
> Trees, planets, rivers, time
> know nothing else. They express it
> moment by moment as the universe.
> Even this fool of a body
> lives it in part, and would
> have full dignity within it
> but for the ignorant freedom
> of my talking mind.[155]

Murray also emphasises the inadequacy of religious language and has implied that it is impossible to speak of God. Protesting against the domination of a scientific paradigm of knowledge, he is inclined to doubt that anything comprehensible can be a reliable guide to reality.[156] For Murray, God is an unnameable reality that prevents closure and the only adequate

---

153 L. Murray, "An Absolutely Ordinary Rainbow," in *The Weatherboard Cathedral* (Sydney: Angus and Robertson, 1969), 47–8.
154 L. Murray, "Poetry and Religion," in *The Daylight Moon* (Sydney: Angus and Robertson, 1987).
155 L. Murray, "The Meaning of Existence," in *Learning Human: Selected Poems of Les Murray* (Sydney: Duffy and Snellgrove, 2003), 199; see also L. McCredden, "The Impossible Infinite: Les Murray, Poetry and the Sacred," *Antipodes* 19 (2005): 166–71.
156 L. Murray, "The Mouthless Image of God in the Hunter-Colo Mountains," in *Collected Poems* (North Ryde, NSW: Angus and Robertson, 1991), 184–5; see also McCredden, "The Impossible Infinite" and L. Murray, "Some Religious Stuff I Know About Australia" in *The Shape of Belief: Christianity in Australia Today*, ed. D. Harris, D. Hynd and D. Millikan (Homebush West: Lancer, 1982), 25–6.

response to the frustrations of experience. Murray's theology is apophatic and uses his disbelief in immanence to outflank the pieties of secular intelligentsias.

Sir John Eccles (1903–1997), a Nobel Prize-winning neurophysiologist and traditionalist Catholic, also combined disbelief with religious faith. Eccles was unusual among Australian scientists in his willingness to proclaim his disbelief in the conventional beliefs to which his fellow scientists subscribed. Like his teacher at Oxford, Sir Charles Sherrington, he advocated a philosophy of the human person as a basis for a world view which made the experience and perceptions of human beings central.[157] Eccles had no faith in a lifeless matter that no-one had actually observed. Rather, following Nobel Laureate Eugene Wigner (1902–1995), Eccles held that mental entities and mental phenomena were ultimate constituents of the world, while the material or objective world had the status of second order or derivative reality.[158] Eccles was convinced that hard thinking would support Christian orthodoxy and, in his later years, he cooperated with British-Austrian philosopher Sir Karl Popper (1902–1994) to defend a form of dualism about the soul.[159]

It may also be possible to detect elements of disbelief in the Catholic political acitivist, B. A. Santamaria (1915–1998). Despite his anti-Communism and his nostalgic advocacy of rural resettlement, Santamaria was a rationalist in some parts of his mind and denied that he had ever had a personal spiritual experience:

> I want to be very clear. People who say that they have spiritual experiences, I envy them, but I don't understand them. My life has been singularly bereft of spiritual experiences. But you naturally – if you went to a school like St. Kevin's, which was only for the last two years of your scholastic life, in what we used to call Leaving and Leaving Honours, just the two years before university, one half hour each day was always devoted to religious instruction, as they called it. And part of the religious instruction was the philosophic foundations of your faith. And it was at that time – and I was already about 14, 13 or 14 – that I began to think autonomously if you like, about God and about

---

157 J. Eccles, *The Brain and the Person* (Boyer Lectures 1965) (Sydney: Australian Broadcasting Commission, 1965): 1.
158 Eccles, *The Brain and the Person*, 5.
159 K. R. Popper and J. C. Eccles, *The Self and Its Brain* (Berlin and New York: Springer International, 1977).

religion. But as for spiritual experiences, I'm afraid I'm not given to them.[160]

Disbelief in the conventional opinions of the day also arguably drove Ronald Conway (b.1927), traditionalist Catholic, clinical psychologist and lay social theorist. Conway denounced the illusions of utopian humanism in books such as *The Great Australia Stupor: An Interpretation of the Australian Way of Life* (1971), *Land of the Long Weekend* (1978), *The End of Stupor: Australia Towards the Third Millennium* (1984), *Conway's Way: Memories, Endeavours and Reflections* (1986) and *The Rage for Utopia* (1992). A friend of Santamaria and also involved in Catholic action, Conway lamented the loss of spiritual depth and cultic mysticism in the Catholic Church as a result of the reforms introduced by the Second Vatican Council. As the Church became more reasonable and democratic, he found his faith receding and turned for spiritual solace to neo-Platonism, the Alexandrian Fathers, and the Sufism of the Islamic mystical poet-philosopher, Ibn Arabi (1165–1204).[161]

For other Catholic intellectuals, however, disbelief purified religion and was not a threat. The literary critic Veronica Brady (1929–2015), a Loreto nun and political activist, for example, was explicit about her disbelief in barracks-style religion. Author of many perceptive books, including a study of the intellectual background to the novels of Patrick White, Brady approaches the numinous against a European cultural background and relies heavily on earlier theorists of religion such as Mircea Eliade (1907–1986) and Rudolf Otto (1869–1937). Brady is sympathetic to religion as an expression of the sacred or the numinous, but much less happy with religion as a system of social control or as a set of irrational beliefs. Indeed, she describes religion of this sort as one of the world's most dangerous drugs. Attacking the Vatican on contraception, abortion, and homosexuality and arguing for the ordination of women, Brady looks down on the literalism of the less intelligent Catholic bishops. Admitting that no-one knows what the word 'God' means and that she cannot explain the Resurrection, she takes disbelief in premature formulations of spiritual mysteries for granted. If the word 'God' means anything, she suggests, it points to what escapes meaning as we know it, and is perhaps best glossed as 'interruption'.[162]

---

160   Bob Santamaria, interviewed by Robin Hughes, 23 April 1997, http://www.australianbiography.gov.au/subjects/santamaria/.
161   See R. Conway, *Conway's Way: Memories Endeavours and Reflections* (Blackburn: Collins Dove, 1988).
162   "The Wisdom Interviews: Veronica Brady", ABC Radio National, Big Ideas, 15 February 2004, http://www.abc.net.au/radionational/programs/bigideas/the-wisdom-

Conversant with French theology and an admirer of mystical strains in Christianity and the writings of Thomas Merton, Brady combines a Celtic openness to the preternatural with an earthy humanism.[163] For her, mysticism is what matters and she has had mystical experiences herself.[164] Without bothering to ask for ecclesiastical permission, she redefines spirituality as being aware of the world's mystery and ultimate goodness:

> ... spirituality is about being home in the world, and being aware of its mystery, and its ultimate goodness but also its terror, and trusting it. But also of the obligation to listen to what's inside you.[165]

Ever independent and influenced by the theology of Dietrich Bonhoeffer and his concept of a 'religionless Christianity', Brady accepts the need to interrogate conventional religiosity and that the God of Christendom is dead. She is strikingly honest about the extent of her disbelief:

> My legs ache.
> The climb up the hill isn't the least of the pains of the pilgrim.
> There's also the pain of disbelieving as much as I do,
> The strain on the muscle of faith.[166]

She does not, however, deny her continuing commitment to her vocation.[167] Brady argues for a religious view from the other side, as it were, as her title *The God-Shaped Hole* (2008) signals. In doing so, she discerns some of the peculiarities of Australian religious thought. In her studies of Australian literature she argues that Australia has produced a crucible of prophets and might produce more in the future, a vision she shared for a time with her friend, Biblical exegete Barbara Thiering.[168] She also suggests that Australian anti-religion implies a negative form of faith, not wholly at odds with the desert God of the Hebrew Scriptures. At the same time, she emphasises the

---

interviews-veronica-brady/3373816.
163 See V. Brady, *The Future People: Modern Culture and the Future* (Melbourne: Spectrum, 1971) and "The Wisdom Interviews".
164 See V. Brady, *The Mystics* (East Malvern, Vic.: Dove Communications, 1974) and K. Jordan, *Larrikin Angel: A Biography of Veronica Brady* (South Fremantle: Round House Press, 2009), especially Epilogue.
165 "The Wisdom Interviews"
166 V. Brady, "Assisi Cycle," quoted in Jordan, *Larrikin Angel*, 4.
167 Jordan, *Larrikin Angel*, 4.
168 See her insightful collection of essays *A Crucible of Prophets Australians and the Question of God* (Sydney: Theological Explorations, 1981); see also B. Thiering, *God's Experiment: Australian Religion* (Walter Murdoch Lecture) (Perth: Murdoch University, 1982).

need for the imagination to be concerned with what is presently invisible and the need to recover the role of symbols. Brady also proposes an exodus Christianity. Influenced by the German Jewish philosopher Ernst Bloch (1885–1977) and thinking of Christians as a people committed to a dynamic process rather than to a static world view, she accepts that Christians may need to reject the ontological assumptions of Greek philosophy in order to arrive at a radically new standpoint.[169] The Australian spirituality she proposes is radically social:

> An Australian spirituality will ... above all be a spirituality of the Way, non-possessive and non-diminutive, a spirituality of giving and receiving ... Talk of an Australian spirituality, therefore, is not something merely individual or inward looking. It has consequences for our society as a whole. A spirituality which helps us to come to terms with our place in the world geographically and historically, and with the indigenous peoples of the land, has profound significance for us as a people.[170]

Indigenous Australian intellectuals brought up in various forms of Christianity also manifested elements of disbelief, sometimes in the context of reasserting their relationship to Aboriginal law. Indigenous playwright Jack Davis (1917–2000), for example, affirmed the intentional promise of the Christian mythology he had been taught by missionaries, but resented its use to justify the oppression of Indigenous people, while the poet Oodgeroo Noonuccal (1920–1993) expressed the distance between the Christian religion and the reality around her:

> I who am ignorant and know so little,
> So little of life and less of God,
> This I do know
> That happiness is intended and could be,
> That all wild simpler things have life fulfilled
> Save man,
> That all on earth have natural happiness
> Save man.[171]

---

169 For different readings of her work, see E. Lindsay, *Rewriting God: Spirituality in Contemporary Australian Women's Fiction* (Amsterdam: Rodopi, 2000).
170 V. Brady, "Toward an Australian Spirituality," cited in Jordan, *Larrikin Angel*, 268.
171 Oodgeroo Noonuccal, "God's One Mistake," in *My People: A Kath Walker Collection* (Milton, Queensland: Jacaranda Press, 1970), 77.

She also complained that the Bible was 'the only book Aboriginals were allowed to be literate about'. Likewise, activist Lorraine Mafi-Williams (1940–2001) anthologised many criticisms of Christianity and the clergy in the first anthology of Aboriginal poetry, *Spirit Song*.[172] Similar attacks on Christianity appeared in Kevin Gilbert's *Inside Aboriginal Australia* (1988).[173] Aboriginal writer and Indigenous theologian David Unaipon (1872–1967) was more indirect and used his retelling of Aboriginal legends to promote Aboriginal values and to offer corrective alternatives to Christian myths.[174]

In other cases Indigenous writers resorted to Christian ventriloquisms to make their point.[175] Novelist Colin Johnson (b. 1938), or Mudrooroo, whose Indigenous status is disputed, insisted that Indigenous people were harmed by the religious faiths that forced their way into their world:

> The road is barred by temples and churches,
> My Lord, Jacky hears your call and tries to run:
> Prophets and gurus trip his feet and shout:
> Your voice is lost in the din of ceaseless babble.
> His soles are sore, his knees bare and bloody,
> He limps on – but his desire for unity
> Dies in a host of faiths screaming TRUTH.
> At last, the door of love – bearing too many locks:
> Krishna and Allah, Jesus and Kali, Mother and Father:
> Poor Jacky sitting and crying in regret and frustration.[176]

Again this was a form of disbelief in both the doctrines and the moral pretensions of Christianity, rather than nostalgic unbelief. Johnson, however, took spiritual concerns seriously enough to study Buddhism.[177] Related

---

172 L. Mafi-Williams (comp.), *Spirit Song: A Collection of Aboriginal Poetry* (Norwood, SA: Omnibus Books, 1993).
173 L. McCredden, "Contemporary Sacredness: The City Poetry of Vincent Buckley and Sam Wagan Watson," in *Luminous Moments*, ch 7.
174 William Ramsay Smith published David Unaipon's *Myths and Legends of the Australian Aboriginals* (London: Harrap, 1930) without acknowledging Unaipon; see also S. Muecke, "'Between the Church and the Stage': David Unaipon at the Hobart Carnival, 1910," *UTS Review* 6, no. 1 (2000), 11–19.
175 See Davidson, *Christian Mysticism and Australian Poetry*, 218–20.
176 Mudrooroo, "The Song Circle of Jacky, Song 2," in *The Oxford Book of Australian Religious Verse*, 145.
177 See Mudrooroo, *The Garden of Gethsemane: Poems from the Lost Decade* (South Yarra, Vic.: Hyland House, 1991), combining Aboriginal, Hindu and Buddhist traditions.

sentiments appear in the Indigenous poet Denis Kevans (1939–2005).[178] Nonetheless, even when Indigenous Australians have adopted a critical attitude to 'whiteman's religion', they have rarely questioned the existence of a nonmundane level of reality.

Wider Disbelief

The patterns discussed in this chapter were modified to some extent after 1960 when diverse spiritual traditions became more obvious, each with their own developmental concerns. For much of the twentieth century disbelief was not prominent among Jewish intellectuals, partly because Jews were self-conscious about their social position and anxious to be accepted as good citizens. Jewish intellectuals were linguistically and spiritually diverse, with secular Jews predominant, alongside Orthodox and Reformed congregations. As colonial non-observance gave way to Anglo-centric establishment, disputes emerged. Sir Isaac Isaacs (1855–1948) and Rabbi Jacob Danglow (1880–1962) in Melbourne, among others, attacked Zionism in the pages of the *Australian Jewish Outlook* as dangerous to Jewish integration into Australian society. Bitter exchanges involving jurist Julius Stone (1907–1985) followed.[179] Jewish disbelief in religious claims was not particularly evident in print, even in the case of Jewish Communists, of whom there were many, although after 1960 some women became critical of Orthodox Jewish sexual stereotypes and some even questioned the idea that Judaism could be understood as the only revealed religion.[180] Jewish attacks on Christianity were largely confined to cultural spaces in which they would not give undue offence. Overall, the Jewish emphasis on laws and rituals meant that disbelieving in particular religious notions or teachings was less important

---

178   For discussion, see K. Gelder and J. M. Jacobs, *Uncanny Australia: Sacredness and Identity in a Postcolonial Nation* (Carlton, Vic.: Melbourne University Press, 1998), chs 1 and 2. More generally, see B. Wheeler (ed.), *A Companion to Australian Aboriginal Literature* (Rochester, NY: Camden House, 2013).

179   W. D. Rubinstein (ed,), *Jews in the Sixth Continent* (Sydney: Allen and Unwin, 1987), chs 8 and 14; see also S. D. Rutland, *Edge of the Diaspora: Two Centuries of Jewish Settlement in Australia* (Sydney: Collins Australia, 1988) and G. B. Levey and P. Mendes (eds.), *Jews and Australian Politics* (Brighton: Sussex Academic Press, 2004). For changing attitudes, see S. D. Rutland, *Pages of History: A Century of the Australian Jewish Press* (Darlinghurst, NSW: Australian Jewish Press, 1995).

180   J. Stern, "Universal Belief," in *Shades of Belonging: Conversations with Australian Jews*, ed. N. Korn (Melbourne: HarperCollins, 1999), 159–62. Stern argued that Judaism could not be the whole truth because it did not free people; see also M. Fagenblat, M. Landau and N. Wolski (eds.), *New Under the Sun: Jewish Australians on Religion, Politics and Culture* (Melbourne: Black Ink, 2006).

than deciding whether or not to practise. Many Jewish intellectuals could become secular without seeing this as a qualification to their Jewishness.

With subsequent migration patterns, modern Jewish Orthodoxy weakened as the younger generation found its moderate rationalism dull, enabling Chabad and other ultra-Orthodox groups to flourish.[181] Younger Jewish intellectuals sometimes engaged in debates about Zionism and post-Zionism and gender issues, especially homosexuality.[182] They also discussed the role of Yiddish culture in the Australian context. There was no major attack, however, on Jewish customs or beliefs. Instead, a distinctive Australian Jewish religious thought began to emerge, which encompassed feminist religious thought and Jewish philosophical theology, in which there were some elements of unbelief, but little disbelief, although some Jews, influenced by the philosopher Martin Buber, argued for secular readings of the Tanach. In Melbourne Sir Zelman Cowen's son, Rabbi Shimon Dovid Cowen (b. 1951), a follower of Rabbi Menachem M. Schneerson, the Lubavitcher Rebbe, argued for an apophatic Judaism, for which the divine cannot be adequately represented in concepts or language. For Jewish thought, he claims, subjectivity and objectivity are different realms with distinct categories.[183] Cowen combines what he takes to be Maimonides' emphasis on the *shechina* as the transcendent other with the immanentist approach to the sacred of Yehuda Arieh Loeve (1526–1609), the Maharal of Prague. In his later works he argues for conservative positions in Jewish ethics.[184]

Australian Muslims have been less intellectually established than Jewish intellectuals and less vocal, although there were occasional explosions of disbelief from Islamic women lamenting patriarchy and what they sometimes saw as the heteronomy of Shariah law,[185] as well as occasional outbursts against assimilation into Australian society. Most Islamic intellectuals have

---

181 Fagenblat, Landau and Wolski, *New Under the Sun*.
182 M. Baker (ed.), *History on the Edge: Essays in Memory of John Foster 1944–1994* (Melbourne University History Monographs 22) (Parkville: History Dept, University of Melbourne, 1997) and *The Fiftieth Gate: A Journey Through Memory* (Sydney, Flamingo, 1997).
183 S. D. Cowen, *Jewish Thought in Context* (East St Kilda, Vic.: S.B. Cowen, 1997) and *Maimonides' Principles: Dialectics and the Structure of Jewish Belief* (Melbourne: Institute for Judaism and Civilization, 2000).
184 S. D. Cowen, *Perspectives on the Noahide Laws: Universal Ethics*, 2nd ed. (East St Kilda, Vic.: Institute for Judaism and Civilization, 2007) and *Politics and Universal Ethics* (Ballan Vic.: Connor Court Publishing, 2011).
185 S. Yasmeen (ed.), *Muslims in Australia: The Dynamics of Inclusion and Exclusion* (Melbourne: Melbourne University Press, 2010).

concentrated on developing an Australian Islam characterised by moderate interpretations of shariah law.

Manifestations of disbelief were sometimes evident among Australian intellectuals converting to Buddhism, many of whom claimed that Buddhism, unlike Christianity, was rational and consistent with science.[186] Many intellectuals attracted to Buddhism acquiesced in Buddhist disbelief in the existence of the objective world and a personal ego, while refusing to believe in the doctrines of the Christian churches. Marie Byles (1900–1979), the first woman to practise as a solicitor in New South Wales and a founder of the Buddhist Society of New South Wales, embodied contraries of this sort. Unable to believe in a personal God and from a rigorous Unitarian background, she wrote four books on Buddhism, but remained hard to locate in any confessional scheme. The Queensland journalist and reclusive Dunk Island naturalist, Edmund James Banfield (1852–1923), also combined Buddhism with ecological and social utopian concerns, without softening his critical assessment of Christianity.[187]

The case of the anti-modernist poet Harold Stewart is also striking. Stewart worked his way through Traditionalist interpretations of oriental doctrines advanced by René Guénon, Ananda Coomaraswamy and Frithjof Schuon (1907–1998), which he encountered as a member of a discussion group at Robb's Bookshop in Melbourne.[188] Subsequently he studied at the Higashi-Hongwangji temple in Japan and became a Buddhist priest. He wrote poetry influenced by Zen twenty years before Kerouac and Ginsberg. For Stewart, Zen aestheticism provided a cultured alternative to Western modernism.[189] The older Stewart accepted the need for faith in 'other power' (*tariki*), but as a Mahayana Buddhist he held that the 'metaphysical' was in the actual world of experience rather than somewhere else. The poet Robert Gray (b. 1945), who claimed to have studied Theravada Buddhism in Sri Lanka, has also married Buddhism and disbelief. Influenced by French poet Francis Ponge (1899–1988) and American poet Charles Reznikoff (1894–1976), Gray merges

---

186 Buddhist influences are found among many Australian poets, including Bruce Beaver (1928–2004), sometimes together with an interest in Christian mysticism.
187 E. J. Banfield, *The Confessions of a Beachcomber* (London: T. Fisher Unwin, 1908).
188 For his response to the Traditionalists and the Melbourne bookshop context, see P. Kelly, *Buddha in a Bookshop: Harold Stewart and the Traditionalists* (North Fitzroy, Vic.: Ulysses Press, 2007), ch. 4.
189 In H. Stewart, *By the Old Walls of Kyoto* (New York: Weatherhill, 1981). Stewart expounded Buddhist and Shinto doctrines as manifestations of the transcendent unity of all spiritual traditions. Similarly, his poem "Autumn Landscape Roll", centring on the Tang Daoist painter Wu Tao-zu, guided the reader through the hells, heavens and purgatories of the Buddhist after-life.

immanence and transcendence in complex patterns. In a poem entitled "To the Master, Dōgen Zenji (1200–1253 AD)", he wrote:

> ... All that's important
> is the ordinary things.
> Making the fire
> to boil some bathwater, pounding rice, pulling the weeds
> and knocking dirt from their roots:
>
> or pouring tea – those blown scarves,
> a moment, more beautiful than the drapery
> in paintings by a Master.
> – "It is this world of the *dharmas*,
> (the momentary particles)
> which is the Diamond."[190]

Other Australians who were inclined to disbelieve in Christianity identified at times with the Chinese religious and philosophical tradition known as Daoism. Western Australian novelist and poet Randolph Stow (1935–2010), for example, changed from being a communicating Anglican with Quaker sympathies to a critic of Augustinian Christianity, before embracing elements of Daoism inflected by disbelief:

> If my words have had power to move, forget my words.
> If anything here has seemed new to you, distrust it.
> I shall distrust it, knowing my words have failed.
> In the truth of the indwelling Tao there is nothing strange.[191]

Daoism has also influenced some environmental philosophers, including Freya Mathews (b. 1949), for whom it modelled a mature and humane engagement with living nature.[192]

---

190 R. Gray, *Selected Poems 1963–1983* (North Ryde, NSW: Angus and Robertson, 1985). Gray can be compared with a range of Australian writers and painters, including the itinerant painter, Ian Fairweather, who translated and identified with the Chinese Zen master Tao-chi.
191 R. Stow, "The Testament of Tourmaline: Variations on Themes of the Tao Teh Ching," in *The Oxford Book of Australian Religious Verse*, 207; see also H. Tiffen, "Tourmaline and the Tao Te Ching: Randolph Stow's Tourmaline," in *Studies in the Recent Australian Novel*, ed. K.G. Hamilton (St. Lucia: University of Queensland Press, 1978) 84–120; A. J. Hassall, *Strange Country: A Study of Randolph Stow* (St. Lucia: University of Queensland Press, 1986) and Hassall's edited volume, *Randolph Stow: Visitants, Episodes from other Novels, Poems, Stories, Interviews and Essays* (St. Lucia: University of Queensland Press, 1990).
192 For discussion of Mathews' work, see Chapter VI.

The situation of Hindu intellectuals is less clear. Hindus came to Australia as cane farm workers in the nineteenth century. In the twentieth century various Hindu religious movements were transplanted onto Australian soil: Vedanta, Hare Krishna, Siddhartha Yoga, Transcendental Meditation, Brahma Kumaris, Sai Baba and many more. However, while autodidact Australians were sometimes happy to put their faith in Indian religious and esoteric teachings, Hindu intellectuals could adopt more refracted positions and stress the cultural value of Hinduism rather than its status as a source of propositional truths. Love for the tradition was not incompatible with a measure of disbelief which construed religion as an effect of social structure. Thus Purushottima Bilimoria (b. 1952), a scholar of Hindu and Parsi origins, brought the experiences of Hindus in Australia to the attention of a wider public in a series of publications. While taking Hinduism seriously as a source of material culture and as a means to community maintenance,[193] Bilimoria subjected Hindu tradition to critical analysis, casting doubt on gurus of all kinds. In due course he explored anticipations of atheism in the Hindu philosophical tradition and discerned a critique of the doctrine that God is among the beings that are, in the Mimamsa tradition,[194] while continuing to observe some Hindu rites and rituals. Eventually his disbelief mellowed to the point where he acknowledged a role for the postcolonial sacred and was happy to participate in Jewish postsacral rites. Perhaps, like other Australians, he began to feel at home in a multifaith pluralism in which literal belief in traditional religious claims was no longer the issue. Bilimoria was an early advocate of a postcolonial approach to the philosophy of religion which sought to get past European models for understanding spiritual traditions around the world.[195] Hindu intellectuals have not, in general, been prominent voices in the national life, although a significant number of Australian writers, including Tasmanian writers such as novelist Amanda Lohrey (b. 1947) and poet James Charlton (b. 1947), have felt a rapport

---

193 Bilimoria himself notes that Hinduism was defended to the Australian Hindu community in terms that implied that religion was subservient to and followed from social structure; see P. Bilimoria, *Hinduism in Australia: Mandala for the Gods* (Melbourne: Spectrum Publications, 1989), 51ff.

194 P. Bilimoria, "Hindu Doubts about God: Towards a Mīmāmsā Deconstruction," *International Philosophical Quarterly* 30 (1990): 481–99, and "The Idea of Authorless Revelation," in R. W. Perrett (ed.) *Indian Philosophy of Religion* (Dordrecht: Martinus Nijhoff, 1989), 143–66; see also his *Yoga, Meditation and the Guru* (Briar Hill, Vic.: Indra Publishing, 1989).

195 P. Bilimoria and A.B. Irvine (eds.), *Postcolonial Philosophy of Religion* (London: Springer, 2010).

with Advaita Vedanta.[196] The first Sikhs to come to Australia arrived in the 1830s, but Sikhs have not yet made an intellectual impression outside their own circles.

Finally, tensions between disbelief and faith can also be found, somewhat differently ordered, in many Australian intellectuals committed to forms of political religion. Many Australian Communists were quick to denounce religion as the opiate of the people, while themselves believing in the utopia of a perfect future society. Some of them were probably closer to the nostalgia of unbelief than to disbelief, an ambiguity heightened by the fact that the Communist Party sometimes allied itself with religious groups to promote particular causes. Nonetheless, in cases of class conflict, Communists tend to regard religion as the ally of reaction and as a system of delusions deployed by reactionaries to prevent social progress. Militant disbelief of this sort could sit easily with elements of the nostalgia of unbelief alongside a profoundly religious political faith. Western Australian novelist Katharine Prichard (1883–1969), for example, spent decades extolling the virtues of the Soviet Union and achieved the status of a Communist saint. Novelist Judah Waten (1911–1985), who was able to converse with Jewish Soviet citizens in Yiddish, also had a foretaste of paradise. Novelist Dorothy Hewett (1923–2002) admitted that her Communism was religious, and spoke of her 'apostasy' when she resigned from the party to which she had given much of her life.[197] Eventually, consistent with a gradual recognition of the religious character of their commitments, some Communist intellectuals sought bridges to Christianity and Judaism. Towards the end of Communism as political religion, a sense of partial convergence with Christianity sometimes became explicit. Former Communist Party leader Eric Aarons (b. 1919), for example, who studied Marxist philosophy in China before evolving into a Marxist revisionist and supporting 'socialism with a human face', embodied a degree of unexpected convergence when he conceded that his views were not far removed from an implicitly spiritual conception of the material universe:

---

196 C. Koch, *Crossing the Gap: A Novelist's Essay* (London: Chatto and Windus, 1987), 16. Charlton has produced fine poetry with an Advaitan tone and a major study, *Non-dualism in Eckhart, Julian of Norwich and Traherne: A Theopoetic Reflection* (New York: Bloomsbury, 2013).

197 See C. MacDonald Grahame, "Dorothy Hewett's Faith in Doubt," *Australian Literary Studies* 20 (2001): 49–61, and D. Hewett, *Wild Card: An Autobiography, 1923–1958* (London: Virago, 1990).

Talking to religious people, I have found it hard to get an answer to the question of what God means to them – means personally, that is. Perhaps the most direct answer I have had came from a Quaker acquaintance. He felt that belief in God meant that he was thereby part of the creative forces of the universe.

I had never thought of it that way before. An atheist, I would like to believe that in a small way I am part of those creative forces too.[198]

Disbelief and Intellectual Structure

The evidence for disbelief assembled here is obviously diverse and the evidence is arguably stronger for men than for women.[199] Elements of disbelief appeared in the eighteenth and nineteenth centuries as intellectuals sought to rethink the status of the Bible, the possibility of miracles, and the credibility of church dogmas. Disbelief also features in agnosticism, freethought, secularism and atheism, although partitions between belief, disbelief and unbelief are often hard to sustain, and a degree of admixture can be found in individual cases. Unbelief, however, tended to go with a kinder interpretation of religious faith than disbelief, which was critical and judgmental within the ranges in which it applied. Among those attracted to what I have dubbed 'esoteric discernments', disbelief tended to be disbelief in institutional religion and the churches. Mostly it did not go to spiritual experiences, or even to the paraphernalia of esoteric religious movements. In the case of what I have dubbed 'confessional verdicts' delivered by those involved in confessional faiths, disbelief often did not go to one's own confession, although it might go to less rational parts of it. It could strike, on the other hand, at belief in other religions and mystical traditions, including secular religions such as scientism.

This chapter has sought to bring nuance and complexity to the standard view that Australian intellectuals can be classified into believers or

---

198   E. Aarons, *What's Left? Memoirs of an Australian Communist* (Ringwood, Vic.: Penguin, 1993), 253.
199   For critical discussion of religious questions among Catholic women, see S. Kennedy, *Faith and Feminism: Catholic Women's Struggle for Self Expression* (Sydney: Dove Communications, 1985). Other cases that deserve further study include the poet Henry Lawson's mother, the newspaper editor, suffragette and poet, Louisa Lawson (1848–1920), who was a combative critic of Christianity, and the radical poet, Lesbia Harford (1891–1927), who wrote "I am No Mystic. All the Ways of God," in *Collected Poems: Lesbia Harford*, ed. Oliver Dennis (Crawley, WA: UWA Publishing, 2014), 129.

unbelievers. It has explored criss-crossed trajectories – trajectories found across many sites and contexts. Given the range and diversity of the evidence, this chapter has opened up fields of inquiry rather than provided definite answers. Many aspects of belief, unbelief and disbelief in Australia remain to be explored. Australian intellectuals often repeated English, Scottish and Irish patterns, just as some of them consciously drew on developments in the United States. However, it is at least possible that some aspects of their religious thought were conditioned by local factors such as physical distance from metropolitan centres and a restricted sense of the complexity and subtlety of religious views other than one's own. These conditions ceased to obtain to the same extent after 1960. Before that, however, intellectuals of many different types were inclined to conclude that particular religious beliefs were false, with the qualified stance towards religious traditions and the limited empathy for the views of others that this often implied. When these attitudes changed, as they did towards the end of the twentieth century, aspects of the structure of Australian intellectual life changed with them.

Chapter II

SACRAL SECULARITY

Although Australians have been widely represented as a secular people, the various forms and meanings of 'the secular' in Australia have not been adequately examined. In much of the historiography the non-religious character of the Australian 'secular' has been taken for granted. Many historians do not distinguish between different concepts of the secular. They also separate the religious from the secular, following usage that became standard in Anglo-Saxon countries in the twentieth century. The secular in Australia, however, was not always discontinuous with the religious, and the tendency to avoid reference to theological doctrines in public life was a form of restraint, not a rejection of the religious. In Australia 'the secular' did not necessarily imply *secularism*, in the sense of an attempt to reduce the influence of religion in human affairs, although it could do so. Indeed, in a range of political and legal contexts, the secular in Australia was widely associated with the need to protect the freedom of religion from governmental interference, rather than with the exclusion of religion from public life.[1] In this chapter I introduce the term 'sacral secularity', and use it to re-read parts of the historical record. In doing so, I draw on the literature reinterpreting secularism more generally – literature with implications for Australian history and jurisprudence.[2] My discussion builds on the work of other scholars and my contribution is to note differences and to place a larger interpretation on well-known examples. I do not cover the whole field.

By 'sacral secularity' I mean the tendency to associate the secular with sacral characteristics, while acknowledging its relative autonomy from ecclesiastical control. There was extensive support in nineteenth- and early twentieth-century Australia for the view that political, social, educational

---

1   M. Maddox, "An Argument for More, not Less, Religion in Australian Politics," *Australian Religion Studies Review* 22 (2009): 348.
2   For literature problematising traditional understanding of both 'the secular' and 'religion', see T. Asad, *Formations of the Secular: Christianity, Islam, Modernity* (Palo Alto: Stanford University Press, 2003).

and legal arrangements should be free from ecclesiastical control, but only very limited support for outright secularism. Moreover, 'secular' often meant open to all, regardless of religious confession. Sacral secularity in the sense in which I use the term differs from the three senses of secularity discussed by the Canadian philosopher Charles Taylor in his monumental study, *A Secular Age* (2007). It does not imply the emptying out of religion from public spaces (Taylor's sense 1); the falling away of religious practice and belief (Taylor's sense 2); or a change in the condition of belief itself from a situation where everyone believed in God to one in which belief in God is understood to be one option among others (Taylor's sense 3). Sacral secularity is *sacral*, in that nonmundane value is pursued as an end. It is *secular*, in that it applies to worldly affairs that do not fall under ecclesiastical control.[3] Sacral secularity is not anti-religious or profane; the sacred and the secular are often intertwined. It involves claims about where and when confessional religion is appropriate, as opposed to questions about its truth.

In this chapter I begin by distinguishing diverse conceptions of the secular that played a role in developments in Australia, in order to alert the reader to the fact that intellectuals did not always understand the secular in the same way, or even in ways that the modern reader will instantly recognise. I then show that sacral secularity appeared in republican and utopian thought, sometimes in surprising forms, that it played a part in debates about educational reform, that it was central to the emergence of public theology, and that it was part of the background to strands of political and social thought in Australia more generally. As in the case of disbelief, sacral secularity is pragmatic nomenclature, encompassing a good deal of diversity. I do not attempt to characterise the whole of governmentality in Australia, or to address the overall patterns of social life.

Diverse Conceptions of the Secular

In nineteenth- and early twentieth-century Australia, neither 'religious' nor 'secular' always carried the sense one might now expect. In this period 'religious' often implied morality or the fulfilment of duties, especially duties to God, while 'secular' did not necessarily imply the nonreligious. There were diverse views of the secular, which sometimes overlapped and sometimes conflicted, and any one individual might draw on one or more of them. It

---

3   C. Taylor, *A Secular Age* (Cambridge, MA: Harvard University Press, 2007), 1–2.

was the interaction between these diverse views that gave the Australian secular its curvature.[4]

Different conceptions of the secular were found in nineteenth- and early to mid-twentieth-century Australia, conceptions that in actual cases were sometimes fused. Firstly, there were Anglican conceptions of the proper relations between church, state and society. In the eighteenth century it was taken for granted that the civil authorities had a duty to promote morality and religion, and the Church of England was often referred to as 'the established religion'.[5] When, however, the Anglican Bishop Broughton insisted that the state should support the church,[6] he was also concerned that the church should be independent of the state in the areas for which it was responsible.[7] Broughton's ecclesiology emphasised that supreme authority in ecclesiastical matters belonged to the Church of England *as a whole*, a view that allowed considerable scope to the civil power, although only the clergy were to define matters of faith.[8] In Broughton's mind, patriotism and true religion were closely linked, and he associated the rise of the English nation with the work of divine providence.[9] Anglicans, however, held diverse views. The Evangelical Anglican minister Samuel Marsden (1788–1853), for example, combined a fierce administration of justice with an evangelical interest in the salvation of souls and had no qualms about performing both religious and temporal duties.[10] Evangelical focus upon the conversion of individuals did not exclude social concern. There was also an imperial dimension to the Second British Empire (1780–1830) that encouraged Anglican clergy to see themselves agents of the Kingdom of

---

4   For recent discussion, see S. Chavura and I. Tregenza, 'Introduction: Rethinking Secularism in Australia (and Beyond)', *Journal of Religious History* 38 (2014): 299–306.
5   See R. Ely, "The View from the Statute," *University of Tasmania Law Journal* 8 (1986): 225–76.
6   R. Ely, "Protestantism in Australian History: An Interpretative Sketch," *Lucas* 5 (1989): 11–20.
7   See B. Kaye, "Broughton and the Demise of Royal Supremacy," *Journal of the Royal Australian Historical Society* 81 (1995): 39–51, and "The Laity in Church Governance According to Bishop Broughton," *Journal of Religious History* 20 (1996): 78–92.
8   G. P. Shaw, *Patriarch and Patriot: William Grant Broughton, 1788–1853: Colonial Statesman and Ecclesiastic* (Carlton, Vic.: Melbourne University Press, 1978), 251.
9   W. G. Broughton, *A Sermon: Preached in the Church of St. James, Sydney, on Thursday, November 12, 1829* (Sydney: Printed by Mansfield, 1829),10.
10 See A. Sharp, "Samuel Marsden's Civility: The Transposition of Anglican Civil Authority to Australasia," in *Law and Politics in British Colonial Thought: Transpositions of Empire*, ed. S. Dorsett and I. Hunter (New York: Palgrave Macmillan, 2010), 129–48, and M. Lake, "Samuel Marsden, Work and the Limits of Evangelical Humanitarianism," *History Australia*, 7, no. 4 (2010): 1–23.

God in the context of the Empire.[11] Another stream of Anglican thought was indebted to a liberal stream in Irish Anglicanism and rejected attempts to convert Catholics.[12] This broad conception of Christianity lay behind Governor Richard Bourke's Church Act of 1836, which sought to establish religious equality by funding the major denominations in New South Wales. There were also differences in view and emphasis between Caroline High Churchmen, inclined to seek accommodations with the state; Tractarians, influenced by the Oxford Movement and wanting independence for the church from political control; and Anglo-Catholics, concerned with the church as an organic community.[13]

Secondly, the secular could be seen as religious in itself. Those of this view, which was often associated with Calvinism, held that the secular realm was under the sovereignty of God and that the godly magistrate was, in principle, as sacral as the minister. This view was unsympathetic to Anglican attempts to unify church and state. It implied a sacral conception of civil society, and might or might not be combined with a focus on the church as a holy society with a distinct collective identity.[14] Views of this type were also found among Particular Baptists and others.[15] Likewise, an emphasis on the theological importance of economic activity and civil society coloured Protestant social and economic thought well into the twentieth century. The free-trade ideology promoted by liberals in nineteenth-century New South Wales, for example, assumed an optimistic natural theology for which providence was active in human affairs beyond the limits of the churches,[16] an approach at times in tension with the Catholic and High Church Anglican sacramental emphases.

---

11   C. A. Bayly, *Imperial Meridian: The British Empire and the World 1780–1830* (London: Longman, 1989).
12   For the influence of Trinity College-educated Anglo-Irish such as Roger Therry and J. H. Plunkett on developments in Australia, see J. Ronayne, *The Irish in Australia, Rogues and Reformers: First Fleet to Federation* (Camberwell, Vic.: Viking, 2003), 10–11. For a study of Bourke, see M. Waugh, *Forgotten Hero: Richard Bourke, Irish Governor of New South Wales, 1831–1837* (Melbourne: Australian Scholarly Publishing, 2005).
13   On Tractarianism, see B. Porter (ed.), *Colonial Tractarians: The Oxford Movement in Australia* (Melbourne: Joint Board of Christian Education, 1989); see also D. Hilliard, "Anglo-Catholicism in Australia, c.1860–1960," in *The Oxford Movement: Europe and the Wider World 1830–1930*, ed. S. J. Brown and P. B. Nockles (New York: Cambridge University Press, 2012), 114–32.
14   Ely, "Protestantism in Australian History."
15   Baptists in Australia were often divided between Reform Calvinist and Finneyist trends.
16   The Reverend John West (1809–1873), for example, colonial politician, historian and editor of the *Sydney Morning Herald*, combined Enlightenment cosmopolitanism, free trade and providential design; see J. West, *The Voluntary Support of the Christian*

Thirdly, there was the positive approach to the secular associated with civic Protestantism. Civic Protestantism was found among Anglicans and among various Protestant churches. For civic Protestantism, a unity of nation and religion should be promoted, and there should be a marriage of law and morality in a nation under God.[17] The assumption was that church and state should work together. A conception of the nation along these lines was probably dominant among Protestants during the First World War, when Protestant clergy hurried to recommend a holy war and defend the Empire. Civic Protestantism blended easily with a pan-Protestant secularity that claimed to be both non-denominational and compatible with the involvement of churchmen and churches in the concerns of the society. It had no objection to non-confessional public religion and was involved in the Anglican and Protestant churches' embrace of imperial citizenship and their support for Australia's involvement on Britain's side in imperial wars.[18] It is fair to note the prevalence of a preference for practical Christianity from the middle of the nineteenth century onwards, but we should be cautious not to assume that such views crossed all denominations.[19]

Fourthly, there was the Catholic conception of 'the *saeculum*', which was formative for parts of Australian political culture. Until the Vatican Council, the Catholic Church regarded the church as a supernatural society and conceived of Christianity's relation to the *saeculum* in terms of the application of Christian principles to temporal affairs. This conception of the secular was not always as conservative as it sounded, and some Catholic bishops in the nineteenth century saw themselves as reformers of the *saeculum*. John Bede Polding (1794–1877), for example, the first Catholic Archbishop of Sydney, a philosopher, theologian, scholar and Benedictine monk, was an admirer of the controversial Italian philosopher and theologian Rosmini (1797–1855), who advocated major reforms of the church and a program of

---

Ministry: Alone Scriptural and Defensible (Hobart, 1849), and G. Melleuish, "Justifying Commerce: the Scottish Enlightenment Tradition in Colonial NSW," *Journal of the Royal Australian Historical Society* 75 (1989): 122–31.

17 Ely, "Protestantism in Australian History," and R. Ely, "The Forgotten Nationalism: Australian Civic Protestantism in the Second World War," *Journal of Australian Studies* 11, no. 20 (1987): 59–67.

18 M. McKernan, *Australian Churches at War: Attitudes and Activities of the Major Churches 1914–1918* (Sydney and Canberra: Catholic Theological Faculty and Australian War Memorial, 1980). For related attitudes in the Second World War, see Ely, "The Forgotten Nationalism".

19 For discussion, see D. Hilliard, "Australia: Towards Secularisation and One Step Back," in *Secularisation in the Christian World: Essays in Honour of Hugh McLeod*, ed. C. G. Brown and M. Snape (Farnham and Burlington, VT: Ashgate, 2010), ch 6.

cultural and social reconstruction.[20] Polding saw the church as having a duty to promote social justice for Aboriginals, prisoners and women and worked for social reforms. Polding's successor in Sydney, Archbishop R. W. B. Vaughan (1834–1883), another Benedictine monk and philosopher, was also concerned about the provision of charity, the education of children and the moral health of the colony. Birmingham Bishop Bernard Ullathorne (1806–1889), having spent time with Polding in Sydney in the 1830s, worked for an end to transportation and other social causes. In due course, and in a related spirit, Australia's first cardinal, Cardinal Moran (1830–1911) from Sydney, took up Leo XII's encyclical *Rerum Novarum* of 1891, recognising the dignity and rights of workers and the socialism of the Labor Party when this was almost unprecedented in the Catholic world.[21] The Catholic conception of the *saeculum*, however, implied that the laity should act as the clergy directed. This meant that Catholic stances varied from city to city and over time.

Finally, there were non-religious conceptions of the secular. These conceptions tended to be indebted to the Enlightenment; to American institutional secularism; and/or to secularist trends in nineteenth-century Britain. They implied that 'the religious' had no place in secular domains and should be strictly excluded from education and politics. Such conceptions were advanced by some critically minded lawyers, journalists and politicians in the nineteenth century; by some members of the labour movement in the late nineteenth century; and by some Labor politicians and by the Greens in the twentieth century.

The fact that there were diverse conceptions of the secular in Australia means that it is a mistake to try to read the historical record in terms of one self-evident 'secular'. On the contrary, in nineteenth- and early twentieth-century Australia the nature of the secular was what was being worked out, and, in many cases, the need to delimit ecclesiastical interference was balanced by concern to promote religion and morality. Between 1788 and 1900 many intellectuals critical of organised religion were mainly hostile to confessionalism rather than of religion or Christianity. They were often not hostile to the sacral and could support forms of sacral secularity, as could

---

20   See L. Victorsen, "The Social Justice Vision of John Bede Polding OSB (1794–1877)" (M.A. thesis, Griffith University, 1996). Polding seems to have appointed Rosminian priests and to have absorbed some of Rosmini's reformist ideas.

21   A. E. Cahill, "Catholicism and Socialism–The 1905 Controversy in Australia," *Journal of Religious History* 1 (1960): 80–101; P. Ford, *Cardinal Moran and the A.L.P.* (Carlton, Vic.: Melbourne University Press, 1966); P. Ayers, *Prince of the Church: Patrick Francis Moran, 1830–1911* (Melbourne: Miegunyah Press, 2007).

many intellectuals sympathetic to organised religion, depending on the issue. Alfred Deakin was not alone in feeling called to divine secular service in his work for Federation,[22] when the idea of creating a Christian nation became almost a crusade.[23] Sacral secularity sentiments were also present in the campaign for recognition of the deity in the preamble to the Constitution.[24] In the same way, sacral secularity emerged strongly after the First World War in the civil religion evident in war memorials in every country town[25] and in the uniquely Australian celebration of Anzac Day.[26] Anzac Day developed into a celebration of what historian Graeme Davison calls 'the binding rituals of the nation',[27] but it is often forgotten that it had Anglo-Catholic beginnings in Brisbane, where Canon D. J. Garland developed most of the features of Anzac Day celebrations in an attempt to sacralise the new nation.[28] Garland's work signals the Christian origins of the Australian nation, a perspective neglected for too long. The fact that Anzac Day became a sacralisation of the secular accepted by many religious and non-religious alike confirms that sacred and secular were often porous in Australia. A degree of sacral secularity was also associated at times with Freemasonry in its hospitals and charitable work.[29]

---

22 A. Gabay, *The Mystic Life of Alfred Deakin* (Cambridge: Cambridge University Press, 1992),152.
23 A. Atkinson, *The Europeans in Australia*. Vol. 3, *Nation* (Sydney: UNSW Press, 2014), ch. 9.
24 See R. Ely, *Unto God and Caesar: Religious Issues in the Emerging Commonwealth 1891–1906* (Carlton, Vic.: Melbourne University Press, 1976), chapters 1, 2, 5, 6 and 14; see also B. Mansfield, "Thinking About Australian Religious History," *Journal of Religious History*, 15 (1989): 333, 343.
25 K. Inglis, "A Sacred Place: The Making of the Australian War Memorial," *War & Society* 3 (1985): 99–126.
26 K. S. Inglis and Jan Brazier, *Sacred Places: War Memorials in the Australian Landscape* (Carlton, Vic.: Miegunyah Press, 1998).
27 G. Davison, *Narrating the Nation in Australia* (Menzies Lecture 2009) (London: Menzies Centre for Australian Studies, King's College, University of London, 2010), 2.
28 See J. A. Moses, "Anzac Day as Religious Revivalism: The Politics of Faith in Brisbane, 1916–1939," in *Reviving Australia*, ed. M. Hutchinson and S. Piggin (Sydney: Centre for the Study of Australian Christianity, Robert Menzies College, Macquarie University, 1994), 170–84; "Anglicanism and Anzac Observance: The Essential Contribution of Canon David John Garland," *Pacifica* 19 (2006): 58–77; and J. A. Moses and G. F. Davis, *Anzac Day Origins: Canon D J Garland and Trans-Tasman Commemoration* (Barton, ACT: Barton Books, 2013). For a different perspective, see K. Inglis, "Anzac, the Substitute Religion," in *Observing Australia: 1959–1999*, ed. C. Wilcox (Carlton, Vic.: Melbourne University Press, 1999), 61–70 (originally published in *Nation*, 23 April 1960). Some recent historians have seen Anzac Day as part of an Australian tradition of militarism; see M. Lake and H. Reynolds, with M. McKenna and J. Damousi, *What's Wrong with ANZAC?: The Militarisation of Australian History* (Sydney: University of New South Wales Press, 2010).
29 For detail, see J. Franklin, "Catholics versus Masons," *Journal of the Australian Catholic Historical Society* 20 (1999): 1–15, and P. Lazar (ed.), *It's No Secret: Real Men*

Against this background of diversity which problematises simple linear schemes that imply a teleological development from religious to secular in Australia,[30] I now turn to sacral secularity in republicanism and utopianism, two tendencies in Australian political and social thought which challenged the existing order. For each tendency, I give only salient examples. I do not suggest that all intellectuals interested in republicanism or utopianism were committed to sacral secularity, but only that it is evident in some outstanding cases.[31]

Republicanism

Republicanism flourished in Australia from early colonial times. It was central, for example, to the thought of Australia's first colonial-born poet, Charles Harpur (1813–1868), in whose writings republicanism implied the conviction that human beings should exercise dominion over their own religious lives. The second son of emancipist parents at Windsor, north of Sydney, and educated at the Government School at Parramatta, Harpur rejected the strife of creeds and denounced all systematised institutional religions. Instead, he advocated a religion of humanity that could be blended with Christianity. Harpur saw the secular as a sphere in which individuals could pursue their goals with autonomy and dignity.

Harpur was indebted to contemporary American religious thinkers, including the Unitarian William Channing (1780–1842) and the Transcendentalist philosopher Ralph Waldo Emerson (1803–1882). He was a friend of Sydney lawyer Daniel Deniehy (1828–1865) and of Henry Parkes.[32] Starting from an anthropology according to which human beings could develop the highest levels of freedom and personality in association with God, Harpur associated the autonomy of each individual and their right to develop and exercise their own powers with a politics of democratic equality, based on the God-given potential of every individual:[33]

Wear Aprons: the Story of Freemasonry in Australia (Sydney: Museum of Freemasonry Foundation, 2000), 67–8.

30 Gregory Melleuish argues that there was no simple transition in Australia from a religious society to a secular one; see his "A Secular Australia? Ideas, Politics and the Search for Moral Order in Nineteenth and Early Twentieth Century Australia," *Journal of Religious History* 38 (2014): 398–412.

31 See also the discussion of several intellectuals in Chapter III of this book.

32 See C. Harpur, *The Bushrangers: A Play in Five Acts, and Other Poems* (Sydney: W. R. Piddington, 1853); *A Poet's Home* (Sydney: Hanson and Bennett Printers, 1862); and *The Tower of the Dream* (Sydney and Melbourne: Clarson, Shallard & Co., Printers, 1865).

33 See M. Ackland, "Charles Harpur's Republicanism," *Westerly* 29, no. 3 (1984): 75–88, and "'Though Urged by Doubt … ': Charles Harpur and the Nineteenth Century Crisis of Faith," *AUMLA* 64 (1985): 154–74.

> I am not only a democratic Republican in theory, but by every feeling of my nature. Its first principles lie fundamentally in the moral elements of my being, ready to flower forth and bear their proper fruit. Hence, as I hold myself, on the ground of God's humanity, to be politically superior to no fellow being, so, on the same ground, I can feel myself inferior to none …[34]

The core of Harpur's religion was a providential theism, requiring no outer cult. 'For what is deep is holy, and must tend/To some divinely universal end,' he wrote.[35] An implicit belief in God's goodness was the fountain head of all true religion, just as a large faith in the capacity of human nature for good was the root of all genuine morality:[36]

> Though of no sect, I was not without religion; it was ever resident in the depths of my nature, like truth in the well – and was drawn thence not unfrequently. But I had a burning – an unconcealable scorn of all eccl[es]iastical pretence; and herein lay my sincerity, though it often caused me to be mistaken for, and pronounced, an infidel, to my great hurt and hindrance in the race of life.[37]

Accordingly Harpur allied himself with Unitarianism, which he believed had been the creed of Milton, Locke, and Newton, and foregrounded 'finality,' or the possibility that every individual could be improved to the full extent and according to the specific character of his capacity.[38] In pursuing 'Humanity', Harpur aimed at an idealistic evolutionist idealism, which would occupy the space of belief in a more rational form.[39]

Presbyterian clergyman John Dunmore Lang (1799–1878) embodied republicanism of a different and specifically Calvinist type, which was to some extent religious. Lang's approach to the secular hung on the claim that the secular realm was under the sovereignty of God. Consistent with the Calvinist view that the secular could be seen as religious for theological reasons, Lang made no distinction between secular and sacred and he located spiritual principles in actual forms of government. For Lang, republicanism

---

34 C. Harpur, "Note to a Republican Lyric," in *Charles Harpur*, ed. A. Mitchell (Melbourne: Sun Books, 1973), 148.
35 C. Harpur, "Life Without and Within," in *Charles Harpur*, 38.
36 E. Perkins, "Providential Design." in *The Poetical Works of Charles Harpur*, ed. E. Perkins (Sydney: Angus and Robertson, 1984): 565.
37 C. Harpur, "A Confession," in *Charles Harpur*, 141.
38 C. Harpur, "Finality," in *Charles Harpur*. 76.
39 See Chapter VI.

was the system of government willed by God and a theological principle, established by divine appointment:

> ... it is matter of sacred history that the only form of human government that was ever divinely established upon earth was the Republican – in the wilderness of Sinai – and that God himself interposed, in the person of his own accredited minister, to protest against the unwarrantable innovation, when that form of government was at length set aside in the commonwealth of Israel, and monarchy established in its stead. Monarchy doubtless prevailed for a long period in that country, *by Divine permission*, as many things else do in this lower world, that are certainly not of Divine appointment; but Republicanism existed from the first *by Divine appointment*; and it cannot, I submit, be a very bad form of government, which can plead such an authority in its favour.[40]

Indeed, he declared:

> Nay, in the original *Magna Charta* of Israel – that famous *Constitutional Act* which came down from Heaven, bearing the *Sign Manual* of the Eternal, for the establishment of a Republic, more glorious, and happier far, while it subsisted, than those of either Greece or Rome – ...
>
> ... we find all the principles of manly freedom established and developed – universal suffrage, perfect political equality (combined with one of the most beautiful and affecting devices imaginable to preserve it) and popular election; the three grand fundamental principles of Republican government.[41]

Lang's republicanism was indebted to the Scottish Presbyterianism that emerged in sixteenth-century Britain as a republican rebellion against the rule of bishops, and, in particular, to the Scottish Presbyterian theologian, Thomas Chalmers (1780–1847), who promoted a radical ecclesiology based

---

40 J. D. Lang, *The Coming Event!, Or, Freedom and Independence for the Seven United Provinces of Australia* (Sydney: J. L. Sherriff, 1870), 124–5; see also D. W. A. Baker, *Days of Wrath: A Life of John Dunmore Lang* (Carlton, Vic.: Melbourne University Press, 1985); D. S. Macmillan, *John Dunmore Lang* (Melbourne: Oxford University Press, 1962); K. Elford, "A Prophet Without Honour: The Political Ideals of John Dunmore Lang," *Journal of the Royal Australian Historical Society* 54 (1968): 161–75; and A. Gilchrist and G. Powell (eds.), *John Dunmore Lang: Australia's Pioneer Republican* (Wantirna, Vic.: New Melbourne Press, 1999).
41 Lang, *The Coming Event!*, 125–6.

on local assemblies.⁴² For Lang republicanism was a matter of the right to local government and self-rule in every state and city, not just nationally; he applied republican principles to a wide range of organisational questions. The same principles led to his active involvement in politics and his insistence, in answering his critics, that the proper government of secular affairs was a sacred matter to be carried out in accordance with the ordinances of God, and he did not modify this view after visiting the United States in 1840.⁴³

Another form of republicanism found in Australia, deriving from revolutionary France, was anti-religious and egalitarian, but it too involved a form of sacral secularity. This was the republicanism of poet Henry Lawson (1852–1922), for example, who, unlike Charles Harpur, had no Transcendentalist sympathies and identified the essence of Christianity with humanism. Lawson summed up the Australian creed, declaring that a true Christian was 'one who is sorry for most men and all women and tries to act to it to the best of his ability'.⁴⁴ While denouncing 'churchism', Lawson identified trade unionism as a new universal religion:

> Trades unionism is a new and grand religion; it recognizes no creed, sect, language or nationality; it is a universal religion – it spreads from the centres of European civilization to the youngest settlements on the most remote portions of the earth; it is open to all and will include all – the Atheist, the Christian, the Agnostic, the Unitarian, the Socialist, the Conservative, the Royalist, the Republican, the black, and the white, and a time will come when all the 'ists', 'isms', etc., will be merged and lost in one great 'ism' – the unionism of labour.⁴⁵

In verse this message could almost take the form of a catechism:

> No church-bell rings them from the Track,
> No pulpit lights their blindness
> 'Tis hardship, drought, and homelessness
> That teach those Bushmen kindness:

---

42   S. J. Brown, *Thomas Chalmers and the Godly Commonwealth in Scotland* (Oxford, Oxford University Press, 1982).
43   See Baker, *Days of Wrath: A Life of John Dunmore Lang*, 163–7, and *Preacher, Politician, Patriot: A Life of John Dunmore Lang* (Carlton, Vic.: Melbourne University Press, 1998).
44   H. Lawson, *Prose Works of Henry Lawson* (Sydney: Angus and Robertson, 1948), 683.
45   H. Lawson, "The New Religion," in *A Camp-Fire Yarn: Henry Lawson Complete Works 1885–1900*, ed. L. Cronin (Sydney: Landsdowne Press, 1984), 112; see also M. Zaunbrecher, "Henry Lawson's Religion," *Journal of Religious History* 11 (1980): 308–19.

The mateship born of barren lands,
Of toil and thirst and danger.
The camp-fare for the wanderer set,
The first place to the stranger ...
They tramp in mateship side by side
The Protestant and 'Roman'
They call no biped lord or 'sir',
And touch their hats to no man![46]

Related views were advanced by the early trade union activist and Protestant Christian, William Guthrie Spence (1846–1926). Spence, originally an active Presbyterian, wrote that Unionism came to the Australian bushman as a religion, bringing salvation from years of tyranny.[47] Spence identified the principles of trade unionism with those of Christ and, like Lawson, held that Christianity was about human brotherhood, not creeds. The writer and sometime organiser of the Australian labour movement, Francis Adams (1862–1893), took these ideas in a more radical direction. Adams, who was influenced by the agnostic English literary critic Matthew Arnold, combined a mystical belief in the struggle for social change with disbelief in popular religion and conventional morality.[48] Like Lawson, he celebrated a religious socialism, based on the spiritual equality of all, without believing in any positive religion.[49] This transformation of Christianity had popular appeal, and Banjo Paterson evoked it in his poem "My Religion" attacking all denominational cant.[50]

Utopianism

The pursuit of transcendent value in ordinary life also manifested in Australian utopianism and flowed into political thought, literature and

---

46 H. Lawson, "The Shearers," in *When I Was King and Other Verses* (Sydney: Angus and Robertson, 1905), 34–5.
47 W. G. Spence, *Australia's Awakening: Thirty Years in the Life of an Australian Agitator* (Sydney and Melbourne: The Worker Trustees, 1909), 53.
48 Adams worked for the *Brisbane Courier*, the *Boomerang* and *The Worker*. He provided brilliant interpretations of Australian social developments in works such as *Australian Essays* (Melbourne: W. Inglis, 1886), *The Australians: A Social Sketch* (London: T. Fisher Unwin, 1893), and *Songs of the Army of the Night* (Sydney: Federal Steam Printing and Building Works, 1888); see also M. Tasker, *Struggle and Storm: The Life and Death of Francis Adams* (Carlton Vic.: Melbourne University Press, 2001).
49 See Adams, *Australian Essays*.
50 See A. B. Paterson (ed.), *The Old Bush Songs: Composed and Sung in the Bushranging, Digging and Overlanding Days* (Sydney: Angus and Robertson, 1905).

art.[51] Utopians looked to new social and political arrangements to achieve religious objectives, often retaining in their thinking redemptionist elements derived from religious sources. In this context, the form of sacral secularity developed by Australia's most important utopian activist, William Lane (1861–1917) is striking. Born in Bristol in 1861, Lane arrived in Brisbane in 1885, having travelled in the United States and Canada. He became active in labour radicalism and started the newspaper *Boomerang* in 1887, becoming editor of Australia's first labour paper, *The Worker* (1890–1974). He was active in the Labor Party during its early years. That he was a religious enthusiast in revolt against the world and its wickedness is often forgotten.[52] In his utopian novel *Working Man's Paradise* (1892), Lane characterised socialism as a religion, demanding deeds as well as words and, in 1893, he established New Australia, a utopian community on unsullied fields in Paraguay.

Like Harpur before him, Lane was inclined to an emotionally tinged physico-theology of an almost seventeenth-century sort – a physico-theology that found God's providence throughout the natural world. He saw himself as dependent upon divine inspiration in his efforts to restore health and harmony to a degenerating race and civilisation:

> To me, turning with aching heart from wrangling and groping, Truth has whispered ... For God has given a task to me, who am unworthy, and has not deserted me altogether, though for years I have tried to do His

---

[51] For an overview, see A. Milner, "Meditations on the Impossible: A Report from Australia," *Spaces of Utopia* 3 (2006): 132–48, http://ler.letras.up.pt/uploads/ficheiros/3067.pdf. For secondary literature on Australian utopianism, see, inter alia, R. Gollan, "American Populism and Australian Utopianism," *Labour History* 9 (1965): 15–21; B. Scates, "The Utopians and Early Socialists Who Lost Their Way: Dreams and Realities," *Royal Historical Society of Victoria Journal* 54, no. 4 (1983): 19–26; G. C. Bolton, "A Whig Utopia in Northern Australia, 1835," *The Push From the Bush* 5 (1979): 120–8; J. A. Daly, "No Class Too Poor to Play: A Democratic Utopia, 1850–1890," in *Elysian Fields: Sport, Class and Community in Colonial South Australia 1836–1890* (Adelaide: J. A. Daly, 1982), 54–111; N. B. Albinski, "Handfasted: An Australian Feminist's American Utopia," *Journal of Popular Culture* 23, no. 2 (1989): 15–32; D. Macken, "Utopia Australia," *The Age*, 28 January–1 February 1983; R. A. Swan, "The Road to Utopia: The Revolutionary and Radical Background to the Creation of the Communist Party of Australia (CPA) in 1922," *Australia and World Affairs* 2 (1989): 38–50; J. Hay, "Deconstructing Utopia: The Blind Metaphors of Colonial Painters and Diarists," in *The Writer's Sense of the Past: Essays on Southeast Asian and Australasian Literature*, ed. Kirpal Singh (Singapore: Singapore University Press, 1987), 133–51; D. Carter, "'Current History Looks Apocalyptic': Barnard Eldershaw, Utopia and the Literary Intellectual, 1930s–1940s," *Australian Literary Studies* 14 (1989): 174–87; and C. Hodges, "Utopia," *Artlink* 10, nos 1/2 (1990): 9–10.

[52] L. Ross, *William Lane and the Australian Labour Movement* (Sydney: L. Ross, 1937) and G. Souter, *A Peculiar People: The Australians in Paraguay* (Sydney: Angus and Robertson, 1968) provide evidence here.

work without declaring him openly, relying on my own intellect rather than on the Supreme Will, and shrinking from the scoffs and jeers of men. It is the reaping of my own sowing. It is that the settlement we have tried to build has been uncemented by the sense of God, without which there can be no firm trust among men.[53]

In Paraguay he wrote:

God speaks in the Springing of the corn, in the march of the stars, in the movements of peoples, and in the wondrous justice which underlies the pains and pleasures of our lives. Never yet has Chaos been; never yet Disorder. Never has the wrong really triumphed; never in all the ages has the right really gone down. To our short-sightedness the comet may seem to wander, the wrong to endure; but the comet moves ever on a set path, and the free-born child shall play in peace on the slaver's forgotten grave. There is Law in all things, ruling the lives of men as the motions of the starts; to fight it is to fail beforehand, for it cannot be fought. To work with it is to win.[54]

Lane interpreted these principles rigidly, in a way that merged politics and religion:

It is the bounden duty of man; even by himself, to try ceaselessly and in spite of his own shortcomings, to put Communism into loving practice in his life. With me that belief springs from an unshakeable faith in what we commonly call 'God'. And when I say God I mean neither the idol built of wood and stone by the hands of savages, nor the idol built of words and phrases by the equal heathenism of higher races. I mean by God the sense of oneness, the lovingness, the completion of that power which, working through matter called us, and all the wondrous universe we see, into living. That power I know and feel is supreme. Nothing is beyond its control. In all the universe, in the whole earth there is none but God who rules – one God and no other ... But one may ask, what has Communism to do with belief in God. This: that to me Communism is part of God's Law.[55]

---

53 W. Lane, Extract from a private letter published in *The Worker*, quoted in Ross, *William Lane and the Australian Labour Movement*, 253.
54 W. Lane, Extract from a Cosme sermon, quoted in Ross, *William Lane and the Australian Labour Movement*, 305.
55 Lane, Extract from a Cosme sermon, quoted in Ross, *William Lane and the Australian Labour Movement*, 305–6.

Here, Lane was endorsing a view of the secular as potentially religious and giving theological reasons for doing so. Lane was not convinced that a utopian society could be built on humanist principles; nor was he sympathetic to those who rejected religion. On the contrary, having decided that 'the Supreme forces' making for harmony in the universe were helping his settlement survive,[56] he blamed irreligion rather than his own leadership for the failure of the community in Paraguay.

Other Australian utopians also attempted to reconcile religion and utopianism without clarifying many of the details. The poet and political activist Mary Gilmore (1865–1962), for example, joined Lane in Paraguay and remained convinced for the rest of her life that the capitalist reduction of everything to money defeated the teachings of Jesus Christ. A friend of Henry Lawson, a founder of the Lyceum Club, and a Foundation Member of the Fellowship of Australian Writers, Gilmore combined disbelief with a religious quietude. Despite her political views (she was associated in her eighties with the Communist paper, *Tribune*), she sometimes attended St Stephen's Presbyterian Church in Sydney and was tolerant of religion, although she was against the rule of any church. In her collection *The Rue Tree* (1931), written mainly in Goulburn between 1920 and 1926 when she was close to the Mercy nuns, she wrote:

> The need of humanity is to lift its heart to something not wholly contained within itself … Man must worship something. Secular, religious, or the toss of a coin, he makes his choice. This book is written in tribute to those who chose the religious – and perhaps, too, with a latent hope that it might help some who, outside the walls, ask for a word to cling to in a dark hour.[57]

Gilmore conceded that the need for worship was basic, but insisted that it could be met in secular forms. She also set limits to Christian equality, declaring:

> All men at God's round table sit,
> And all men must be fed;
> But this loaf in my hand,
> This loaf is my son's bread.[58]

---

56   Souter, *A Peculiar People*, 161.
57   M. Gilmore, "Introductory," in *The Rue Tree* (Melbourne, Robertson and Mullens, 1931).
58   M. Gilmore, "Nationality," in *The Penguin Book of Australian Verse*, comp. J. Thompson, K. Slessor and R. G. Howarth (Harmondsworth, Middlesex: Penguin, 1958), 21; see also W. H. Wilde, *Courage a Grace: A Biography of Dame Mary Gilmore* (Carlton, Vic.: Melbourne University Press, 1988).

Gilmore left it unclear how religion and socialism were to be reconciled and never spelt out the type of institutions that might function in place of churches over the longer term.

From the cases of republicanism and utopianism discussed, it will be clear that those who pursued transcendent value in secular life were not necessarily politically quiescent. Nor, however, was sacral secularity confined to those with radical political or social views. Indeed, when, in the nineteenth century and the early to mid-twentieth century, attempts were made to determine the proper role of the government in education, the tendency to pursue sacral goals in the secular, while accepting the autonomy and legitimacy of the secular, was once again apparent. As we shall see, sacral concepts of the secular played a part in approaches to education in the nineteenth century, and in the emergence of public theology discourse after 1920. In the case of education, the issue was whether religious education should be publicly provided and, if so, in what form. In the case of public theology, the issue was whether concern for the welfare of the public should be a fundamental principle of the national life, reflected both in policy and in arrangements based on public provision.

Public Education

Issues about the proper role of religion in education arose repeatedly in the Australian colonies and were bound up with questions of what should be provided publicly. Contrary to the earlier historiography, which has attributed secularisation to various nineteenth century educational initiatives, including Governor Bourke's Church Act of 1836, educational reformers in nineteenth-century Australia usually assumed that education had a religious purpose. A view of this kind can be found, for example, in Enlightenment programs of secular education proposed by those who were hostile to churchism and the clergy. The former Presbyterian minister Benthamite rationalist, Henry Carmichael (1796–1862), did not, as is sometimes suggested, assume a secular conception of education when he set up the Normal Institution in Elizabeth Street in Sydney in 1835. Hired by John Dunmore Lang to teach at his proposed Australian College, Carmichael turned against what he saw as Lang's sectarian approach to education and argued that clerical-style religious education had no place in public education. Carmichael was Governor Bourke's main supporter in the struggle for non-denominational schools and a major promoter of mechanics' institutes. Nonetheless, he was not a secularist in the sense of an enemy of religion and he assumed that non-denominational education would be religious because there was a religious faculty in every human being.[59]

A friend of Jeremy Bentham and associated with the strong utilitarian strand in colonial culture, Carmichael claimed that religion in the positive sense was a matter of opinion and could not be part of knowledge. On the other hand, he maintained that human beings had religious instincts prior to the imposition of religious opinions and beliefs upon them. Carmichael took it for granted, therefore, that religion in the non-ecclesiastical, natural sense should be the basis of education. In his view, children needed to be taught to form their own opinions on matters of religion and should be exposed to the Bible only as a work of reference. 'True religion' for Carmichael was a religion of humanity instilling the foundations of universal brotherhood, and could be known by all.[60]

In nineteenth-century Australia religion and education were closely linked. There was also a widespread notion of morality as something that secular knowledge and employments served to promote[61] – a theme that underlay many discussions, including Jewish discussions, of non-denominational public education. Allied with this, there was a general confidence among many clergy that science and religion supported one another and that Christianity would only benefit from higher educational standards. Thus, in Hobart, Presbyterian minister, philosopher and scientist John Lillie (1806–1866) championed non-denominational schools, resisted Anglican educational pretensions, and lectured to the Mechanic's Institute, convinced that Christianity had everything to hope for from the progress of science.[62] The cause of secular education could be seen, therefore, as the cause of religion.

---

59 See G. Nadel, *Australia's Colonial Culture: Ideas, Men and Institutions in Mid-Nineteenth Century Eastern Australia* (Melbourne: F. W. Cheshire, 1957), 264–5.
60 See Carmichael's Maitland Lecture, reprinted in *Empire*, 12 March 1857, 174ff, and Nadel, *Australia's Colonial Culture*. There was also a sacral secularity dimension to the education provided for workingmen by the mechanics' institutes; see P. Candy and J. Laurent (eds.), *Pioneering Culture: Mechanics' Institutes and Schools of Art in Australia* (Adelaide: Auslib Press, 1994).
61 R. Ely, "Now You See It: Now You Don't!: Issues of Secularity and Secularisation in Publicly Funded Elementary Schools in the Australian Colonies during the Middle Third of the Nineteenth Century," in *Journal of Religious History* 38 (2014): 377–97. Ely locates what came to be called secular education within civic Protestantism.
62 J. Lillie, *Lecture upon the Advantages of Science* (Hobart Town: J. C. Macdougall, 1839), 16–17. For discussion, see S. Petrow, "Intellectual Life in Hobart: The Contribution of John Lillie 1838–1856," *Tasmanian Research Association Papers and Proceedings* 52, no. 2 (2005): 74–84.

Likewise, the conception of secular instruction, as it had been developed in Ireland and Scotland in the context of civil Protestantism, was often understood by Protestants as a preparation for the Gospel.[63] Among Protestants, secular education often meant education based on our 'common Christianity' rather than denominationalism. This was the background to Governor Bourke's Church Act of 1836 in New South Wales, which gave equal official recognition to the Anglican, Catholic, Presbyterian and Wesleyan Methodist churches. Drawing on the experience of liberalism in Ireland, Bourke advocated religious equality and was opposed to attempts to convert Catholics since they were already Christians. He acted as a Protestant of the established Church, confident that reason would lead human beings to Christian belief.[64]

Conflicting conceptions of religion and the secular were also at the heart of the fierce denominational rivalries that emerged in the context of debates over religious education.[65] Earlier historiography sometimes understood these debates as a victory of secularism over denominational religion. Many of the combatants in these debates, however, assumed a sacral view of the secular from Bishop Broughton at one extreme, proposing a public education that would be exclusively Anglican, to John Dunmore Lang at the other, campaigning against state aid to church schools. Similarly, when Robert Lowe (1811–1892), in the pages of his weekly, *The Atlas*, attacked Bishop Broughton in the 1840s for betraying Protestantism, he was anti-clerical, not anti-Christian, even according to a recent account 'an Enlightenment Protestant', who favoured non-denominational Christian education.[66] In the same way, the term 'secular' in the New South Wales Education Act of 1870 meant non-sectarian, rather than free from religion. Free, compulsory and secular education encompassed 'general religion' and permitted the churches to come into school for an hour a day.

---

63   Ely, "Protestantism in Australian History".
64   D. Stoneman, "The Church Act: The Expansion of Christianity or the Imposition of Moral Enlightenment" (PhD diss., University of New England, 2012), ch 1.
65   For standard treatments, see A. G. Austin, *Australian Education 1788–1900: Church, State and Public Education in Colonial Australia* (Carlton, Vic.: Pitman, 1972) and J. S. Gregory, *Church and State: Changing Government Policies Towards Religion in Australia, with Particular Reference to Victoria since Federation* (North Melbourne, Vic.: Cassell, 1973). For the Catholic experience, see R. Fogarty, *Catholic Education in Australia 1806–1950* (Melbourne: Melbourne University Press, 1959).
66   For an excellent study of Robert Lowe and his attacks on Bishop Broughton, see S. Chavura, "'… But in Its Proper Place …': Religion, Enlightenment and Australia's Secular Heritage: The Case of Robert Lowe in Colonial NSW 1842–1850," *Journal of Religious History* 38 (2014): 356–76. Chavura shows that even the notorious Robert Lowe was an Enlightened Protestant of sorts.

The views of politician and newspaper editor Sir Henry Parkes, one of the leading advocates of secular education and an enemy of state aid to churches, should also be seen against this background. Parkes took a Christian conception of education for granted, partly because a socially engaged conception of Christianity was part of his Chartist background.[67] Parkes was committed to both Christian and Enlightenment conceptions of the public. It is true that he modified his position over time, but he did so, paradoxically, by moving closer to a more Christian view of the secular. Parkes was sympathetic to non-denominational Christianity and initially sought to limit the educational influence of Anglicans and Catholics.[68] He saw the rearing of children in the free use of their faculties as the cause of light versus darkness, and did not hesitate to argue that enlightenment was the antidote to the superstitious fears that gave the Catholic priesthood its power.[69] Subsequently, Parkes modified his approach for reasons of political expediency and supported Christian secular education in New South Wales.

Consistent with these ambiguities, 'free, compulsory and secular' education was interpreted differently in each state. In Victoria, the term 'secular' was construed more in the spirit of Enlightenment by Justice George Higinbotham, an Anglican layman, to exclude the clergy and specifically Christian content. Higinbotham accepted that education should include religious education, but denied that any sectarian beliefs or practices should be taught and suggested that religious teaching could be imparted by any honest man. His anticlericalism, however, had little popular support and his approach to secular education was abandoned in 1878 in favour of systematic partnership with the churches and the teaching of Christianity, both in Religious Instruction and in ordinary subjects.[70] Further, the nonreligious 'secular' dimension of Australian education arguably diminished in the course of the nineteenth century in the context of concern for the formation of the future citizens of a white Christian nation.[71] It is important to remember, however, that the tendency to emphasise 'common Christianity' in educational contexts was a Protestant view. Public education continued

---

67   B. Kaye, "From Anglican Gaol to Religious Pluralism: Re-casting Anglican Views of Church and State in Australia," in *Church and State in Old and New Worlds*, ed. H. Carey and J. Gascoigne (Leiden: Brill, 2011), 287–306.
68   For a capable account, see C. Byrne, "'Free, Compulsory and (Not) Secular': The Failed Idea in Australian Education," *Journal of Religious History* 37 (2013): 20–38.
69   H. Parkes, "Darkness or Light—Which is to Conquer?," *Empire*, 13 October 1851, 250.
70   Byrne, "'Free, Compulsory and (Not) Secular'", 8–9.
71   Byrne, "'Free, Compulsory and (Not) Secular'", 9.

to be rejected by Catholics as likely to produce infidelity, immorality and lawlessness.[72]

Related accounts could be given of the tendency to make education a sacral goal in the work of intellectuals concerned with civics education and workers' education in Australia. Early contributions to civics were made by the South Australian feminist reformer Catherine Helen Spence and by journalist Walter Murdoch (1874–1970), who adopted the idea of compulsory education as a preparation for citizenship from the British idealist political philosopher T. H. Green (1836–1882).[73] A related view later inspired much of the work of educational reformer Peter Board (1858–1945) and his efforts to use education as a means to promote democratic citizenship. A mixture of civil theology and social idealism also played a crucial role in the emergence and development of adult education in Australia. Here, the Anglican clergyman, G.V. Portus (1883–1954), who had studied history and economics at Oxford University under the historian H. A. L. Fisher, played a leading role. A student of Francis Anderson (1858–1941), Professor of Logic and Mental Philosophy at the University of Sydney, and also influenced by Mungo MacCallum, Portus worked with the Student Christian Movement nationally[74] and attempted to promote a more contemporary and socially aware form of Christianity. He engaged with Marxism as a contemporary religion, while emphasising that the churches needed to recognise the justice of the protest against bad social and economic arrangements embodied in Communism.[75] Convinced that the church must disengage from unjust social structures or perish, Portus turned to education as an area due for reform, becoming a Director of Tutorial Classes at the University of Sydney and, in 1934, Professor of History and Political Science at the University of Adelaide. As the second director of the Anglican-influenced Workers' Educational Association,[76] Portus promoted the cause of adult education

---

72 "Roman Catholics and Education" Pastoral Letter from Archbishop Vaughan and New South Wales Bishops, *Sydney Morning Herald*, 25 July 1879, 3.
73 See W. Murdoch, *The Australian Citizen An Elementary Account of Rights and Duties* (Melbourne: Whitcombe & Tombs, 1912).
74 The SCM was an important outlet for progressive Christian thought and was supported by Francis Anderson, Boyce Gibson, Ernest Burgmann and Samuel Angus. It shaped the thinking of many significant Australians, including H. V. Evatt, who was Francis Anderson's student; see R. Howe, *A Century of Influence: The Australian Student Christian Movement 1896–1996*, (Sydney: UNSW Press, 2009).
75 G. V. Portus, *Marx and Modern Thought* (Sydney: WEA, 1921) and *Communism and Christianity* (Morpeth NSW: St. John's College Press, 1931), 66.
76 The WEA continued to be a source of progressive religious ideas for decades to come. G. Stuart Watts, in particular, promoted enlightened thinking about religion in books such as *Why I Believe: The Rational Basis of Religious Faith* (Sydney, 1940).

as a secular ministry.[77] At the end of his life Portus doubted traditional doctrines such as original sin, the virgin birth, the atonement, the efficacy of prayer and, probably, personal immortality, but his activism did not recede as his Christian orthodoxy did.[78]

The tendency to hold that public provision was consistent with sacral but not confessional goals was not confined to education. In the twentieth century, attempts to enhance the status of the public in Australian social thought were promoted by Christian intellectuals engaged in what would later be called 'public theology'. I now turn to this public theology and read it as a policy-oriented engagement with the secular on sacral principles.

Public Theology

Although the term 'public theology' was not widely used in Australia until the 1960s, when it was imported from the United States, attempts to address issues in public life from a theological perspective in terms that could be understood by a wide public were made in Australia before that. A form of Christian Socialism was promoted among Anglicans at St. Paul's College in Sydney and in Melbourne and Adelaide. The British Christian Socialists, F. D. Maurice and Charles Kingsley (1819–1875), together with the writings of William Temple (1881–1944), Archbishop of York and, later, of Canterbury, were much read. In Newcastle, Christian Socialists associated between 1890 and 1916 with low-church Protestant groups, especially Primitive Methodists, and had links with the Reverend Charles Strong and his Australian Church.[79] Christian Socialists were concerned to alleviate the situation of the poorest groups in society and their ideas lay behind the founding of the Brotherhood of Saint Laurence, an Anglican religious order set up by Anglo-Catholic Father Gerard Kennedy (1885–1974) in a working-class parish in Newcastle. Through him, the Anglo-Catholic concern to reform the public world acquired a powerful social voice in Australia. Some broad-church Anglicans also inclined to Christian Socialism, including John Moyes (1884–1972), the Bishop of Armidale, who was dubbed the Anglican Church's social conscience.

---

77 See G. V. Portus, *Free, Compulsory and Secular: A Critical Estimate of Australian Education* (Joseph Payne lectures 1936-7) (London: Oxford University Press for the Institute of Education, 1937).
78 For Portus, see I. Tregenza, "The Political Theology of *The Morpeth Review*. 1927–1934," *Journal of Religious History* 38 (2014): 413–28.
79 T. Laffan, "Christian Socialism in Newcastle, 1890 to 1916," *The Hummer* 3, no. 6 (2001).

A public dimension also emerged in some forms of Catholic social thought before the emergence of an explicit public theology discourse. Strands of Catholic social thought, some of them inspired by the distributism advocated in Britain by the leading English Catholic thinkers, G. K. Chesterton (1874–1936) and Hilaire Belloc (1870–1953), were particularly important in the first half of the twentieth century.[80] For example, the Jesuit William Philip Hacker (1874–1954) devoted considerable energy to defending the social teachings of the Popes. There were also attempts to evaluate Fascist developments in Spain and Italy and to counter the threat of international Communism.[81] In Melbourne Frank Maher founded the Campion Society in 1931 for intellectuals who wanted to develop a Christian social philosophy. Subsequently, a monthly journal, *The Catholic Worker*, emerged which was highly critical of both capitalism and Communism. Influenced by Chesterton and Belloc, by the historian Christopher Dawson (1889–1970) and by the American Catholic social radicals, Dorothy Day (1897–1980) and Peter Maurin (1877–1949), *The Catholic Worker* was concerned with the rights of workers, profit-sharing, industrial councils, a just wage and the equitable distribution of property.[82] Such concerns re-emerged in the 1960s after the Second Vatican Council, when there was a renewed emphasis on Catholic social teaching and 'mission' was often redefined as work for justice and peace in the context of building the Kingdom of God.[83]

The need to relate Christian responses to political, social and economic issues emerged explicitly in the public theology developed by Ernest Burgmann (1885–1967), Anglican Bishop of Goulburn from 1934 to 1960, Warden of St. John's College, Morpeth, near Newcastle, and subsequently Bishop of Canberra. Burgmann adhered to the theological approach to the secular associated with civic Protestantism and sought to promote a marriage of law and morality in a nation under God. Responding to what he saw as the general failure of Australian Anglicans to develop technical analyses of social and cultural processes, even though there were perfectionist and utopian streams in nineteenth-century Anglicanism,[84] he believed that the church should have

---

80   See C. H. Jory, *The Campion Society and Catholic Social Militancy in Australia 1929–1939* (Sydney: Harpham, 1986), 33–4.
81   Jory, *The Campion Society and Catholic Social Militancy in Australia 1929–1939*, chapters 9 and 10.
82   See C. H. Jory, "The Campion Era: The Development of Catholic Social Idealism in Australia" (M.A. Thesis, Australian National University, 1974).
83   E. Campion, *Australian Catholics: The Contribution of Catholics to the Development of Australian Society* (Ringwood, Vic.: Viking, 1987), ch. 5.
84   W. J. Lawton, *The Better Time to Be: Utopian Attitudes to Society Among Sydney Anglicans 1885 to 1914* (Kensington, NSW: UNSW Press, 1990).

a central role in Australian society and lead national thought. A passionate critic of capitalism who stood up for the disadvantaged in the Hunter Valley during the Depression of the 1930s,[85] Burgmann was critical of Western capitalism as a distorted form of political economy and sought to defend its victims by encouraging organisations like the Unemployed Workers Movement. He became known as 'the Red Bishop'.[86]

A leading social critic, keen to advance and support new initiatives in many areas,[87] Burgmann held that the task of the church was to reform society, to lead it in thought and in the formulation of new social policies. Christianity, he argued, was wider than the church. Driven by a profound sense of service to the community and sustained by a sociologically complex understanding of religion as a resource for the building up of the collective life, Burgmann helped found the *Morpeth Review* (1927–1934), an intellectual journal for those on the borderland of institutional religion dealing with economics, anthropology, religion and current affairs. In the same spirit, he championed quality theological education. For Burgmann, a truly public Christianity was implicit in the Christian conception of the Kingdom of God and the church needed to work for human betterment in all areas of social life. He added to this, however, his own distinctive analysis of the division imposed by modernity, which could only be overcome by working in every aspect of society and culture to achieve unity of life.[88]

Although Burgmann was a broad-church evangelical who criticised the ecclesiasticism and ritualism of the high-church Oxford Movement, his sense of publicity was shaped by his sympathy for attempts to combine the teachings of Christ with socially progressive or even socialist views. Influenced by liberal British churchmen such as Charles Gore, J. R. Illingworth and William Temple, Burgmann fused a modernist commitment to the new with attempts to revive a more communitarian and enchanted past. Drawing upon Platonism, the Alexandrian Fathers, and the German Rhineland mystic Meister Eckhart (1260–1328), he attempted to ally mystical views with a sacramental view of nature. The religious sense, he held, grew out of nature, and human beings had a natural capacity to move towards an increasingly integrated spiritual existence and to

---

85 One of the best treatments of Burgmann's thought can be found in G. Melleuish, *Cultural Liberalism*, ch. 6; see also P. Hempenstall, *The Meddlesome Priest: A Life of Ernest Burgmann* (St Leonards, NSW: Allen and Unwin, 1993).
86 P. Hempenstall, "The Bush Legend and the Red Bishop: The Autobiography of E. H. Burgmann," *Historical Studies* 19 (1981): 568.
87 Hempenstall, *The Meddlesome Priest*, chapters 6, 7 and 10.
88 Melleuish, *Cultural Liberalism*, 146.

enter into the Divine.[89] Burgmann used this theological anthropology to underwrite his theological vision and it enabled him to combine a modern emphasis on emerging natural scientific disciplines with a rich conception of personality to which scientific materialism was inadequate.[90] In effect, he married Platonism with evolutionism and vitalism.[91] Burgmann's vast synthesis included both a project of overcoming the alienations of modern industrial society and a Patristic conception of salvation involving the whole cosmos.[92]

For Burgmann, the sacred was about the whole of life, and the modern separation of religious and secular, science and religion needed to be overcome. In this uncompromising spirit, he sought to develop an integral and encompassing modernist outlook, with applications across the whole range of human concerns. Accordingly, Burgmann recommended psychology as a key resource for clergy, following the Australian social theorist and industrial psychologist Elton Mayo (1880–1949), who insisted that psychology had to be applied to religious data.[93] Mayo insisted that religion had to be understood as a human fact answering to human needs and wants. But he also accepted that the church was the proper guardian of past and future human values through which the individual could aspire to union with the universe.[94] Understanding religion in human terms did not imply a low view of its importance. Burgmann also championed psychoanalysis as a fundamental discipline for all humanistic studies and envisaged a vast role for it in educating humanity.[95] Even more radical, Burgmann supported a greater role for scientific and technical experts in the management of human life and advocated a form of eugenics.

Burgmann's philosophical outlook was shaped by his philosophy teacher Francis Anderson,[96] whose undergraduate Ethics course he followed, and by the ideas of the British philosopher C. C. J. Webb (1865–1954), whom he heard lecture at Oxford in 1914. Following Webb, he insisted that personality, the heart of Christianity, was something that scientific materialism was

---

89　E. Burgmann, *God in Human History* (Morpeth, NSW: St. John's College Press, 1931).
90　E. Burgmann, *The Regeneration of Civilization* (Moorhouse Lectures 1942) (Sydney: Robert Dey, 1943).
91　Melleuish, *Cultural Liberalism*, 139.
92　Melleuish, *Cultural Liberalism*, 138–148.
93　E. Mayo, *Psychology and Religion* (Melbourne: Macmillan, 1922).
94　*Psychology and Religion*, 9–17, 27–37 and G. Melleuish, "Liberal Intellectuals in Early Twentieth Century Australia: Restoring the Religious Dimension" in *Australian Journal of History and Politics* 35 (1989), 1–12, especially 6.
95　J. Damousi, *Freud in the Antipodes: A Cultural History of Psychoanalysis in Australia*, (Sydney: UNSW Press, 2005), 81–5.
96　See Chapter III.

unable to explain.[97] Burgmann held that the goal of historical development was the creation of a world in which every human being would be recognised as a personal spiritual being. To achieve this, religion needed to become an active force in the life of society and the world. For Burgmann, Christianity was a liberation movement in human history, of which the church was only one form.[98]

Grounded in the sociology and psychology of the period, and informed by developments in the natural and the social sciences, Burgmann's theology aimed to provide a Christian response to the emergence of modernity, which he interpreted in terms of a breakdown of the harmony between the spiritual and the rational which should exist within the human personality.[99] In the modern world, Burgmann claimed, it was impossible for the human being to be a rational soul or to attain harmony. The restoration of harmony required the work of the church and of the state, as well as a balance between different parts of the soul.[100] According to Burgmann, the solution to the problem of modern disunity was a universal democracy that would harmonise the various parts of the group mind. To strike a balance between the community and the individual, it was essential to recognise the human being as a personal spiritual being who developed his personality best through serving the community.[101] On Burgmann's principles, the challenges of scepticism and freethought could be met by a Christianity that accepted rationalism and naturalism within their proper limits. Christianity called human beings to the task of setting humanity free. It was an adventure of faith, the truth of which could become as sure in the realm of experience as the sense of beauty in art.[102] In the same way, Burgmann advocated a wide ecclesiology for which the church was larger than Christendom. Against this holistic background, Burgmann preached a Jesus who drew no distinction between the secular and the sacred, a Jesus for whom politics was religion.[103]

---

97 I. Tregenza, "The Idealist Tradition in Australian Religious Thought," *Journal of Religious History* 34 (2010): 335–53.

98 E. H. Burgmann, *Religion in the Life of the Nation* (Morpeth, NSW: St. John's College Press, 1930).

99 Here again Burgmann's views resemble those of Elton Mayo. Mayo originally believed that religion could motivate individuals to aspire to union with the universe but gradually gave up this belief and turned instead to secular human understanding as a substitute; see E. Mayo, *Democracy and Freedom* (Melbourne: Macmillan, 1919) and the detailed discussion in G. Melleuish, "Australia and the Servile State," *Political Theory Newsletter* 3, no. 2 (1991): 126.

100 Melleuish, *Cultural Liberalism*, 144–5.

101 Burgmann, *Religion in the Life of the Nation*, 41–4; Melleuish, *Cultural Liberalism*, 140.

102 Burgmann, *Religion in the Life of the Nation*, 41–4.

103 Burgmann, *Religion in the Life of the Nation*, 33.

Another leading high-church Anglican, a friend of Burgmann and member of the Morpeth circle, A. P. Elkin (1891–1979), also tended to identify religion with the social. Elkin was Professor of Anthropology at the University of Sydney, Vice-Rector of St. John's Theological College, Newcastle, and policy advisor on Aboriginal assimilation. Having worked his way through Kant's critique of metaphysics and a crisis of faith, Elkin became an anthropologist and adopted a basically Durkheimian conception of religion as a social reality concerned with creating and maintaining community.[104] While accepting a power that is creator and life-giver, he combined a suspicion of religious intellectualising with a strong commitment to the social reality of practice. This allowed him to combine a collectivist sociology with a critical outlook. Elkin emphasised personal experience and ritual over theology and belief, but he took religious practices seriously as public facts.[105]

Like his mentor Burgmann, Elkin drew on critical insights from sociology and cultural anthropology to gain a more informed understanding of what human beings were doing in their religious lives. Theology was recast accordingly. For Elkin, God was to be approached by 'moral faith' rather than intellectual understanding, and he supplemented this Kantian position with Durkheimian perspectives on the role of religion in society.[106] For Elkin, religion served to bind societies together and religious experience mattered more than creeds.[107] This viewpoint made it possible for him to appreciate the Aborigine who danced his religion.[108] As Gregory Melleuish notes, Elkin believed that religion could provide inspiration for an inter-

---

104 T. Wise, *The Self-Made Anthropologist: A Life of A.P. Elkin* (Sydney: Allen and Unwin, 1985), 32–6. For his studies of 'Aboriginal religion', see A. P. Elkin, *Studies in Australian Totemism* (Sydney: Australian National Research Council, 1933), *The Australian Aborigines: How to Understand Them* (Sydney: Angus and Robertson, 1938), and "Elements of Australian Aboriginal Philosophy," *Oceania* 40 (1969): 85–98.
105 A. P. Elkin, "Religion and an Anthropologist," *Morpeth Review* 20 (1932): 38ff.
106 See the discussion in Wise, *The Self-Made Anthropologist*, 32–6; see also R. McGregor, "From Old Testament to New: A. P. Elkin on Christian Conversion and Cultural Assimilation", *Journal of Religious History* 25 (2001): 39–55.
107 See A. P. Elkin, "The Function of Religion in Society" in *Morpeth Review* 2, no. 16 (1931) 8–17 and "The Present Social Function of Religion" *Morpeth Review* 2, no. 18 (1931) 23–33; also the analysis in G. Melleuish, "Liberal Intellectuals in Early Twentieth Century Australia: Restoring the Religious Dimension" 10.
108 Elkin was unusual in taking seriously the nonmundane aspects of Aboriginal law, including the possession of spiritual knowledge and telepathy, although his interpretations in terms of magic and sorcery were anachronistic; see A. P. Elkin, *Aboriginal Men of High Degree*, 2nd ed. (St Lucia: University of Queensland, 1977). Despite his assimilationist views, he campaigned hard for justice for Aborigines; see his *Citizenship for the Aborigines* (Sydney: Australasian Publishing, 1944).

group ethics and the basis for the development of the human being as a free social personality. And, like Burgmann, he argued that the role of religion in the modern world was the creation of a universal order through the development of a universal individual self.[109]

Burgmann, Elkin and the high-church Vice-Rector of St. John's Theological College, the Reverend R. S. Lee, formed the core of the Morpeth circle.[110] Their activities, especially in the context of the *Morpeth Review*, assisted the emergence of a public sphere of policy-edged debate and discussion in Australia.[111] This public sphere was theologically inspired, even though the matters discussed were not always explicitly religious. Burgmann, Elkin and Lee derived an incarnational theology from the path-breaking Anglican theological collection of essays, *Lux Mundi*, which appeared in Britain in 1889, and from Anglo-Catholic theologians such as Charles Gore (1853–1932) and Henry Scott Holland (1847–1914). According to this theology, divine immanence was working itself out in the temporal order or the *saeculum*.

The Morpeth circle drew on this theology in order to advocate contemporary applications of the Gospel. They did so with a strong sense of religious citizenship, a conception of the relationship between politics and religion known in Australia through the reception of the political thought of T. H. Green.[112] Moreover, they brought their concerns to the attention of relevant professional audiences. The Morpeth circle included a range of public intellectuals, including leading historian Keith Hancock (1888–1988), trade union leader and activist Lloyd Ross (1901–1987) and political scientist and Professor of Public Administration at the University of Sydney, F. A. Bland (1882–1967), who defended a conception of citizenship that resisted any division between sacred and secular.[113] The whole social order was to be judged, Bland maintained, by what he called 'Christ's way of life'.[114]

---

109 Melleuish,"Liberal Intellectuals", 10.
110 Lee was a leader of the Christian Socialist Movement in Newcastle and sympathised for a time with the Soviet Union. He left Australia for Britain, where he became Rector of the Anglo-Catholic Church of St. Mary, Oxford; see T. Moore, "'The Morpeth Mind' and Australian Politics 1927–1934." Paper presented at the Australasian Political Science Association Conference, University of Newcastle, 25–27 September 2006, 38–40.
111 Moore, "'The Morpeth Mind' and Australian Politics 1927–1934".
112 A. Vincent, "T.H. Green and the Religion of Citizenship," in *The Philosophy of T. H. Green*, ed. A. Vincent (Aldershot: Gower, 1986), 48–61.
113 See W. Maley, "The Political Philosophy of F. A. Bland," *Political Theory Newsletter* 5, no. 1 (1993): 25–38.
114 F. A. Bland, "Citizenship in the Light of Christ's Way of Life," *Morpeth Review* 23 (1933): 13–27, and Tregenza, "The Political Theology of *The Morpeth Review*,

The Australian Broadcasting Commission religious affairs broadcaster, Kenneth Henderson (1881–1965),[115] also played a role in the Morpeth circle. Henderson, a theological modernist and pupil of the Melbourne personal idealist philosopher, W. R. Boyce Gibson, promoted broadcasting as a religious opportunity in a culture in which Christianity was declining in influence.[116] Well-read in the work of the German theologian and social historian, Ernst Troeltsch (1865–1923), who brought a sternly objective analysis to the social history of the churches, Henderson argued that Christianity was plain, personal and experimental, and not corporate and traditional'.[117] Like others influenced by the incarnational theology of *Lux Mundi*, he assumed that Christ's incarnation was continuing and could be looked for in the ideals of the age and in the emergence of a new world accommodating ethics.[118] He too was concerned to relate Christianity and citizenship.

The members of the Morpeth circle tended to adopt a sociological conception of religion as socially integrative and rejected attempts to confine religion to the private sphere. Likewise, they tended to adopt a 'church in society' conception of church and sought to overcome the separation of religion and the secular, and of science and religion, in modern industrial societies. 'Religion' was not to be reduced to a private hobby, or to one department of life. A philosophy of civilisation, requiring harmony and balance, was central to their views.[119] Several members of the Morpeth circle tended to allegorise historical Christianity in social civilisational terms. Their theological modernism involved a certain emergence out of traditional religion and its understandings of incarnation and atonement, even though this was concealed in some respects by their adherence to

---

1927–34"; see also K. T. Henderson, *Prayers of Citizenship* (London: Longmans, Green, 1940); A. Healey, "Nerve and Imagination: Kenneth Thorne Henderson in Retrospect", *St. Mark's Review* 148 (1992): 13–19.

115 For an outstanding discussion of the importance of the Morpeth circle for Australian conceptions of citizenship and the secular, see Tregenza, "The Political Theology of *The Morpeth Review*, 1927–34"; see also T. Moore, "'The Morpeth Mind' and Australian Politics 1927–1934".

116 K. Henderson, *Broadcasting as a Religious Opportunity* (Sydney: ABC, ca. 1940).

117 K. Henderson, *Christian Tradition and Australian Outlook* (Melbourne: Australian Student Christian Movement, 1923), 11–12.

118 K. Henderson, "Christianity as Originality," *Morpeth Review* 21 (1932): 16, and R. Trumble, *Kenneth Thorne Henderson: Broadcaster of the Word* (Richmond, Vic.: Spectrum Publications, 1988). For discussion, see Tregenza, "The Political Theology of *The Morpeth Review*, 1927–1934".

119 M. Hughes-Warrington and I. Tregenza, "State and Civilization in Australian New Idealism 1890–1950," *History of Political Thought* 29 (2008): 89–108.

traditional liturgical forms. Circle members were also often involved in promoting enhanced international relations through the Round Table and the League of Nations Union.[120]

Morpeth's approach to social thought was influential beyond Anglican circles through the work of the leading Methodist minister and publicist, Alan Walker (1911–2003), who studied for his doctorate under Elkin and wrote some forty popular books. Following receptions of the work of American-based German Protestant theologian Paul Tillich (1886–1965), who spoke of a 'God above God' or 'ultimate concern', the publication of Bishop Robinson's *Honest to God* (1963), and the positive account of secularisation found in Harvey Cox's *The Secular City* (1965), sacral secularity flourished in Methodist circles in Australia. Indeed, many Methodist and, later, Uniting Church leaders believed that God was working through the secular world and saw work for human development as their religious duty.[121]

These concerns continue to be promoted in Anglican circles through the work of St Mark's National Theological Centre in Canberra, which has grown out of the library Burgmann founded in 1957, and through the writings of Anglican churchman Bruce Kaye (b. 1939). Deploying his training at Durham and Basel, Kaye looks to the ecclesial vision of the sixteenth-century Anglican divine Richard Hooker for a model of an incarnational contextual Anglicanism.[122] Rejecting the Sydney-based Moore College tradition, which related Anglicanism back to the English Reformation, Kaye has argued that Anglicanism originated in the *Ecclesia Anglicana* of the seventh and eight centuries. He has also defended both the legacy of the High Church Bishop Broughton and the revisionary theologies of the nineteenth-century liberal theologians, D. F. Strauss and F. C. Baur. Kaye rethinks the character of Australian Anglicanism in light of a public theological conception of church and has written a series of

---

120 See D. Garnsey, *Arthur Garnsey, a Man for Truth and Freedom* (Sydney: Kingsdale Press, 1985); see also Arthur Garnsey's work on the theological dimensions of citizenship, *The Problem of Social Unity: Social Unity and the Responsibility of Citizenship* (Sydney: Social Problems Committee, Diocese of Sydney, 1918).
121 These ideas were central to the work of the US-based Australian Methodist theologian, Colin Williams; see his *Where in the World?: Changing Forms of the Church Witness* (London: Epworth Press, 1965) and *What in the World?* (New York: National Council of the Churches of Christ, 1964).
122 Kaye investigates the model in, among other works, *A Church Without Walls: Being Anglican in Australia* (North Blackburn, Vic.: Dove, 1995). For discussion, see S. Pickard, "Placing Theology: Traditions and Challenges for Australian Anglicans," in *Agendas for Australian Anglicanism: Essays in Honour of Bruce Kaye*, ed. T. Frame and G. Treloar (Hindmarsh, SA: ATF Press, 2006), 85–122.

books relating Trinitarian theology to a 'church in society' ecclesiology. The public theology tradition is also continued by a group of scholars working in the Centre for Public and Contextual Theology in Canberra,[123] as well as the publications of Anglican Evangelical Tom Frame (b. 1962), until 2006 the first full-time Bishop to the Australian Defence Force. Frame's writings show that public theology can also take a conservative form. In *Church and State: Australia's Imaginary Wall* (2006), Frame argues that the Australian Constitution does not formally separate church and state and endorses the view of the British theologian Frederick Maurice that the church ought to be active in the public square. In *Living By the Sword: The Ethics of Armed Intervention* (2004), he argues that war cannot be abolished so long as human sinfulness prevails.[124] Much more could be said about public theology in the Australian context, but here my intention is to emphasise its importance as evidence that a sacral approach to the secular has continued to be possible in the twentieth century and beyond.

Wider Influences on Political and Social Thought

The tendency to pursue transcendent value within the secular domain could also be found in the thought of radical Christians such as the Reverend Archibald Turner (1843–1901), who founded a labour church in Bourke Street, Melbourne, Hugh Gilmore (1842–1891), and the Reverend Frank Hartley (1909–1971). Religious activist intellectuals played a role in the emergence of Fabianism in Australia, among them Charles Marson (1859–1891), the high-church Anglican cleric who founded the South Australian Fabian Society. For these intellectuals, what mattered was the conviction that daily life in the present world should be radiant with depth and meaning. For all of them, the *saeculum* should be seen to be ethically transformed as a matter of public fact.

Thinkers influenced by political liberalism also evidenced sacral secularity at times.[125] The Victorian Charles Henry Pearson (1830–1894), for example, brought a religiously coloured moralism to the search for secular alternatives to external religion. A Professor of Modern History at King's College, London from 1855 to 1864 and lecturer in History at the University of Melbourne, Pearson was originally a Christian Socialist influenced by J. S.

---

123 See D. J. Neville (ed.), *The Bible, Justice and Public Theology* (Sheffield: Sheffield Phoenix Press, 2014).
124 T. Frame, *Church and State: Australia's Imaginary Wall* (Sydney: UNSW Press, 2006) and *Living By the Sword?: The Ethics of Armed Intervention* (Sydney: UNSW Press, 2004).
125 G. Melleuish, *The Power of Ideas: Essays on Australian Politics and History* (North Melbourne, Vic.: Australian Scholarly Publishing, 2009), 31–37.

Brewer (1810–1879), an English historian of the Reformation, and F. D. Maurice. Over time, however, Pearson became convinced that religion and religious interests were no longer things to be captured and confiscated by ecclesiastics and theologians. Forecasting the decline of the church, along with other traditional institutions, in the context of the rise of the modern state,[126] Pearson sought to realise religious values in secular arrangements. How far a version of sacral secularity can be found in nineteenth-century liberal social thinkers, such as Bernard Wise (1858–1916) and the Congregational minister and newspaper editor John West (1809–1873), is perhaps harder to measure, but some elements of sacral secularity may have been present.[127]

The case of Frederic William Eggleston (1875–1954), the twentieth-century Australian theorist of liberalism, is clearer. Eggleston understood social transformation as a religious work and one that was, indeed, able to survive religion's demise. In *Search for a Social Philosophy* (1941), he advocated an idealistic pragmatism for which individuals would serve the common good and work for the welfare of humanity as a way of preserving religious perspectives in a no longer religious age.[128] As a Deakinite liberal, Eggleston sympathised with T. H. Green's critique of utilitarianism and analysed the contemporary social condition as a period of disillusionment in which individuals were unable to fully develop their personalities, falling instead under the sway of a superficial economism. Eggleston envisaged God as realising Himself in human life. His political and social thought remained neo-Christian and he wrote of the need to achieve a spontaneous order based on duty, unselfishness and brotherly love.[129]

Secularity in Transition

Intellectuals with Christian social concerns informed Australian approaches to public education, broadcasting and, sometimes, social welfare,[130] just as

---

126 C. H. Pearson, *National Life and Character: A Forecast* (London: Macmillan, 1893), 222; see also J. Tregenza, *Professor of Democracy: The Life of Charles Henry Pearson 1830–1894* (Carlton, Vic.: Cambridge University Press, 1968) and S. Macintyre, *A Colonial Liberalism: The Lost World of Three Victorian Visionaries* (South Melbourne: Oxford University Press, 1991).

127 See, however, G. Melleuish, "Liberal Intellectuals in Early Twentieth Century Australia: Restoring the Religious Dimension," *Australian Journal of Politics and History* 35 (1989): 1–12.

128 Eggleston left significant unpublished writings and his work deserves extended treatment; see W. Osmond, *Frederic Eggleston: An Intellectual in Australian Politics* (Sydney: George Allen and Unwin, 1985).

129 Melleuish, *Cultural Liberalism*, 171–174.

130 For the complexities of their involvement in social welfare, see J. Murphy, *A Decent Provision: Australian Welfare Policy, 1870 to 1949* (Farnham, Surrey: Ashgate, 2011).

they contributed to the emergence of spaces in which to debate public issues, which would come to be called the public sphere.[131] The tendency to pursue sacral goals in the secular realm became less important in the course of the twentieth century, as the influence of Christianity declined and as approaches to citizenship indebted to the thinking of the British philosopher T. H. Green gave way to statist conceptions of citizenship, whether derived from British theorist of citizenship T. H. Marshall (1893–1981)[132] or neoliberal in character. Nonetheless, the role of Christianity in constructing conceptions of the public in Australia should not be underestimated.[133]

The evidence discussed in this chapter shows that sacral secularity appears among a range of intellectuals and across various sites. It played a role in utopianism and republicanism and in debates about public education. It was central to the emergence of public theology as a policy-oriented engagement with the secular. Sacral secularity also, as we shall see in the next chapter, had a role in many forms of religious liberalism.

Similarly, John Flynn of the Australian Inland Mission was inspired by social gospel ideas; see B. Hains, *The Ice and the Inland: Mawson, Flynn, and the Myth of the Frontier* (Carlton, Vic.: Melbourne University Press, 2002), 146–47.

131 T. Moore, "'The Morpeth Mind' and Australian Politics 1927–1934".
132 See B. Howe and A. Nichols (eds.), *Spirit of Australia: Religion in Citizenship and National Life* (Hindmarsh, SA: ATF, 2001–2003).
133 Many Australian Prime Ministers were influenced by Christian social thought; examples include: Labor leader Ben Chifley (1885–1951), whose 'Light on the Hill' mantra echoed a Biblical reference; H. V. Evatt (1894–1965), who was active in Christian circles as a young man and an admirer of Scottish Hegelian Henry Jones; Presbyterian Robert Menzies (1894–1978), whose influential collection, *The Forgotten People and Other Studies in Democracy*, (Sydney: Angus and Robertson, 1943), was indebted to Christian sources; and Gough Whitlam (1916–2014) and Bob Hawke (b. 1929), both of whom came from socially concerned Protestant families; see R. Williams, *In God They Trust?: The Religious Beliefs of Australia's Prime Ministers 1901–2013* (Sydney: Bible Society Australia, 2013). In the same way, some policy-makers in Australia bordered on a sacral approach to the secular, including the Governor of the Reserve Bank, H. C. Coombs (1906–1997), an agnostic alienated from Christianity, but not from the Aboriginal sacred. Other examples might include the distinguished economist and Chancellor of the Australian National University, John Crawford (1910–1984), Secretary of the Commonwealth Treasury Roland Wilson (1904–1996), and eminent lawyer and public servant Kenneth Bailey (1898–1972), all of whom had been active members of the Student Christian Movement.

Chapter III

RELIGIOUS LIBERALISM

Religious liberalism in Australia was to revise how both religion and Christianity were understood. Religious liberals sought to modernise and reform religious beliefs and practices; some also promoted social reform. Religious liberalism in Australia was to be found in several cities and cannot be separated too strictly from other tendencies and movements; it was one element that tended to promote the sacral secularity already discussed. My coverage in this chapter is selective. I focus on prominent religious liberals in order to show that religious liberalism went both to the reform of traditional religious beliefs and to a wide range of social concerns, often summed up as what 'true' or 'modern' Christianity required. I also emphasise its transnational character in Australia, the extent to which religious liberals drew on advanced ideas from elsewhere and interacted with intellectual allies overseas in order to promote ideas and attitudes in advance of the society in which they lived. My discussion focuses on Unitarianism and modernism.

Religious liberals in Australia were of diverse sorts and their outlooks were shaped, to varying degrees, by philosophical and/or theological developments overseas. Some were influenced by Scottish Hegelianism and/or by personal idealism.[1] Some were responding to German theological developments and new research on church history. Some were in contact with English theological modernists and/or indebted to the political philosophy of T. H. Green, which, with its emphasis on active citizenship and social reform, provided a real-world translation of religious ideals. Some developed liberal theological ideas under the influence of Platonism, as it was being reinterpreted in Britain.[2] Some transposed concern with the sacred into concern for social reform and looked forward to a future society characterised by rationality and harmony.[3]

---

1   For discussion of these movements, see ch IV.
2   G. Melleuish, *Cultural Liberalism*, 19, 87–100, 52–56.
3   Melleuish, *Cultural Liberalism*, chs 3 and 4, especially 101–102.

Some religious liberals were inclined to ask whether the nation or the university or civil society could play the role once played by the church. Others joined open religious societies. Criticism of church doctrines and practices did not necessarily cut religious liberals loose from ecclesial frameworks. Most accepted that Christianity could contribute to the reformation of humanity and were inclined to reinterpret traditional doctrines in social and ethical terms rather than to break with them altogether.

The common factor among religious liberals was that they remained religious and worked for the reform of religion, rather than its abolition. They did not reject belief in God, although they could call for a new concept of God. Nor did they did not deny the need for sacred narratives, even if they adopted critical attitudes towards the Scriptures. Similarly, most religious liberals accepted that some sort of 'faith' was necessary. Even though many leading religious liberals were clerics, there was also a laicist side to religious liberalism. Some religious liberals emphasised, in the spirit of American Unitarian William Ellery Channing (1780–1842), that everyone was able to participate in the divine. Most religious liberals were not troubled by nihilism; for them the world remained meaningful and beautiful, and a good life was a life of moral action to make it better. In the context of cultural and social change, religious liberals held that Christianity should adjust to modern thought, keep up with developments in the natural and human sciences, and refocus theology on the main problems of human life.

Unitarianism

Unitarianism was a form of theological minimalism. Unitarians rejected the doctrine of the Trinity and other traditional church dogmas, but did not develop theological dogmas of their own. Unitarianism in Australia was influenced both by the rationalism of the scientist theologian, Joseph Priestley (1733–1804), and by the subsequent radicalisation of the movement by British Unitarian leader and Principal of Manchester New College, James Martineau. Priestley's Unitarianism focused on natural religion, on evidences for Christianity, and on the philosophical doctrine of necessity, whereas Martineau's New School of Unitarianism focused more on freedom and an inner experience of the divine. Attracting members from among the thoughtful, Unitarians in Australia combined a quest for spiritual autonomy with a commitment to spiritual values and social progress. They were open to a diversity of spiritual traditions, while being single-minded in their insistence that 'true religion' was about expressing sacral values in ordinary life. As 'dissenters from dissent',[4] Unitarian intellectuals took nonconformity further, challenging a range of accepted dogmas and social norms from the standpoint of higher and more universal ethical principles. They were often open to various forms of freethought and republished many of the ideas and arguments put forward by eighteenth-century freethinkers. Indeed, mixtures of critical disbelief and creedless piety often existed in the one person. Unitarians took reason as the best guide in religion and emphasised individual regeneration rather than doctrines or creeds.[5]

One of the most important Unitarians in South Australia, and one definitely of Martineau's New School, was the writer, novelist, preacher, feminist and political reformer Catherine Helen Spence (1825–1910). In an early Adelaide full of preachers and sects,[6] Spence revolted against Calvinist doctrines of election and maintained that nothing should be believed on any authority that was unworthy of the highest conception of God.[7] From 1850 on, she did not take communion because she was not a 'converted Christian'.[8] In stages, her religion came to consist in benevolence and the pursuit of justice. Denying the divinity of Christ and the infallibility of Scripture, she emphasised the discrepancy between human conceptions of God and the scale of the universe:

> When we think of thirty millions of suns with worlds revolving round them which is far as modern astronomy has reached – when the six days of creation are infinitely extended – and when we think of all things *becoming* rather than existing – when we turn from the infinitely great to the infinitely small and distinguish and divide and even subdivide the infinitesimal atom into even more infinitesimal atoms, the most recent discovery – and when we see that one great spirit is in us all, and through all, as well as above all, we stagger at the greatness of the thought of God.[9]

---

4   D. Hilliard, "Dissenters from Dissent: The Unitarians in South Australia," *Journal of the Historical Society of South Australia* 11 (1983), 92–104.
5   Consistent with this, Higinbotham, at the opening of the new Unitarian Church in East Melbourne in 1887, appealed for a system of belief shorn of paradox and contradictions.
6   D. Pike, *Paradise of Dissent: South Australia 1829–1857* (London: Longmans, Green, 1957); see also G. Walter, *The Gospel of Unitarianism* (Melbourne: George Robertson & Co., 1885).
7   C. H. Spence, Sermon on the basis of belief, 23 October 1898, p. 1 (State Library of South Australia, MS PRG 88/8, Records of Catherine Helen Spence 1866–1910).
8   See S. Magarey, *Unbridling the Tongues of Women: A Biography of Catherine Helen Spence* (Sydney: Iremonger, 1985), 64.
9   C. H. Spence, Sermon on the three reverences, 24 November, no year indicated, p. 3 (State Library of South Australia, MS PRG 88/8, Records of Catherine Helen Spence 1866–1910), quoted in Magarey, *Unbridling the Tongues of Women*, 67.

Spence continued to be interested in rethinking religion in the light of science or the manifestation of God in nature, but she blamed theology for giving thought a wrong direction and sought to reinterpret religion in non-anthropomorphic terms.[10]

Spence emerged from the despair of her early years with the help of the Adelaide Unitarian minister John Crawford Woods (1824–1906), who rejected Jesus' divinity and the doctrines of original sin and the atonement.[11] Spence substituted on occasion for the minister at the Adelaide Unitarian Christian Church by reading published sermons. She was also associated for a time with Wellington Square Primitive Methodist Church in Adelaide, where there was an emphasis on Christian Socialism and an involvement with social concerns. Nonetheless, there was a transition in her thinking from religious belief to righteous action in the world.[12] In *An Agnostic's Progress From The Known To The Unknown* (1884) Spence sought to satisfy herself that reverent agnostics were by no means materialists; that the nature of the human being might or might not be consciously immortal, but was spiritual; and that there was scope for spiritual energy and emotion in the duties that lay before each of us towards ourselves and towards our fellow creatures. She held that mistake and misapprehension, violence, ambition and greed, had kept back the unfolding of the 'Gospel germ' for nearly 2000 years. Spence was especially critical of the repressive functions of religious institutions and of the religion of fear they sometimes promoted.[13] Like the writers Joseph Furphy and Bernard O'Dowd (1866–1953) after her, she advocated an egalitarian, cooperative and republican society as the realisation of the real content of Christianity. At other times she spoke of the need to devise a non-supernatural religion, one that brought spiritual energy and emotion to the performance of secular duties.[14]

Spence's vision for the reconstruction of society was influenced by Jane Hume Clapperton's *Scientific Meliorism and the Evolution of Happiness* (1885). In her socialistic novel *Handfasted* (1879) and in *A Week in the Future* (1889),

---

10 C. H. Spence, *Each in his Own Tongue: Two Sermons Delivered in the Unitarian Christian Church, Adelaide, July 17 and 24, 1904* (Adelaide: printed by Vardon and Pritchard, 1904), 7, 10, 19.

11 J. C. Woods, *Unitarian Christianity: Scriptural as well as Reasonable* (Adelaide, 1858).

12 For discussion, see R. B. Walker, "Catherine Helen Spence, Unitarian Utopian," *Australian Literary Studies* 5 (1971): 31–41.

13 C. H. Spence, *An Agnostic's Progress From The Known To The Unknown* (Adelaide: Williams and Norgate, 1884), 5.

14 Drafts of sermons Spence delivered at the Unitarian Church, Adelaide, from 1896 to 1908 are among her records at the State Library of South Australia (MS PRG 88/8); see also Walker, "Catherine Helen Spence, Unitarian Utopian".

Spence promoted a vision of a utopian secular order in which the churches would be reduced in number, liberal in doctrine, and served by unpaid part-time ministers. God was more pleased, she implied, with a world in which there was less prayer, but more happiness. On the other hand, while the new world was much less formally religious, nothing was secular, and everything was 'profoundly religious' in a non-ecclesiastical sense.[15] Spence's views varied somewhat over the years, as her commitment to immortality was at times somewhat uncertain, but these changes in her beliefs were less important than the fact that she moved out of positive religion and adopted religion based on the pursuit of social improvement and kindness. Conscious of being a new kind of woman, Spence pursued this new religion with passion and conviction. A campaigner for women's suffrage, Vice-President of South Australia's Women's Suffrage League and an advocate of electoral reform, she, like British feminists Mary Wollstonecraft and Mary Shelley, spent her life fighting for the rights of women and trying to reform government and society so that humanity might move closer to perfection. Nonetheless, for Spence sacral secularity was allied to a conception of science and government that gave a leading role to the state. She saw herself as attempting to understand the laws of nature governing human lives, an accomplishment that was part of humanity's progress towards perfection. Spence held that the state should play a crucial role in social reform[16] and wrote the first civics textbook used in Australian schools.[17]

Another prominent Unitarian, Alexander Sutherland (1852–1902), a journalist, schoolmaster and poet from Glasgow, developed one of the first responses in Australia to the challenges of Darwinism. Sutherland's study of the evolution of the human mind, *The Origin and Growth of the Moral Instinct* (1898), was praised by leading British scientists, such as Francis Galton, Herbert Spencer and Alfred Russel Wallace.[18] Headmaster of Carlton College in Melbourne and later a lecturer in English at the University of Melbourne, Sutherland was co-editor of *The Melbourne Review* and a contributor to the Unitarian monthly, *Modern Thought*. A close friend of the

---

15   C. H. Spence, *A Week in the Future*, a novel serialised in the *Centennial Magazine*, January–June 1889.
16   C. H. Spence, *Autobiography* (Adelaide: W. K. Thomas, 1920), especially chapters XIX, XXI and XXIII.
17   C. H. Spence, *The Laws We Live Under* (Adelaide: Government Printing Office, 1880).
18   *The Journal of Mental Science* called *The Origin and Growth of the Moral Instinct* 'the most original and important work of mental science that has appeared for more than forty years'; see H. G. Turner, *Alexander Sutherland, M.A.* (Melbourne: T. C. Lothian, 1908), 27.

radical Melbourne clergyman, Charles Strong, and politically active in the city, he was critical of external religion and advocated a secularist form of religious education, integrated into the curriculum as a whole rather than the teaching of positive doctrines.[19]

Andrew Inglis Clark (1848–1907), a Tasmanian engineer who became a lawyer, intellectual and leading constitutionalist was more explicit about his lack of belief in traditional Christianity and drew conclusions from it. Clark's upbringing in the strictly Calvinist environment of the Particular Baptists had a strong influence on his subsequent religious development. Until the age of twenty-four, Clark was thoroughly immersed in this highly disciplined, strictly exclusivist, but congregationally governed sect, of which he became a communicant at the age of twenty-two. As soon as he was baptised, on 21 April 1870, he threw himself into the life of the chapel, but his discontent soon surfaced and he was responsible for the resolution of 1872 that dissolved the chapel by a unanimous vote.[20] Just two years later Clark had undergone a religious transformation. In his introduction for the journal *The Quadrilateral*, he referred to a 'Universal Church of Conscience and Commonwealth of Righteousness' in which 'no separation of heaven and earth, of Christian, Greek or Jew was recognised.[21] In due course, Clark became both a political and a religious liberal, influenced by the English political philosopher John Stuart Mill (1806–1873), who believed that in religious matters one should look outside the sects.[22]

Sometime in the 1880s Clark wrote of the kind of church in which he would feel comfortable:

> [the] great want of the world today is a church capable of constructing out of the religious instincts of humanity a moral and social ideal in harmony with the conclusions of reason and the revelations of science.[23]

He also talked of his approach to faith as 'the happy mean between unreasonable credulity and invincible scepticism'.[24] It is possible to detect here the influence of American Unitarian writers such as William Ellery

---

19 Turner, *Alexander Sutherland, M.A.*
20 M. Haward and J. Warden (eds.), *An Australian Democrat: The Life, Works and Consequences of Andrew Inglis Clark* (Hobart: Centre for Tasmanian Historical Studies, University of Tasmania, 1995).
21 A. I. Clark, "Prelude," *The Quadrilateral* 1 (1874): 2.
22 Haward and Warden, *An Australian Democrat*, 101,107.
23 *A. I. Clark Papers* (University of Tasmania Library, Special Collection, C4/F18).
24 A. I. Clark, "An Untrodden Path of Literature," in *A. I. Clark Papers* (University of Tasmania Library, Special Collection, C4/F31a).

Channing and Ralph Waldo Emerson and traces of English Unitarian thought. Indeed, in his paper 'The Relations of Morality and Religion Under Paganism and Under Christianity', Clark referred to James Martineau as his 'revered master in theology'.[25] Clark followed Martineau both in his emphasis on the need to take account of modern science and in advocating a politics of dissent. His attitude to Christianity, however, was guarded:

> I decline to identify the Church in any age, or any branch of it, with Christianity ... Christianity is a purely moral force that was implanted in humanity by Jesus Christ ... and which has propagated itself with increasing volume from age to age by the contact of soul with soul, without depending on any special organization or particular ritual or book.[26]

Clark also exhibited an unequivocal distrust of churches:

> The Church throughout the larger part of its career presents itself to our contemplation as an organisation aspiring to the performance of political functions and to the control of men's conduct by dogmas and penalties, and, as such, its career is marked with all the evidences of human weakness, selfishness, ambition, arrogance, intolerance, cruelty and crime.[27]

Clark saw the idea that there must be an organised church as unnecessary and as an often dangerous spiritual crutch whose temporal power needed to be restrained.[28] In 1896 he joined a small Unitarian congregation, known as Our Father's Church, and continued to call himself a Unitarian until his death.[29] He was also the Tasmanian correspondent for the Unitarian monthly, *Modern Thought* from 1885.[30]

---

25 A. I. Clark, "The Relations of Morality and Religion Under Paganism and Under Christianity," in *A. I. Clark Papers* (University of Tasmania Library, Special Collection, C4/F15).
26 A. I. Clark, "The Influence of Christianity on Morals and Civilisation," in *A. I. Clark Papers* (University of Tasmania Library, Special Collection, F16(a)), quoted in R. Ely, "Andrew Inglis Clark and Church-State Separation," *Journal of Religious History* 8 (1975): 274.
27 Clark, "The Influence of Christianity on Morals and Civilisation," quoted in Ely, "Andrew Inglis Clark and Church-State Separation", 274.
28 Ely, "Andrew Inglis Clark and Church-State Separation," 274.
29 See *The Harbinger of Light*, 1 December 1907; *Tasmanian News*, 18 November 1907.
30 Ely, "Andrew Inglis Clark and Church-State Separation," 273.

Clark's commitment to anti-establishment traditions of dissent and nonconformity has sometimes been interpreted as secularism,[31] but this is misleading. In the run-up to the 1884 elections for the Tasmanian House of Assembly, in which Clark stood as a candidate, one of his neighbours wrote a letter to the editor of the *Mercury*, asserting that it was inconsistent of Clark to 'call on the name of the Supreme Being so much when we know him to be a staunch advocate of Bradlaugh the atheist'.[32] Clark was swift in his rebuttal: 'I ... have never entertained at any period in my life the slightest sympathy with Bradlaugh's atheistic opinions, or with any opinion of a similar type'.[33] Clark's formative role in the negotiation of Australian secularity needs to be seen against this background. Clark was deeply interested in constitutional and law reform and greatly admired American republican institutions.[34] He corresponded with Oliver Wendell Holmes (1809–1894), followed debates about American approaches to law reform, and argued for a strict separation of church and state in the Australian Constitution. He opposed state support of religious schools vehemently and successfully prevented the teaching of theology at the University of Tasmania.[35]

Clark's many papers on religious and theological topics, as well as his largely unpublished poetry, show him to have been a man of deep religious sensitivity, alert to the presence of the sacred in the world. His legal and constitutional efforts to separate religion and the state grew out of a concern that the government should never be able to exert influence over the religious choices of the people. He was determined that mainstream or orthodox churches should not be given power or precedence over dissent. Clark held that there was a natural tendency for religious institutions to subvert man's civil and religious liberty.[36] He took a social realist view of churches as self-interested organisations, led by largely unreformed humanity. Accordingly, he questioned the motives of churches that accepted state support for their schools, and sought to restrict clerical participation on the Council of the University of Tasmania.

Consistent with this, the older Clark was a religious independent, who remained open-minded and willing to consider the claims of spiritualism and

---

31 Haward and Warden, *An Australian Democrat*.
32 *The Mercury*, 26 August 1884.
33 *The Mercury*, 27 August 1884.
34 Ely, "Andrew Inglis Clark and Church-State Separation", 272.
35 Ely, "Andrew Inglis Clark and Church-State Separation", 271–89, and Haward and Warden, *An Australian Democrat*, ch. 10.
36 Ely, "Andrew Inglis Clark and Church-State Separation", 274.

theosophy, while tending to disbelieve in traditional Christian doctrines.[37] Breaking with what he saw as the spiritual tyranny and bibliolatry of the Reformation, Clark rejected traditional forms of Protestant worship apart from the sermon.[38] While abhorring the God of the Old Testament, he interpreted the coming of Jesus as an evolutionary leap, disclosing a new world of responsibilities and relations.

The Melbourne liberal theologian, Frederick Sinclaire (1881–1954), in contrast, was more explicitly concerned with the reform of Christian doctrine and apologetics. Educated at Manchester College, Oxford, Sinclaire was the minister of the Eastern Hill Unitarian Church in Melbourne from 1907 to 1911. A prolific essayist and a bitter critic of Melbourne's Protestant clergy, he described himself as a rationalist with a Voltairean mind.[39] Following his resignation from the Eastern Hill Unitarian Church, he set up his own Free Religious Fellowship, operating freelance without a pulpit, and a monthly magazine of undogmatic religion and social and literary criticism. Sinclaire's sermons, informed by the Edwardian literary socialism of Oscar Wilde and Bernard Shaw, were heard by Melbourne intellectuals such as the poet Bernard O'Dowd, publisher and poet Frank Wilmot (1881–1942), literary critic Nettie Higgins (later Palmer) and dramatist Louis Esson (1878–1943), most of whom shared his vision of a harmonious society.[40] In his sermons Sinclaire argued for a 'Living Theology' that would make a Wordsworthian turn and deal with common experience in ordinary language. This theology would also respond to modern spiritual emotions, such as the new feeling for nature and the passion for social justice evident in advanced circles.[41] Sinclaire's rousing alternative, 'Free Religion', combining intellectual openness and creativity, would not imprison the realities of spiritual experience within rigid intellectual forms, but would be socially radical.[42]

---

37 Ely, "Andrew Inglis Clark and Church-State Separation", 274.
38 Clark edited the short-lived journal, *The Quadrilateral*; weekly meetings of a coterie of his followers in his Hobart home became the centre for original thought on the island; see Ely, "Andrew Inglis Clark and Church-State Separation".
39 H. W. Rhodes, *Frederick Sinclaire: A Memoir* (Christchurch: University of Canterbury, 1984), 10–11.
40 Rhodes, *Frederick Sinclaire*, chs 2 and 3; for Sinclaire generally, see D. Walker, *Dream and Disillusion: A Search for Australian Cultural Identity* (Canberra: Australian National University Press, 1976), especially ch. 5.
41 F. Sinclaire, *Fellowship: A Monthly Magazine of Undogmatic Religion and Social & Literary Criticism*, March 1917. Sinclaire's magazine was a source of radical religious writing in Australia.
42 Walker, *Dream and Disillusion*, chapters 5 and 6.

Unlike some writers of the 1930s who tended to make socialism their religion (Jean Devanny, Eleanor Dark, Dymphna Cusack, Betty Roland and Katharine Susannah Prichard), Sinclaire criticised Western civilisation for its empty secularism and lack of moral ideals.[43] His alternative was a world informed by sacral values, but not by ecclesiasticism. Sinclaire preached and lectured for the Reverend Charles Strong and, like him, opposed both the First World War and conscription. A powerful critic of the existing social and economic order, he characterised the labour movement as the instrument of God and humanity, whose sacred mission was to accomplish the overthrow of capitalism.[44] He became co-editor of the *Socialist*, the journal of the Victorian Socialist Party, and condemned those Christian churches that supported the ruling classes against the poor.

Other leading Victorian intellectuals associated religious liberalism with socialism. Thus the Melbourne poet Bernard O'Dowd, for example, found Unitarianism a convenient shelter for his independent religious ideas, as he developed away from commitment to external religious forms. From a Northern Irish Catholic background, the young O'Dowd was an agnostic, whose radical views cost him a teaching position. He was also an agent for a secular journal and participated in anti-God meetings. A 'bush heretic',[45] O'Dowd was bitterly critical of the external religion of the Old Testament and attacked revealed religion generally. Involved with both freethought and spiritualism, he joined a variety of literary, religious and political clubs, including the Melbourne Progressive Lyceum Movement, for which he produced *The Lyceum Tutor* in 1888. O'Dowd was associated with W. H. Terry (1836–1913) and Melbourne spiritualism. He was involved, at different times, in the Melbourne New Thought Movement, the Theosophical Society, Strong's Australian Church, and Frederick Sinclaire's Religious Fellowship. In 1913 he was President of the Victorian Rationalist Association. After 1929, however, O'Dowd became reconciled to Christianity as a result of his reading of the German philosopher Immanuel Kant (1724–1804), from whom he learnt that religious postulates could be understood as regulative postulates, and not empirical, assertions. Subsequently, O'Dowd attended the Unitarian Church regularly, where he conducted the Sunday meditation services.[46]

---

43 F. Sinclaire, *Fellowship* 1, no. 2 (1914) and "Science and Religion," *Fellowship* 2, no. 5 (1915): 3–4.
44 Walker, *Dream and Disillusion*, op. cit. p.132.
45 H. Anderson, *The Poet Militant: Bernard O'Dowd* (Melbourne: Hill of Content, 1968), 14.
46 Anderson, *The Poet Militant*, 113.

O'Dowd was an eclectic free spirit who by the age of twenty-three had read the works of a great number of intellectuals, such as Spencer, Mill, Goethe, Proudhon, Dante, Petrarch, Camões, the Kalevala and the Mahabharata.[47] He was a member of the Walt Whitman movement in Melbourne, being attracted to the American prophet's vision of democracy based on the divinity of man.[48] He sometimes saw literature as an alternative to traditional religion, construing poetry as a 'little sister' to religion, and as more appropriate to modern materialist society than outmoded creeds.[49] Like Alfred Deakin, O'Dowd believed that radical religious views could be combined with new religious forms and composed various parareligious rituals, including a burial service. He linked his parareligion with a post-rationalist psychology, holding that the function of the poet in every age was to create 'gods' or powers on the boundary between this world and the next.[50] Immersing himself in Buddhism and Vedanta, O'Dowd argued that faith in the transcendental could replace the cruelties of positive religion. A 'Common Room' of the unconscious, he suggested, explained the mystical unity of all.[51] In *The Silent Land* (1906), O'Dowd, like Harpur, envisaged a single Emersonian 'Over-Soul' for all humanity:

> Whene'er we sacrifice our need
> To still the weary's moans,
> We have obeyed, whate'er our creed,
> God's Silent Overtones.[52]

Under contemporary conditions, however, things were more difficult:

> But now, for trust mayhap betrayed
> Or pride too loosely checked,
> The Silent Oracles evade
> Our questions too direct.[53]

---

47 Anderson, *The Poet Militant*, 31–7, 97ff.
48 See W. Gay, *Walt Whitman, The Poet of Democracy* (Melbourne: E.A. Petherick, 1893).
49 B. O'Dowd, "A Little Sister of Religion," *Notes on Address to Pleasant Sunday Afternoon at Wesley Church, October 17, 1943* (State Library of Victoria, O'Dowd Papers 1885–1966, Box 1/2).
50 B. O'Dowd, "The Gods," in *The Silent Land and Other Verses* (Melbourne: T.C. Lothian, 1906), 21–8, and Anderson, *The Poet Militant*, 97ff, 105–6; see also B. O'Dowd, *Dominions of the Boundary* (Melbourne: T.C. Lothian, 1907).
51 B. O'Dowd, "The Common Room," in *The Silent Land*, 16–19.
52 B. O'Dowd, "The Tones of Silence," in *The Silent Land*, 43.
53 B. O'Dowd, "Evensong," in *The Silent Land*, 45.

In more theosophical mood, he envisaged a universal appearance of truth in religion and myth:

> Though Reason claim omniscient worth
> And lush her dogmas thrive:
> Our present home is more than earth,
> Our senses more than five
> And the mystic who sees the star-folk throng
> Where we but the noonday blue
> Knows no religion yet was wrong
> And never a myth untrue.[54]

Once again, scepticism about positive religion went with spiritual idealism and a commitment to social reform. With early Fabian affiliations, O'Dowd was a founding member of the Victorian Socialist Party and took part in Charles Strong's Collingwood Workingmen's Club. He was a member of the Australian Natives' Association, a friend of the anarchist theoretician, Jack Andrews (1865–1903), and wrote for the radical weekly *Tocsin*. In his poetry O'Dowd celebrated the sacrality of the Australian bush. His cultural nationalism had strong spiritual components that included premonitions of spiritual reality to come:

> You are the brooding comrade of our way,
> Whispering rumour of a new Unknown,
> Moulding us white ideals to obey,
> Steeping whate'er we learn in lore your own,
> And freshening with unpolluted light
> The squalid city's day and pallid night
> Till we become ourselves, distinct, Australian,
> (Your native lightning charging blood and nerve),
> Stripped to the soul of borrowed garments, alien
> To that approaching Shape of God you serve.[55]

Another key Victorian literary figure, novelist Joseph Furphy, was not a Unitarian, but in his intellectual development he covered some of the same terrain. The son of Irish Protestant immigrants, Furphy belonged to a small Evangelical church, the Church of Christ, in Shepparton, but gradually

---

54 B. O'Dowd, "Mystic," in *Poems of Bernard O'Dowd* (Melbourne, Vic.: Lothian, 1941), 111.
55 B. O'Dowd, *The Bush* (Melbourne: T.C. Lothian, 1912), 32.

became more radical. As a young rationalist, Furphy rejected traditional interpretations of the Scriptures and clerical authority, although, like other radicals of the period, he took spiritualism seriously as a movement that tried to make empirically testable claims.[56] As the years passed, he became convinced that the churches failed to teach the truth of Christianity, although he admired the Reverend Charles Strong and read that radical churchman's monthly publication *The Commonweal*. Furphy did not accept the authority of the Bible, but, like the German dramatist Lessing, he distinguished the religion of Christianity from the religion of Christ.[57] With the help of the libraries in the mechanics' institutes established in many country towns, Furphy read himself out of conventional religion. He also read Edward Bellamy (1850–1898) and William Morris (1834–1896) and became committed to a form of Christian socialism. Furphy refused to separate religion from society and based his creed on spiritual equality and the betterment of humanity. For Furphy, the New Testament was the textbook for an ideal socialism[58] and a true Christianity would seek to establish a just social system:

> The best hope of religion rests not in the distorted Christianity which fences monopoly and points the plundered toiler to a heaven won by mental suicide and moral self-abasement, but in the restored gospel of equal rights to the fullness of God's earth and equal liability to the consecrated penalty of work.[59]

The Kingdom of God was to be realised in the collective history of humanity.

Furphy's social mission was nuanced, however, by Augustinian reservations about corrupted human nature. His criticism of church religion did not mean that working people did not need to follow an exacting code based

---

56 J. Barnes, *The Order of Things: A Life of Joseph Furphy* (Melbourne: Oxford University Press, 1990), 271–3, 332–3.
57 Barnes, *The Order of Things*, 155.
58 Early Victorian socialists often believed that socialism was closer to the true spirit of Christianity than the teachings and practices of the churches. Tom Mann, founder of the Victorian Socialist Party, attacked the 'Ungodly Religious', but drew parallels between socialism and 'true Christianity'. Mann set up Socialist Sunday Schools, delivered 'Socialist Sermons' and performed socialist baptisms; see C. Tsuzuki, *Tom Mann 1856–1941: The Challenges of Labour* (Oxford: Clarendon Press, 1991).
59 J. Furphy, "Essay 12: In Favor," in E.W. Cole (ed.), *Cyclopaedia of Short Prize Essays on the Federation of the Whole World: Illustrated with Representative Portraits of All Nations: First Series Containing Fifty Essays by Fifty Australasian Writers* (Melbourne: E.W. Cole, 1890), 55.

on work, self-discipline, self-education and temperance.⁶⁰ His scepticism struck at traditional supernaturalism, but not at the Christian view that human beings stood in need of redemption. Hence, the religious themes in his writing were allied to social and political goals. In his novel *Rigby's Romance*, he implied that Christianity was about acting well and very different from the craft of priests.⁶¹ In *Such is Life* (1903) Furphy still seemed to believe that 'the kingdom of God is within us; our embracing duty is to give it form and effect, a local habitation and a name'.⁶² Nonetheless, his own views were probably not those of his character, Tom Collins, and there were indications in the novel that human beings lived in an ambiguous world of contingency and chaos. Furphy's personal views seem to have been syncretic and there is some suggestion that he came to see theosophy as the religion taught by Christ.⁶³

Unitarianism represented an intellectually serious strand in Australian religious thought, associated with wide and international cultural learning and with work for social reform. Unitarians were critics of the pathologies of the Christian churches, but also aware of the writings of progressive intellectuals in Britain and the United States. They were inclined to radical social views, even if as individuals they sometimes retained pessimistic assumptions from their upbringing in more conservative churches.

Theological Modernism

Unitarians tended to be theological minimalists with progressive social views. Many of the most important religious liberals in Australia, however, were theological modernists, for whom questions about theological doctrine, the historical reliability of the Scriptures, and questions about church history were central. Professionally concerned to reinterpret Christianity, they were not on the fringe of society, but at its centre. An intellectual élite, they were immersed in the classics, in the history of theology, and in Scottish and German philosophical and theological authors, about whom ordinary Australians knew little.

---

60 See J. Croft, *The Life and Opinions of Tom Collins: A Study of the Works of Joseph Furphy* (St. Lucia: University of Queensland Press, 1991), ch. 6.
61 J. Furphy, *Rigby's Romance: A "Made in Australia" Novel* (Sydney: Angus and Robertson, 1946), 214. In this novel Rigby debates with a clergyman whether Christianity was compatible with state socialism.
62 J. Furphy, *Such Is Life: Being Certain Extracts from the Diary of Tom Collins*, ed. C. Hartley Grattan (Chicago: University of Chicago, 1948), 118.
63 Barnes, *The Order of Things*, 382.

Some theological modernists drew heavily on Scottish idealism, both Scottish Hegelianism and personal idealism. The Scottish idealists identified the renewal of Christianity with its realisation in political, social and economic life.[64] They advanced reinterpretations of religious belief and church history, seeking to relate Christianity to a new critical temper. Conceiving of the state as a moral agent with a duty to provide a nurturing environment for its citizens, they valorised positive over negative liberty, promoted a conception of active citizenship as the way to self-realisation, and acknowledged a duty of care in the public sphere. In international affairs, they emphasised a moral conception of Empire, international cooperation, and the need to resist militarism and imperial wars. The Scottish idealists promoted the democratisation of universities and the provision of popular liberal education for working people, especially through the WEA, efforts to alleviate the poor through university settlements, compulsory education, the introduction of old age pensions, prison reform, and the development of industrial arbitration law. All of these concerns were also promoted by intellectuals in Australia who were influenced by Scottish idealist ideas. And for many of them building the Kingdom of God was the central concern, even though this is now sometimes forgotten.[65]

The influence of idealist philosophy on Australian religious liberalism and on social reform was extensive, partly because many of the intellectuals concerned were Protestant clergymen, and partly because idealist philosophy allowed intellectuals to reinterpret Christianity as social activism. Idealists were inclined to adopt an immanent conception of God, to refuse all dualisms, to manifest faith in moral and spiritual progress, and to believe in the value of personality.[66] This gave them a powerful framework for thinking about political, social and economic life and about international affairs.

Some religious liberals were indebted to Anglican modernist churchmen, such as Charles Gore, the liberal Catholic Principal of Pusey House, Oxford, J. R. Illingworth, and William Temple, who emphasised the need for critical

---

64 See D. Boucher (ed.), *The Scottish Idealists: Selected Philosophical Writings* (Exeter: Imprint Academic, 2004).
65 The full story is yet to be told. It includes the social achievements of Australian women, who were often theologically motivated, to which Marian Sawer has rightly drawn attention. For excellent discussion of the role of women in promoting social liberalism, see M. Sawer, *The Ethical State?: Social Liberalism in Australia* (Carlton, Vic.: Melbourne University Press, 2003).
66 M. Hughes-Warrington and I. Tregenza, "State and Civilisation in Australian New Idealism, 1890–1950," in *History of Political Thought* 29 (2008): 92.

methods in the study of theology and the Scriptures.[67] Some modernists also tended to follow British churchmen in emphasising the need to revisit Platonism and the theology of the Church Fathers. Modernists, in general, were culturally privileged and their radicalism was a radicalism from above. All of them, however, tried to face new challenges to Christianity as they came to hand.

John Woolley (1816–1866), a liberal clergyman appointed first Principal and Professor of Classics and Logic at the University of Sydney in 1852, combined classical learning, Scottish Enlightenment sympathies and a concern with natural theology going back to eighteenth-century authors such as William Paley (1743–1805). He was the friend of Dean Arthur Stanley (1869–1947), the church historian, biographer of Matthew Arnold and leading English liberal theologian of his time. Stanley advocated a close connection between church and state and held that the religious expression of the faith of the community on the most sacred and most vital of all its interests should be controlled and guided by the whole community through the supremacy of law. Stanley favoured making the creed as wide as possible and was prepared to allow English Nonconformists and Scottish Presbyterians to preach in Anglican pulpits.[68] Woolley shared Stanley's relaxed approach to church membership. He drew on the German liberal theologian and church historian August Neander (1806–1850), who argued from the position that diverse tendencies appeared successively in church history and that the development of the spiritual life ought not to be forced into a single dogmatic form.[69] Woolley combined these liberal conceptions of the church with sympathy for Platonic theology and the views of the Christian Platonist Josiah Bunsen (1791–1860) in particular.[70]

Woolley was endowed with considerable learning and brought significant transnational intellectual influences to New South Wales. He was a capable philosopher who adopted the 'logic of the concrete' developed by John Henry Newman (1801–1890) and wrote a refutation of John Stuart Mill's *A System of Logic*.[71] Following the Scottish philosopher Sir William Hamilton

---

67 C. Gore, *The Reconstruction of Belief* (London: John Murray, 1926). Gore turned to the Fathers and Platonism in his attempt to rethink Christianity as a rational philosophical outlook.
68 J. Witheridge, *Excellent Dr Stanley: The Life of Dean Stanley of Westminster* (Wilby: Michael Russell, 2013).
69 For fine discussion, see G. Melleuish, "The Theology and Philosophy of John Woolley," *Journal of Religious History* 12 (1983): 418–32.
70 Melleuish, "The Theology and Philosophy of John Woolley", 421.
71 Melleuish, "The Theology and Philosophy of John Woolley", 418.

(1788–1856), Woolley advocated an epistemological agnosticism, in which what was not subject to conditions could never be an object of thought. According to Woolley, although human beings were driven to pursue pure truth, they were only able to arrive at discursive reasoning.[72] There were tensions in Woolley's thought between his epistemological agnosticism, which denied that human beings could know the supernatural, a sense that providence was working to achieve its designs in human history, and Enlightenment optimism about the future.

Like other religious liberals in the early nineteenth century, Woolley believed in 'true religion' rather than in theological dogmas and was inclined to understand Christianity in terms of its role in human history. He saw the history of the human spirit as a process through which humanity gradually reached higher levels of development. Christianity, he argued, had not realised its full potential and could only do so when it was freed of extraneous elements.[73] A Freemason with rationalist sympathies, Woolley was critical of the churches and sought to establish Christianity outside them. He saw the churches as obstacles to a proper public enactment of what he, like many Protestants of his day, called 'our common Christianity'.[74] Consistent with these principles, Woolley argued that religious education should take place within a strictly non-confessional framework and for a clear separation between theology and secular learning. He sought to confine the church colleges within the University of Sydney to an ancillary role, on the grounds that they tended to disrupt social unity,[75] and in this respect had an impact on the development of theology and religious thought in Australia.

Woolley dreamt of a harmonious society brought about by the unimpeded operation of natural laws, in which active souls could play a central role. Like other religious liberals, he believed in continuous revelation and in the need to harmonise society and religion, and looked forward to a society characterised by democracy and justice. Drawing upon strands in Scottish Calvinist theology, Woolley focused on civil society as an arena in which religion, politics and culture could come together. Understanding history as tending to an ultimate harmony, Woolley, in his *Lectures Delivered in Australia* between 1852 and 1860, reasserted what he took to be the ancient

---

72 Melleuish, "The Theology and Philosophy of John Woolley".
73 J. Woolley, *Lectures Delivered in Australia* (Cambridge: Macmillan, 1862), 169.
74 Woolley, *Lectures Delivered in Australia*, 81.
75 J. Woolley, *Religious Education: the Safeguard of the State, A Sermon* (London, 1850).

view of the religiousness of social union. The state and the church, he argued, could not be separated from one another:

> Civil society is the great school of humanity: the appointed trial of steadfastness and faithfulness; the battle-ground of good and evil in the soul; the discipline of self-control and benevolence. And, therefore, perfect virtue, as a citizen, is, in one sense, more rare and difficult than genuine religion.[76]

This implied a merger of the sacred and the secular, in which the sacral was realised in a secular form.

For Woolley, God's moral government was the true type of human government, and the law was a schoolmaster with the capacity to bring the human being into communion with the law-giver.[77] Similarly, civil government was religious, and the education owed to the younger generation also had to have a religious or moral character. Later Woolley appealed to social sympathy and the affections and to reverence for man, seemingly promoting a religion of humanity as a perspective on which all colonists could agree. He opposed all metaphysical speculation and endorsed a natural theology from which moral principles could be derived independently of religious doctrines. In this natural theology the state acquired civil religious significance as a symbol of sacramental brotherhood.[78] Woolley assumed that a unification of religion and art could sustain the spiritual life of human beings and was committed to the intellectual and moral improvement of the colony and, therefore, to education as a means to such improvement. He lectured at schools of art and mechanics' institutes and was involved with teacher education in New South Wales.[79]

The tendency to reinterpret religion as being about social concerns also characterised the thought of James Jefferis (1833–1917), South Australian Congregational Church leader and liberal evangelical. For some years Jefferis was a champion of religious liberty, arguing for the separation of church and state and the secularisation of Australian politics. As conditions changed, he modified his views and became a champion of civic Protestantism, a creed broad enough to attract widespread support. Jefferis was prepared to come to terms with developments in the sciences,

---

76   Woolley, *Lectures Delivered in Australia*, 125.
77   Woolley, *Lectures Delivered in Australia*, 123, 125.
78   G. Nadel, *Australia's Colonial Culture: Ideas, Men and Institutions in Mid-Nineteenth Century Eastern Australia* (Melbourne: F.W. Cheshire, 1957), 266–70.
79   For useful detail, see Nadel, *Australia's Colonial Culture*, ch. 21.

although he resisted the more radical views associated with British Congregational theologian R. J. Campbell (1867–1956), whose theology had advocates in South Australia. Favouring a culturally rich Christianity, Jefferis combined evangelical piety with a willingness to respond to the times. In a series of Sunday evening lectures in April 1882 at the Congregational Church in Sydney on 'Other Bibles and Other Beliefs' to young men who were 'bold enough to think freely', he dismissed modern freethinkers as reincarnations of the sceptics of ancient Greece and recommended a sophisticated interpretation of religion, based on his experiences in Ceylon, India and Egypt, as well as on his reading of the German Indologist Max Müller (1823–1900).[80] Like the great Protestant theologian Friedrich Schleiermacher (1768–1834), who rethought theology in experiential terms in order to respond to religion's cultural despisers, Jefferis addressed those inclined not to take Christianity seriously and conceded that many forms of disbelief were well grounded. In response to criticisms of traditional religion, Jefferis was prepared to change the form of religion and to transform its political and social role. Noting that his contemporaries did not want a divorce between religion and politics, he advocated a vital union between Christianity and the state.[81] Jefferis championed a civic Christianity and a Catholic Church, independent of creeds and confessions and concerned with social justice rather than with narrowly religious concerns.[82]

The case of the Reverend Charles Strong also illustrates the tendency for theological modernists to identify Christianity with ethical and social activism. Strong is a major figure in the history of Australian religious thought whose trial for heresy and subsequent decision to establish his own Australian church arguably had an impact on the parameters of Australian citizenship. Strong came to Melbourne in 1875 to become the minister of its principal Presbyterian Church, Scots Church. He was a member of the Established Church of Scotland and had a doctorate of divinity from the

---

80 J. Jefferis, *Other Bibles and Other Beliefs: A Series of Eight Lectures delivered at the Pitt Street Congregational Church as a Help to Young Men of Free Thought* (Sydney: Samuel E. Lees, 1882).

81 See J. Jefferis, "The Relations of Australian Christianity with Australian Citizenship," in *New South Wales Congregational Year Book* (Sydney, 1888); "The Religious Celebration of the Centenary of the Colony," in *New South Wales Congregational Year Book* (Sydney, 1887); and W. Phillips, *James Jefferis: Prophet of Federation* (Melbourne: Australian Scholarly Publishing, 1993).

82 J. Jefferis, *A Free Church in a Free State: its Claims and Conflicts* (Sydney: Foster and Fairfax, 1878); and Phillips, *James Jefferis*, 166.

University of Glasgow,[83] where he had studied with the Scottish Hegelian, John Caird, from whom he learnt that a fundamental recasting of Christianity was called for, involving both the reform of worship and the elaboration of a Christian critique of the existing social order.[84] Strong's Scottish Hegelianism made him a formidable progressive thinker, up-to-date with new developments in many areas of knowledge. Strong, who had considered becoming a Unitarian minister, held to principles that were, in Scotland, within the limits of Presbyterianism, broadly conceived, but were far removed from Melbourne Calvinists' understanding of Christianity as a set of propositional beliefs authorised by and contained in the Scriptures.

Strong did not believe that Christianity depended on the historical accuracy of the Scriptures and he held no positive belief that Jesus' death could be understood as a literal atonement for the sins of mankind. In these beliefs he owed much to the Scottish theologian John McLeod Campbell (1800–1872), who rejected substitutionary theories of the atonement and argued that salvation was for the whole world. He also continued the critical revisionism of the Presbyterian Biblical scholar, William Robertson Smith (1846–1894), and the Presbyterian divine, Thomas Erskine (1788–1870), who rejected standard Calvinist accounts of the atonement and emphasised personal religious experience rather than objectivist historical claims.[85] Strong was further influenced by Scottish debates about alternative understandings of the church.[86] This Scottish background in the development of religious liberalism in Australia is of greater importance than has always been realised.

Strong promoted Scottish and German liberal theological ideas in Melbourne.[87] He also corresponded with leading British liberal theologians, including John Caird and the Unitarian James Martineau.[88] Following Caird's *The Fundamental Ideas of Christianity* (1899), Strong made no distinction between natural and revealed religion. He also distinguished between faith as assent to beliefs and faith as an inner spiritual process. Then

---

83 See the introductory study by C. R. Badger, *The Reverend Charles Strong and The Australian Church* (Melbourne: Abacada Press, 1971).
84 See J. Caird, *The Fundamental Ideas of Christianity: with a Memoir by Edward Caird*, (Gifford Lectures 1892/3 and 1895/6), 2 vols (Glasgow: J. MacLehose, 1899).
85 Badger, *The Reverend Charles Strong and The Australian Church*, 213ff.
86 For the Scottish background, see A. C. Cheyne, *Studies in Scottish Church History* (Edinburgh: T. & T. Clark, 1999), especially chs 4 and 8.
87 C. Strong, *Some Recent Protestant Theology: Being Six Lectures on the Drift of Modern Thought as Illustrated by Representative Books of Today* (Melbourne: J. Haase, 1896).
88 Badger, *The Reverend Charles Strong and The Australian Church*, 158–205.

Strong was immersed in the writings of the major German liberal Protestant theologians, and held that the true Christianity was its most recent form, rather than its primitive form. Following the German liberal Protestant theologian Albrecht Ritschl (1822–1889), he insisted that the truth of theology was practical rather than theoretical – a matter of how we should act rather than what we should believe.[89] Strong adopted many of the views of Ritschl's disciple, Adolf von Harnack (1851–1930), the church historian who claimed that the early church councils had replaced the simple ethical religion of Jesus with metaphysical dogmas.[90]

Further, like the theologian Albert Schweitzer (1875–1965), Strong identified Christianity with work to realise the Kingdom of God in history,[91] which he held was the sole justification for the church as a civil institution. Accordingly, the sacerdotal, the dogmatic, and the monarchical elements in Christianity could disappear. Instead, worship should be simple and ministers should be prophets, teachers and spiritual guides of a freethinking educated laity. In an age in which traditional religion and theism no longer convinced many of the educated, Strong sought to recall the church to the Christianity of the primitive church, which, in his view, had focused on morality and mutual service. Christians were to remain faithful to the principles of free spiritual and social religion, on which Jesus' concept of the Kingdom was originally based, and to try to realise these principles under contemporary conditions.

Empowered by these radical theological ideas, Strong proposed the re-interpretation of religion, as Copernicus and Galileo had reinterpreted astronomy.[92] He promoted the scientific study of religion and argued for a natural theology, grounded in scientific and psychological investigations. Strong approached religious questions from the standpoint of comparative religion and contemporary developments in sociology.[93] He treated the

---

89   Badger, *The Reverend Charles Strong and The Australian Church*, 209–38.
90   For Ritschl's anti-metaphysical theology, see A. E. Garvie, *The Ritschlian Theology* (Edinburgh: T. & T. Clark, 1899).
91   C. Strong, "The Relation of the Australian Church to Creed and Dogma: Anniversary Address," 6 December 1896, 14, and "The Broad Church: A Sunday Evening Lecture," 1889, 6, in the *Papers of Charles Strong, 1875–1961* (National Library of Australia, MS 2882, Series 4); see also I. Tregenza, "The Idealist Tradition in Australian Religious Thought," *Journal of Religious History* 34 (2010), 335–53.
92   C. Strong, *Christianity Re-interpreted and Other Sermons* (Melbourne: George Robertson, 1894), 9; see also N.Habel, "The Hermeneutics of Charles Strong," paper delivered at the Charles Strong Symposium, July 2006, http://normanhabel.com/wp-content/uploads/2013/09/Charles-Strong-Hermeneutics.pdf.
93   Badger, *The Reverend Charles Strong and The Australian Church*, 232, 283–6.

Bible as a collection of the sacred books of the Hebrews, rather than as revealed text, and dismissed inconvenient Biblical stories, such as the story of Abraham and Isaac, as allegories. Mature religion, he taught, should be based on the study of human experience, rather than on the Bible.[94] Strong was equally dismissive of traditional ecclesiology. In works such as *The Old Theology and the New* (1888), he cited the latest British and German Protestant scholarship in presenting the view that Jesus did not found a church and the claim that the church organisation had changed over the centuries from its original democratic constitution to a monarchical system of government.[95] Like the German theologians he admired, Strong argued for a more spiritual conception of religion, based on what was divine in humanity. He conceived of God in immanentist terms as an indwelling, energising force or spirit. According to Strong, Christian faith was not a system of beliefs communicated once and for all, but the gradual unveiling of truth in reason and in the heart. It did not need an infallible book, support from evidence, or fixed dogmas; nor did it need to posit the supernatural or miracles. The essence of Christianity was to be found in the life of Jesus, not in the Christologies adopted by the early church councils.

Strong did not hide the radical nature of his views. Instead, he advanced a comprehensive New Theology in place of the Old:

> The New Theology I should say in the first place recognises Theology as *fluid*, that is subject to change. The Old Theology regarded it as necessarily a fixed and final dogma.
>
> The New Theology, I should say, secondly, thinks of God as the indwelling, Energising Spirit, informing Force of all life, the centre of the radiated circle of being 'in whom, through whom, to whom are all things', 'in all, through all, above all'. The Old Theology thought of him more as (a) external, (b) most manifested in the past, (c) most manifested in the abnormal.
>
> The New Theology, I should say, thirdly, thinks of God as manifested in Humanity, and of Humanity as essentially God's Son. The Old Theology regarded man as a creature, as utterly debased, and a rebel, deserving eternal torments. Jesus was what all are potentially.

---

94 Badger, *The Reverend Charles Strong and The Australian Church*, 282.
95 C. Strong, *The Old Theology and the New: A Sunday Evening Lecture* (Melbourne, 1888).

The New Theology, I should say, fourthly, regards God's as love and justice not as two things needing to be reconciled, but as one, and God as essentially a reconciling Father drawing the world into Himself.

The New Theology, I should say, fifthly allies itself with Science.

The New Theology, I should say, sixthly, bases Religion on Human Experience, and not on the letter of an infallible book.[96]

Preaching to influential Melburnians and other enthusiastic supporters, Strong proclaimed the end of credal Christianity and demanded the reform of the existing ecclesiastical institutions, in so far as they were harmful to religion and morality. According to Strong, individuals should be self-reliant in matters of religion and not dependent upon external ecclesiastical authorities. In this respect, Strong's religious republicanism went well with his radical social views.

Strong was a controversial figure in Melbourne, both because he proposed radical reform of the Westminster Confession and because he drew radical social conclusions from his theological views. Strong's willingness to admit that the Bible contained textual and historical errors aroused concern in the churches and these tensions heightened when he declared his belief in evolution and referred to Genesis as a 'Creation myth'. When Strong rejected the atonement as a morally repulsive idea in his contribution to an 1880 symposium in *The Victorian Review*,[97] the Assembly of the Presbyterian Church branded him a heretic. Some critically minded Presbyterians, including the Reverend Professor J. L. Rentoul (1846–1926), who accepted both the results of Higher Criticism and Darwinism, opposed Strong because they believed that his conception of Christianity tended towards naturalism or an immanentist conception of reality.[98]

After Strong's expulsion from Scots Church, many of his congregation followed him to set up the Australian Church, with a radical progressive agenda. Within a year average weekly attendances at Strong's church had built up to 1000, amongst whom were Charles Pearson, George Higinbotham,

---

96   C. Strong, "Address to the Australian Church Guild in 1908", in Badger, *The Reverend Charles Strong and The Australian Church*, 285.
97   C. Strong, "The Atonement," *The Victorian Review* 2 (1880): 763–73; see also his *Christianity Re-interpreted and Other Sermons*.
98   D. Chambers, "Theological Hall" in *Ormond College Centennial Essays*, ed. S. Macintyre (Melbourne: Melbourne University Press, 1984), 108–111.

Alfred Deakin, H. B. Higgins, and Bernard O'Dowd.[99] The aims of Strong's Australian Church were not modest:

> Believing that theology is a progressive science, that genuine religion is confined to no one form of belief, and that to fetter the minds and bind the consciences of minister or people is not only ridiculous folly but a sin in this Nineteenth Century ... the promoters of the Australian Church have sought to found a society that while reserving whatever is venerable in the past, will ever be open to any new light of God and which may unite men in many shades of opinion in the unity of the religious spirit and practical Christianity.[100]

Strong and his followers claimed the right to make up a new and more contemporary version of Christianity, even though they were forced to do so outside the existing churches. They identified Christianity with work to realise the Kingdom of God. Strong's experiment with a national church without creed implied that Australians could teach Europeans how to organise their religious lives. His comprehensive Australian Church, which was not based on creeds or ecclesiastical forms, was a remarkable feature of Melbourne life in the 1880s. He continued to preach in support of the rights of working people, international peace, and intellectual freedom for the next sixty years, even though his views estranged many well-to-do members of his church over the years. In effect, Strong embodied a model of liberal religious citizenship, a model that eventually came to be widely accepted, which allowed the individual to judge religious questions for themselves, provided they did not degrade the views of others, and to arrive at views inconsistent with their social location or the official positions of churches.

As Strong grew older, he described himself as a Liberal Christian and then as a Modernist. By 'Modernism' he meant not only the attempt to express the language of the past in the language of the present, but the effort to lift Christianity to a higher spiritual level.[101] Although he rejected extrinsicist supernaturalism, the Resurrection and miracles,[102] Strong's views were not naturalistic, and, like some of the English Modernists, he expected fresh revelations once obsolete dogmas were displaced.[103] Consistent with this,

---

99 Sawer, *The Ethical State?*, 37ff; Badger, *The Reverend Charles Strong and The Australian Church*, ch. 9.
100 Prospectus of the Australian Church, quoted in J. Roe, "Challenge and Response: Religious Life in Melbourne 1876–86," *Journal of Religious History* 5 (1968): 165.
101 Badger, *The Reverend Charles Strong and The Australian Church*, 309, 312.
102 Badger, *The Reverend Charles Strong and The Australian Church*, 297.
103 Badger, *The Reverend Charles Strong and The Australian Church*, 279–83, 289–93.

although Strong was controversial in Melbourne, he was not seen as a heretic internationally, and his views on a range of matters converged with those of the leaders of the Modernist movement within the Church of England. He had personal links with Charles Gore,[104] and was well regarded in Scotland, receiving a Doctorate of Divinity from Glasgow University in 1887. To this extent, Strong saw himself as a transnational voice in 'colonial' Melbourne.

Strong identified the practical realisation of Christianity with socialism. He was a passionate advocate of social reform, pacifism and feminism, and attacked unjust social conditions, such as land and money monopolies, relentlessly.[105] Strong opposed rigid Sabbatarianism and argued for the opening of libraries and art galleries on Sunday. He contributed to a variety of social organisations and helped establish the Social Improvement Friendly Help and Children's Aid Society and the Criminology Society in Melbourne. His Free Religious Fellowship and its associated reform groups, which were financially supported by leading Victorians, such as Alfred Deakin and George Higinbotham, became a hub for social liberal and feminist ideas in Melbourne.[106] Strong worked for the underprivileged and sided with organised labour in various controversies, speaking to workers against sweating, supporting strikers, and holding radical economic and social views.[107] During the 1890s, Strong cooperated with his friend Horace Tucker (1849–1911) on a resettlement scheme for the unemployed in country areas.[108] Strong campaigned for justice for Aborigines and worked actively for prison reform and for the rights of women, giving women leadership roles in all his projects.[109] A convinced anti-militarist, he opposed the Boer War and founded the Melbourne Peace Society in 1905 and the Sisterhood of International Peace in 1918. Strong vigorously opposed capital punishment and campaigned for the proper care of mentally handicapped children. He showed interest in utopian experiments and was involved in the Village

---

104 Gore, *The Reconstruction of Belief*. Unlike Strong, Gore turned to the Fathers and Platonism and attempted to rethink Christianity as a rational philosophical outlook.
105 C. Strong, *Thoughts for the Times: Personality, Land and Money: Substance of Address* (Melbourne: Australian Church, 1918).
106 Among those involved were H. B. Higgins, journalist Alice Henry and suffragists Isabella and Vida Goldstein; see Sawer, *The Ethical State?*, ch. 2, especially 37–8.
107 Sawer, *The Ethical State?*, 28ff.
108 Tucker set out his ideas in many articles and in his novel, *The New Arcadia: an Australian Story* (Melbourne: George Robertson, 1894).
109 Sawer, *The Ethical State?*, 38.

Settlement Movement.[110] His wife, Jane, set up the first crèche for working mothers in Melbourne.[111] Strong had a major impact on socially concerned intellectual circles in Melbourne, through people like Joseph Furphy and Bernard O'Dowd. He tirelessly encouraged his followers to work for the transformation of the world in which they lived.

Although Strong's Scottish Hegelian version of Christianity lost support over time, the sacral secularity he sought to achieve in many different social contexts proved more enduring. His attempts in the convergence between radical theology and sacral secularity were not confined to Victoria; his liberalism had parallels elsewhere in Australia. Adelaide was particularly receptive to liberalism, where local religious liberals included the Reverend Charles Bright of Norwood Baptist Church, who was a founder of the Society for the Study of Christian Sociology, Congregationalists, William Roby Fletcher (1868–1947), Vice-Chancellor of the University of Adelaide,[112] and Alfred Depledge Sykes (1871–1940), who propagated the conception of a rational arguments-based Christianity associated with views found in radical *New Theology* (1907) of the British Congregationalist R. J. Campbell.[113] It is also appropriate to identify some continuation of Strong's approach in present-day statements on a range of social issues by the Uniting Church of Australia. Strong's intellectual legacy is honoured by the Charles Strong Trust and the annual Charles Strong Lecture.

Another influential religious liberal in Australia, the philosopher and educationist Francis Anderson, also came from a Scottish theological and philosophical background. Anderson had studied in Glasgow under, and then assisted, Edward Caird (1835–1908), the Scottish Presbyterian leader, idealist philosopher and Kant scholar, before he migrated to Melbourne in 1886 to become an assistant to Charles Strong in his Australian Church. Subsequently, he became the first Challis Professor of Logic and Mental Philosophy at the University of Sydney and played a prominent part in Sydney's intellectual life. He became the first editor of the *Australasian*

---

110 Sawer, *The Ethical State?*, 290–1 and Badger, *The Reverend Charles Strong and The Australian Church*, ch 8.
111 See Sawer, *The Ethical State?*, ch. 2, especially 38.
112 W. R. Fletcher, *Modern Aspects of the Flight of Faith and the Higher Criticism of the Bible, in the Light of Modern Discoveries* (Sydney: "Australasian Independent" Office, 1892).
113 D. Hilliard, "Unorthodox Christianity in South Australia," *Journal of the Historical Society of South Australia* 2 (2005): 38.1–38.10 and "Strong's Liberal Contemporaries: Adelaide, 1870–1914," http://users.esc.net.au/~nhabel/symposium/Hilliard%20on%20Strong.pdf.

Journal of Psychology and Philosophy. Anderson's outlook, like Strong's, was sophisticated and complex.[114] He combined expertise in the classics with wide contemporary reading and was influenced by Edward Caird's Hegelianism and the identification of Christianity with work to realise the Kingdom of God. In addition, Anderson was indebted to T. H. Green, for whom Christianity implied an active conception of citizenship,[115] and Charles Gore. Less immersed in German theological writers than Strong, Anderson was a personal idealist who held that 'God' was to be understood as a living fact of spiritual experience. 'Not until we have this intimate personal experience do we know what exists in fact, namely, that God is within us as part of our own existence', he wrote.[116] Like other personal idealists, he was convinced that the principle of personality was realising itself in human history,[117] and that society was reconstructing itself in the enlightened hearts and consciences of its citizens.[118]

The strong transnational elements in Anderson's background made him an eminence in Australia who, as those who appointed him intended, connected Sydney to the metropolitan worlds of Britain and the Empire. Anderson was concerned with large ideas and civilisational issues, rather than with philosophy in a technical sense. His synthesis of Christianity with utopian optimism, ethical activism and philosophical idealism was nothing if not comprehensive. Anderson brought an anthropological interpretation of faith to bear on an evolutionary view of human social, cultural and economic development. He redefined religion as a form of life and a living stream of energy, not a body of literal propositions, and as practical rather than a

---

114 For an excellent overview of Anderson, including his different phases, see Melleuish, *Cultural Liberalism*, 87–95.

115 Anderson was one of a group of like-minded thinkers at the University of Sydney. The Professor of History, George Arnold Wood (1865–1928), also promoted a sacral civil religion based on spiritually active individuals, which combined a Franciscan concern to apply the Gospel with an attempt to educate active men; see R. M. Crawford, *"A Bit of a Rebel": The Life and Work of George Arnold Wood* (Sydney: Sydney University Press, 1975), 135–42. David Stow Adam (1859–1925), Professor of Systematic Theology at Ormond College, Melbourne, also endorsed the Scottish Hegelianism of the Glasgow school; see his *Cardinal Elements of the Christian Faith* (London: Hodder and Stoughton, 1911).

116 F. Anderson, *The Religion of the Christian Student* (Sydney: Angus and Robertson, 1930), 17.

117 Melleuish, *Cultural Liberalism*, 90–1.

118 F. Anderson, *Christian Liberty and Ecclesiastical Union: An Examination of the Proposed "Basis of Union of the United Church of Australia"* (Sydney: Angus and Robertson, 1923), 6.

matter of dogmatic theology.[119] This view implied not only that doctrinal tenets and practices would vary in the course of history, but that religions were important for their impacts on human ethical development rather than for the ideational constructs they deployed. Ranging over the main questions of cultural and intellectual life, Anderson's idealist philosophy of civilisation emphasised moral philosophical issues and perspectives from sociology. Anderson advocated a new social form for Christianity. "The progress of religion consists in the freeing of man's spirit from the bondage of the external and the material," he wrote.[120] Like other religious liberals, Anderson took the religious sense of the human being to be a more reliable basis for religion than the scriptures.[121] Humanity's essential religiosity was intuitive and non-dogmatic. It was a form of poetic religious sentiment that could guide the creation of a purer society. Anderson had faith in a higher humanity and in the possibility of a future society based on cooperation.[122] Humanity, he believed, was organising itself into a kingdom of justice.[123]

Anderson's account of the history of Christianity was more critical. In *Liberty, Equality and Fraternity* (1922) Anderson wrote of the rise of humanity as the cumulative work of four revolutions: the moral revolution known as Buddhism; the religious revolution known as Christianity; the political revolution of which France was the standard bearer; and the economic revolution still underway.[124] This implied that religion needed to develop and change with the advances of history. Historical Christianity, however, had failed to fulfil the promises of its social gospel, partly because the passive elements had been emphasised at the expense of the active virtues, just as the individualistic aspect had been stressed at the expense of the socialistic aspect.[125]

Anderson's conception of the church was also expansive and he held that spiritual matters were no longer things to be confiscated by ecclesiastics and theologians.[126] Against this background, Anderson advocated a radical

---

119 Melleuish, *Cultural Liberalism*, 90 and F. Anderson, "Religious Faith and Modern Thought," in Francis Anderson papers, University of Sydney Archives v, 26.
120 Anderson, *Christian Liberty and Ecclesiastical Union*, 39, quoted in Melleuish, *Cultural Liberalism*, 89.
121 Melleuish, *Cultural Liberalism*, 90.
122 Melleuish, *Cultural Liberalism*, 90, 94.
123 Melleuish, *Cultural Liberalism*, 88.
124 F. Anderson, *Liberty, Equality and Fraternity* (Sydney: Australasian Association of Psychology and Philosophy, 1922).
125 Anderson, *Liberty, Equality and Fraternity*, 18.
126 Anderson, "The Present Religious Situation," *Australasian Journal of Psychology and Philosophy* 1 (1923): 222.

revision of Christianity for which the goal of humanity became the Kingdom of righteousness. Christianity was mainly an ethical inspiration and the realities to which theology referred were to be found in the inner life. In this advocacy Anderson merged Christianity with a program of social idealism, which his students attempted to realise in diverse institutional contexts. Like Strong in Melbourne, he believed that religious evolution was still continuing and to be located within the wider context of a philosophy of civilisation:

> Religious thought and sentiment now, as at every previous stage of development, contain relics of previous stages, survivals of myth and magic; and there is perhaps not a single religious institution to-day in which these survivals are not more or less actively functioning. But this simply signifies that religious progress has not yet ceased. The progress of religion consists in the freeing of man's spirit from the bondage of the external and the material.[127]

In Anderson's mind, Christianity was a forward motion in history that was not crucially ecclesiastical, just as it was not secular. It was visible in its historical effects and did not rest upon any separation of the church and the world. In Anderson's theology, the Scottish Hegelian emphasis on evolution was dominant and the distinction between philosophy and religion was blurred, since philosophy was the ally of religion. Like many other modernists, Anderson and his wife Maybanke were also active in a range of social causes, including the Workers' Educational Association.[128] He made contributions to education and teaching in New South Wales,[129] and advocated a new international civilisation, supporting the League of Nations Union during the crisis in international relations in the 1930s.[130] The example of Anderson shows how, for many decades, theological modernism and idealist philosophy combined to promote social and educational development in Australia. The alliance was transitory, however, and, under Anderson's successor, Bernard Muscio (1887–1926), philosophy at the University of Sydney moved closer to realism and the natural sciences.[131]

---

127 Anderson, *Christian Liberty and Ecclesiastical Union*, 39, also 36.
128 Sawer, *The Ethical State?*, 45ff.
129 F. Anderson, *The Public School System of New South Wales* (Sydney: Angus and Robertson, 1901) and *Tendencies of Modern Education with Some Proposals of Reform* (Sydney: Angus and Robertson, 1909).
130 F. Anderson, *Peace or War* (Sydney: Angus and Robertson, 1935).
131 Melleuish, *Cultural Liberalism*, 87–96, 108–9.

Later Modernism

Most modernists were located within Christian orthodoxy, even if sometimes at its edge. Later modernists, influenced by German theological developments, Biblical criticism and church history, were, however, sometimes prepared to make a more a radical break with Christianity as it had been interpreted by the churches. They held a variety of political and social views and could be progressive, sympathetic to free market liberalism, or conservative. Among the later modernists, the case of Samuel Angus (1881–1943) deserves particular study. A major figure in the history of Australian religious dissent who only just escaped expulsion from the Presbyterian Church for heresy, Angus has not had the scholarly attention he deserves, and his many books on religious topics have not been studied in depth by Australian historians.[132] Angus was a distinguished classical scholar and an historian of international repute, some of whose views became less controversial in the decades after his death.

Angus came from a conservative Ulster background. After attending Queen's College in Galway, he studied at Marburg in Germany with the eminent philologist Adolf Deissmann (1866–1937) and with the theological faculty in Berlin, then at Princeton University and at Princeton Theological Seminary under the conservative theologian Benjamin Warfield (1881–1921), who defended the inerrancy of Scripture and other fundamentalist views. Armed with a strong grasp of early church history, including a deep knowledge of the mystery religions and Gnosticism, in 1915 Angus became Professor of Theology at St. Andrews Theological College at the University of Sydney, which had a tradition of theological and New Testament learning.[133]

---

132   Among Angus's books were *The Environment of Early Christianity* (London: Duckworth, 1914); *The Mystery Religions and Christianity: A Study in the Religious Background of Early Christianity* (London: John Murray, 1925); *The Religious Quests of the Graeco-Roman World: A Study in the Historical Background of Early Christianity* (London: John Murray, 1929); *Christianity and Dogma: Professor Angus to His Critics* (Sydney: Angus & Robertson, 1933); *Jesus Lives in the Lives of Men* (Sydney: Angus & Robertson, 1933); *Religion in National Life* (Sydney: Angus & Robertson, 1933); *Truth and Tradition: A Plea for Practical and Vital Religion and for a Reinterpretation of Ancient Theologies* (Sydney: Angus & Robertson, 1934); *Essential Christianity* (Sydney: Angus & Robertson, 1939); *Man and the New Order* (Sydney: Angus & Robertson, 1941); and *Alms for Oblivion: Chapters from a Heretic's Life* (Sydney: Angus & Robertson, 1943).

133   For discussion of Angus, see S. E. Emilsen, *A Whiff of Heresy: Samuel Angus and the Presbyterian Church in New South Wales* (Kensington, NSW: New South Wales University Press, 1991); see also A. A. Dougan, *A Backward Glance at the Angus Affair* (Sydney: Wentworth Books, 1971); R. D. Linder, "Apostle to the Australians: The Rev Dr Samuel Angus in Australia, 1915–1943," in *The Furtherance of Religious Beliefs: Essays on the History of Theological Education in Australia*, ed. G. Treloar (Sydney:

Anticipating later scholarship, Angus revalued the Gnosticism that had flourished in and beside the early church as an attempt to make religion at once rational, uplifted and enthusiastic. He preferred what he took to be the generous views of the Greeks to the materialistic Jewish eschatology he believed that traditional Christianity had adopted.[134] The tension between his early church historical studies and what his contemporaries took to be 'Christian orthodoxy' persisted throughout his career.

Angus combined sophisticated interpretations of late antiquity with sympathy for English modernism, a movement in the Church of England that sought to reconcile Christianity with modern Biblical scholarship and the findings of the sciences. Like the eminent German liberal theologians and historical critics F. C. Baur and D. F. Strauss, he was committed to the study of the early development of Christianity, to stripping off the dogmatic formulations of the church, and to getting back to the concrete, historical human personality of Jesus. Like other religious liberals, including the French Protestant theologian Auguste Sabatier (1839–1901), Angus taught that religion should be understood as life rather than doctrine, as did. Like Dean Inge and many of the English theological modernists, he argued for a renewed emphasis on the Platonic tradition in Christianity as a response to the complexities of the modern age.[135]

Angus, like Anderson and Strong, was a transnational intellectual who kept in contact with intellectuals around the world, especially with intellectual allies in Britain, Germany and the United States. In 1924 he stayed with the English modernist Henry D. A. Major (1871–1961), Principal of Ripon Hall, Oxford, with whom Angus agreed on many points and whose approval he sought for some of his works.[136] Angus also shared critical scholarly perspectives on the Old and New Testaments with the distinguished Biblical

---

Centre for the Study of Australian Christianity for the Evangelical History of Association of Australia, 1997); and M. S. Parer, *1933 – Australia's Last Heresy Hunt: Samuel Angus* (Sydney: Wentworth Books, 1971).

134 Angus, *Alms for Oblivion*, 14.
135 Inge was Professor of Divinity at Cambridge and wrote many influential books, including *Christian Mysticism: Considered in Eight Lectures Delivered Before the University of Oxford* (London: Methuen, 1899); *Personal Idealism and Mysticism: The Paddock Lectures for 1906, Delivered at the General Seminary, New York* (London: Longmans, Green, 1907); and *The Philosophy of Plotinus: The Gifford Lectures at St Andrews, 1917–1918* (London: Longmans, Green, 1918).
136 On modernism, see A. R. Vidler, *A Variety of Catholic Modernists* (London: Cambridge University Press, 1970) and A. Stephenson, *The Rise and Decline of English Modernism: The Hulsean Lectures 1979–80* (London: SPCK, 1984); see also C. Pearson, A. Davidson and P. Lineham (eds.), *Scholarship and Fierce Sincerity: Henry D.A. Major: The Face of Anglican Modernism* (Auckland: Polygraphia, 2006).

scholar Kirsopp Lake (1872–1946) at Harvard University. Angus denied that he was a Unitarian, continued to believe in the Holy Catholic and Apostolic Church and the Communion of Saints, liberally interpreted, and claimed to be close to the incarnational school of Anglican theology led by Archbishop William Temple and John Baillie (1886–1960).[137] He also drew on mystical writers in Britain such as Evelyn Underhill (1875–1941) and Baron von Hügel (1852–1925). His liberal Catholic sympathies were, however, balanced by his Presbyterian background, with its republican emphasis on the religious lives of autonomous individuals. According to Angus, Jesus made the individual human being the supreme court of appeal for truth.[138] A human being's religion was not merely what he professed, but what operated spontaneously in his or her life. Angus added to this concept ideas drawn from liberal French Protestantism and, like the French Protestant liberal theologian Eugène Ménégoz (1838–1921), whose works he studied, Angus insisted that faith was quite different from belief in doctrines and that religious truth could not be put into words.[139]

Angus posed a problem for the Presbyterian Church in New South Wales because he claimed the right as a properly appointed officer of the United Free Church of Scotland to combine a confessional appointment with modernist views. He survived two attempts in the New South Wales Assembly of the Presbyterian Church to have him declared a heretic in the 1930s. Faced with a stagnating church in need of revitalisation in which there was little working-class involvement, Angus attempted to hold onto the wealthy and the educated. In the process, he shocked Australians of the working and lower middle classes, as he mediated the most advanced European scholarship to those of higher social standing. The radical civic content of his message was that no traditional creeds or ancient Christologies or external forms had any authority over the spiritual experience and conscientiously formulated free thought of the individual.

Angus's modernism was comprehensive. He rejected not only the traditional Calvinist doctrines of the atonement and propitiation, as well as any idea of a God who could only be approached through a mediator, but

---

137 Emilsen, *A Whiff of Heresy*, 260ff.
138 Angus, *Essential Christianity*, 202.
139 Emilsen, *A Whiff of Heresy*, 186. Angus can be compared with the New Zealand Presbyterian modernist theologian Lloyd Geering (b. 1918); see L. Geering, *God in the New World* (London: Hodder and Stoughton, 1968) and *Resurrection: A Symbol of Hope* (London: Hodder and Stoughton, 1971). Charges of heresy similar to those brought against Geering in 1967 were brought against Peter Cameron, Master of St. Andrew's College, Sydney, in 1993.

also the Trinity, the Virgin Birth, Augustinian supernatural grace, and any conception of a supreme being in another order.[140] According to Angus, not one of the doctrines of historic Christianity, certainly not the notion that Jesus was God, derived with certainty from Jesus.[141] Moreover, Angus raised the possibility that Jesus was ignorant of the new Gospel that his followers proclaimed after his death.[142] He also denied that either Jesus' miracles or the Resurrection had happened in a literal sense. The truth of the Resurrection of Jesus was not the disputable fact of an empty grave, but that Christ's spirit still moved the souls of human beings.[143] Similarly, all theological doctrines were psychologically and historically conditioned, and it mattered little what anyone believed about Christ. What mattered was how much of Christ lived in them.[144] In place of the supernaturalism preached by the clergy, Angus argued that what was needed was a religion relevant to the real problems of the age, based on an inclusive creed intelligible to the laity. Like other modernists, Angus held that the world was moving away from external religion towards a more inward faith and he advocated that Christianity become a religion of personal and spiritual consciousness, rather than a religion of legalism and superstition.[145] Like Strong earlier, Angus had hopes that the coming religious revival would be neither antiquarian nor emotional-evangelistic, but would be marked by the dominant ethical note which marked Jesus' view of true religion.[146]

Unlike Strong, with whom he corresponded, Angus based his Christianity on a Pietist faith in Jesus rather than on a transposition of Christianity into a philosophical system. Again, like others influenced by personal idealism, he identified Christianity with the emergence and further development of personality.[147] Angus was loyal to the 'religion of Jesus', which could not be found in any form of institutional religion. True religion, Angus argued, was not to be confused with the 'metaphysics' that had contaminated theological teaching and preaching. Christianity was a way of life, not a system of dogmas. Christians were to be united not by a uniformity of theological

---

140 Angus, *Truth and Tradition*.
141 S. Angus, *Forgiveness and Life: Chapters from an Uncompleted Book, The Historical Approach to Jesus*, ed. E. H. Vines (Sydney: Angus and Robinson, 1962), 2; *Truth and Tradition*, 36.
142 Angus, *Forgiveness and Life*, 89.
143 Angus, *Truth and Tradition*, 109.
144 Angus, *Essential Christianity*, 3–59.
145 Angus, *Essential Christianity*, Foreword.
146 Angus, *Essential Christianity*, 59.
147 Angus, *Essential Christianity*, 27; see also his *Truth and Tradition*, 120.

opinions, but by common ideals of service.[148] Angus's Christianity implied both a revised doctrine of God and a transposition of traditional Christian doctrines into a social theology oriented towards action. These were sentiments that liberation and feminist theologians were to amplify after his death.

As an historian, Angus was indebted to Historical Criticism and to the Berlin church historian and theologian Adolf von Harnack. Following Harnack's *Lehrbuch der Dogmengeschichte* (1894–97), he lamented the transposition of the simple Jesus of Nazareth into the cosmic Logos and criticised the early church history for occluding true Christianity in metaphysical dogmas.[149] Consistent with this, Angus rejected every attempt to identify Christianity with a particular world outlook. Indeed, his erudite studies of the early church were designed to demonstrate that Christianity could not be equated with particular historically changing doctrines. Christianity's notion of God needed to be purged, he argued, of the traces of oriental despotism still to be found in the Old and New Testaments.

Angus was never as socially radical as Strong and he retained a Calvinist suspicion of all utopias. Hence, even though he sympathised with social justice concerns and egalitarian aims as part of a program of social reconstruction,[150] he warned against collectivism. The state was putting its gyves on every department of human life, he complained, and would reduce the human being to citizenship and nothing more. Indeed, the state should provide its members with incentives to bear their own burdens, rather than undermine their self-help and initiative.[151] Angus's conservatism also led him to oppose proposals for church union and to advocate a strong presence of the church at the centre of the national life. It also made him sympathetic for a time with authoritarian politics and even, on one account, fascism.[152]

Like Strong, Angus refused to separate the sacral and the secular and, at the end of his life, he attacked what he saw as the growing secularism in

---

148 Angus, *Christianity and Dogma*, 17. For a contemporary assessment, see R. G. Macintyre, *The Theology of Dr Angus: A Critical Review* (Sydney: Angus and Robinson, 1934), 129.
149 Angus, *The Environment of Early Christianity*; *The Mystery Religions and Christianity*; and *The Religious Quests of the Graeco-Roman World*.
150 Angus, *Man and the New Order*, 6–7, 20.
151 Angus, *Man and the New Order*, 17, 24–5.
152 Angus, *Man and the New Order*, 29. Angus became more conservative in reaction to the depression of the 1930s. In the mid-1930s he was close to R. W. Gillespie, the founder of the Old Guard, an admirer of fascism and of Hitler's Germany. In 1935 he travelled in Germany and in 1936 sided with the Arabs against the Jews in Palestine. His enthusiasm for Hitler's Germany was short-lived.

the universities. A properly sociologically formed view of the function of religion, Angus believed, overcame simple-minded objections to it of the kind made by the Sydney atheist philosopher John Anderson:

> The main purpose of religion is not to supply us with a stereotyped set of opinions or a ready-made scheme of doctrines, but to steady us in allegiance to our ideals, to maintain our faith in the moral values, and to strengthen us in increasing truth and goodness upon earth. Religion gives no clear proof of the existence of God or of the objective existence of moral values, but it increases our faith that the things which we love deepest have in them an imperious degree of reality.[153]

There was also a Presbyterian republican element at the heart of Angus's thought, an opposition to the rule of external authority which he believed had distorted Christianity since the seventeenth century. For him 'essential Christianity' was about the development of a Christ-like autonomous personality and was compatible with freedom of conscience.[154] A view of the religious dimensions of citizenship followed from Angus' principles. The traditional view that the citizenship of the Christian was in heaven needed to be qualified by an emphasis on Christians taking out full citizenship in the state and in society.[155] Granted that both citizenships needed to run concurrently, Angus emphasised that Christians should work the Sermon on the Mount 'into their lives':

> Man is a creature of two worlds – of spirit and of sense, in both of which he must fulfil himself. Because as citizens we look at the things that are unseen and eternal, we do not lose our selves amid the things that are seen and temporal, and that are requisite to us as citizens and as human beings.[156]

Like Edward Caird in Scotland, Angus understood religion as the attitude, conscious or unconscious, of the entire personality towards the problems and needs of life,[157] and not a matter of the opinions one chose to adopt. This enabled him to promote Christianity as a vital practical religion relevant to real life, while revising traditional doctrines such as the divinity of Christ, the Atonement, the Resurrection and the Trinity in a humanistic direction.

---

153 Angus, *Religion in National Life*, 21.
154 Angus, *Essential Christianity*, 129–30.
155 Angus, *Man and the New Order*, 55.
156 Angus, *Religion in National Life*, 22.
157 Angus, *Religion in National Life*, 15–23.

He provided a version of Christianity that made it relevant to the whole of public and private life.

Angus had followers in Sydney, among them G. Stuart Watts (1899–1988), an Anglican priest who had studied with Angus and with the philosopher John Anderson. Watts was also a transnational intellectual, who sympathised with the ethics of reverence for life advocated by Albert Schweitzer, with the impersonal theism argued for by Scottish theologian John Laird (1887–1946) in his 1939 and 1940 Gifford Lectures, and with the revisionist views of Kirsopp Lake. Apart from quoting Angus with enthusiasm, Watts spoke of the living Christ and of a restatement of the faith in terms of the best thought of the day. He promoted a theological outlook for which beliefs were irrelevant. What mattered was to live in accordance with the laws of the universe:

> I hold that man to be genuinely religious, whatever his theoretical position, who tries to live in harmony with those laws, and with the evolutionary process which flows from obedience to them. "Reverence for Life" is the one universal, indispensable creed. The man who professes it may be a theist, an agnostic, an atheist or whatnot; but if he reverences life and seeks to serve under the Purpose of Life he is an authentically religious man.[158]

Like Angus, Watts combined liberal Catholic and modernist sympathies.[159] He too seemed to want to remain within the church, while fundamentally revising its beliefs, and, in 1940, he addressed an uncompromising 'Open Letter' to the Anglican bishops on behalf of modernist clergy, outlining their difficulties with divine personality, immortality, prayer, revelation, Christology and miracles.[160] Watts lectured on religious topics for the Workers' Educational Association for many years. In his many courses on Asian religion and mysticism he sought to reconcile Christianity with a more universal outlook and thus to commend it to an educated public. Watts also produced a substantial work on the philosophy of religion, *The Revolution of Ideas* (1982), in which he developed an inner empiricism in what he took to be an Andersonian spirit, seeking to bring out the meaning of religious ideas in terms of spatio-temporal experience.[161] Eventually he

---

158 Watts, *Why I Believe*, 5.
159 G. Stuart Watts, *The Church at the Crossroads: An Open Letter to the Australian Episcopate* (Casino, NSW, 1942), 7.
160 Watts, *The Church at the Crossroads*.
161 G. Stuart Watts, *The Revolution of Ideas: Philosophy, Religion and Some "Ultimate Questions"* (Marrickville: Hale & Iremonger, 1982), xiv.

abandoned supernaturalism altogether and argued for a new conception of God as natural, rather supernatural,[162] an outlook amounting to naturalism with immanent transcendence and involving a Platonic theory of forms.[163]

In the longer term Angus's main successor was perhaps the energetic, talented lay theologian and lecturer in the School of Divinity at the University of Sydney, Barbara Thiering (b. 1930).[164] A disbeliever in orthodox views, Thiering was influenced by the German philosophers Nietzsche (1844–1900) and Heidegger (1889–1976), by the radical German Lutheran theologian and New Testament scholar Rudolf Bultmann (1884–1976), and by American feminist theology. She combined a hermeneutical approach to the study of the scriptures with an evangelical commitment to a prophetic liberation theology, which was, in part, her own invention. Thiering saw herself as at the front of contemporary Biblical research. She became controversial in the 1990s when she claimed that the Gospels referred in code to actual historical happenings, although not the happenings associated with them by ordinary Christians. A gifted lecturer and linguist, Thiering took her radical views to the public through books and television programs. Predictably her identification of the Wicked Priest in the scrolls at Qumran as Jesus and the Teacher of Righteousness as John the Baptist led to extended controversy. Thiering implied that the Virgin Birth and the Resurrection were myths that the authors of the Gospels knew had never happened.[165] On Thiering's account, the history behind the New Testament texts bore only limited resemblance to the interpretations placed on them by the Christian churches and the public had a right to be acquainted with this fact.

Although Thiering seemed to some to be trying to subvert Christian orthodoxy, her commitment to finding concealed meanings in the letter of the New Testament suggests continuities with her evangelical background.

---

162 Watts, *The Revolution of Ideas*, xi, section II.
163 Watts, *The Revolution of Ideas*, 154. Watts seems to have derived his Platonism from Angus.
164 Barbara Thiering wrote *Jesus the Man: A New Interpretation from the Dead Sea Scrolls* (Sydney: Transworld Doubleday, 1992), also published as *Jesus and the Riddle of the Dead Sea Scrolls* (San Francisco: Harper Collins, 1992); *Jesus of the Apocalypse: The Life of Jesus After the Crucifixion* (Sydney: Transworld Doubleday, 1995); *The Book That Jesus Wrote: John's Gospel* (Sydney: Transworld Doubleday, 1998); *Redating the Teacher of Righteousness* (Sydney: Theological Explorations, 1979); *The Gospels and Qumran* (Sydney: Theological Explorations, 1981); *God's Experiment: Australian Religion (Walter Murdoch Lecture)* (Perth, WA: Murdoch University, 1982); *The Qumran Origins of the Christian Church* (Sydney: Theological Explorations, 1983).
165 For discussion of Thiering's controversial views, see L. Star, *The Dead Sea Scrolls, the Riddle Debated* (Crows Nest, NSW: ABC Books, 1991), 102.

Indeed, she was something of an evangelist herself and quickly emerged as a controversial public figure. When her first book, *Redating the Teacher of Righteousness* (1979) was dismissed by international scholars, she continued with her project, justifying what many regarded as her sensational results by her own interpretation of the *pesher* method, a Jewish interpretative practice that looked for concealed meanings relevant to the present in scriptural texts.[166] Like Angus, Thiering insisted that she was deeply religious and only disbelieved in obsolete dogmas. Her radical hermeneutics, influenced by her personal experiences of clericalism and patriarchy, allowed her to articulate her disbelief in Christianity, as the clergy interpreted it, while claiming to support original or primitive Christianity as a sociopolitical movement that freed human beings from ritualistic superstition.[167] Consistent with this, Thiering was committed to women's liberation in the church and elsewhere.[168] Her type of religious liberalism was continued in part by later religious modernists in Australia, influenced by religious progressives in the United States.

Religious Liberalism and the Reform of Christianity

Religious liberalism in Australia did not completely succeed in changing what people understood by 'religion', although it certainly promoted more liberal conceptions of religion among educated minorities. It focused rather more on the reform of Christianity. In this regard, it had only limited success, developing as a cultural and intellectual movement only with difficulty. Doubting the supernatural did not produce a new synthesis, and there was always the danger that liberals would end up professing the enlightened views of their secular contemporaries. With important exceptions, religious liberalism tended to erode the basis from which it sprang – commitment to historical Christianity. In the nineteenth and early twentieth centuries it was the cause of religious reform that occasioned charges of heresy. Most Australians accepted the existence of God and providence in an undefined sense, especially in the context of ancient Israel, the Empire, and the emerging horizon of a Protestant nation, although Catholics, for obvious reasons, were more inclined to associate the supernatural with Christ's true church. As the century progressed, the tendency to believe that history

---

166 Thiering, *Redating the Teacher of Righteousness*, part 1, and *Jesus and the Riddle of the Dead Sea Scrolls*, ch. 4.
167 Thiering, *The Gospels and Qumran*, and *The Qumran Origins of the Christian Church*.
168 B. Thiering, *Created Second?: Aspects of Women's Liberation in Australia* (Sydney: Family Life Movement of Australia, 1973).

was under divine governance was less noticeable, supernaturalism declined, and some religious liberals seemed less concerned about whether they were Christians or not. This made their concern about the incarnation or miracles seem less central. In the same way, where nineteenth-century liberals sought to soften Christian supernaturalism, without doubting that reason supported the existence of God, later twentieth-century religious liberals questioned theism as well, thus finding themselves involved in more radical forms of exodus from tradition. They were also, for the same reason, harder to distinguish from secular humanists.

This does not imply that the courageous stand religious liberals made for critical thought and freedom of expression was unimportant in Australia. What became less important later in the twentieth century was the social reform side of religious liberalism, which had contributed so much to the development of civil society and notions of active citizenship before 1945. In the second half of the twentieth century, conservative forces arguing for neoliberal conceptions of economics either ignored religious considerations entirely or allied themselves with conservative Christians, for whom revisions of traditional religious dogmas were anathema. Religious liberals tended to promote religious individualism. In the nineteenth century many of them were committed to social reform and the common good, including the need to educate a morally informed public. In the later twentieth century religious liberals might favour the use of public instrumentalities to educate and improve the public, but they were not deeply rooted in the wider community and could display considerable suspicion of the modern state. On the other hand, in so far as religious liberals understood religion in evolutionary terms and expected better religion to come, their expectations received some support from cultural and social changes after 1960, when the question of whether spirituality and self-made religious mixes could replace religion in an organisational sense could no longer be ignored.

Chapter IV

RELIGIOUS THOUGHT AND PHILOSOPHY

Intellectuals with philosophical concerns are discussed in several chapters of this book.[1] In this chapter, I turn to religious intellectuals for whom changes in philosophy were central, and not ancillary concerns. I begin with formative philosophical traditions that provided major resources for and/or challenges to religious thought. I then discuss three religious intellectuals who worked the religion–philosophy interface in creative ways. Each was a transnational agent, abreast of international developments, who drew on various disciplines and cultural geographies. Although none of these intellectuals could be described as typical, they related to wider intellectual and cultural changes. Finally, I briefly note some Australian contributions to the philosophy of religion.

Formative Philosophical Traditions

Although a number of different philosophical traditions have impacted on Australian religious thought, none of them has gained a wide enough acceptance to form a national outlook. The early influences were English and Scottish, although several European traditions, including some forms of Catholic scholasticism, came to the colonies. Utilitarianism, for example, understood as a stance on government and reform rather than as a body of technical doctrines, played a formative role in the colonial period through the presence of Benthamites such as Henry Carmichael and the penal reformer Alexander Maconochie (1787–1860). Utilitarian ideas were relevant to penology and educational reform.[2] They were not necessarily anti-religious,

---

1   See, especially, Chapters II and VI. Nietzschean philosophy, vitalism, process philosophy, Marxism, environmental philosophy and postmodernism are all discussed to some extent, but as influences rather than as technical philosophical movements.
2   For the view that utilitarianism had a major influence on Australian institutions, see H. Collins, "Political Ideology in Australia: The Distinctiveness of a Benthamite

although some of utilitarians followed Bentham's personal irreligious views, and the utilitarian tendency to sidestep religion in public affairs arguably influenced some national institutions. Scottish realism was also widely received in nineteenth- and early twentieth-century Australia, and had a religious dimension, although this is now sometimes forgotten. Much of the interest in realism had Scottish origins and many realists were Scots with Presbyterian connections. As in Scotland, realists in Australia were concerned to reject the representationalist doctrines of British empiricists such as Locke and Hume, and to claim instead that human beings had direct knowledge of objects. As in Scotland, there was a convergence between philosophical realism and the idea that human beings could rely on common sense, and this claim could involve the further claim that some ideas were simply given to human beings, including some religious ideas, in which case many of the epistemological problems that empiricism presented for religious thought were easily solved. Some Scottish realists were inclined to adopt German philosophical doctrines such as intellectual intuition, in which case a philosophy of religion was close at hand.

Scottish realism was promoted in New South Wales by the Congregational and Presbyterian minister Barzillai Quaife (1798–1873), Professor of Mental Philosophy and Divinity at Dunmore Lang's Australian College in Sydney. Quaife gave lectures based on the commonsense philosophy of Scottish philosopher Thomas Reid (1710–1796) as early as 1850. Quaife's interpretation followed that of Scottish philosopher Sir William Hamilton, who held that Reid's insistence that some notions are simply given to common sense contained the elements of an answer to Kant's critical philosophy, in which the Scots were well versed.[3] Realism, however, was not as crucial to the defence of Christianity in Australia, in contrast to the United States, where it was a major part of Protestant apologetics.

Society," in *Australia, The Daedalus Symposium*, ed. R. Graubard (North Ryde, NSW: Angus & Robertson, 1985), 147–69; see also G. Nadel, *Australia's Colonial Culture: Ideas, Men and Institutions in Mid-Nineteenth Century Eastern Australia* (Melbourne: F. W. Cheshire, 1957). Associations of utilitarianism with racism and Empire are contested in B. Schultz and G. Varouxakis (eds.), *Utilitarianism and Empire* (Lanham, MD: Lexington Books, 2005).

3 Quaife's lectures were published as *The Intellectual Sciences: Outline Lectures Delivered Chiefly at the Australian College, Sydney, in the Year 1850, 1851*, 2 vols (Sydney: Gibbs Shallard; Melbourne: Robertson, 1872). For his sermons, see *A Condensed View of the Design and Proper Uses of the Lord's Supper* (Parramatta, NSW: Benjamin Isaacs, 1845); *The Rules of the Final Judgement: A Sermon, the Substance of which was Preached at Scots Church* (Parramatta, NSW: Benjamin Isaacs, 1846); and *Lectures on Prophecy and the Kingdom of Christ* (Sydney: Colman, Piddington & Ford, 1848).

From the late nineteenth century until the 1930s, Scottish and British idealism, which sometimes overlapped, were major influences on philosophical thought in Australia.[4] Scottish idealism came to Australia in at least two forms – Scottish Hegelianism and personal idealism. Scottish Hegelianism flourished at the University of Glasgow and among the disciples of T. H. Green who taught there. The Scottish Hegelians held that Hegel and Darwin could be combined in a philosophy of cosmic evolution.[5] According to Edward Caird, Professor of Moral Philosophy at the University of Glasgow, Christianity no longer needed to be wrapped in types and symbols of an earlier faith.[6] Instead, it had to be reinterpreted in the context of the evolution of religion in general and should be studied by naturalistic methods. Caird took it for granted that evolution applied to religion as much as to nature. He identified Christianity with the service of humanity, not with acquiring outworn beliefs.[7] He also reinterpreted the doctrine of God, so that God became the principle of unity, presupposed by all differences. John Caird, Edward's brother, was even more explicit about making Christianity primarily a matter of morality and work for social reform. Both Cairds questioned the traditional distinction between natural and revealed religion and rejected the Calvinist conception of predestination. Both were committed to working for human betterment in all areas of human life on principles at once philosophical and religious. Their stance was taken up by intellectuals with Scottish connections in Australia, including, as we have seen, Charles Strong and Francis Anderson, who made it possible

---

4   For discussion, see M. Davies and S. Helgeby, "Idealist Origins: 1920s and Before," and R. Sinnerbrink and M. S. Russell, "Black Swan: A History of Continental Philosophy in Australia and New Zealand," in *History of Philosophy in Australia and New Zealand*, ed. G. Oppy and N.Trakakis (Dordrecht: Springer, 2014), vol. 1, ch. 1 and vol. 2, ch.19. Historians have sometimes tended to blur the differences between Scottish and British idealism. For the Scottish idealists, see D. Boucher (ed.), *The Scottish Idealists: Selected Philosophical Writings* (Exeter: Imprint Academic, 2004); see also S. A. Grave, *A History of Philosophy in Australia* (St. Lucia: University of Queensland Press, 1984).

5   See D. G. Ritchie, *Darwin and Hegel: with Other Philosophical Studies* (London: Swan Sonnenschein, 1893) and the essay written by Samuel Alexander for the 1887 T. H. Green Prize in moral philosophy at Oxford, published as *Moral Order and Progress* (London: Trubner, 1889).

6   For Edward Caird, see H. Jones and J. H. Muirhead, *The Life and Philosophy of Edward Caird* (Glasgow: Maclehose, Jackson, 1921). Caird's texts, including *The Critical Philosophy of Kant* (Glasgow: Maclehose, 1889) and *The Evolution of Religion: The Gifford Lectures 1890–91 and 1891–92*, 2 vols. (Glasgow: Maclehose, 1893), made the most advanced Scottish thought available in Australia and raised philosophical and theological issues to which Australians returned for the next 100 years.

7   Caird, *The Evolution of Religion*.

for intellectuals working in Australia to be at the forefront of international discussions, a fact that is sometimes neglected in the standard national histories.

Personal idealism, in contrast to Scottish Hegelianism, was more oriented towards the development of personality and philosophical psychology. Personal idealists based their idealism on the presence of the ideal in the life of each person, not, like the British idealists, on a metaphysical absolute. They promoted a social humanism, based on personality, and encouraged the study of psychological issues, as well as an engagement with the sciences.[8] Personal idealism was a major influence on three early professors of philosophy in Australia and on some of the courses they taught. Henry Laurie (1837–1922) and William Ralph Boyce Gibson (1869–1935), the first and second Professors of Philosophy at the University of Melbourne, and Scott Fletcher (1868–1947) at the University of Queensland,[9] were all personal idealists.[10] The Scottish philosopher and personal idealist, Andrew Seth Pringle-Pattison (1856–1931), was well known to philosophers in nineteenth and twentieth-century Australia. Apart from rejecting the absolute idealism of British idealists such as Bradley and Bosanquet, Pringle-Pattison advanced a non-classical theism, for which God was not a transcendent, unchanging, self-sufficient being. In books such as *Man's Place in the Cosmos* (1897), *The Idea of Immortality* (1912) and *The Idea of God in the Light of Recent Philosophy* (1917), he held that God and man were not independent facts and that God was not transcendent or external to the world, but present in the consciousness of each person. Substance, in this view, was the wrong model for understanding either the individual or God, which were porous to one another.[11] These were radical views and they made an impact.

In Australia, Scottish idealism, especially as it was embodied in visitors such as the Welsh Hegelian Henry Jones (1852–1922), who gave lectures on

---

8 See H. Sturt (ed.), *Personal Idealism: Philosophical Essays by Eight Members of the University of Oxford* (London: Macmillan, 1902).
9 Scott Fletcher traced the development of personality to the New Testament in *The Psychology of the New Testament* (London: Hodder and Stoughton, 1912), to which the personal idealist philosopher Hastings Rashdall wrote the introducton.
10 See Gibson's contribution to Sturt's collection, *Personal Idealism*; see also "Problems of Spiritual Experience," in *Australasian Journal of Psychology and Philosophy* 2 (1924): 183–196. Hastings Rashdall also rejected substitutionary theories of the atonement in *The Idea of Atonement in Christian Theology: Being the Bampton Lectures for 1915* (London: Macmillan, 1919).
11 See A. Seth Pringle-Pattison, *Hegelianism and Personality: Second Series of Balfour Lectures* (Edinburgh: William Blackwood, 1887).

'Idealism as a Practical Creed' at Sydney University in 1908,[12] was a source of both theological rationalism and progressive social thought. Those shaped by Scottish philosophy included Mungo MacCallum at the University of Sydney and William Mitchell at the University of Adelaide. Henry Laurie's *Scottish Philosophy in its National Development* (1902) was widely studied and there was a tendency to see the history of philosophy through Scottish lenses. Scottish idealism provided philosophers in Australia with personal links with contemporaries working in Scotland, England, Canada and the United States. It allowed them to see themselves as international protagonists of radical philosophical and theological ideas.

British idealism, on the other hand, made a more limited impact on Australian thinking. The central thesis of British idealism – the claim that the reality was a single interconnected system – was not widely adopted in Australia, and it has been argued that it is better to refer to 'New Idealism', since the Australians rarely adopted an organic conception of the state and placed a greater emphasis on Empire, history and the international order than the British idealists.[13] What resonated in Australia was a body of ideas supporting activist approaches to citizenship and the construction of political and social institutions, and not the absolute idealism of F. H. Bradley (1846–1924) or Bernard Bosanquet (1848–1923). Here the key figure was T. H. Green, who rejected the social atomism and the negative theory of freedom of English liberalism, arguing instead that the state had a duty to act to achieve ethical ends. He also argued for an active, even a religious, concept of citizenship.[14] Again, Green's conception of Christianity was practical and ethical and involved an obligation to work for social reform. His view of Christianity was influential in Australia, not least because it converged with a major thrust of Scottish idealism. In Sydney, Green's work

---

12 H. Jones, *Idealism as a Practical Creed* (Glasgow: Maclehose, 1909); the lectures and his *The Working Faith of the Social Reformer and Other Essays* (London: Macmillan, 1910) were widely discussed. For Jones' work on citizenship, see D. Boucher and A. Vincent, *A Radical Hegelian: The Political and Social Philosophy of Henry Jones* (Cardiff: University of Wales, 1993), ch. 3; and D. Boucher, "Practical Hegelianism: Henry Jones's Lecture Tour of Australia," *Journal of the History of Ideas* 51 (1990): 423–52.
13 For the view that it is better to speak of New Idealism in the Australian context, see I. Tregenza, "The Idealist Tradition in Australian Religious Thought," *Journal of Religious History* 34 (2010): 335–53, and M. Hughes-Warrington and I. Tregenza, "State and Civilisation in Australian New Idealism, 1890–1950," *History of Political Thought* 29 (2008): 89–108.
14 A. Vincent and R. Plant (eds.), *Philosophy, Politics and Citizenship: The Life and Thought of the British Idealists* (Oxford: Blackwell, 1984); D. Boucher (ed.), *The British Idealists* (Cambridge: Cambridge University Press, 1997); and D. Boucher and A. Vincent, *British Idealism and Political Theory* (Edinburgh: Edinburgh University Press, 2000).

was promoted by Mungo MacCallum, who had studied in Scotland with Edward Caird.

Idealism gave religious thinkers in Australia an alternative to utilitarian and materialist forms of social thought. It also provided them with draft positions on a large range of issues, including the contemporary roles of psychology, biology and sociology, comparative religion, ethics, political and economic issues, and the scientific study of religion. It allowed them to present themselves as being at the front of contemporary thought and to construe Christianity as a forward evolutionary development, rather than a relic of the past.

As the twentieth century progressed, idealist philosophy in Australia gave way to realism. Scottish philosophical realism had originally supported religious claims by grounding them in common sense, without a need to derive such claims from sense data. Once realism became associated with the notion that philosophy should be based on the natural sciences, religion was more vulnerable.[15] The tendency to move from idealism to realism was accentuated by the arrival in 1927 of the Scottish philosopher John Anderson in Sydney. As we have seen, Anderson's views were complex, influenced more by his training in the Classics than a simple summary might suggest. Many of his followers, however, took for granted a robust realism, the need to defer to the natural sciences, and hostility to unclear meaning. After Anderson, a good deal of philosophy in Australia was anti-religious and many Protestant religious thinkers abandoned the philosophical arena entirely. Philosophers influenced by Wittgenstein and the philosophy of language could still maintain religious positions by insisting on more sophisticated conceptions of language and meaning, but this advantage also declined as Wittgenstein's views, at least as interpreted in Britain, were displaced in stages in philosophy

---

15   The transition to realism was facilitated by the work of Bernard Muscio (1887–1926) at the University of Sydney who recommended realism over idealism, and to the influence of William Mitchell (1861–1962), the first Professor of Philosophy at the University of Adelaide, who attempted to integrate realism with a non-reductionist philosophy of mind that took account of the results of the natural sciences in his well-regarded *Structure and Growth of the Mind* (London: Macmillan, 1907) and then in two series of Gifford Lectures (*The Place of Minds in the World* (London: Macmillan, 1933); see also W. Martin Davies, *The Philosophy of Sir William Mitchell (1861–1962): A Mind's Own Pace* (Lampeter: Edwin Mellen Press, 2003)). Mitchell produced a remarkable philosophy of mind emphasising the need for an internal as well as external perspectives and making our capacity to experience itself the basis for an inference to a notion of mind; see H. J. Allen, "Mitchell's Concept of the Human Mind," (Masters diss., University of Adelaide, 1984), 7, and Davies and Helgeby, "Idealist Origins: 1920s and Before".

departments by Frege's philosophy of logic, which privileged the reference of terms rather than how language was used in practice.

The strongest philosophical challenges to religious thought in Australia came from the combination of materialism and natural scientific reductionism in 'Australian materialism'. Natural scientific reductionism held that the world was a single physical system, the study of which should be left to the natural sciences. This conception of science was widely rejected in the nineteenth century, but in the twentieth century it came to be seen as the philosophy of the natural sciences. Materialism in itself was not a major problem for religious thought. After all, the ancient Stoics had promoted a materialism that was religious and some theologians found various forms of materialism in the Bible. French and German mechanical materialism and Marxist historical materialism were more problematic because they implied that religious entities could play no role in causal explanations. The philosophical tendency that became known as 'Australian materialism' was a threat because it denied both that religious claims were meaningful and that anything with religious characteristics could exist.

Australian materialism emerged in Adelaide in the context of technical attempts to resolve the mind–body problem by resort to physicalism and a mind–brain identity theory by analytical philosophers such as U. T. Place (1924–2000) and J. Smart (1920–2012), both of whom accepted some form of scientific reductionism. Subsequently, Sydney philosopher David Armstrong (1926–2014) championed materialism as the ontology of science and what contemporary naturalism required. His *A Materialist Theory of the Mind* (1968) became a standard contribution to attempts to achieve a coherent materialist account of mind. Armstrong wrote many well-argued books in which he defended technical accounts of the nature of universals, states of affairs, truthmakers and a systematic metaphysics.[16] Australian materialism confronted religious thinkers with natural science coming in against them,

---

16   D. M. Armstrong, *A Materialist Theory of the Mind* (London: Routledge and Kegan Paul, 1968); *Belief, Truth and Knowledge* (London: Cambridge University Press, 1973); *Universals and Scientific Realism* (Cambridge: Cambridge University Press, 1978), 2 vols; *The Nature of Mind and Other Essays* (Ithaca: Cornell University Press, 1981); *What is a Law of Nature?* (Cambridge: Cambridge University Press, 1983); *A Combinatorial Theory of Possibility* (Cambridge: Cambridge University Press, 1989); *Universals: An Opinionated Introduction* (Boulder, CO: Westview Press, 1989); *A World of States of Affairs* (Cambridge: Cambridge University Press, 1997); *Truth and Truthmakers* (Cambridge: Cambridge University Press, 2004); and *Sketch for a Systematic Metaphysics* (Oxford: Oxford University Press, 2010). For the Sydney scene more generally, see J. Franklin, *Corrupting the Youth: A History of Philosophy in Australia* (Paddington, NSW: Macleay Press, 2003).

with a theory of meaning that rendered them speechless and with a coherent conception of reality that excluded God and all other supernatural entities. Thus it put Christian claims under pressure. In the same way, a tradition of utilitarianism, brilliantly exemplified by the philosopher Peter Singer, provided a powerful alternative to any form of religious ethics,[17] especially ethical thought that made realist or absolutist claims. Absolutist standpoints of this kind underlay a great deal of Catholic ethical thought, including the works of Archbishop Anthony Fisher (b. 1960).[18] They were also sometimes shared, in part, by those without the benefit of religious commitments.[19] Ethical absolutism struggled, however, to redeem its claims discursively.

Given these philosophical traditions, intellectual and cultural relations between religious thought and philosophy in Australia have been various and sometimes difficult. The distinction between philosophy and religious thought has not always been sharp, with some forms of philosophy, Scottish idealism for example, arguably themselves being forms of religious thought, and some anti-religious forms of philosophy, including perhaps Andersonianism, at times amounting at times to secular confessions. In a new society with diverse philosophical traditions, religious intellectuals needed to be sensitive to both local and international audiences. They also needed to promote the reception of new international developments in philosophy, to offer a view of the religion–philosophy interface which suggested what were the best philosophical resources that religious thought could draw upon, and to explain how some of the challenges to religious thought from philosophy could be met.

I now discuss three important religious intellectuals who negotiated the relationship between religious thought and philosophy in creative ways. Each of them stood out as exceptionally learned in the Australian context, and each engaged with European philosophical developments, as most of their Australian contemporaries did not. Each of them also showed independence of mind and intellectual courage, which could be argued to have derived in part from their experiences in Australia.

---

17 See P. Singer, *Animal Liberation: A New Ethics for our Treatment of Animals* (New York: Random House, 1975); *Practical Ethics* (Cambridge: Cambridge University Press, 1979); *How Are We to Live? Ethics in an Age of Self-interest* (Melbourne: Text Publishing, 1993); and *Rethinking Life and Death: The Collapse of Our Traditional Ethics* (Melbourne: Text Publishing, 1994).
18 A. Fisher, *Bioethics for a New Millennium* (New York: Cambridge University Press, 2012).
19 The agnostic Raimon Gaita (b. 1946), for example, attacked moral scepticism and defended an absolutist account of ethics based on moral experiences. See his *Good and Evil: An Absolute Conception* (London: Macmillan, 1991) and *A Common Humanity: Thinking about Love and Truth and Justice* (Melbourne: Text Publishing, 1999).

William Ralph Boyce Gibson and Personal Idealism

The philosopher William Ralph Boyce Gibson (1869–1935) exemplifies the case of a thinker who sought to bring the latest developments in philosophy and science to Australia.[20] He did so as part of a wider project of promoting harmonious relations between contemporary philosophy and Christianity.

The gifted son of a Methodist minister, at home in both mathematics and in the major European languages, Gibson won an open scholarship to Queen's College, Oxford, where he studied mathematics with a view to becoming an astronomer. Later he went to Jena in Germany, where he became well-informed about the latest debates in German philosophy and psychology and the work of the German philosopher Rudolf Eucken (1846–1926) in particular. Eucken was a philosopher of the *Lebensphilosophie* movement in Germany, a religio-ethical movement that sought to integrate philosophy with real life. Gibson also worked in Paris with the eminent philosopher of science and religion Émile Boutroux (1845–1921), for whom he wrote a treatise on Descartes' geometry, subsequently published in the *Revue de Métaphysique et de Morale*. Between 1895 and 1897 he studied at Glasgow University with Henry Jones. The young Gibson developed his own philosophical outlook, influenced by the British philosopher Herbert Spencer and by elements of aesthetic humanist pragmatism derived from the British German philosopher, F. C. S. Schiller (1864–1937).

Appointed to the Chair of Mental and Moral Philosophy at the University of Melbourne, Gibson arrived in Melbourne in 1912 as a transnational intellectual in contact with other intellectuals in Britain, Europe and the United States. He had already published a volume of essays, *God With Us: A Study in Religious Idealism* (1909) and subsequently became the foremost interpreter and translator of Rudolf Eucken's ideas. Gibson sympathised with Eucken's activism and with his notion of a constructive philosophy that required spiritual work. Like Eucken, he was convinced that naturalism could not generate value and meaning, and saw the need for a decision about one's stance on life, which then had causal consequences for one's own life and for society. Nonetheless, although Gibson shared Eucken's proto-existentialism, he was not persuaded by many details of Eucken's philosophy, which, Gibson argued, did not provide adequate account of either personal freedom or religious mysticism. Moreover, according to Gibson, Eucken's treatment of

---

20   For an analysis, see S. Helgeby, "*Personal Idealism*, Criticism and System: The Philosophy of William Ralph Boyce Gibson (1869–1935)," *Collingwood and British Idealism Studies* 12 (2006): 75–102.

psychology was methodologically unsatisfactory. Gibson further objected that Eucken underestimated the role of properly constructed logical categories and did not integrate his interpretation of consciousness and self-knowledge with a proper philosophical account of nature.[21] These alleged deficits gave Gibson his opportunity, and he sought to provide Eucken's religious ethical philosophy with the adequate psychological basis and the philosophy of nature that it lacked.

In due course Gibson reconstructed Eucken's religious ethical philosophy in the direction of personal idealism. Like the leading Scottish personal idealist philosopher Pringle-Pattison, Gibson construed personal idealism as an alternative to naturalism, although he placed more emphasis than Pringle-Pattison on an idealism which was monistic, monotheistic and monocosmic – an idealism for which reality was ultimately spiritual and rational.[22] Philosophy, he argued, needed to begin with the human being rather than with nature, and with the ideal as a super-personal reality present in the life of each person, which alone made it possible for the human being to understand God. Gibson followed Pringle-Pattison in adopting an anthropotheistic standpoint which denied that human beings could see things from a divine or absolute standpoint. Instead, a religious idealism had to be based on a concept of God as inclusive of us and our freedom – on 'God with us' or 'spiritual life'.[23] Gibson denied that God and the human being were separate, and he interpreted traditional theological attributes in anthropological terms. Omniscience, for example, could be construed in terms of our freedom's demand that love should eventually prevail.[24] In this way, he was able to rethink theism from an anthropocentric standpoint that did not posit an external divine being. Nonetheless, Gibson understood personal experience as God-dependent and he rejected the pluralism, meliorism and anthropocentrism, which he associated with William James' pragmatism. Indeed, he advocated a dynamic spiritual monism, for which freedom had a basis in the universe in the form of real but not yet actualised possibilities.[25]

---

21   W. R. B. Gibson, *Rudolf Eucken's Philosophy of Life* (London: Adam and Charles Black, 1906), chapters 7 and 10; see also R. Eucken, *Christianity and the New Idealism: A Study in the Religious Philosophy of To-day*, translated by L. J. and W. R. B. Gibson (London: Harper, 1909) and see also R. Eucken, *The Problem of Human Life as Viewed by the Great Thinkers from Plato to the Present Time*, translated by W. S. Hough and W. R. B. Gibson (London: T. Fisher Unwin, 1910).
22   W. R. B. Gibson, *God With Us: A Study in Religious Idealism*, (London: Adam and Charles Black, 1909), 190, 212, 213.
23   Gibson, *God With Us*, 213, 214.
24   Gibson, *God With Us*, 214, 215.
25   Gibson, *God With Us*, 211.

The key to Gibson's version of religious idealism was the study of the personal experience of the experient. Gibson insisted that the ideal was present even in the most ordinary experiences and that human experience was intrinsically purposive. Human beings had immediate knowledge of ideals, values and real possibilities.[26] It followed, Gibson argued, that experience needed to be understood in teleological terms. Indeed, he went so far as to argue that indicative inference was only applicable to the inorganic.[27] Like others influenced by personal idealism, Gibson was convinced that philosophy should be based on careful psychological analysis and a teleological method.[28] Philosophy was to pursue the inward objectivity and to differ fundamentally from natural science. As a philosophical psychologist, Gibson held that a science of mind could be constructed from immediate consciousness and conceived of a psychology based on the inward point of view of the individual as a science of free agency.[29] He maintained that a concrete teleological psychology dealing with the actions of individual consciousness yielded a standpoint on human freedom, by which the rest of experience could be judged.[30] Here he drew a sharp distinction between causal, or physical, psychology and inward teleological psychology, based on the experient, not the observer.[31]

Gibson sought to develop his philosophy of personality and freedom on this phenomenological basis and advanced idealist accounts of psychological states in interactions with William James, G. F. Stout (1860–1944) and Alexander Shand (1858–1936), all leading international philosophical psychologists of the period. Consistent with this emphasis on consciousness, Gibson followed the emergence of phenomenology as a philosophical science of consciousness closely and spent part of 1928 studying in Freiburg

---

26 Gibson, "What is Philosophy?," *Australasian Journal of Psychology and Philosophy* 11 (1933): 93.

27 See W. R. B. Gibson with A. Klein, *The Problem of Logic* (London: Alan and Charles Black, 1908). Gibson argued that logic, and not only psychology, should be placed on an experiential foundation. See his "The Relation of Logic to Psychology with Special Reference to the Views of Dr. Bosanquet," *Proceedings of the Aristotelian Society* 3 (1903): 166–86.

28 W. R. B. Gibson, "Does the Ideal Really Exist?," *Australasian Journal of Psychology and Philosophy* 3 (1925): 159–78.

29 W. R. B. Gibson, "The Problem of Freedom in its Relation to Psychology," in Sturt, *Personal Idealism*, 134–92.

30 Gibson, "The Problem of Freedom in its Relation to Psychology"; see also his later formulations in "What is Philosophy?".

31 W. R. B. Gibson, *A Philosophical Introduction to Ethics: An Advocacy of the Spiritual Principle in Ethics from the Point of View of Personal Idealism* (London: Swan Sonnenschein, 1904), 192.

with Edmund Husserl (1859–1938), the philosopher who founded the phenomenological school. In Freiburg he met Martin Heidegger, Emmanuel Levinas (1906–1995) and other philosophers in Husserl's circle who were convinced that phenomenology made possible a new beginning for philosophy.[32]

Husserl was one of the most original philosophers of the twentieth century. He attempted to re-establish philosophy as an exact science by basing it on a strict phenomenological method. In his hands, philosophy became a matter of research into content that could be intuited, rather than primarily a matter of theory or argument. Husserl's claims were complex, because, while seeming to move philosophy towards experience, he also related it to a form of transcendental logic, influenced by Kant. Many later philosophers, including Heidegger, attempted to reformulate Husserl's ideas in a way that retained some of his advances, while avoiding the difficulties to which they gave rise. Gibson did not attempt a complete reconstruction of Husserl, partly because he read Husserl through a personal idealist lens and was inclined to understand phenomenology in psychological rather than in logical terms. Instead, as with his earlier involvement with Eucken, Gibson sought to make the new German thought available in English, publishing the first English translation of Husserl's *Ideas* in 1931 pioneering his reception in English-speaking circles. Gibson remained committed to psychologism – the attempt to identify concepts with mental states – an approach that Husserl had abandoned. Ideal meanings, Gibson insisted, were inseparable from the ego's real existence.[33] He was critical of Husserl's account of the self, of the way he gave priority to the ideal in his analyses, of his reliance upon intuitive evidence, of his dualism between meaning and object, and of his notion that the pure ego could be conceived of as an essence.[34] Gibson also considered translating Heidegger's *Sein und Zeit*.

Like others influenced by personal idealism, Gibson believed that philosophical psychology could provide a foundation for a religious approach to life. Whether Gibson could in fact find support for a religious approach to life in philosophical psychology was less clear. As a personal idealist, Gibson held that 'the Ideal' was the presence of God in personal life.[35] Naturalism,

---

32 W. R. B. Gibson, "From Husserl to Heidegger: Excerpts from a 1928 Freiburg Diary," *Journal of the British Society for Phenomenology* 2 (1972): 58–83.
33 W. R. B. Gibson, "The Problem of Real and Ideal in the Phenomenology of Husserl," *Mind* 34 (1925): 326.
34 Gibson, "The Problem of Real and Ideal in the Phenomenology of Husserl".
35 Gibson, *God With Us*, chapters 1 and 11, and W. R. B. Gibson, "A Peace Policy for Idealists," *Hibbert Journal* 5 (1906/7): 407–24.

in contrast, Gibson held, led to a psychology without a soul, a political philosophy without community, and a society based only on contract. Personal idealism allowed Gibson to bring philosophy and psychology together in a religious quest. It also made it possible for him to remain a Christian, while attempting to replace folk religious beliefs with more rational concepts. For Gibson religion was not concerned with salvation hereafter, but with the redemption of the present world. He was inclined, following the Scottish Hegelians Edward and John Caird, to translate Christian doctrines into existential terms.

Given these principles, Gibson argued that Christianity needed to be expressed in a new form:

> … with all respect to Christianity, we demand its expression in a new form. We require that Christianity shall identify itself more definitely with a religion of Spiritual Life, as opposed to a religion that merely ministers to human frailty, and that it shall show greater decision in casting off the antiquated accessories which hamper its movement.[36]

Following Auguste Sabatier, who exalted faith over belief, Gibson insisted that religious doctrines were necessarily symbolical.[37] At the same time, he insisted that faith was the foundational and universal form of rationality.[38] According to Gibson, God was super-personal and could be conceived in rational terms.[39] Like Rudolf Eucken in Germany, he held that God was immanent within the life of the soul and that every human being had something like a subliminal perception of Him. He also held that the immediate presence of a spiritual life superior to time in the soul was the basis for belief in immortality.[40] For the young Gibson, religious idealism offered a Christian philosophy and a framework for a normatively grounded approach to social reform, so the problem of the relationship

---

36 Gibson, *Rudolf Eucken's Philosophy of Life*, 180.
37 For Sabatier's liberal Protestantism, see his *Les Religions d'Autorité et la Religion de l'Esprit* (Paris: Librairie Fischbacher, 1904).
38 W. R. B. Gibson, "Religion and Rationality (with Special Reference to Dr.Otto's 'Idea of the Holy')," *Australasian Journal of Psychology and Philosophy* 4 (1926): 241–2.
39 W. R. B. Gibson, "Problems of Spiritual Experience: II. The Personal Bond," *Australasian Journal of Psychology and Philosophy* 2 (1924): 194.
40 The claim that the individual was conscious of a supersensual fact in his or her own experience inspired Gibson's essay "The Problem of Freedom and its Relation to Psychology" and his later three articles "The Ethics of Nicolai Hartmann," *Australasian Journal of Psychology and Philosophy* 11 (1933): 12–28; 12 (1934): 33–61; and 13 (1935): 1–23. Gibson's *A Philosophical Introduction to Ethics* criticised the theories of T. H. Green and A. E. Taylor.

between religion and philosophy was less acute. Gibson was convinced that Christianity called for a new social order and attempted to ground his ethical and moral philosophy in the inviolate spiritual experience of the individual. He argued for ethical perspectives on economic affairs, and believed that the League of Nations should be used to abolish war.[41] With his gifted wife Lucy, who also translated philosophical works by Eucken, he was a significant figure in Melbourne's cultural landscape.

In his later years, Gibson was occupied with developments in the natural sciences that offered the prospect of a richer naturalism and even a metaphysics that encompassed qualitative features of the world. He retained the idea that philosophy and ethics should be teleological, while returning to the work of Émile Boutroux and Henri Bergson on the philosophical status of the natural sciences, in which he had been interested as a young man. Like Bergson, he argued for a non-reductionist metaphysics that was compatible with natural science.[42] Gibson recognised Bergson as one of the great contemporary thinkers and taught a course on his ideas. He took up Bergson's doctrine of lived time and argued that it was more fundamental than measured time, on the general principle that the subjective was the basis from which the objective emerged.[43] In 1928 he published a survey of the thought of the Hungarian philosopher and physicist Melchior Palágyi (1859 1924), emphasising the originality of his dynamicist view of space as flowing and changing and the prospects for a unitary but non-reductionist naturalism, which it implied. He also discussed the affinity between the idealism of the Italian philosopher Benedetto Croce (1866–1952) and developments in the new physics that implied that interpretation had physical effects.[44]

The close relationship between psychology, philosophy and religion championed by Gibson did not continue later in the twentieth century. Accordingly, his influence in Melbourne was perhaps more a matter of reputation than of substantive views. Nonetheless, the religious ethical outlook he promoted encouraged Australian intellectuals to construe philosophy as intrinsically relevant to social reform and public affairs.[45] His

---

41 See Helgeby, "Personal Idealism, Criticism and System - The Philosophy of William Ralph Boyce Gibson (1869–1935)", 99–100.
42 Gibson continued to engage with developments in science throughout his life and dealt with the theory of relativity in *The Problem of Logic*.
43 Grave, *A History of Philosophy in Australia*, 43.
44 "Obituary: William Ralph Boyce Gibson," *Australasian Journal of Psychology and Philosophy* 13 (1935): 85–92.
45 Gibson, "A Peace Policy for Idealists".

view that the pursuit of ethical progress was the proper aim of human life influenced his sons, Alexander Boyce Gibson (1900–1972), his successor in the Chair of Philosophy at the University of Melbourne, and Ralph Siward Gibson (1906–1989), a prominent Australian Communist, as well as other leading Melbourne intellectuals.[46] Although more conservative than his father, Alexander Boyce Gibson was a leader of the Student Christian Movement and gave religious talks for the Australian Broadcasting Commission. He applied his personalism to political and social questions, attacking utilitarian views, arguing that social life should be understood in terms of mutual relations between persons, and defending democracy as the only political system that promoted the development of personality.[47]

Max Charlesworth and Pluralism

With the decline of Scottish philosophy and idealism more generally, religious thought in Australia lacked a strong philosophical partner. Apart from scholastic philosophy, phenomenology often seemed the form of philosophy most amenable to religious thought, and Boyce Gibson had grasped its significance. There was a significant reception of phenomenology in Australia, but a link with religion was not dominant.[48] Alexander Boyce Gibson continued working, as did other philosophers influenced by Wittgenstein, but Protestant religious thought often evaded philosophy where possible, while Catholic religious thinkers struggled with the legacies of scholastic philosophy. Against this background, another philosopher, Max Charlesworth (1925–2014), emerged in Melbourne with the capacity to renew the relationship between philosophy and Christianity. Charlesworth was exceptional among Australian philosophers for his integrity, for his capacity to change and develop as the balance of evidence shifted, for his willingness to pioneer new developments, and for his familiarity with both scholastic philosophy and contemporary European philosophy. Like Boyce Gibson, Charlesworth brought extensive knowledge of contemporary European philosophy to the interpretation of religious thought and worked

---

46   D. Watson, *Brian Fitzpatrick: A Radical Life* (Sydney: Hale and Iremonger, 1979).
47   For his application of Christianity to politics, see A. B. Gibson, *Christianity, Democracy and Dictatorship* (The Christian and the War, no.1) Perth, WA: Sands & McDougall, Printers, 1940).
48   See M. Harney, "The Contemporary European Tradition in Australian Philosophy," in *Essays on Philosophy in Australia*, ed. J. Srzednicki and D. Wood (Dordrecht: Kluwer, 1992), ch. 7, and R. Small (ed.), *A Hundred Years of Phenomenology: Philosophical Perspectives on the Phenomenological Tradition* (Aldershot: Ashgate, 2001).

as a transnational intellectual with links to Western Europe and the United States.

Charlesworth's work needs to be seen against the background of the scholastic philosophy that prevailed in Catholic institutions in Australia until the 1960s. Scholastic philosophers argued against Kant that the existence of God and the world were knowable as they were in themselves. In doing so, they relied on the derivative interpretations of medieval philosophers of systematisers such as Josef Kleutgen (1811–1883) in Germany, and on a range of French, Italian, Spanish commentators.[49] Before the Second Vatican Council, scholastic philosophy was taught in seminaries and used to rationalise Catholic teaching about abortion, euthanasia, homosexuality and contraception. Scholastic philosophy was also drawn upon as a form of international cultural capital in debates about socialism and the labour movement, in debates about conscription, and in debates about Franco and Spanish fascism.[50] It played a significant part in the fight against Communism and, in the late 1940s, was present in the popular apologetics of Patrick Joseph (Paddy) Ryan (1904–1969).[51]

The importance of scholastic philosophy in Australia, where it was not simply a body of philosophical doctrines, but a set of orientations by which Catholics ordered their lives, is often overlooked by secular historians. Scholastic philosophy was particularly significant in the area of ethics because of its implications for sexual life and medical practice. Scholastic philosophers argued for an objectivist view of ethics that had bearings on many debates about sexuality and medicine, just as they explored neo-Aristotelian approaches to economics and law.[52] For scholastic philosophers it was possible to determine either what was consistent with natural law and what was not or what the moral constitution of our nature called for by resort to reason without reference to church authorities or the scriptures. In this view, certain acts were intrinsically immoral, just as certain arrangements were intrinsically unjust. A scholastic understanding of natural law may perhaps have played a role in the celebrated Harvester decision of 1907 which

---

49 Franklin, *Corrupting the Youth*, ch. 4.
50 C. H. Jory, *The Campion Society and Catholic Social Militancy in Australia 1929–1939* (Sydney: Harpham, 1986).
51 J. Franklin, *Catholic Values and Australian Realities* (Bacchus Marsh, Vic.: Connor Court, 2006), ch. 2.
52 For a Catholic version of human rights, based on an acceptance that human beings are made in the image of God, see J. Franklin (ed.), *Life to the Full: Rights and Social Justice in Australia* (Bacchus Marsh, Vic.: Connor Court, 2007).

ensured that workers in Australia were paid a fair basic wage.[53] Scholastic philosophy was also part of the background, nearly ninety years later, to the Mabo decision acknowledging the prior Aboriginal ownership of the land.[54]

A tough-minded form of scholastic philosophy was also promoted in Sydney by Father Austin Woodbury (1899–1979), who had studied with the eminent Thomist philosopher–theologian Réginald Garrigou-Lagrange (1877–1964) in Rome. Woodbury founded the Aquinas Academy and introduced Australians to an uncompromising European tradition of scholastic philosophy, for which knowledge had ontological, and not merely epistemological, status.[55] A milder form of Catholic philosophy was advanced in Melbourne with the Jesuit Eric D'Arcy (1877–1964) of the Melbourne University Philosophy Department. Unlike the Sydney Thomists, Father D'Arcy endorsed the linguistic turn in philosophy associated with the views of the Austrian philosopher Ludwig Wittgenstein (1889–1951) and recommended using Wittgenstein to elucidate philosophical and theological questions.[56]

Max Charlesworth began his intellectual career in Melbourne with these concerns. A leading Catholic intellectual and a respected bioethicist, he was trained in scholastic philosophy, but became adept at the style of analytical philosophy favoured at the University of Melbourne, where several philosophers (G. A. Paul, Douglas Gasking and A. C. 'Camo' Jackson) had links to Wittgenstein at Cambridge. These philosophers promoted a turn to 'ordinary language', which allowed religious language to be taken seriously, as one language among others. As a Lecturer, later Senior Lecturer, in the University of Melbourne Philosophy Department, Charlesworth remained interested in the problem of religious language, especially, following Wittgenstein, in how language was actually used. His doctoral dissertation at the Catholic University of Louvain in Belgium was on linguistic philosophy and he continued to emphasise how linguistic analysis led religious thought away from metaphysical riddles.[57] Appointed to the University of Melbourne in

---

53   Franklin, *Corrupting the Youth*, 393.
54   Franklin, *Corrupting the Youth*, 388–98 and J. Franklin, "The Mabo High Court and Natural Law Values" in J. Franklin, *Catholic Values and Australian Realities* (Ballan, Vic, Connor Court, 2006), ch 10. The case for natural law was also renewed in contemporary theoretical terms by the South Australian philosopher John Finnis, among others.
55   Franklin, *Corrupting the Youth*, 80–2.
56   E. D'Arcy S.J., *Conscience and the Right to Freedom* (London: Sheed and Ward, 1961) and *Human Acts: An Essay in Their Moral Evaluation* (Oxford: Clarendon Press, 1963).
57   M. Charlesworth, *Philosophy and Linguistic Analysis* (Pittsburgh, PA: Duquesne University Press, 1961).

1960, Charlesworth worked under Professor Alexander Boyce Gibson, and was influenced by the way he thought about religious questions in terms of a fruitful tension between doubt and belief. He also adopted Alexander Boyce Gibson's emphasis on a pluralism of viewpoints in philosophy – a position that contrasted with convergent hard-edged philosophical outlook prevailing at the University of Sydney in the 1960s.

After the Second Vatican Council, Catholic philosophy in Australia moved away from scholasticism towards existentialism and then continental philosophy, and Charlesworth played a role in this transition. The young Charlesworth sought to defend Catholic principles and their application to ethical questions in terms of a rich humanist cultural framework. To do so, he made use of his immersion in French cultural life. Charlesworth had experienced first-hand contemporary developments in European philosophy, being a friend of Jean-Paul Sartre (1905–1980) and Simone de Beauvoir (1908–1986). Persuaded that French philosophy offered depths that Anglo-American philosophy lacked, he sought to promote an understanding of phenomenology and existentialism in Australia. This mixture of Melbourne-style analytical philosophy, French existentialism, phenomenology, and Catholic scholasticism enabled Charlesworth to appear urbane and balanced on a wide range of Catholic-related philosophical issues. It also made it possible for him to revive, in some respects, the proto-existentialism pioneered much earlier by W. R. Boyce Gibson.

Charlesworth, believing that philosophy should concern itself with the problems of society and not only with technicalities, remained engaged with the world all his life. At the same time, he held that contemporary philosophy could learn from the medieval philosophical tradition. Accordingly, he translated the writings of Aquinas and wrote a commentary on and translation of Anselm's *Proslogion*.[58] In the 1960s Charlesworth introduced the first course in what came to be called Continental Philosophy in Australia, emphasising the contemporary relevance of Sartre's existentialism and French responses to Husserl.[59] He argued for the importance of phenomenology, as Boyce Gibson had done long before him, but with a

---

58   St. Thomas Aquinas, *Summa Theologicae. Vol. 15. The World Order*, translated and with a commentary by Max Charlesworth (London: Blackfriars, 1970); *St. Anselm's Proslogion*, translated and introduced by Max Charlesworth (South Bend, IN: University of Notre Dame Press, 1979).
59   M. Harney, "The Contemporary European Tradition in Australian Philosophy," ch, 7; see also *Ten Lectures on Contemporary Continental Philosophy* (Melbourne: Melbourne Philosophical Society, 1962), and M. Charlesworth, *The Existentialists and Jean-Paul Sartre* (St. Lucia: University of Queensland Press, 1975).

focus on its impact on Sartre and Merleau Ponty. Christianity, he implied, could find support in the latest French philosophy.

Charlesworth integrated his liberal philosophical views with a progressive social vision. Active as a young man in the Melbourne Campion Society, he co-edited *The Catholic Worker* in the early 1960s, attacked B. A. Santamaria's Movement and denounced Australia's involvement in the Vietnam War. Subsequently he adopted some of the liberal views of the American Jesuit John Courtney Murray (1904–1967) and argued that Catholicism was compatible with liberalism, freedom and democracy.[60] Catholics, he insisted, could embrace the idea of a free and an open society. In stages Charlesworth changed from an erudite and impressive spokesperson for the Catholic Church and member of the Vatican's Secretariat for Unbelievers into a philosophical and religious independent, respectful of many traditions. Charlesworth was convinced that philosophy and religion should be brought together. To this end, he helped found the journal *Sophia* to promote research in philosophical theology and the philosophy of religion and worked for many years with the Australian Catholic philosopher and ethicist Tony Coady (b. 1936).

In 1975 Charlesworth became Founding Dean of Humanities at Deakin University in Geelong, where he became involved in interdisciplinary studies. At Deakin Charlesworth collaborated with the Anglo-Irish philosopher Patrick Hutchings (b. 1929), with Purushottima Bilimoria and other scholars. In this new interdisciplinary Charlesworth explored the sociology of science and became interested in social anthropology, with its emphasis on the social construction of knowledges. In effect, he became less inclined to study concepts, understood as somehow given, and more inclined to study how knowledges were constructed and by whom, in particular contexts. Here he benefited from new conceptions of knowledge associated with the sociology of science.[61]

Against this background, Charlesworth returned again and again to the interpretation of Aboriginal religion in an attempt to bring about a cultural revolution in the way Australians understood Aboriginal people.[62]

---

60 M. Charlesworth, *Church, State and Conscience* (St. Lucia: University of Queensland Press, 1973).
61 M. Charlesworth et al., *Life among the Scientists: An Anthropological Study of an Australian Scientific Community* (Melbourne: Oxford University Press, 1989).
62 M. Charlesworth, *The Aboriginal Land Rights Movement* (Waurn Ponds, Vic.: Deakin University, 1983); *Religion in Aboriginal Australia: An Anthology* (St Lucia: University of Queensland Press, 1984); and *Religious Business: Essays on Australian Aboriginal Spirituality* (Cambridge: Cambridge University Press, 1989).

In partial correction of his earlier attempts to deal with Aboriginal religions within a comparative religions framework, he came to recognise that 'Aboriginal religion' was itself a construct.[63] Charlesworth's work on Aboriginal religion made him aware of deeper spiritual traditions than those of popular Catholicism, and by his work on comparative religion, which alerted him to the diversity of trends world-wide. Drawing on the lessons of the complexity and diversity of Aboriginal law and on international developments in the theory of religion, Charlesworth produced some of the most innovative essays on religion written in Australia. In these essays he advanced the idea that religions were to be understood as creative inventions.[64] He also moved towards a more complex notion of 'revelation', which recognised both the extent of human agency and the heterogeneity of the different patterns found in actual 'religious inventions'.[65] In the same way, Charlesworth's work in ecumenical contexts made him aware of the need for a less triumphalist hermeneutics.

Almost against his will, Charlesworth moved beyond confessional confines and became an advocate of interreligious theology for whom there could be no established morality in a liberal society. In bioethics he adopted liberal views on a range of questions, emphasising the difficulty of resolving such issues in a society in which there was no common morality.[66] He remained, however, committed a humanist utopia, according to which there could be a society in which people made free and autonomous decisions about what kinds of people there should be.[67] In addition to embracing pluralism openly, Charlesworth discovered the originality of Australia's geography and cultural space and became open to mystical intimations that a creative religious explosion could occur in the twenty-first century in the ancient land of Australia.[68]

In his later years, Charlesworth remained sympathetic to a sacral dimension, but was less inclined to believe that any one set of symbols could be regarded as normative. He was a critic of the revival of papal authority and Vatican bureaucracy under John Paul II and Benedict XVI and an advocate

---

63 M. Charlesworth, *Religious Inventions: Four Essays* (Melbourne: Cambridge University Press, 1997), ch. 2.
64 Charlesworth, *Religious Inventions*.
65 Charlesworth, *Religious Inventions*, especially Essay 3; see also Charlesworth, *Religious Business*.
66 M. Charlesworth, *Bioethics in a Liberal Society* (Cambridge: Cambridge University Press, 1993).
67 M. Charlesworth, *Life, Death, Genes and Ethics* (Crows Nest, NSW: ABC, 1989), 95, and Bioethics and a Liberal Society.
68 M. Charlesworth, "Terra Australis and the Holy Spirit," in *2000 A.D. Millennium*, ed. H. Daniel (Melbourne: Penguin, 1992), 280–7.

of a radically democratised church.[69] He rejected clericalism and centralised Roman bureaucracy, advocating a return to the democratic practices of the early church. Charlesworth became convinced that Christianity had nothing to do with clericalist heteronomy. Indeed, his final understanding of Catholicism was closer to the Christianity of Boyce Gibson and the Scottish idealists than could have been predicted by anyone who knew him as a young man. Like Gibson, Charlesworth believed that Christianity was consistent with advances in the sciences, but that it needed an update to align it with democracy and with a wide program of social and economic reform. By the end of his life, Charlesworth had arrived at a radical position, in which philosophy needed to work with other disciplines in the search for wisdom. In the same way, without abandoning his personal Catholicism, Charlesworth, embraced the more stringent implications of pluralism within the framework of liberal political philosophy. He accepted the need to reshape religious thought radically in order to allow for the primacy of individual decision and the immanence of the human being in changing cultures and societies.

Kevin Hart and Theological Phenomenology

Both W. R. Boyce Gibson and Charlesworth sought to bring the major developments in European philosophy to the attention of Australians, and both accepted the need for the revision of Christianity to enable it to come to terms with contemporary scientific and social changes. Just as W. R. Boyce Gibson reworked Rudolf Eucken's proto-existentialism, Charlesworth moved away from his scholastic beginnings by assimilating French existentialsm, American liberal political philosophy, and the challenges of Aboriginal spirituality and comparative religion. A third religious intellectual, the poet, literary critic and Professor of Christian Studies at the University of Virginia and Eric D'Arcy Professor of Philosophy at the Australian Catholic University, Kevin Hart (b. 1954), also turned to European philosophy, primarily to French theological phenomenology, as a resource for rethinking the relationship between religious thought and philosophy.

Before 1925 significant commentary on French philosophy was found in Australia. J. McKellar Stewart published *A Critical Exposition of Bergson's Philosophy* (1911) and J. Alexander Gunn (1896–1975) published *Bergson and His Philosophy* (1920) and *Modern French Philosophy* (1922) for which

---

69   M. Charlesworth, *A Democratic Church: Reforming the Values and Institutions of the Catholic Church* (Melbourne: John Garratt, 2008).

Bergson wrote an introduction, as well as a study of Spinoza. After the 1920s French philosophers were studied in university departments of French and, from the 1960s on, French philosophy impacted on Australian scholarship more generally, in part influenced by British and American patterns of interpretation. Contemporary French philosophy was initially interpreted as 'structuralism', 'anti-humanism' and 'Marxism', and then as 'postmodernism' and 'poststructuralism'. In due course the works of Jacques Derrida (1930–2004), Emmanuel Levinas (1906–1995) and Michel Foucault (1926–1984), and Gilles Deleuze (1925–1995), Luce Irigaray (b. 1930), Hélène Cixous (b. 1937) and Michèle le Doeuff (b. 1948) became well known. Exposure to these philosophers gave rise to many books, articles and theses in the areas of religious studies, biblical studies and theology.[70]

The most sustained engagement with French writers in a theological context can be found in the works of Kevin Hart. Born in London, Hart migrated to Australia in 1966 at the age of twelve. He attended Oxley State High School in suburban Brisbane and the Australian National University, gaining a doctorate at the University of Melbourne. In Australia he developed transnational knowledge that he subsequently took to the University of Notre Dame in Indiana and the University of Virginia, returning for some of each year to give seminars at the Australian Catholic University in Melbourne. Hart is a transnational intellectual working mainly on French thinkers – a thinker who is at home in Paris and in Britain who reads at least five European languages. Adept in the study of languages, Hart was originally interested in pure mathematics and logic, especially Husserl's *Logical Investigations*. Immersing himself in French philosophy and literature, he worked his way with systematic rigour through the output of the intellectual and literary figure, Georges Bataille (1897–1962), the philosopher and Christian mystic, Simone Weil (1909–1943), and the poet and essayist, Yves Bonnefoy (b. 1921), to the work of Derrida.

A convert to Catholicism, Hart combines a deep knowledge of contemporary French philosophical authors of literary disposition open to an apprehension of

---

[70] See, for example, E. Grosz, *Sexual Subversions: Three French Feminists* (Sydney: Allen and Unwin, 1989); M. Deutscher, *Subjecting and Objecting: An Essay on Objectivity* (St. Lucia: University of Queensland Press, 1983); M. Deutscher (ed.), *Michèle le Doeuff: Operative Philosophy and Imaginary Practice* (New York: Humanity Books, 2000) and *Genre and Void: Looking Back at Sartre and Beauvoir* (Aldershot: Ashgate, 2003); P. Patton, *Deleuze and the Political* (London/New York: Routledge, 2000); P. Patton and John Protevi (eds.), *Between Deleuze and Derrida* (London and New York: Continuum, 2003); S. Bignall and P. Patton (eds.), *Deleuze and the Postcolonial* (Edinburgh: Edinburgh University Press, 2010); and P. Patton, *Deleuzian Concepts: Philosophy, Colonization, Politics* (Palo Alto: Stanford University Press, 2010).

a mysterious imageless God. In the context of tactical bows to postmodernism and postmodern philosophy,[71] Hart mobilises his skills as a poet to provide acute and rigorous readings of philosophical and theological texts.[72] He achieves a powerful theological vision for which God is not a being and cannot be thought of in terms of metaphysics, where 'metaphysics' means, as it does for Heidegger, a form of ontotheology in which reality is reduced to being. Hart accepts the standard Heideggerian view that metaphysics in this sense occludes both our selfhood and our relation to God. Like Heidegger, Hart holds that metaphysics in the sense of ontotheology can be overcome and he reads Derrida as extending Heidegger's argument in this respect.

In his *The Trespass of the Sign* (1989), Hart showed that Derrida's deconstruction could be read as involving a quasi-transcendental argument that any discourse contains the means to call its metaphysical claims into question.[73] In addition, Hart argued that deconstruction was neither atheistic nor destructive of theology, as had been claimed, but rather could be related to negative theology and, indeed, opened up discussion about the possibility of a non-metaphysical theology. Negative theology, Hart insisted, was a form of deconstruction and this pointed to the fact that a beyond that could never be grasped in logical or conceptual terms manifested in experience. Accordingly, Hart distinguishes between *theiology* as the study of the highest grounds and *theology* as the study of God, as revealed in thinking and praying. He rejects any attempt to think of God within metaphysics and suggests that God cannot be thought of as a cause, ground, or source.

When, in due course, Derrida rejected negative theology interpretations of his work, Hart continued the project in his own terms, drawing on other French philosophical writers. Hart accepts elements of the deconstruction of the subject argued for by Derrida, Levinas and Lacan, but then continues the deconstructionist program beyond its Derridanian beginnings. He does so by turning to the work of the French philosophical novelist Maurice Blanchot (1907–2003), to whom he has devoted four books.[74] Hart takes

---

71   K. Hart, *Postmodernism: A Beginner's Guide* (Oxford: One World, 2004).
72   For Hart as a religious poet, see Davidson, *Christian Mysticism and Australian Poetry*, ch 6.
73   K. Hart, *The Trespass of the Sign: Deconstruction, Theology, and Philosophy* (Cambridge: Cambridge University Press, 1989), xi.
74   K. Hart, *Nowhere Without No In Memory of Maurice Blanchot* (Sydney: Vagabond Press, 2003); *The Dark Gaze: Maurice Blanchot and the Sacred* (Chicago: Chicago University Press, 2004); with Yvonne Sherwood (eds.), *Derrida and Religion: Other Testaments* (London: Routledge, 2004); with Barbara Wall (eds.), *The Experience of God* (New York: Fordham University Press, 2005); with Geoffrey Hartman (eds.), *The Power of Contestation: Perspectives on Maurice Blanchot* (Baltimore, MD: Johns

from Blanchot the merging of philosophy and literature, the deconstruction of the Cartesian subject or the claim that the subject can never be self-present, and the critique of any philosophy based on representation.

Hart is the outstanding example of an Australian religious thinker committed to what theologians call 'apophaticism'.[75] The term 'apophatic' (from the Greek ἀπόφημι – *apophēmi*, to deny) is associated with the tradition of negative theology, which maintains that anything said of God is more false than true. It is used to describe theologies that deny that God can be represented directly. For apophatic theology, which is the dominant tradition in the Eastern, as opposed to the Western, church, negations of positive theological statements are necessary to preserve the unrepresentable character of what transcends creatures. In Eastern Orthodoxy apophaticism is associated with high levels of theological and philosophical training and with austere monastic practices. Apophaticism in Australia, however, is associated with the tendency to avoid positive religious statements, which has been noted by several observers,[76] including the Catholic theologian Anthony Kelly, who noted that, for Australians,

> God, then, is the silence in which we belong, the silence in which every voice is heard, all wounds are healed and all our times have a future, God of the 'no-thing', God of the centre, God of the common dish.[77]

Hart rethinks theology in radically apophatic terms, as a discourse that deals with content that exceeds thought, content that can be recognised, but not cognised. Drawing on his studies of Christian mysticism, especially Pseudo-Dionysius (5th century CE) and Meister Eckhart (1260–1328), in order to develop a version of theological deconstruction, he envisages the divine as in continual movement and irreducible to presence. Hart is sympathetic

---

Hopkins University Press, 2005); *Counter-Experiences: Reading Jean-Luc Marion* (South Bend, IN: Notre Dame University Press, 2007); and *Clandestine Encounters: Philosophy in the Narratives of Maurice Blanchot* (South Bend, IN: Notre Dame University Press, 2010), among other volumes.

75 For discussion of apophatic tendencies in Hart's poetry, see Davidson, *Christian Mysticism and Australian Poetry*, ch. 6.

76 The theologically trained philosopher, Richard Campbell, also captured this apophatic dimension of Australian religious intellectual life in 1977 when he characterised the religious sense in Australia as that our lives stand out into an emptiness which is not nothing, but the uncanny limit to human endeavour; see R. Campbell, "The Character of Australian Religion," *Meanjin* 36 (1977): 188.

77 See A. Kelly, *A New Imagining: Towards an Australian Spirituality* (Melbourne: Collins Dove, 1990): 132.

to attempts to rethink the divine with call, withdrawal and gift, and as a reality that addresses human beings but cannot be understood by them. He defends Dionysius's mystical theology against Derrida's reservations and, in particular, accepts Dionysius's claim that good rather than being should be taken to be the first divine name – in effect, that ethical call has priority over being.

Taking up the French turn to Pseudo-Dionysius and the neo-Platonic emphasis on a God above being as a way of responding to Heidegger's 'critique of ontotheology', or the tendency to locate God within the order of being, Hart proposes a theology without 'the God of metaphysics' – one that emphasises the non-conceptual aspects of religious experience. He identifies with French writers who construe the existential situation of the human being as already theologically shaped. These resources may not be sufficient, however, to give negative theology the intellectual credibility that it needs. To achieve such credibility, Hart turns to recent French attempts to rethink phenomenology so that it can take account of Christian revelation, at least as a phenomenological possibility.[78] In these writers the givenness of *phenomenality* replaces the Husserlian idea of *phenomena* for a subject. Specifically, Hart engages at length with Derrida's former student, theological phenomenologist Jean-Luc Marion (b. 1946). Hart locates Marion in his German context, while drawing attention to lacunae in his work. Marion attempts to provide a new foundation for phenomenology as first philosophy by rethinking what Husserl and Heidegger mean by 'the phenomenon' and proposes a 'third reduction', based on the self-giving of the phenomenon itself. He does so by interpreting phenomenology as radical empiricism for which intuition goes beyond the sensible and includes all givenness. Marion revises phenomenology to include the 'saturated phenomenon', that is, the phenomenon in which there is an overwhelming givenness or excess going beyond the intentional acts that saturate it.[79] Such phenomena fall outside phenomenology as Husserl classically conceived it. Hart insists that we have no right to set limits in advance to what counts as a phenomenon and seeks to exploit the resources of this extension of phenomenology for apophatic theology. He also interrogates Marion's notion that the divine can be recognised in an experience of the impossible.[80]

---

[78] See B. E. Benson and N. Wirzba (eds.), *Words of Life: New Theological Turns in French Phenomenology* (New York: Fordham University Press, 2010).

[79] For an excellent introduction to these difficult ideas by one of Hart's students, see R. Horner, *Jean-Luc Marion: A Theo-Logical Introduction* (Aldershot: Ashgate, 2005).

[80] Hart (ed.), *Counter-Experiences*.

Blending elements of Blanchot, Marion and theological phenomenologists, such as Jean-Louis Chrétien (b. 1952) and Jean-Yves Lacoste (b. 1953), as well as the radical phenomenology of life proposed by French philosopher and novelist Michel Henry (1922–2002), Hart's negative theology takes it for granted that our relation to the divine cannot be based on presence or representation as an object of knowledge, although it does involve careful attention to experience and to the problem involved in any attempt to speak of the experience of God.[81] For Hart no proper account of experience that does not include God as a transversal is adequate. At the same time, he emphasises that such experience is non-thetical and cannot come within the hermeneutic circle.[82] Hart accepts that negative theology of this sort abounds in *aporiae* and is always to some extent unfinished.

For Hart neither philosophy nor theology nor poetry can grasp 'the whole thing',[83] although they can achieve a good deal in dialogue with one another. In his most recent major study,[84] Hart sees phenomenology as at the centre of all his scholarly writing in philosophy, theology and literature and carefully analyses different senses of what Husserl means by the *epoché*, or reduction.[85] Phenomenology for Hart, however, is not to be narrowly identified with the phenomenology of Kant, Husserl or Heidegger. It is a matter of attending to the things themselves and letting them disclose themselves in their own ways. Hart argues that such phenomenology can look more deeply at issues than the disciplines of either philosophy or theology sanction.[86] Applying this extended sense of phenomenology, Hart introduces his own version of phenomenological theology, which begins from a formal point of view with Jesus' parables, and, substantively, with Jesus' relation to the Father, rather than with a doctrine of God.[87] According to Hart, Jesus performs a reduction from 'world' to 'Kingdom' in his telling of the parables. The parables for Hart offer pre-thetic experience of the Kingdom.[88] For Hart, Jesus' words and acts, as recorded in the Christian scriptures, disclose the meaning of God's

---

81 See Hart and Wall (eds.), *The Experience of God*.
82 See K. Hart, "The Kingdom and the Trinity," in J. Bloechl (ed.), *Religious Experience and the End of Metaphysics* (Bloomington, IN: Indiana University Press 2003), 153–73.
83 For a brilliant interpretative essay, see C. Watkin, "De Omni Re Scibili: Kevin Hart Philosopher, Theologian, Poet," *Parrhesia* 18 (2013): 36–40.
84 For Hart's remarkable monograph on the basileia tou theou, see K. Hart, *Kingdoms of God* (Bloomington, IN: Indiana University Press, 2014).
85 Hart, *Kingdoms of God*, 2.
86 Hart, *Kingdoms of God*, 4.
87 Hart, *Kingdoms of God*, 151.
88 Hart, *Kingdoms of God*, 154.

kingly rule,[89] and what is revealed by the parables is the invisible coming forth of love itself.[90] As usual, Hart clarifies the act of reading with literary brilliance, even though his theology remains narrowly focused (God cannot be known except as revealed by Jesus of Nazareth) and remote from discursive arguments.

Indeed, Hart, even though he is sensitive to the difficulty of reconciling the Christian emphasis on the Kingdom with the doctrine of the Trinity, retains from his reading of Protestant theology the overwhelming sense of the unconditionality of God, associated with Swiss theologian Karl Barth (1886–1968). For Hart, human beings can only experience God through grace, and God does not appear in experience. He also places heavy emphasis on the unique role of Jesus Christ. Hence Hart critiques Derrida's tendency to treat the otherness of God and the human person as the same, and has related doubts about the work of Marion. Similarly, under the influence of rabbinical interpretations of Judaism, Hart retains a commitment to the primacy of Scripture. In contrast to ultra-radical contemporary religious thinkers, such as John Caputo (b. 1940) and Gianni Vattimo (b. 1936), who abandon both theism and Christian orthodoxy, Hart seeks to renew such orthodoxy by applying phenomenology to scriptural texts. At the same time, he foregrounds the theological doctrine of the *kenosis*, or the self-emptying of Christ. In this way, he seeks to relate his negative theology of unsayable effects to a Kingdom of God theology, with implications for the human social world. In doing so, he remains with the contemporary French emphasis on philosophy tied to personal experience, and makes no attempt to provide a sociology of theology or a sociology of religion. The tension between experience as revelation and a God who does not appear also remains, and central Christian concepts such as the Trinity, become not conceptually graspable, but only available in the life that reaches towards them.

Hart's commitment to contemporary French philosophy of religion means that his work draws on materials that remain largely inaccessible to lay audiences. It is also far from clear that theological phenomenology will persuade analytical philosophers. Hart assumes that phenomenology can provide substantial clarifications of experience, on which, among other resources, theology can draw. It is not clear, however, how such phenomenology will be seen in the light of more metaphysically oriented French

---

89   Hart, *Kingdoms of God*, 143.
90   Hart, *Kingdoms of God*, 135.

philosophy. Nonetheless, Hart's sophisticated discussion of philosophical theological issues sets a high bar for subsequent work and is perhaps the most consistently erudite contribution yet made by an Australian.

A rigorous approach to textual reading can also be found in the work of one of Hart's students, Melbourne Jewish philosopher Michael Fagenblat (b. 1972). Fagenblat wrote his doctorate at Monash University under Hart before going on to post-doctoral studies at the Hebrew University and the Shalom Hartman Institute in Jerusalem. Where Hart follows the French phenomenological theological tradition, which brings philosophy close to literature, Fagenblat proposes a radical reinterpretation of the work of the Jewish philosopher Emmanuel Levinas by reading it against a Jewish background. Like Hart, Fagenblat is a multilingual, transnational intellectual who works from multiple locations (Melbourne, Paris, Jerusalem, New York) and, like Hart, he tends towards stringent readings.

Levinas is often read as an ethical thinker who rethinks Husserl's phenomenology in order to interpret existence and transcendence in light of the birth of ethical meaning. Levinas' wider phenomenology goes beyond Husserl and Heidegger to include new levels of experience, above all, face-to-face encounters, and to explore pre-intentional affective experience in which transcendence comes to pass. His emphasis on preconceptual sensibility opens up new possibilities for ethical and religious thought. Fagenblat, however, rejects the standard moralist interpretations of Levinas and what he calls the myth of Levinas' ethics. Instead of attributing a kind of theological Protestantism to Levinas, Fagenblat reads Levinas in terms of the Jewish tradition, and, specifically, in the context of Midrash, the homiletic stories told by Jewish rabbis to explain passages in the Torah – stories that tend to draw out the irreducibly difficult and contradictory character of human affairs.[91] For Fagenblat, Levinas advances Judaic ethical negative theology. Fagenblat also relates Levinas' alleged ethics to a secularisation of the Jewish covenant of faith.[92] In effect, he sets up the Jewish idea of permanently and irreducibly difficult ethical thought, instantiated in hard cases, against the quest for clear principles and rules that has dominated ethical philosophy since Kant. According to Fagenblat, Jewish faith should be understood phenomenologically rather than cognitively, and theological beliefs are derived from the noncognitive experience of covenantal faith.[93]

---

91 M. Fagenblat, *A Covenant of Creatures: Levinas's Philosophy of Judaism* (Palo Alto: Stanford University Press, 2010).
92 Fagenblat, *A Covenant of Creatures*, xxv.
93 Fagenblat, *A Covenant of Creatures*, xxv.

In the same relentless spirit, Fagenblat draws out the critical elements in Jewish readings of the Bible, which emphasise insurmountable difficulties in order to construct an outlook that recognises the gap between ethics and law.[94] Influenced by Heidegger, he rejects any neutral ontology and accepts the need to move from metaphysics to hermeneutics. Rejecting every easy position, Fagenblat writes that:

> By situating evil in the heart of transcendence we situate ourselves within the battle against it. The task ahead is to show how the transcendence of the good is distinguishable from evil by a covenantal commitment to its *interpretation*. In that way mythical theology can become part of history and our response to transcendence can remain politically engaged even as we take responsibility for its meaning.[95]

Fagenblat follows the negative theology implicit in the philosophical theology of the most famous medieval Jewish philosopher Maimonides (1135–1204), according to which God's name is known, but nothing else is known about him.[96] Further, like Maimonides, Fagenblat argues from the fact that philosophical reason can provide very little help where religious questions are concerned to the need for Jews to be guided by the Torah. Even more radical, like the Israeli religious and political critic Yeshayahu Leibowitz (1903–1994), who championed an Orthodox approach to Judaism on the principles of existential atheism, and to whom he is indebted, Fagenblat explores a philosophical theology which does not depend on the existence of God. This theology takes atheism to be the natural condition of human beings, and then argues that Jews need to accept and follow the heteronomy of revealed law precisely because they can acquire no substantial knowledge of God by rational means. This is a tough-minded position with few parallels in Christian thought. It allows Fagenblat to address contemporary atheism, without surrendering Jewish tradition. It also allows him to defend a very modest account of philosophy's ability to address religious concerns.

Despite the dates and contexts that separate them, Boyce Gibson, Charlesworth and Hart exemplify significant currents in religious thought

---

94 See M. Fagenblat, "How Is Ethics Possible?" (PhD, Monash University, 1998).
95 M. Fagenblat, "Back to the Other Levinas: Reflections prompted by Alain P. Toumayan's *Encountering the Other: the Artwork and the Problem of Difference in Blanchot and Levinas*," *Colloquy* 10 (2005): 298–313, especially 309; see also M. Fagenblat, "Levinas and Maimonides: From Metaphysics to Ethical Negative Theology," *Journal of Jewish Thought and Philosophy* 16 (2008): 95–147.
96 Fagenblat, *A Covenant of Creatures*, ch. 4.

in Australia. They were all concerned with contemporary developments in philosophy, and they all worked in and from several cultural geographies: France, Belgium, Germany, Britain and the United States. Moreover, each of them assayed the religion–philosophy interface, albeit in different ways – by arguing that personality and philosophical psychology brought religious thought and philosophy together (Gibson); by turning to interdisciplinary studies that implied that traditional religious studies and philosophical approaches were inadequate (Charlesworth); and by turning to theological phenomenology as a tradition which assayed religious terrain from an intra-philosophical perspective (Hart). Each of these religious intellectuals approached the issues they worked on by referring to the greatest minds they could find engaged with such topics. Moreover, in each case they proposed major shifts in the way Christianity should be presented to their contemporaries – a shift to ethical social life (Gibson); a shift to a social pluralism beyond any imposed intellectual synthesis (Charlesworth); and a shift to an apophatic awareness of the nonmundane and the reduction Jesus performed in telling his parables (Hart). All three turned to personal experience as providing a basis for a defensible theology in an age of science. The phenomenology central to Gibson's approach to the relationship between religious thought and philosophy reappears in Hart's work on theological phenomenology, just as Gibson's proto-existentialism has parallels in Charlesworth's promotion of French existentialism. In all three thinkers there are tensions between a voluntarist tendency to emphasise the need to choose a standpoint and the desire to find features of experience that compatible with religious claims.

Rethinking the Philosophy of Religion

A number of philosophers in Australia have made significant contributions to the philosophy of religion, widely construed. Many of them have done so in a context in which university philosophy has been predominantly anti-religious. Apart from the major figures already discussed, note should be taken of the achievement of Alexander Boyce Gibson. In the course of his long career at the University of Melbourne, Gibson emerged as a significant philosopher of religion, although, it can be argued, he was underestimated in the English-speaking philosophical world in his lifetime.[97] Gibson

---

97 Alexander Boyce Gibson defended orthodox theological views; see, especially, his *Theism and Empiricism* (London: SCM Press, 1970); also his *The Philosophy of Descartes* (New York: Russell and Russell, 1967); *Muse and Thinker* (London: Watts, 1969);

denied that he was an idealist, but he engaged with both idealism and with the realism of Samuel Alexander long after it was fashionable to do so. In the same way, he insisted that philosophy was metaphysics at a time when this was not a well-regarded view.[98] Indebted to his tutor at Balliol, A. B. Lindsay, and to the British personalist philosopher, John Macmurray (1891–1976), Gibson contended for a realistic personalism and for a blend of theism and empiricism, understanding empiricism as a wide conception that included personal activity, responsibility and discovery.[99] He also promoted a religious existentialism in Melbourne, inspired by the Danish philosopher Søren Kierkegaard and the Russian novelist Dostoevsky (1821–1881). Gibson agreed with Kierkegaard that religion was existential, but insisted that religious experience was not outside the scope of reason.[100] Although in some ways a conservative Christian thinker, especially when compared with his father, Gibson also saw the need for new theological thought, and, following the American philosophical theologian Charles Hartshorne (1897–2000), whose work he admired, he accepted that God must be in time.[101] At his best, he offered a sophisticated philosophical theism based on dialectical features of spiritual experience, one that implied a double-aspect view, according to which God is prolongated into the world, but we are only able to grab at His fringes, while the order, creativity, morality and personality found in the world are fringes for us, but also prolongations of God into the world.[102] Gibson's philosophical theology was refracted and refined, and deserves more notice than it has received.

Apart from Alexander Boyce Gibson, who encouraged an interest in existential phenomenology at Melbourne, religiously-inclined philosophers produced fine work in a mixture of scholastic, analytical and continental styles on the problems of theism and theodicy, which appeared in *Sophia*, the journal Charlesworth founded in 1962 and co-edited for many years by Patrick Hutchings, or came out of the Catholic Institute of Sydney and the Melbourne College of Divinity, now the University of Divinity. Nothing like an analytically coherent Christian metaphysics was proposed, however, and

---

The Religion of Dostoevsky (London: SCM Press 1973). For an excellent study, see S. Helgeby, "Alexander Boyce Gibson: Theism, Empiricism and Idealism," *Collingwood and British Idealism Studies* 14 (2008): 96–127.

98   A. Boyce Gibson, "Preface to a Future Metaphysics," *Australasian Journal of Psychology and Philosophy* 25 (1947): 129–51.

99   Gibson, *Theism and Empiricism*, 10–11,18–21, 40.

100   A. Boyce Gibson, "Existential Religion and Existential Philosophy," *Danish Yearbook of Philosophy* 8 (1971): 94–114, especially 94–5.

101   A. Boyce Gibson, "God is not Timeless," *Crux* 71, no. 4 (1968), 8.

102   Gibson, *Theism and Empiricism*, 64, 78, and Helgeby, "Alexander Boyce Gibson", 122.

it became unclear whether any metaphysical support for religious claims could be found. Some Anglicans were sympathetic to philosophically-inclined British theologians, such as Austin Farrer (1904–1968), Eric Mascall (1905–1993) and John Macquarrie (1919–2007), just as some Protestants were attracted to the project of Christian philosophy. Reformed philosophy of a Calvinist variety was promoted at Ridley College in Melbourne and at Emmanuel College at the University of Queensland. Some Catholic philosophers trained in scholasticism blended medieval knowledges and analytical philosophy-style argumentation to good effect. the Marist priest and philosophical theologian Barry Miller (1923–2006), for example, rejected the perfect being theism that dominated the Catholic tradition. He also argued against Kant and Frege that existence was a real property. Miller further proposed that God was simple existence and identical with his attributes.[103] Miller's ideas were subsequently taken seriously in the United States. Other philosophers who were also religious intellectuals achieved international distinction by combining analytical training with insights from other disciplines.

Richard Campbell (b. 1939), for example, who had training in analytical philosophy and theology, produced internationally distinguished work by combining the sharpness of analytical philosophy with deep theological reading and sensitivity to the action based ontology of the Hebrew language. A student of the Scottish Presbyterian theologian Crawford Miller at St Andrew's Hall in Sydney, Campbell gained international attention in 1976 with his monograph, *From Belief to Understanding: A Study of Anselm's Proslogion Argument on the Existence of God*. He argued that Anselm's argument had been radically misunderstood and was concerned only with the scope of what is said (*quod dicitur*), and not with some ontological proof, as had long been assumed. In subsequent publications he spelt out Anselm's account of the rationality of faith and his understanding of freedom and truth. As well as emphasising that Anselm's conceptions were bound up with his philosophy of language, Campbell showed that an argument could be made for the view that God cannot be coherently *said* not to be, a theme to which other philosophers have returned.[104] He also implied that

---

103 See B. Miller, *From Existence to God: A Contemporary Philosophical Argument* (New York: Routledge, 1992), and *A Most Unlikely God: A Philosophical Enquiry into the Nature of God* (South Bend, IN: Notre Dame University Press, 1996).
104 See R. Campbell, "Anselm's Theological Method," *Scottish Journal of Theology* 32 (1979): 541–62; "Anselm's Background Metaphysics," *Scottish Journal of Theology* 33 (1980): 317–43; and "'Freedom as Keeping the Truth' – The Anselmian Tradition," in *Anselm Studies II*, ed. J.C. Schnaubelt et al. (White Plains, NY: Kraus International, 1988), 297–318.

Anselm's subtle reasoning and refusal to separate reason from faith were of contemporary relevance.

In his later work Campbell has drawn closer to Heidegger and the concerns of European philosophy, but he has also built out from his theological training and his knowledge of Hebrew to promote an event-based account of the relation between historicity and truth, in effect breaking with the Greek bias of most Western philosophy and religious thought. In his later work he rejects the linguistic concept of truth as transmuted Platonism, disposes of any conception of God as an entity, and defines the Christian stance in anti-Platonist and non-Cartesian terms as living with historicity and contingency in openness to the future. Campbell has developed a novel conception of truth and a process-philosophy ontology in opposition to the physicalism widely accepted in the philosophy departments of Australian universities.[105] He has yet to address the implications of this non-Whiteheadian process philosophy for religious thought, although overcoming reductive naturalism is obviously important.

Another analytically trained philosopher, Peter Forrest (b. 1948), brings an original metaphysical mind to bear on difficult questions in the philosophy of religion, drawing on his background in pure mathematics and his knowledge of Indian metaphysical views. Although a Catholic with Thomist sympathies, Forrest accepts the philosophical materialism of his teacher, Sydney philosopher David Armstrong, within limits, and uses it to challenge theory of possible worlds put forward by American philosopher David Lewis. He also defends a realist interpretation of quantum physics and physicalism. Forrest is concerned to bring philosophical principles and contemporary physics together on speculative principles.[106] He is prepared to consider the necessary structure of an ether pervading the universe and to reject the standard interpretation of General Relativity. Armed with hard-nosed doctrines and considerable technicality, he develops an original non-traditional theism that does not involve supernaturalism.[107]

---

105   See also R. Campbell, *Truth and Historicity* (Oxford: Clarendon Press, 1992) and *The Concept of Truth* (Basingstoke: Palgrave Macmillan, 2011). For religious applications, see R. Campbell, "Truth, Process and Faithfulness," in *God Down Under: Theology in the Antipodes*, ed. W. W. H. Lamb and I. Barns (Adelaide: ATF, 2003), 171–200. For Campbell's work on process philosophy, see *The Metaphysics of Emergence* (London: Palgrave Macmillan, 2015).
106   See P. Forrest, *The Necessary Structure of the All-Pervading Aether: Discrete or Continuous? Simple or Symmetric?* (Frankfurt: Ontos, 2012).
107   P. Forrest, "Physicalism and Classical Theism," *Faith and Philosophy* 13 (1996): 178–200, and *The Dynamics of Belief: A Normative Logic* (Oxford: Blackwell, 1986), and many papers in major journals.

Forrest argues that God is the best explanation for certain features of the universe discovered by the contemporary sciences. He concedes, however, that the state of the world cannot be reconciled with traditional claims for divine omnipotence and omniscience. Instead, he posits an ontologically limited God who changes over time.[108] This theism is non-classical, and goes with a 'tough theodicy'. Similarly, in *Developmental Theism: From Pure Will to Unbounded Love* (2006), Forrest shows how such a theism might alleviate intractable issues about evil, the incarnation and the Trinity.

Logically exact work was also done on arguments about miracles, for the existence of God and for theodicy by the evangelical philosopher Bruce Langtry (b. 1946) at the University of Melbourne.[109] In his 2008 monograph, *God, the Best and Evil*, characterised by exceptional rigour, Langtry addresses the challenges posed for traditional theism by the problem of evil, with reference to the work of leading British and American analytical philosophers. To do so, he draws a distinction between an agent's intrinsic causal powers and cognitive capacities and the ways in which they can be exercised in current circumstances. Some philosophers were influenced by the reformed epistemology associated with the American Calvinist philosopher, Alvin Plantinga (b. 1932), and/or by the philosophical theism defended by British philosophers such as Richard Swinburne (b. 1934). Many religious thinkers, however, did not take up technical developments in philosophy (including the discovery of paraconsistent logics and possible world theory) that might have been useful to them, although a number enlisted the views of philosophers such as British philosopher Alasdair MacIntyre (b. 1929), who challenged the notion of a pure or impartial reason.[110]

Consistent with this, the case against the traditional arguments for the existence of God has been made in detail in a series of books by Graham Oppy (b. 1960), who also advocates a revised world-views approach to the

---

108 P. Forrest, *God Without the Supernatural: A Defense of Scientific Theism* (Ithaca, NY: Cornell University Press, 1996).
109 B. Langtry, "Hume on Testimony to the Miraculous," *Sophia* 11 (1972): 20–25; "God, Evil and Probability" *Sophia* 28 (1989): 32–40; and *God, the Best, and Evil* (Oxford: Oxford University Press, 2008); see also the discussion in G. Oppy and N. N. Trakakis (eds.), *A Companion to Philosophy in Australia and New Zealand* (Melbourne: Monash University Publishing, 2010). For earlier analytical philosophy critical of the coherence of theism, see C. B. Martin *Religious Belief* (Ithaca, NY: Cornell University Press, 1959). Religiously minded philosophers also defended theism with reference to current debates; see Gibson, *Theism and Empiricism*.
110 See, for example, the books of the Catholic theologian Tracey Rowland (b. 1963), who in her *Culture and the Thomist Tradition after Vatican II* (London: Routledge, 2003) reinterpreted Thomism in terms derived from Alasdair MacIntyre.

philosophy of religion has not been answered in depth.¹¹¹ A few religious intellectuals, however, reacted to analytical-philosophy style criticisms of traditional philosophy of religion by rethinking the foundations of the field. Nick Trakakis (b. 1972), for example, a philosopher at the Australian Catholic University with theological training in the Greek Orthodox tradition, argued in *The God Beyond Belief* that facts regarding evil provide at least some evidence against the existence of God.¹¹² He subsequently moved away from the analytical philosophy approach to the philosophy of religion altogether and in *The End of Philosophy of Religion* argued for a new style of philosophy of religion, based on a conception of philosophy that was not restricted to the norms of scientific thought.¹¹³

Prospects

These individual contributions, it may be suggested, do not add up to an edifice. Relations between religious thought and philosophy in Australia were often happenstance. Many Protestant theologians saw no need for philosophical foundations, although hermeneutical philosophy, from Schleiermacher to Heidegger and Gadamer, was enlisted to help with the interpretation of religious texts. German philosophy, which was arguably the most important philosophical tradition for religious thought, was received in Australia from the nineteenth century onwards. However, it often came in a somewhat muted form, partly, because it was often read through the lens of Scottish idealism. When Scottish idealism declined, it took decades for a more philologically exact understanding of German philosophy to emerge. Apart from W. R. Boyce Gibson's internationally important work on Rudolf Eucken and Edmund Husserl, McKellar Stewart, at the University of Adelaide from 1923 to 1950, researched on Kant at the University of Marburg, lectured on Nietzsche, published on Husserl and wrote a manuscript on Husserl's philosophical thought.¹¹⁴ P. R. Le Couteur

---

111 See, G. Oppy, *Philosophical Perspectives on Infinity* (Cambridge: Cambridge University Press, 2006); *Arguing about Gods* (Cambridge: Cambridge University Press, 2006); *The Best Argument Against God* (Basingstoke: Palgrave Macmillan, 2013); *Describing Gods: An Investigation of Divine Attributes* (Cambridge: Cambridge University Press, 2014); and *Rethinking Philosophy of Religion: An Opinionated Introduction* (Basingstoke: Palgrave Macmillan, 2014).
112 N. Trakakis, *The God beyond Belief: In Defence of William Rowe's Evidential Argument from Evil* (Dordrecht: Springer, 2007).
113 N. Trakakis, *The End of Philosophy of Religion* (London: Continuum, 2008).
114 J. McKellar Stewart, "Husserl's Phenomenology," *Australasian Journal of Psychology and Philosophy* 11 (1933): 221–31, and "Husserl's Phenomenological Method,"

(1885–1958), at the University of Western Australia from 1913, studied with Oswald Külpe in Bonn, while Morris Miller (1881–1964) at the University of Tasmania wrote books on Kant.[115]

The early interest in German philosophy continued into the 1920s, at a time when Australians showed relatively little interest in major British philosophers such as Bertrand Russell. Interest in German philosophy receded thereafter for some decades, although theologians read Heidegger, European hermeneutics and literary theory when philosophers generally did not. After the Second World War, Australian awareness of German philosophy expanded and, with the arrival of members of the Hungarian Lukács circle, Ágnes Heller (b. 1929), Ferenc Fehér (1933–1994), György Márkus (b. 1934) and Maria Márkus, Australians had access to more European interpretations of Hegel and Marx. There was a significant opening to European social thought in Melbourne around the Icelandic historical sociologist, social philosopher and former student of Habermas, Jóhann Árnason (b. 1940), who came to La Trobe University in 1976. William Doniela, trained at the University of Freiburg, worked on Hegel at the University of Newcastle, and Jan T. J. Srzednicki, at the University of Melbourne, published on the Austrian philosopher Franz Brentano.[116] Phenomenology was studied at several universities and Max Deutscher (b. 1937), among others, worked on Husserl, while interest was also taken in the work of the Czech phenomenologist Jan Patočka (1907–1977).

From the 1980s there was significant interest in German philosophy at the University of Sydney, the University of New South Wales, the University of Tasmania, and at the Australian National University, but its impact on religious thought has been very slow. Some Australians worked on the contemporary significance of German philosophers, mainly Benjamin, Bloch, Heidegger, Arendt and Schelling,[117] often with an eye

---

Australasian Journal of Psychology and Philosophy 12 (1934): 62–72.
115 E. Morris Miller, *Kant's Doctrine of Freedom* (Melbourne: George Robertson, 1913); *The Basis of Freedom: A Study of Kant's Theory* (Sydney: Australasian Association of Psychology and Philosophy, 1924); *Moral Law and the Highest Good* (Melbourne: Macmillan, 1928).
116 J. T. J. Srzednicki, *Franz Brentano's Analysis of Truth* (The Hague: Nijhoff, 1965).
117 See, among other texts, A. Benjamin, *Working with Walter Benjamin: Recovering a Political Philosophy* (Edinburgh: Edinburgh University Press, 2013); W. Hudson, *The Marxist Philosophy of Ernst Bloch* (London: Macmillan, 1982); J. Malpas, *Heidegger's Topology: Being, Place, World* (Cambridge, Mass.: MIT Press, 2007); S. G. Crowell and J. Malpas (ed.), *Transcendental Heidegger* (Palo Alto: Stanford University Press, 2007); M. Deutscher, *Judgment after Arendt* (Aldershot: Ashgate, 2007); and P. D. Bubbio and P. Redding (eds.), *Religion After Kant: God and Culture in the Idealist Era* (Cambridge: Cambridge Scholars Publishing, 2012).

on the religious implications of their thought. At the University of Sydney, Paul Redding (b. 1948) imported the American pragmatic interpretation of German idealism into Australia and did original work on Hegelian thought and German idealist philosophy of logic.[118] Although personally an atheist, Redding argues that God is a fact of reason.[119] Redding's interpretation of philosophy as the self-knowledge of reason offers the prospect of contributions to religious thought that go beyond the impasses of theism and atheism. Paradoxically, his work in some ways returns to themes explored by Scottish idealist philosophers in the nineteenth century, especially those who, like Edward Caird and Pringle-Pattison, saw a convergence between Scottish philosophy and Hegel's idealism.

Overall, religious thought and philosophy have not come together in Australia as they might, especially not with regard to the specific problems and concerns of Australian society. Most philosophy has been divorced from concerns with place, although this is changing with the work of Jeff Malpas (b. 1958)[120] Religious thought, for its part, has often relied heavily on literature in English, turning only to French and German philosophical resources as they have been taken up in English-language works, initially by the Scottish idealists and then by American and British scholars. Reception of Russian philosophical thought has been limited, although major figures, such as Lev Shestov (1866–1938) and Nikolai Berdyaev (1874–1948), are cited in translation. In recent decades religious intellectuals in Australia have become more aware of the potential of Asian philosophies to recast traditional religious questions, thanks in part to journals such as *Sophia*, and in part to high-quality work on Indian, Tibetan and Chinese philosophy by philosophers in Australia, which often questions the metaphysical assumptions of Western Christianity. Nonetheless, a sustained engagement with Asian philosophies is yet to come. On the other hand, as this chapter has shown, some religious intellectuals have negotiated the religion–

---

[118] P. Redding, *Hegel's Hermeneutics* (Ithaca, NY: Cornell University Press, 1996); *The Logic of Affect* (Ithaca, NY: Cornell University Press, 1999); *Analytical Philosophy and the Return of Hegelian Thought* (Cambridge: Cambridge University Press, 2007); and *Continental Idealism: Leibniz to Nietzsche* (London: Routledge, 2009).

[119] P. Redding, "Kantian Origins: One Possible Path from Transcendental Idealism to a Post-Kantian Theology," in Bubbio and Redding, *Religion After Kant*, ch. 1.

[120] Malpas explores the holy without use of religious terms, making extensive use of an individual interpretation of Heideggerian topology. He has argued for the importance of place with nonmundane characteristics in several books, including *Place and Experience: A Philosophical Topography* (Cambridge: Cambridge University Press, 1999), *Heidegger's Topology, and Heidegger and the Thinking of Place: Explorations in the Topology of Being* (Cambridge, Mass: MIT Press, 2012).

philosophy interaction in creative ways and produced imaginative and courageous work that is internationally recognised, and others have made substantial contributions to the philosophy of religion. It seems likely that further receptions in Australia of global philosophical resources and further developments in analytical philosophy will offer opportunities for richer interaction between religious thought and philosophy in the future.

Chapter V

THEOLOGY IN DEVELOPMENT

Theology in Australia has a rich and complex history, but it has received relatively little scholarly attention.¹ My discussion emphasises the extensive presence of theological resources, the quality of theological discussion, and the gradual emergence of independent theology, as confidence grew and as more attention was paid to local contexts and Australia's location in the Asia-Pacific region. I do not address the technicalities of theology as such; nor do I discuss the substantial contributions Australians have made to Biblical studies,² except where the theological import seems primary.

Cultural Capital

A capacity for theological controversy emerged relatively early in Australia. As the colonies consolidated, theological writings arrived in both Australia and New Zealand.³ In the nineteenth and early twentieth centuries, Australians interested in religious ideas were generally familiar with debates in Britain and the United States. There were caches of books and

---

1 See, however, R. Banks, "Fifty Years of Theology in Australia, 1915–1965. Part One," *Colloquium* 9, no. 1 (1976): 36–42. and "Part Two" 9, no 2 (1977): 7–16; E. Osborn, "Tendencies in Australian Theology," *Colloquium* 12, no. 1 (1979): 2–16, and "Variety in Australian Theology," *Australian Biblical Review* 34 (1986): 59–64; G. P. Shaw, "Beyond Discipline?: The Historical Context of Theological Thought in Australia," *St Mark's Review* 133 (1988): 14–20; and A. Hamilton, "200 Years of Australian Theology," *Compass* 22 (1988): 32–8.
2 William Dalton, Leon Morris, Frank Anderson, John Painter, Anthony Campbell, Gerald O'Collins, Francis Moloney, Brendan Byrne, Norman Habel, Dorothy Lee, and Elaine Wainwright are among Australia's internationally recognised Biblical scholars.
3 Contact between Australian and New Zealand theologians was extensive, some of it through meetings of the Australian and New Zealand Society for Theological Studies, see R. Campbell, "The Philosophical Environment for Theologising in Australia," in *Australian and New Zealand Religious History 1788–1988: A Collection of Papers and Addresses Delivered at the 11th Joint Conference of the Australian and New Zealand Society of Theological Schools and Society for Theological Studies … September 1988*, ed. R. S. M. Withycombe (Canberra: Australian and New Zealand Society of Theological Schools and Society for Theological Studies, 1988), 33–43.

journal articles in university libraries, in theological colleges,[4] and in institutions associated with religious orders. The number of languages theology students learnt – Hebrew, Greek, Latin, French, Italian or German – admittedly to varying levels of mastery, is often forgotten, and the Catholic religious orders selected their most talented recruits to send to Ireland, Italy, France, Belgium and Germany. The Jesuits provided a liberal classical education for the Catholic élite and religious orders, such as the Redemptorists, Marists, Dominicans, Sacred Heart, Columbans, Carmelites, Franciscans, Augustinians and Loreto, had European-educated professionals in their ranks, many of whom studied in Rome or at Louvain in Belgium.[5] Luther Seminary in Adelaide had a major German theological library, and the Greek Orthodox imported significant theological resources.

In the twentieth century, theology was studied in most major cities in Australia, although theology was not taught in universities until after 1960, before which religion was often unwelcome in Australian universities, partly because of the widespread sectarianism found in the nineteenth century. This may have delayed the development of original theological thought and established conditions that were different from those in the United States, where Chairs of Theology were relatively common in universities. It also meant that seminaries and training colleges were dominated by the pastoral needs of the churches.[6] Small concentrations of theologians, church historians and biblical scholars kept abreast of international developments, but their influence was limited. For colonial Australia's first 150 years, Australian theologians were intellectually oriented towards Britain, Europe and the United States. Many studied at British, European or American universities, often publishing a major book based on their doctoral studies and placing articles in the best international journals. Returning to Australia, expert in ancient and often modern languages, their cultural capital sometimes made

---

4   These included St. Patrick's in Manly, Ormond College in Melbourne, and St. Andrew's College, Leigh College and Camden College in Sydney.
5   U.M.L. Bygott, *With Pen and Tongue: The Jesuits in Australia* (Carlton, Vic.: Melbourne University Press, 1980); D. Strong, *Jesuits in Australia: An Ethnographic History of the Society of Jesus in Australia* (Richmond, Vic.: Aurora, 1995); E. Lea-Scarlett, *Riverview, A History* (Sydney: Hale and Iremonger, 1989); and G. Dening, *Xavier: A Centenary Portrait* (Kew, Vic.: Old Xaverians Association, 1978). For education abroad, see J. Franklin, *Corrupting the Youth: A History of Philosophy in Australia* (Paddington, NSW: Macleay Press, 2003), ch. 4.
6   G. Treloar (ed.), *The 'Furtherance of Religious Beliefs': Essays on the History of Theological Education in Australia* (Sydney: Centre for the Study of Australian Christianity for the Evangelical History Association of Australia, 1997).

it hard for them to relate to members of their own denominations, let alone to the wider Australian public.

In the twentieth century several international theologians visited Australia and a few of them stayed for long periods. Hans Küng, John Macquarrie, Eduard Schweizer, Dietrich Ritschl, Fritz Buri, Francis Fiorenza and Oliver Donovan were among those who came. The Scottish theologian John McIntyre (1916–2005), for example, was educated in Scotland, but was Professor of Theology at St. Andrew's Theological Hall in Sydney from 1946 to 1956 before becoming Professor of Divinity at the University of Edinburgh and Moderator of the General Assembly of the Church of Scotland. McIntyre worked through the quarrel between Swiss Reformed theologian Karl Barth and his former ally, Emil Brunner (1889–1966), over the possibility of natural theology based on analogy. He left a sophisticated body of thought about the relationship between theology and history, on which many Australian Protestants drew. Another Presbyterian, Crawford Miller (1913–2001), a high churchman, brought a high level of theological learning to Sydney, although he published little.[7] The presence of such figures encouraged Australian theologians to follow international debates and to read theological literature in German. It did not encourage them to attempt to lead such debates.

As theological expertise consolidated, a rich theological culture developed in the twentieth century,[8] evident in various theological journals, especially *Pacifica: Australasian Theological Studies*, edited in Melbourne. *Pacifica* published substantive articles by internationally well-regarded Australian theologians and Biblical scholars, such as John Honner, Neil Ormerod, Patricia Fox, Maryanne Confoy, Norman Habel, Merrill Kitchen and Denis Edwards. Other journals such as *Australian Catholic Record*, *Australian eJournal of Theology*, *Colloquium*, and *St. Mark's Review* diffused an understanding of current theological debates among religious audiences. Australian theologians also proved excellent ecumenists (James Haire, Robert Gribben, Charles Sherlock, Peter Carnley, Michael Putney, John D'Arcy May, John Thornhill).[9]

---

7   See Richard Campbell's obituary for Miller in the *Sydney Morning Herald*, 16 July 2001.
8   Few have attempted to acknowledge the originality of Australian theologians. For two preliminary Protestant efforts, see G. Lilburne, "Australian Theology: Protestant Contributions," *Colloquium* 28, no. 2 (1996): 19–30, and G. R. Treloar, "Three Contemporary Christian Radicals in Australia: Robert Banks, Stuart Piggin, and Bruce Kaye," in *Agendas for Australian Anglicanism: Essays in Honour of Bruce Kaye*, ed. T. Frame and G. R. Treloar (Adelaide: ATF Press, 2006), ch. 8.
9   See, for example, J. D'Arcy May, *After Pluralism: Towards an Interreligious Ethic* (Münster: LIT-Verlag, 2000).

Three central questions for Australian theologians in the twentieth century were: What is the nature of the church?, What is the nature of the Trinity?, and What is meant by 'mission'? Theologians responded to these questions in different ways.

Ecclesiology

Much of the early theology in Australia was evangelical. From the first colonial chaplains (Richard Johnson, Samuel Marsden and William Cowper) on, evangelicals attempted to rethink the nature of mission in the new context. Often this took the form of social concern. The first chaplain of the New South Wales prison colony, Richard Johnson, for example, was engaged in several forms of social welfare. The Baptists were also in the vanguard of attempts to develop a theology to transform the social world, combining influences from the London evangelist C. H. Spurgeon (1834–1892) with elements of the Anabaptist tradition and the Baptist seminary at Rüschlikon in Switzerland.[10] As well as the Particular Baptist Calvinist views of Henry Dowling (1780–1869) in Tasmania and the mystical Quaker sympathies of G. H. Morling (1891–1974) in New South Wales, a social gospel tradition associated with Samuel Pearce Carey (1862–1953) flourished in Melbourne. The Baptist tradition has been continued by a range of Christian activists, including Timothy Costello in Melbourne, and in Queensland by Athol Gill (1937–1993), who studied under the Swiss Baptist theologian Eduard Schweizer at Rüschlikon and identified Christianity with radical discipleship, the critique of social and economic structures, and cooperating with God in initiating a new order.[11] Although Americanised theology, preaching and music came to dominate in many Baptist churches, the more intellectual tradition, oriented to social justice, survives in Melbourne and Canberra, where it is represented by the German Australian Baptist theologian Thorwald Lorenzen (b. 1936), who strives in his studies of the Trinity to relate Christian spirituality to justice concerns and effective participation in the contemporary world.[12]

---

10   On the Baptists, see J.D. Bollen, *Australian Baptists: A Religious Minority* (London: Baptist Historical Society, 1975) and K. Manley, *From Woolloomooloo to 'Eternity': A History of Australian Baptists*, 2 vols. (Milton Keynes: Paternoster, 2006).
11   Gill set up Christian communities, including the House of the Gentle Bunyip; see A. Gill, *Life on the Road: The Gospel Basis for a Messianic Lifestyle* (Homebush West, NSW: Lancer Books, 1989) and D. Neville (ed.), *Prophecy and Passion: Essays in Honour of Athol Gill* (Hindmarsh, SA: Australian Theological Forum, 2002), ch. 1.
12   T. Lorenzen, *Resurrection and Discipleship: Interpretative Models, Biblical Reflections, Theological Consequences* (New York: Orbis, 1995) and *Resurrection, Discipleship, Justice: Affirming the Resurrection Jesus Christ Today* (Macon, GA: Smyth & Helwys, 2003).

Concerns with context and mission also led Sydney evangelicals to make contributions to church practice. Part of the background can be found in the federal theology imported from Northern Ireland by T. C. Hammond, Principal of Moore College and Grand Master of the Loyal Orange Institution in New South Wales. Federal theology was a development in Calvinism whose adherents read the Scriptures in terms of a series of covenants between God and man. Hammond's theology, however, was more eclectic than this might suggest and his ecclesiology was closer to that of the sixteenth-century Anglican divine, Richard Hooker (1554–1600) and, indeed, the Book of Common Prayer, than was later common among evangelicals in Sydney.[13] Similarly, although he tended to a strong form of Biblical rationalism and was opposed to any 'philosophic scheme', Hammond's culture and social views were broader than has sometimes been suggested and his legacy to the Sydney archdiocese was perhaps less in the area of doctrine than in apologetical style.[14]

Canon David Broughton Knox (1916–1994) continued this style, advancing a distinctive evangelical view of ecclesiology, based on the primacy of the local church. Of Northern Irish descent and with Brethren elements in his background, Knox was an Oxford-trained historian, learned in Protestant understandings of 'faith' in the reign of Henry VIII, who identified with Calvinist federal theology, in general, and with William Tyndale in particular.[15] Knox was also influenced by Scottish philosophical realism, by the rationalism and literalism prevailing at Princeton Seminary in the United States under the conservative leadership of Benjamin Warfield, and by an emphasis on coherence, sometimes associated with philosophy in Sydney. As a philosophical realist, Knox believed in a single truth that corresponded with the relations prevailing in reality.[16] In the spirit of the Princeton Seminary, he opposed the subjectivism of modernist theologians and argued that the revelation of God consisted of propositions that could be articulated in preaching. According to Knox, metaphor was the mother of heresies, and

---

13 For a sympathetic view, see J. McIntosh, "Anglican Evangelicalism in Sydney 1897–1953: the Thought and Influence of Three Moore College Principals – Nathaniel Jones, DJ Davies and TC Hammond" (PhD thesis, University of New South Wales, 2014).

14 T. C. Hammond, *In Understanding Be Men*, 5th ed. (London: Inter-Varsity Fellowship, 1954).

15 D. B. Knox, *The Doctrine of Faith in the Reign of Henry VIII* (London: J. Clarke, 1961); *Justification by Faith* (London: Church Book Room Press, 1959); and *The Everlasting God* (Welwyn: Evangelical, 1982).

16 D. B. Knox, "Propositional Revelation, the Only Revelation," in *D. Broughton Knox: Selected Works*, vol. 1: *The Doctrine of God* (Sydney: Matthias Media, 2001), 307–18.

human religions were the products of man's rebellion against God.[17] This revelational positivism could make Knox seem fierce, but he also defended what might be called a form of evangelical Catholicism, for which the true church was a heavenly reality and denominationalism was a false sacralisation of purely human arrangements.[18] For Knox, Christianity was a matter of obedience to God and he did not hesitate to argue against the ordination of women and for male supremacy within the household.[19] After initial reservations, he also came to sympathise to some extent with apartheid and ended his days working for the Church of England in South Africa.

Knox's views helped shape a distinctive Sydney Anglicanism, which proved influential internationally. Knox's critics, some of them leading evangelicals (Robert Banks, Graham Cole, Bill Lawton), charged that Knox made no attempt to take account of theological research or Biblical scholarship, that his writings ignored major scholarly contributions of international renown, that he used crucial terms such as 'faith' inconsistently, and that he had no developed theology of the Holy Spirit.[20] Nonetheless, Knox's combative style was influential, despite the fact that views sometimes depended on a literalist account of meaning. Consistent with this, Knox's approach to the nature of the church gained some exegetical support from his colleague D. W. B. Robinson (b. 1922), a classical philologist and a careful New Testament scholar, who became the Anglican Archbishop of Sydney and a statesman of Australian Evangelicalism. Educated at Cambridge, where he worked with British Biblical scholars C. F. D. Moule and C. H. Dodd, Robinson focused on the nature of the church as an assembly, on the distinction in the New Testament between Jews and Gentiles, and on the authority of the New Testament canon. He used philology to determine what he took to be the 'original intent' of New Testament texts.[21] Influenced by the distinguished German New Testament scholar Oscar Cullman (1902–1999),

---

17 Knox, *The Everlasting God*, 161.
18 M. Cameron, *An Enigmatic Life: David Broughton Knox, Father of Contemporary Sydney Anglicanism* (Brunswick East, Vic.: Acorn Press, 2006), 296–7.
19 For a committed feminist view, see M. Porter, *The New Puritans: The Rise of Fundamentalism in the Anglican Church* (Carlton, Vic.: Melbourne University Press, 2006) and *Sydney Anglicans and the Threat to World Anglicanism: The Sydney Experiment* (Farnham: Ashgate, 2011).
20 R. Banks, "The Theology of D. Broughton Knox – A Preliminary Estimate," in *God Who is Rich in Mercy: Essays Presented to D. B. Knox*, ed. P.T. O'Brien and D.G. Peterson (Homebush West, NSW: Lancer, 1986), 377–403; and E. F. Osborn, "Reason and Revelation," *Australian Biblical Review* 8 (1960), 29–37.
21 D. W. B. Robinson, *Faith's Framework: The Structure of New Testament Theology* (Sutherland, NSW: Albatross, 1985) and *Donald Robinson: Selected Works*, ed. P. G.

Robinson developed a typological reading of the Bible that assumed that it was possible to relate each Biblical text to every other.[22]

Knox's follower, Peter Jensen (b. 1943), gave Knox's theology practical expression as Archbishop of Sydney. Trained like Knox as an historian at Oxford, Jensen advanced a Puritan rationalism designed to convert a new generation for which the trappings of British liturgical Anglicanism had become alien. Like Knox, Jensen follows federalist covenantal theology and insists that revelation involves information as well as relationship.[23] Nonetheless, Jensen now rejects Knox's creationism in favour of a theistic view of evolution and has refined his approach to the Trinity in response to attacks on what were construed as his subordinationist views. In his later writings he deviates from Knox's rejection of religious experience and human religions and admits general as well as special revelation, while insisting that general revelations are not 'saving'.[24] He also accepts that Biblical research and the progress of the sciences may require some reformulations of traditional positions.[25] Jensen combines social and moral conservatism with a commitment to the preaching of the Word at the expense of the Eucharist. He also supports lay presidency and admission to communion without baptism and confirmation. He has confronted Lambeth Palace on the issues of women's ordination, male supremacy in the family and homosexuality.[26] Although some see in him a Puritan hostility to liturgical forms, vestments, art and ceremonies,[27] Jensen's minimalism has what might be called a 'postreligious' dimension:

> I don't really want to talk about the institutional church or even religion. Such things are of marginal interest to me. Even though I quite like

---

Bolt, and M. D. Thompson (Sydney: Australian Church Record, 2008). For studies, see D. Peterson and J. Pryor, *In the Fullness of Time: Biblical Studies in Honour of Archbishop David Robinson* (Homebush West, NSW: Anzea, 1992), especially xvii–xxviii.

22 G. Goldsworthy, *Christ-Centred Biblical Theology: Hermeneutical Foundations and Principles* (Downers Grove: InterVarsity Press, 2012), chapters 9 and 10.

23 P. Jensen, *The Revelation of God* (Leicester: Inter-Varsity Press, 2002), 82, 90–94; see also P. Jensen, "An Agenda for Australian Evangelical Theology," *Reformed Theological Review* 42, no. 1 (1983): 1–9.

24 Jensen, *The Revelation of God*, 85–7, 98–108.

25 See P. Jensen, *The Future of Jesus* (Kingsford, NSW: Matthias Media, 2008); *The Revelation of God and At the Heart of the Universe: What Christians Believe* (Leicester: Inter-Varsity Press, 1991).

26 See Jensen's views on homosexuality in "Ordination and the Practice of Homosexuality," in *Doctrine Panel of the Anglican Church of Australia, Faithfulness in Fellowship: Reflections on Homosexuality and the Church* (Mulgrave, Vic.: John Garratt Publishing, 2001), 161–80.

27 For a critical account, see Porter, *The New Puritans*, and *Sydney Anglicans and the Threat to World Anglicanism*.

going to church, I find it hard to like the institutional organisation. And I don't really think of myself as a religious person.[28]

In his later writings Jensen accepts that Jesus' primary concern was with the Kingdom of God rather than with personal salvation. However, he understands Christian praxis in terms of a covenantal life-style, based on obedience and love. It remains to be seen whether Sydney approaches to ecclesiology will be enduring, especially since scholars influenced by Knox and Robinson, such as Graeme Goldsworthy and William Dumbrell, are beginning to give way to scholars more sympathetic to the dialectical theology of Karl Barth and the Greek Church Fathers, which turn far less on propositional revelation.[29] The tendency among evangelical theologians, however, to believe that Christian theology can be derived from a rigorous reading of the Scriptures remains strong.[30]

Another contribution to evangelical ecclesiology was made by the Sydney historian, Robert Banks (b. 1931). At Clare College, Cambridge in the 1960s Banks completed a doctorate on Jesus' attitude to the law. Subsequent studies of Paul and the house churches in the New Testament led him to reject the traditional understanding of the church and to attempt to restore what he took to be the church of the New Testament.[31] Banks promoted a home church movement that dispensed with the need for clergy and promoted Christianity beyond denominationalism and the church on the hill. He advocated a radical theology of everyday life and the ideal of theology of, by, and for the people – as opposed to theology for the university lecture hall. In a stream of semi-popular books, he related Christianity to money, technology, media and other popular concerns. Banks' work on these issues has been taken up in the United States, where he was the Foundation Professor in the Ministry of the Laity at Fuller Seminary in Los Angeles in the 1990s.

Theologians belonging to other traditions have also made contributions to ecclesiology. Anglo-Catholics wrote studies of the Eucharist with

---

28 Jensen, *The Future of Jesus*, 11.
29 M. Jensen, "Krisis? Kritik?: Judgment and Jesus in the Theology of Rowan Williams," in M. Russell (ed.), *On Rowan Williams: Critical Essays*, ed. M. Russell (Eugene, OR: Cascade Books, 2009), 68–84; cf B. Myers, *Christ the Stranger: The Theology of Rowan Williams* (Edinburgh: T. & T. Clark, 2012).
30 C. Sherlock, *Words and the Word: Case Studies in Using Scripture* (Preston: Mosaic Press, 2013).
31 R. Banks, *Paul's Idea of Community: The Early House Churches in their Historical Setting* (Homebush West, NSW: Lancer, 1979).

ecclesiological dimensions.³² Gabriel Hebert (1886–1963), for example, a monk of the Society of the Sacred Mission, wrote learned books on liturgical, eucharistic and ecclesiastical matters, as well as *Fundamentalism and the Church of God* (1957), which had a major impact in the United States. There was also a strong ecclesial dimension to *The Structure of Resurrection Belief* (1987), by Archbishop Peter Carnley (b. 1937). Drawing on the Greek Fathers, Carnley denied that the Resurrection could be adequately understood merely as an historical event, not out of scepticism, but from a conviction that the risen Jesus was revealed from heaven. The emergence in 1977 of the Uniting Church of Australia from the merger of a group of mainstream Protestant churches also had an ecclesiological basis in the work of the Davis McCaughey (1914–2005) and in the work of contemporary theologians such as James Haire, William Emilsen and D'Arcy Wood. In due course, the Uniting Church played a role in the struggle for reconciliation and land rights in Australia and was consistently at the forefront in advocating for social justice.³³ Among Catholics, there were few original approaches to ecclesiology, with the exception of the work of the Brisbane-based theologian Ormond Rush (b. 1950). Rush applies German reception hermeneutics to theological contexts and argues for recovering 'the sense of the faithful' (*sensus fidelium*),³⁴ with the implication that the teachings of the Popes need to be received by the church in order to have validity.

The Trinity

The need for original work on the Trinity was recognised by theologians from many churches and taken up most powerfully perhaps in Catholic theology, where it was associated with the need to modernise the presentation of the Church's teachings. For much of Australia's history, Catholic theology was taken from Roman manuals and scholastic philosophy, although there were elements of Patristic theology and French spirituality as well. After the Second Vatican Council, however, Catholic theology blossomed under the influence of a new awareness of the implications of Biblical Studies and a greater freedom to express a diversity of views. Many Catholic theologians

---

32 Anglicans were engaged extensively in theologies of the Eucharist – from high-church theologians (Gabriel Hebert, Keith Rayner, Peter Carnley) to extreme nominalist (Broughton Knox, D. W. B. Robinson, Peter Jensen, Robert Doyle). For details, see B. Douglas, *A Companion to Anglican Eucharistic Theology* (Leiden: Brill, 2012), vol. 2.
33 W.W. and S. Emilsen, (eds.), *The Uniting Church in Australia: The First 25 Years* (Armadale, Vic.: Circa, 2003).
34 O. Rush, *The Eyes of Faith: The Sense of the Faithful and the Church's Reception of Revelation* (Washington, DC: Catholic University of America Press, 2009).

responded to the need to modernise the presentation of Catholic doctrine. The theologian Charles Hill (1931–2007), for example, sought to use discourse analysis and a Christology that identified Christ with the Wisdom figure of the inter-testamental Biblical literature in order to generate a believable Christianity.[35] Likewise, Marist theologian John Thornhill (b. 1929), whose central concern was the theology of culture, wrote about the foundations of ecclesiology in *Sign and Promise: A Theology of the Church for a Changing World* (1988) and produced an ecumenically open and historically aware incarnational theology designed to be compatible with modernity.[36]

Among Catholic systematic theologians, renovation of the philosophical tradition known as Transcendental Thomism by the German Jesuit, Karl Rahner (1904–1984), and the writings of Canadian Jesuit Bernard Lonergan (1904–1984) were influential.[37] Rahner held that theology was anthropology and that all human beings have an unthematic perception of God. He taught Australian theologians to re-express traditional doctrines in contemporary terms. Lonergan proposed a version of transcendental method for which the subject could come to understand what it is to understand by self-appropriating the invariant normative patterns of the recurrent operations of conscious intentionality involved in all cognitive activity.[38] His radicalisation of Transcendental Thomism was taken up by Catholic intellectuals because he applied it to concerns Australian theologians faced: the nature of interpretation; the challenge of an evolutionary cosmology; the need to relate theology to the contemporary sciences; and the problem of how to develop a coherent version of interdisciplinarity. Drawing on these international resources, Catholic theologians sought to move way from revelational positivism or an approach that implied that what was later believed was somehow present in the Biblical resources. Instead, they sought to make allowance for human agency, change in the course of history, and the need to adapt to contemporary cultures.

---

35 R. C. Hill, *Mystery of Life: A Theology of Church* (Melbourne: Collins Dove, 1990); *Jesus and the Mystery of Christ: An Extended Christology* (North Blackburn, Vic.: Collins Dove, 1993).

36 J. Thornhill, *Modernity: Christianity's Estranged Child Reconstructed* (Grand Rapids, MI: W. B. Eerdmans, 2000); see also *Sign and Promise: A Theology of the Church for a Changing World* (London: Collins, 1988) and *Christian Mystery in the Secular Age: The Foundation and Task of Theology* (Westminster, MD: Christian Classics, 1991).

37 Lonergan's work made an impact through the work of Peter Beer at Canisius College in Sydney and through theologians studying at Boston College in the United States.

38 See B. Lonergan, *Understanding and Being: An Introduction and Companion to Insight: The Halifax Lectures*, ed. E. A. and M. D. Morelli (New York: Edwin Mellen, 1980). For other major texts, see E. A. and M. D. Morelli (eds.), *The Lonergan Reader* (Toronto: University of Toronto Press, 1997).

The turn to the Trinity in Australian theology was partly a response to the declining credibility of popular theism or the idea of God as a supreme being outside the universe who miraculously intervenes in it. It involved rethinking the Biblical evidence, reappropriating elements of the Greek Fathers, and opening up a historically new relation to Eastern Orthodoxy, which had always foregrounded a dynamic account of the Holy Spirit. By moving away from the tritheism of popular theology and rethinking the Trinity in process and relational terms, theologians were able to begin to overcome the dualism that has arguably distorted Latin Christianity and to reconnect theology with ecological and social concerns.

In this spirit, Brisbane-born Redemptorist Anthony Kelly (b. 1938), reasserts classical Christian claims in an idiom informed by both classical European theology and high cultural trends. A stylist and a poet, who draws on his training in Rome at the Anselmianum and at Boston College in the United States where he specialised in Lonergan studies, Kelly is attuned to the relations between faith and culture and has the capacity to enliven many traditional themes, including the notion of a natural law. His *An Expanding Theology*[39] and many subsequent books are outstanding texts in the correlationist mode advocated by the American Catholic theologian David Tracey. In his influential work, *The Trinity of Love*, Kelly defends a Thomist psychological analogy approach to the Trinity, based on an analogy between the faculties of the psyche and the three divine persons.[40] In *The Resurrection Effect* he deploys both Lonerganian categories and themes from philosophers writing in French, such as Levinas and Marion, to give a phenomenological and more experiential account of the Christian mysteries.[41] His student, Anne Hunt (b. 1952), has made an advance in Trinitarian theology by relating the Trinity to the Paschal mystery, as the Catholic tradition had largely failed to do, and is regarded internationally as an important theologian.[42]

Another transcendental theologian and follower of Rahner, Denis Edwards (b. 1943) developed an ecological creation theology, integrating Christology

---

39 See A. Kelly, *An Expanding Theology: Faith in a World of Connections* (Newtown, NSW: E. J. Dwyer, 1993).
40 A. Kelly, *The Trinity of Love: A Theology of the Christian God* (Wilmington, DE: Michael Glazier, 1989).
41 A. Kelly, *The Resurrection Effect: Transforming Christian Life and Thought* (Maryknoll, NY: Orbis Books, 2008).
42 A. Hunt, *The Trinity and the Paschal Mystery: A Development in Recent Catholic Theology* (Collegeville, MN: Liturgical Press, 1997); *Trinity: Nexus of the Mysteries of Christian Faith* (Maryknoll, NY: Orbis Books, 2005) and subsequent publications.

and Trinitarian theology with contemporary science and ecological concerns. Edwards defends a non-interventionist theism, for which God needs to be conceived in Trinitarian terms as *being in relation*, rather than as a supreme being outside the universe.[43] His theology is indebted to classic Christian writers such as Irenaeus (d. 202), Richard of St. Victor (d. 1173) and Bonaventure (1217–1274), all of whom developed cosmic Christologies. In Edward's cosmic Christology, which is indebted to contemporary American Catholic theological writing, Christianity is about the transformation of the universe. God works in the universe through secondary causes to bring nature to wholeness and healing. Edwards' Christology extends Teilhard de Chardin's visionary indications in more contemporary scientific and ecological terms and is close to Eastern Orthodox theology with its emphasis on cosmic mysticism, its doctrine of *theosis* or divinisation, and its account of the 'uncreated energies' through which God deals with humanity and acts in the world.

A third Rahnerian transcendentalist, David Coffey (b. 1934), who studied at the Ludwig Maximilian University in Munich under Karl Rahner and Michael Schmaus (1897–1993), developed a non-classical Christology drawing on Augustine's model of mutual love between the members of the Trinity, which differed from traditional Christologies in emphasising that Christ was led throughout by the Spirit. Coffey sought to replace the traditional processions model of the Trinity with a Christology 'from below', which took full account of Jesus' humanity. He also developed a new account of grace. Subsequently, Coffey became known for his mutualist theory of the Trinity, according to which the three persons were co-involved, rather than subordinate to each other, for which he was to a certain extent indebted to Anthony Kelly.[44] His work on the Trinity, which is generally referred to as 'Spirit Christology' had a major impact that has resulted in at least three monographs devoted to his work.[45]

---

43 D. Edwards, *Breath of Life: A Theology of the Creator Spirit* (Maryknoll, NY: Orbis Books, 2004); also *Human Experience of God* (New York: Paulist Press, 1983); *Jesus and the Cosmos* (Homebush, NSW: St Paul's Publications, 1991); *Made from Stardust: Exploring the Place of Human Beings within Creation* (North Blackburn, Vic.: Collins Dove, 1992); *Jesus, the Wisdom of God: An Ecological Theology* (Homebush, NSW: St Paul's Publications, 1995); and *The God of Evolution: A Trinitarian Theology* (New York: Paulist Press, 1999).

44 See, especially, D. Coffey, *Grace: The Gift of the Holy Spirit* (Manly, NSW: Catholic Institute, 1979) and *Deus Trinitas: The Doctrine of the Triune God* (Oxford: Oxford University Press, 1999).

45 R. Del Colle, *Christ and the Spirit: Spirit Christology in Trinitarian Perspective* (New York: Oxford University Press, 1994); D. O'Byrne, *Spirit Christology and Trinity in the Theology of David Coffey* (Bern: Peter Lang, 2010); and S. M. Studebaker, *The Trinitarian Vision of Jonathan Edwards and David Coffey* (Amherst, NY: Cambria Press, 2011).

A fourth Rahnerian, the distinguished Jesuit theological writer Gerald O'Collins (b. 1931), Emeritus Professor at the Pontifical Gregorian University in Rome, has had hundreds of papers published in international journals and has written or edited fifty-nine books, including works on the Trinity, local Christology and the salvation of all peoples.[46] Yet another Catholic theologian, indebted to both Rahner and Lonergan, layman Neil Ormerod (b. 1954), has criticised a range of Trinitarian theologies influenced by Eastern Orthodoxy and reasserted the logical superiority of the Thomist psychological model of the Trinity.[47] Taken together, Australian Catholic theologians have had an impact on contemporary Trinitarian theology worldwide and have addressed the question of how Christian doctrine can be renewed in a potentially post-theistic era. Their work shows the increasingly independent spirit of Australian theology.

Feminist Theology

The question of mission was addressed by theologians of all churches in Australia, but it acquired particular force when mission was associated with justice concerns and redefined with reference to the audiences being addressed. Australian theology changed when theologians were forced to rethink theological categories in more inclusive terms and to include feminist and gay perspectives. Feminist theologians have been significant in Australia, both as creative writers and as activists. They have introduced Christian women to the work of French feminist philosophers and their radical accounts of sexual difference, and to the hermeneutics of suspicion applied to Biblical texts by the Harvard feminist scripture scholar Elisabeth Schüssler Fiorenza (b. 1938). Australian feminist theological writers include Erin White (b. 1941) and Marie Tulip, editor of the feminist religious magazine *Magdalene*, Muriel Porter (b. 1948), Elizabeth Evatt (b. 1933), Elaine Lindsay (b. 1948) and Patricia Brennan (1944–2011).[48] More recently,

---

46   See G. O'Collins, *Jesus Today: Christology in an Australian Context* (New York: Paulist Press, 1986); *Christology: A Biblical, Historical, and Systematic Study of Jesus Christ* (Oxford: Oxford University Press, 1995); *Living Vatican II: The 21st Council for the 21st Century* (New York: Paulist Press, 2006); and *Salvation for All: God's Other Peoples* (Oxford: Oxford University Press, 2008).
47   N. Ormerod, *The Trinity: Retrieving the Western Tradition* (Milwaukee, WI: Marquette University Press, 2005).
48   See the special issue of *Pacifica* on "Feminist Theology: The Next Stage", ed. D. A. Lee and M. Porter, *Pacifica* 10, no. 2 (1997); see also E. Lindsay (ed.), *Towards a Feminist Theology: Papers and Proceedings from a National Conference called together by MOW, National WATAC, Women-Church, 18–20 August 1989, Collaroy Centre, Sydney*

leading Australian Biblical scholars, such as Elaine Wainwright (b. 1948) and Dorothy Lee (b. 1953), have offered fresh readings of New Testament texts and problematised the traditional reliance on male epistemologies.[49] Feminist theological scholars have also been at the forefront of theological attempts to rethink patriarchy, injustice and racism. Over several decades, Australian feminist theological scholars have contributed to rethinking the nature of the church, especially to debates about the ordination of women[50] and homosexuality. They have also attempted to develop conceptions of the divine with which women can identify, while avoiding ecclesiastical censure.[51]

Contextual Theology

Mission was also central to debate about the need to develop a theology suitable to Australia's geographic and cultural contexts. Here a major issue for Australian theologians was how to relate to Aboriginal law. Until the second half of the twentieth century, Australian theologians had only

---

(Helensburgh, NSW: Conference Committee, 1990); E. Lindsay (ed.), *Women Authoring Theology, Papers and Proceedings from a National Conference Called Together by MOW, National WATAC, Women-church, Feminist Uniting Network, 24–26 May 1991, Strathfield, Sydney* (Petersham, NSW: Conference Committee, 1992); M. Confoy, D. Lee, and J. Nowotny (eds.), *Freedom and Entrapment: Women Thinking Theology* (North Blackburn, Vic.: Dove, 1995); M. Joy and P. Magee (eds.), *Claiming our Rites: Studies in Religion by Australian Women Scholars* (Adelaide: AASR, 1994) and D. McRae-McMahon, *Everyday Passions: A Conversation of Living* (Sydney: ABC Books, 1998).

49 See E. M. Wainwright, *Shall We Look for Another: A Feminist Rereading of the Matthean Jesus* (Maryknoll, NY: Orbis Books, 1998); *Women Healing/Healing Women: The Genderization of Healing in Early Christianity* (London: Equinox, 2006); M.-T. Wacker and E. M. Wainwright (eds.), *Land Conflicts, Land Utopias* (London: SCM Press, 2007); E. M. Wainwright, L.-C. Susin and F. Wilfred (eds.), *Eco-Theology* (London: SCM Press, 2009); and P. L. Culbertson and E. M. Wainwright (eds.), *The Bible in/and Popular Culture: A Creative Encounter* (Atlanta: Society of Biblical Literature, 2010); see also D. A. Lee, *Hallowed in Truth and Love: Spirituality in the Johannine Literature* (Preston, Vic.: Mosaic, 2011).

50 The Movement for the Ordination of Women, led by the former medical missionary Patricia Brennan, made a significant contribution to the decision to ordain women in the Uniting Church and in parts of the Anglican Church; see M. Porter, *Women in the Church The Great Ordination Debate in Australia* (Ringwood, Vic.: Penguin, 1989).

51 M. Rose, *Freedom from Sanctified Sexism: Women Transforming the Church* (MacGregor, Qld: Allira, 1996); and also the work of the evangelical theologian Kevin Giles, *Women and their Ministry: A Case for Equal Ministries in the Church Today* (Melbourne: Dove, 1977) and *Created Woman: A Fresh Study of the Biblical Teaching* (Canberra: Acorn Press, 1985); A. Nichols (ed.), *The Bible and Women's Ministry: An Australian Dialogue* (Canberra: Acorn Press, 1990); and G. Davies, "Homosexuality in the New Testament.", in *Doctrine Panel of the Anglican Church of Australia, Faithfulness in Fellowship*, 63–74.

a limited understanding of Aboriginal law, largely because of the way Europeans represented Aboriginal beliefs and practices. Nineteenth- and early twentieth-century sociologists and anthropologists imposed European conceptions of religion, myth, magic and ritual on the substantially different pattern of ideas and practices that made up Aboriginal law.[52] Influenced by positivism and functionalism, they saw 'Aboriginal religion' as a form of pre-scientific and pre-logical consciousness. Christian missionaries were at first inclined to hold that Aboriginal people had no religion because they had no priesthood, sacrifices or services. In a related spirit, in his 1899 articles and his multivolume work, *The Golden Bough*, the British anthropologist James Frazer, argued that Aborigines had only 'magic' and not 'religion'.[53] Subsequently, the French sociologist Émile Durkheim, in his celebrated study of totemism in Australia, argued that there was Aboriginal religion, but that it was the most primitive and elementary form of human social organisation.[54] British anthropologist A. R. Radcliffe-Brown, the founding Professor of Anthropology at the University of Sydney from 1926 to 1931, adopted the functionalist view that Aboriginal religion was a manifestation of Aboriginal society rather than something important in itself.[55] Empathetic interpretations, on the other hand, were advanced by a range of writers open to the numinous. The Lutheran missionary Pastor C. F. T. Strehlow (1871–1922), in particular, emphasised the richness and inventiveness of the cultural forms he explored.[56] Strehlow's approach was challenged by the anthropologist Sir Walter Baldwin Spencer (1860–1929)

---

52   To be fair, Mircea Eliade, the Romanian doyen of religious studies still applied Western conceptions of 'religion' to Aboriginal law without embarrassment in his classic study, *Australian Religions: An Introduction* (Ithaca, NY: Cornell University Press, 1973).
53   J. G. Frazer, "The Origin of Totemism," *Fortnightly Review* 45 (1899): 647–65, 835–52); *The Golden Bough* (London: Macmillan, 1960), 72
54   E. Durkheim, *Les Formes Élémentaires de la Vie Religieuse: Le Système Totémique en Australie* (Paris: Presses Universitaires de France, 1960) (originally published 1912).
55   A. R. Radcliffe-Brown, "The Social Organization of Australian Tribes," *Oceania* 1 (1930), reprinted as *Oceania Monographs*, no. 1 (Melbourne: Macmillan, 1931).
56   C. F. T. Strehlow, *Die Aranda- und Loritja-Stämme in Zentral-Australien*, 5 vols (Frankfurt: Joseph Baur, 1907–1920). Other sympathetic studies were produced by A. P. Elkin, E. A. Worms, Phyllis Kaberry, Ursula McConnel, W. L. Warner and Géza Róheim; see E. A. Worms and H. Petri, *Australische Eingeborenen-Religionen* (1968), translated by M. J. Wilson, D. O'Donovan and M. Charlesworth as *Australian Aboriginal Religions* (Richmond, Vic.: Spectrum Publications for Nelen Yubu Missiological Unit, 1986); W. L. Warner, *A Black Civilization: A Social Study of an Australian Tribe* (New York: Harper & Brothers, 1937); P. M. Kaberry, *Aboriginal Woman, Sacred and Profane* (London: Routledge and Sons, 1939); and G. Róheim, *The Eternal Ones of the Dream: A Psychoanalytic Interpretation of Australian Myth and Ritual*

and the ethnographer Francis James Gillen (1855–1912). In *The Native Tribes of Central Australia*, *Native Tribes of the Northern Territory of Australia*, and *The Arunta*, Spencer and Gillen argued that Aborigines were primitives at a lower level of social development.[57]

A better understanding of Aboriginal law came slowly. A. P. Elkin, an Anglican priest and Professor of Anthropology at the University of Sydney, took an unusual position in defending a view of Aboriginal religion as 'Aboriginal philosophy'. He also undertook a study of Aboriginal high men and their spiritual powers.[58] His student, humanistic anthropologist W. E. H. Stanner (1905–1981), argued that Western approaches to ethnography threatened to trivialise what was unique and important in Aboriginal culture, which, he insisted, had high cultural status in its own right.[59] In the 1968 Boyer Lectures, Stanner called out the failure to incorporate black experience into the image of the national past as 'the great Australian silence'.[60] He rejected the reductionist methods favoured by most social scientists and sought to relate Aboriginal religion as high culture to the universality of transcendent value.[61] Stanner drew attention to the fact that European Australians refused to see the vast difference between Aboriginal and European culture and concepts, and insisted that, in their sacred activities,

---

(New York: International Universities Press, 1945). Kaberry's work was particularly outstanding for its treatment of gender roles and its recognition of the ritual life of Aboriginal women, issues that resisted easy interpretations in European terms.

57 B. Spencer, and F.J. Gillen, *The Native Tribes of Central Australia* (London: Macmillan, 1899) and *The Arunta: A Study of a Stone Age People*, 2 vols (London: Macmillan, 1927).B. Spencer, *Native Tribes of the Northern Territory of Australia* (London: Macmillan, 1914)

58 A. P. Elkin, *Aboriginal Men of High Degree: Initiation and Sorcery in the World's Oldest Tradition* (St. Lucia: University of Queensland Press, 1977). For Elkin's assimilationist views, see R. McGregor, "From Old Testament to New: A. P. Elkin on Christian Conversion and Cultural Assimilation," *Journal of Religious History* 25 (2001): 39–55.

59 See W. E. H. Stanner, "Religion, Totemism and Symbolism," in *Aboriginal Man in Australia*, ed. R. M. and C. H. Berndt (Sydney: Angus & Robertson, 1965), 207–37; *On Aboriginal Religion* (Sydney: University of Sydney, 1966); *Whiteman Got No Dreaming: Essays 1938–1973* (Canberra: Australian National University Press, 1979), 17; and R. Manne (ed.), *The Dreaming and Other Essays* (Melbourne: Black Inc, Agenda, 2009)

60 W. E. H. Stanner, *After the Dreaming: Black and White Australians: An Anthropologist's View* (1968 Boyer Lectures) (Sydney: Australian Broadcasting Commission, 1968), 27.

61 P. Sutton, "Stanner's Veil: Transcendence and the Limits of Scientific Inquiry," in *An Appreciation of Difference: WEH Stanner and Aboriginal Australia*, ed. M. Hinkson and J. Beckett (Canberra: Australian Aboriginal Studies Press, 2008), 115–25.

Aborigines achieved a magnification of life.[62] He also argued that Aboriginal societies demonstrated a spirit of cooperation and kinship from which Western societies could learn.[63] Stanner's work, although not without its difficulties,[64] was a major step forward.

Once it was suggested that there were many 'Aboriginal religions' and not just one; that Aboriginal law varied around the continent; and that 'Aboriginal religion' was not changeless or static, but evolving, interactive and sometimes coloured by contact with Christian missionaries, detailed studies made generalisations difficult. It emerged that account had to be taken of major regional differences and of the practices of Torres Strait Islanders.[65] It was also argued that the term translated as 'the Dreamtime' had no temporal implications. Similarly, Aboriginal ancestral beings proved difficult to assimilate into European ideas of spirits, were not clearly separated from the material world and were not what Europeans understood by 'deities'.[66] These issues were difficult to resolve, partly because some Aboriginal people internalised European language and concepts to some extent and made claims about their culture and spirituality that were adapted to European ideas, especially in the context of political and cultural struggles, including for land rights. A literature on Aboriginal spirituality, written by Christians, emerged, in which the distinctiveness of Aboriginal cosmology and philosophy were to some extent elided.[67] Indeed, there were tensions at times

---

62 J. Beckett and M. Hinkson, "'Going More Than Half Way to Meet Them': On the Life and Legacy of WEH Stanner," in *An Appreciation of Difference*, 1–26, especially 17.
63 Stanner, *After the Dreaming*, 15.
64 For Stanner's commitment to transcendent value, see "Part 2. In Pursuit of Transcendent Value," in *An Appreciation of Difference*.
65 See R.M. Berndt, *Kunapipi: A Study of an Australian Aboriginal Religious Cult* (Melbourne: F.W. Cheshire, 1951); *The Sacred Site: The Western Arnhem Land Example* (Canberra: Australian Institute of Aboriginal Studies, 1970), *Australian Aboriginal Religion* (Leiden: Brill, 1974); R. M. and C. H. Berndt, *The World of the First Australians*, (Sydney: Ure Smith, 1964); T. Swain, *Interpreting Aboriginal Religion: An Historical Account* (Bedford Park, SA: Australian Association for the Study of Religion, 1985); M. Charlesworth, "The Invention of Australian Aboriginal Religions," in *Religious Inventions: Four Essays* (Oakleigh, Vic.: Cambridge University Press, 1997); S. Poirier, *A World of Relationships: Itineraries, Dreams, and Events in the Australian Western Desert* (Toronto: University of Toronto Press, 2005); and H. Onnudottir, A. Possamai and B. Turner, *Religious Change and Indigenous Peoples: The Making of Religious Identities* (Farnham: Ashgate, 2013). On Christian missionaries, see T. Swain and D.B. Rose (eds.), *Aboriginal Australians and Christian Missions* (Bedford Park, SA: Australian Association for the Study of Religions, 1988).
66 T. Swain, "Dreaming, Whites and the Australian Landscape: Some Popular Misconceptions," *Journal of Religious History* 15 (1989): 345–50.
67 See A. Pattel-Gray (ed.), *Aboriginal Spirituality: Past, Present, Future* (Blackburn, Vic.: HarperCollins Religious, 1996).

between European discourses that often failed to grasp that Aboriginal conceptions did not map onto European notions of 'religion' or 'spirit', and Aboriginal interpretations of their traditions.[68]

The anthropologist Deborah Bird Rose (b. 1946) addressed these issues with exceptional clarity. Based on her extensive fieldwork among the Yarralin people of the Victoria River region in the Northern Territory, Rose denied that Aboriginals accepted the dualistic notions that Europeans attributed to them. In an attempt to reduce European misunderstandings, she declared:

> I use the term 'spirit' with some trepidation. The English term cannot but signal a body-soul dichotomy which is inappropriate to the Yarralin context. Were I able to find a better term, I would avoid 'spirit' altogether, but as it is, I must state emphatically that spirit is immanent in body and even death does not wholly disrupt this immediacy. Death terminates the unique, separating out different parts, but spirit lives and continues to be embodied. As we will see, Yarralin people believe that a human being embodies several spirits at least one of which remains embodied on earth; this idea is widespread across Aboriginal Australia.[69]

European Australian theologians, however, have largely lacked the training to address such matters. The challenge of Aboriginal law to Christian theology has been substantial. As Swain and others have argued,[70] Aborigines confronted Europeans with radically different ideas of place, time and agency and with a nonmundane, nontheistic system of action, based on the sacredness of the land, its animals and fauna, and a rich meaning system

---

68   For some of the differences between Aboriginal law, for which the spirits are intra-worldly material beings, and Christian claims, see W. H. Edwards, *Recovering Spirit: Exploring Aboriginal Spirituality* (Charles Strong Memorial Trust Lecture, 2001) (Adelaide: Charles Strong Memorial Trust, 2002), 23ff.
69   D. B. Rose, *Dingo Makes Us Human: Life and Land in an Australian Aboriginal Culture* (Cambridge: Cambridge University Press, 1992), 58; see also D. B. Rose, "Consciousness and Responsibility in an Aboriginal Religion," in *Traditional Aboriginal Society: A Reader*, ed. W. H. Edwards (Melbourne: Macmillan, 1987); *Nourishing Terrains: Australian Aboriginal Views of Landscape and Wilderness* (Canberra: Australian Heritage Commission, 1996); *Reports from a Wild Country: Ethics for Decolonisation* (Sydney: UNSW Press, 2004); D. B. Rose and R. Davis (eds), *Dislocating the Frontier: Essaying the Mystique of the Outback* (Canberra: ANU E Press, 2005); D.B. Rose with S. D'Amico, *Country of the Heart: An Indigenous Australian Homeland* (Canberra: Aboriginal Studies Press, 2011); and D. Mowaljarlai with J. Malnic, *Yorro Yorro=Everything Standing Up Alive: Spirit of the Kimberley* (Broome, WA: Magabala Books, 1993).
70   T. Swain, *Aboriginal Religions in Australia: A Bibliographical Survey* (New York: Greenwood Press, 1991) and *A Place For Strangers: Towards A History of Australian Aboriginal Being* (Melbourne: Cambridge University Press, 1993).

enacted in narratives with fluid rather than fixed meanings. In this meaning system, 'country' has causal power and, in a sense, ownership over human beings. Identities are local and, in that sense, contingent; all existents have place, and no distinction between nature and culture is possible. Europeans were also disoriented by a meaning system based on initiation. They did not know what to make of ancestral beings who came outside from the inside in the past and left tracks, beings who metamorphosed into the landscape and produced material objects. They struggled with rhythmed dreaming events, complex kinship systems, animal totems and gender-specific secret knowledges. They were less than at ease with spiritual realities expressed in ceremonies, dance, painting, music, burial and rites. European attempts to construe the Aboriginal meaning system as 'Aboriginal religion' were perhaps premature in some respects and not sufficiently sensitive to Aboriginal difference. There may be no Western-type distinction between the sacred and the profane in Aboriginal law.

Some Aboriginal religious intellectuals responded to the lack of understanding displayed by European Australians by relativising 'whiteman's Christianity' and by rethinking Christianity for Aboriginal people in Indigenous terms. This response was perhaps best articulated by Djiniyini Gondarra (b. 1945), a Uniting Church theologian and lecturer in theology at Darwin's Nungalinya College, in *Series of Reflections on Aboriginal Theology*, *Series of Reflections on Aboriginal Religion* and other writings.[71] Gondarra was the leader of the 1976 revival on Elcho Island when he had a Christian vision expressed in Aboriginal totemic terms, in which God said to him:

> You lay down every totem and ceremony. In each of them there is good and bad. All of them must come under my Lordship, be washed by the blood of Jesus Christ, and then you will see a new Aboriginal culture. I don't want to destroy and leave you empty. I will restore and renew what is good.[72]

---

71 D. Gondarra, *Series of Reflections on Aboriginal Theology* (Darwin, NT: Bethel Presbytery, Northern Synod of the Uniting Church, 1986); *Series of Reflections on Aboriginal Religion* (Darwin, NT: Bethel Presbytery, Northern Synod of the Uniting Church, 1996); "Overcoming the Captivities of the Western Church Context," in *The Cultured Pearl: Australian Readings in Cross-Cultural Theology and Mission*, ed. J. Houston (Melbourne: Victorian Council of Churches, 1986) 176–82. See also the approach of Tony Tjamiwa, an Uluru elder within the Uniting Church, in Edwards, *Recovering Spirit*.

72 J. Blacket, *Fire in the Outback* (Sutherland, NSW: Albatross, 1997), 20; see also S. Piggin, "Jesus in Australian History and Culture," in *Mapping the Landscape: Essays in Australian and New Zealand Christianity*, ed. S. and W. W. Emilsen (New York: Peter Lang, 2000), 159.

God, he argued, had worked in and through the ancestors and that Christianity came to fulfil the aspirations of Aboriginal law, in which Jesus was present. Gondarra compared Aboriginal law with the ancient religion of Israel in order to envision a Christian afterlife for Aboriginal traditional culture.[73] His declaration 'Father You Gave Us the Dreaming' became a slogan for future Aboriginal religious leaders. Gondarra's theology implied not only that the law was sacred for Aboriginal Christians, but also that Aboriginal communalism had providential elements that could be used to convert the white church to the Gospel. It promoted a social theology as a correction of Western individualism and reasserted the dignity and worth of Indigenous cultures.[74] In recent years attempts to integrate Aboriginality and Christianity have generated a growing genre of 'Aboriginal Theology',[75] emphasising that Aboriginal people lived for thousands of years guided by Aboriginal law until a new Dreaming came to them in Christianity. This synthesis is based on 'the knowledge of finding the Lord in the soil of the wonderful land where the Ancestors once walked'.[76] Once Christian theological thought opened up to take account of the negative consequences of white settlement, including the loss of land, the stolen generation and white racism,[77] reconciliation and justice became among the most important themes in theological writing in Australia.[78] In the process, the automatic superiority of European cultures and knowledges were questioned and theologians had to consider to what extent Aboriginal knowledges involved alternative forms of science.

---

73 For the view that Indigenous Christian theologians should expand their canonical resources to include Indigenous 'Old Testaments', see M.G. Brett, "Canto ergo sum: Indigenous Peoples and Postcolonial Theology," *Pacifica* 16 (2003): 247–56.

74 N. Loos, *White Christ Black Cross: The Emergence of a Black Church* (Canberra: Aboriginal Studies Press, 2007).

75 See, for example, G. Rosendale, *Rainbow Spirit Elders, Rainbow Spirit Theology: Towards an Australian Aboriginal Theology* (Melbourne: Harper Collins Religious, 1997); J. Hendriks and G. Hall, "Aboriginal Australian Witness," in M. Carrara et al, *Spirit of Religion: A Project for Meeting and Dialogue directed by Raimon Panikkar* (Milan: Servitium, 2011); see also J. Hendriks and G. Hall, "The Natural Mysticism of Indigenous Australian Traditions," *Australian eJournal of Theology* 13, no.1 (2009), http://aejt.com.au/2009/issue_13/?article=158315. On the blending of Biblical and Indigenous elements in the life of Tony Tjamiwa, see Edwards, *Recovering Spirit*.

76 These are words of the theology teacher Evelyn Parkin; see E. Stockton with T. O'Donnell, *Aboriginal Church Paintings: Reflecting On Our Faith* (Lawson, NSW: Blue Mountains Education and Research Trust, 2010) 43.

77 F. Brennan, *Land Rights: The Religious Factor* (Charles Strong Memorial Lecture, 1992) (Adelaide: Charles Strong Memorial Trust, 1993).

78 M. Porter, *Land Of The Spirit?: The Australian Religious Experience* (Geneva: World Council of Churches, 1990).

Attempts to syncretise Aboriginal spiritual traditions with Christianity continued, but the independent greatness of Aboriginal thought and culture, including what came to be called 'the Aboriginal sacred', came to be accepted by many Australians.[79]

Some theologians responded to this changed situation by attempting to come closer to an Aboriginal understanding of the sacredness of the land. After 1960 a number of theologians explored the possibility of a uniquely 'Australian' theology – one which would relate to the ancient land, to Indigenous spiritual traditions and to emerging national identity in a language the people speak.[80] This conception of 'Australian' theology plays an important role in the Uniting Church. Geoffrey Lilburne (b. 1943), for example, a Uniting Church theologian, argues that Australia can be the place where the myths of Christendom are unravelled:

> ... it seems to me that the chastened methods of a Barthian theology might enable us to begin to clear the space into which the God of the Gospel could be distinguished from the gods of the historical projects of the colonisers and imperialists. The place and the pattern of this timeless land and the dialogue its human habitations offer might pose the radical question of the Gospel to all this culture, all this history, all this civilisation. Here the dubious inheritance of Christendom might finally be faced and an essential condition for the manifestation of the true God be realised.[81]

Rejecting 'Christendom' and critical of creation theologies and theologies of nature as lacking a basis in the New Testament, Lilburne produces a theology in the Calvinist Reform tradition for which land was central to the Old Testament in ways parallel to its place in Aboriginal spirituality.[82] Lilburne sees no contradiction between a Biblically oriented theology of land and an incarnational sense of place appropriate to the particularities of Australia.[83] In

---

79 Cf Davidson, *Christian Mysticism and Australian Poetry*, ch 7 "Christian Mystical Poetics and Indigenous Australia".
80 V. C. Hayes (ed.), *Toward Theology in an Australian Context* (Bedford Park, SA: ASSR, 1979) and P. Malone, (ed.), *Developing an Australian Theology* (Homebush, NSW: St Pauls, 1999); see also G. Goosen, *Australian Theologies: Themes and Methodologies into the Third Millennium* (Strathfield, NSW: St Pauls Publications, 2000).
81 G. Lilburne, "Contextualising Australian Theology: An Enquiry into Method," *Pacifica* 10 (1997): 364, and Tony Kelly's reply, "Whither 'Australian Theology'?: A Response to Geoffrey Lilburne," *Pacifica* 12 (1999): 192-208.
82 G. Lilburne, *A Sense of Place: A Christian Theology of the Land* (Nashville: Abingdon Press, 1989), ch. 6.
83 Lilburne, *A Sense of Place*, 89.

a related spirit, Uniting Church minister Chris Budden (b. 1949) draws on the theology of the United Aboriginal and Indigenous Christian Congress to argue for a 'second people's theology', sensitive to Aboriginal ownership of the land – a theology that overcomes the European Christian reliance on a story that prevents this place from being 'country'.[84]

Other Australian theologians have attempted to restructure their theologies around the spiritual meaning of the land. Lutheran Biblical scholar and theologian Norman Habel (1932), for example, declares:

> I knew the Spirit of God through the story of the cross ... I now realise that this Spirit has been experienced in a radically different way by the indigenous people of the land as the Spirit of the Land. I no longer relate to the Creator exclusively with the images and symbols inherited from European Christianity. I can now reach out to the Spirit within this land – not only in the landscape but in the history of suffering and resistance in this land ...
>
> The land – the symbol of the Spirit of the Land, a deep creative presence experienced for many centuries and a profound suffering presence experienced since colonisation – an indigenous holy land. The cross – the symbol of a suffering God known to Christians is the ultimate power behind all reconciliation. For me, all these spiritual forces are integrated in the soul that is Australia's.[85]

Habel was not alone in this response,[86] but he stands out because he has pioneered Australian theo-ecological hermeneutics in his five-volume *Earth Bible* series, identifying a hermeneutics that treats the Bible from the perspective of the earth rather than from the perspective of human beings.[87]

---

84   C. Budden, *Following Jesus in Invaded Space: Doing Theology on Aboriginal Land* (Cambridge: James Clarke & Co., 2011), 72.
85   N. Habel, *Reconciliation Searching for Australia's Soul* (Pymble, NSW: HarperCollins, 1999), 162–3.
86   See S. S. Charkianakis, *Australian Passport*, translated by V. Karalis (Blackheath, NSW: Brandl and Schlesinger, 2002), and V. Adrahtas, "Innovation within Greek Orthodox Theology in Australia: Archbishop Stylianos and the Mystique of Indigenous Australian Spirituality," in *Innovation in the Christian Orthodox Tradition?: The Question of Change in Greek Orthodox Thought and Practice*, ed. T. St. Willert and L. Molokotos-Liederman (Farnham: Ashgate, 2012), 231–52.
87   Among many books, see N. Habel, *The Land is Mine* (Minneapolis: Fortress Press, 1995) and the five volumes of *The Earth Bible*, including: N. Habel and S. Wurst (eds.), *The Earth Story in Genesis* (Sheffield: Sheffield Academic Press, 2000); *The Earth Story in Wisdom Traditions* (Sheffield: Sheffield Academic Press, 2001); and N. Habel (ed.), *The Earth Story in the Psalms and the Prophets* (Sheffield: Sheffield Academic Press, 2001). For discusssion, see A. H. Cadwallader with P. L. Trudinger (eds.),

Contextually oriented postcolonial theology has also appeared, some of it informed by the work of American Indian theologians. There are also works that read the Bible in the light of postcolonialism and postmodernism,[88] as well as attempts to address the problem of context that draw on South American liberation theological insights.[89] In these discourses there is some tension between an emphasis on unique geographic and historical features of the Australian continent, Aboriginal narratives, and high cultural ideas imported from overseas. Anglican theologian Stephen Pickard (b. 1952), for example, explores the ambiguities of place, space and land and relates a specifically Australian church 'on the verandah' to a theological systematics for postmodern times.[90] For Pickard, God is 'in between all things' and the church is God's ecclesial space, wherever it is to be found.

Australia's context also extends to Asia, and Australian theology, for the most part, has yet to come to terms with it. Despite Australian missionary involvement with Korea, China, India, Vietnam and the Philippines, Australian theology is still to engage with Asian cultures in depth. The need to engage with Asian Christianity has been consistently championed by the Reformed theologian James Haire (b. 1946), who spent thirteen years in Halmahera in the North Moluccas and has worked to contain Muslim–Christian violence in Indonesia. Haire argues that public theology should be at the heart of theological and dogmatic reflection, just as all theology is intercultural and contextual. Drawing on his extensive work on Christianity in India, Sri Lanka, Taiwan, China, Japan, Korea and Indonesia, he emphasises that Western ideas cannot be assumed in Asian contexts in which a distinction between public and private is often not found and that the radically contextual nature of theology has to be faced.[91] Haire's work

---

Where the Wild Ox Roams: Biblical Essays in Honour of Norman C. Habel (Sheffield: Sheffield Phoenix Press, 2013) and M. G. Brett, *Genesis: Procreation and the Politics of Identity* (London: Routledge, 2000); *Decolonizing God: The Bible in the Tides of Empire* (Sheffield: Sheffield Phoenix Press, 2009) and "Canto ergo sum: Indigenous People and Postcolonial Theology".

88   See Brett, Genesis and R. Boer, *Last Stop Before Antarctica: The Bible and Postcolonialism in Australia* (Sheffield: Sheffield Academic Press, 2001).
89   J. Wilcken, "To Liberate Theology: Pursuing Segundo's Project in an Australian Context," *Pacifica* 17 (2004): 55–70.
90   S. Pickard, *In-Between God: Theology, Community and Discipleship* (Adelaide: ATF, 2011), chapters 4 and 7.
91   J. Haire, "'Should We Do It In Public?': Public Theology in the Asia Pacific Region," Ferguson Lecture, delivered in Auckland, 3 August 2007; *The Character and Theological Struggle of the Church in Halmahera, Indonesia, 1941–1979* (Studien zur interkulturellen Geschichte des Christentums 26) (Frankfurt-am-Main: Peter Lang, 1981).

implies that theology in Australia should learn from Asian Christianity and engage with the real problems of Australian society in a realistic but critical fashion. There are also Catholic attempts to deploy Asian cultural traditions as resources for Australian theology, including Hinduism and Daoism. Here the work of the Australian French priest and Sanskrit scholar John Dupuche (b. 1940) deserves to be better known. In his studies of Tantra and Kashmiri Śaivism, Dupuche argues that Asian traditions can provide resources for a renewal of Christianity. Dupuche reads Christian texts through an Asian non-dualist lens.[92] The results of his work are challenging and have not yet been taken up by Australian theologians. It is likely, however, that theology in Australia will be more regionally inflected in the future.

It is also fair to suggest that many areas of theological research have yet to link up with one another. No developed theology of sexuality has been written in Australia, despite attention to Biblical perspectives by Anglican scholars, by Baptist Keith Dyer of Whitley College, Melbourne, and by Uniting Church New Testament scholar Bill Loader, who reassessed the role of sexuality in the Old and New Testaments as well as in Qumran in exceptionally learned studies.[93] There have been only limited contributions to theology and economics.[94] Lutherans have contributed to debates about the relationship between theology and science,[95] and Pentecostals have written on theological topics. Greek Orthodox theology in Australia has been mainly the concern of clergy, although this is now changing.[96] The

---

92 J. Dupuche, *Towards a Christian Tantra: The Interplay of Christianity and Kashmir Shaivism* (Melbourne: David Lovell Publishing, 2009) and *Jesus, the Mantra of God* (Melbourne: David Lovell Publishing, 2005); see also J. Dupuche, "Renewing Christian Anthropology in Terms of Kashmir Shaivism," *Australian eJournal of Theology* 4, no. 1 (2005), http://aejt.com.au/; "The Goddess Kali and the Virgin Mary," *Australian eJournal of Theology*, 19, no. 1 (2012), http://aejt.com.au/.

93 See W. Loader, *The Septuagint, Sexuality and the New Testament: Case Studies on the Impact of the LXX in Philo and the New Testament* (Grand Rapids, MI: Eerdmans, 2004); *Sexuality and the Jesus Tradition* (Grand Rapids, MI: Eerdmans, 2005); *The Dead Sea Scrolls on Sexuality: Attitudes towards Sexuality in Sectarian and Related Literature at Qumran* (Grand Rapids, MI: Eerdmans, 2009); and *The New Testament on Sexuality* (Grand Rapids, MI: Eerdmans, 2012).

94 There were attempts to include economics in theology and to recognise that theology could critique economics; see I. Hore-Lacy, *Creating Common Wealth: Aspects of Public Theology in Economics* (Sutherland, NSW: Albatross Books, 1985), and P. Oslington (ed.), *The Oxford Handbook of Christianity and Economics* (New York: Oxford University Press, 2013).

95 M. Worthing, *God, Creation and Contemporary Physics* (Minneapolis: Fortress Press, 1996) and the contributions of M. Worthing, J. Puddefoot and A. Foest in T. J. Kelly and H. D. Regan (eds.), *God, Life, Intelligence and the Universe* (Adelaide: ATF, 2002).

96 See D. Costache and P. Kariatlis (eds.), *Cappadocian Legacy* (Sydney: St Andrews Orthodox Press, 2013).

journal *Phronema* is published and the many works of John Chryssavgis (b. 1958) explore Orthodox theology in general and the work of John Climacus in particular. Reflecting his Australian upbringing and his ecumenical exposure to Protestant, Catholic and Orthodox theologies, Chryssavgis argues for Orthodoxy 'without delusion', given the shattered divine image in ourselves and in our world.[97] The Russian Orthodox churches in Australia, however, have generally deferred to authorities overseas.

Heritage and Horizon

What can we conclude from such a wealth of diverse and rich materials? Firstly, considerable theological cultural capital came to Australia. The extent of cultural capital transfer has been largely overlooked by historians, as has the transcultural agency involved in working in theology as an international discipline. Here, it is important to remember that theological knowledges were found widely among academics, clergy and lawyers before 1970, so that the notion that theology was the concern of a tiny élite requires qualification.[98] Secondly, theology in Australia has struggled with problems of distance and colonial habits of mind. It has taken time to engage with the Australian context and the region, despite major responses to Indigenous cultures, the experience of presenting the Gospel in the Pacific, and minority interests in Hinduism and Sufism.[99] There are also continuing and unresolved problems about how high traditions of theological learning and publication relate to more practical 'lived theology' concerns, and about how theologies based on exclusive religious identities relate to contexts characterised by religious pluralism.[100]

Thirdly, internationally important contributions to theology have been made here, especially to the theology of the Trinity. Theologians have not

---

97   J. Chryssavgis, *Light Through Darkness: The Orthodox Tradition* (Maryknoll, NY: Orbis Books, 2004) 16–17.
98   Among academics there were many outstanding classicists, Patristic scholars and church historians including Eric Osborne, Duncan Reid, Edwin Judge, Bruce Mansfield, Ian Breward and Raoul Mortley.
99   Here Australians influenced by forms of theosophy play a role, as they did at the beginning of the twentieth century; see, for example, the books of Harry (Kenneth) Oldmeadow, written from a Traditionalist standpoint, such as *Traditionalism: Religion in the Light of the Perennial Philosophy* (Colombo: Sri Lanka Institute of Traditional Studies, 2000), and Rodney Blackhirst's *Primordial Alchemy and Modern Religion Essays on Traditional Cosmology* (San Rafael CA: Perennis, 2008).
100 See G. Bouma, "Australian Anglicans and Religious Plurality: Exclusive Theologies vs. Theological Affirmations of Diversity - A Tale of Two Cities," *Journal for the Academic Study of Religion*, 26, (2013): 139–156.

ignored other areas, including theological anthropology.[101] Some have been concerned to keep theology up-to-date with a society moving further and further away from tradition. Among evangelicals, as a common belief in God gave way to personal spiritualities, Charles Sherlock, among others, has insisted on the need for contemporary equivalents of traditional theological formulations.[102] On the other hand, no outstanding theological system has been produced in Australia.

Fourthly, many theologians have contributed to applied and practical theology,[103] ranging from the activism of David Millikan to the work of publicly minded ethicists such as Gordon Preece and Robert Gascoigne to the practical theology of Gerard Hall, Terry Veiling and the Sri Lankan-born Anglican priest Ruwan Palapathwala.[104] Likewise, theologians such as the Uniting Church leader Gordon Dicker and the evangelical Anglican Bill Lawton have sought to relate theological issues to real-life contexts such as work, health, sport, the environment and the economy. Many theologians have been concerned to address national issues such as poverty, the condition of Indigenous peoples and racism.[105] Other theologians have concerned themselves with popular theology and with the challenges of doing theology in radically new social and cultural contexts.[106] Such world-centred theology often seeks to take account of sociological analyses. There is also the empirical theology of Paul McQuillan at the Australian Catholic University in Brisbane. It is less certain that Australian theologians have been able to adequately respond to the cultural changes associated with what

---

101 See, for example, C. Sherlock, *The Doctrine of Humanity Contours of Christian Theology* (Downers Green: InterVarsity Press, 1996).

102 C. Sherlock, "From 'Mate Upstairs' to 'Spirituality Sponsor': God Images in Australian Society," in P. Malone (ed.), *Developing an Australian Theology* (Strathfield: St Pauls Publications, 1999), ch 2; *Words and the Word: Case Studies Using Scripture* (Preston, Vic.: Mosaic Press, 2013).

103 David Millikan attempted to pioneer a practical theology engaged with local social realities. He founded the Zadok Institute for Religion and Society in 1971; see also D. Millikan, *The Sunburnt Soul: Christianity in Search of an Australian Identity* (Homebush West, NSW: Anzea, 1981).

104 R. Gascoigne, *The Public Forum and Christian Ethics* (Cambridge: Cambridge University Press, 2001) and *The Church and Secularity: Two Stories of Liberal Society* (Washington DC: Georgetown University Press, 2009).

105 See A. Dutney, *Sex and Death: A Personal Account of Christianity* (Melbourne: Uniting Church Press, 1982) and *Manifesto for Renewal: The Shaping of a New Church* (Melbourne: Uniting Church Press, 1986); G. Preece, *Changing Work Values: A Christian Response* (Brunswick, Vic.: Acorn, 1995); and D. Hynd, J. Barr, and G. Preece (eds.), *Theology in a Third Voice* (Hindmarsh, SA: ATF, 2006).

106 See F. J. Moloney, "A Theology of Multiculturalism," in P. Malone (ed.), *Discovering an Australian Theology* (Homebush, NSW: St Paul Publications, 1988), 133–46.

are sometimes called 'postmodern cultures' or with electronic technologies. It is also fair to note a capacity for innovation in the context of major social problems. Internationally influential work has been done, for example, on spirituality and ageing from a practical theology perspective by Elizabeth MacKinlay at the Centre for Ageing and Pastoral Studies, established as part of St Mark's National Theological Centre in Canberra in 2001.[107]

In sum, it is fair to see Australian theology as in development and as showing signs of growing independence and originality. It deserves a place in any broad-minded history of Australia.

---

107 E. MacKinlay, *The Spiritual Dimension of Ageing* (London: Jessica Kingsley, 2001) and *Spiritual Growth and Care in the Fourth Age of Life* (London: Jessica Kingsley, 2006).

Chapter VI

POSTSECULAR CONSCIOUSNESS

The postsecular is not a well-established category in Australian historical writing. Some of the international literature on the postsecular may have application to Australia,¹ not least in the context of changing understandings of 'the sacred' and 'the mystical'.² The term 'postsecular' has many meanings and is a label rather than a concept. It is used to describe a changed relationship between the state and religion, to imply some kind of return to religion after secularity, to capture a change in postcolonial thinking that associates secularisation with colonialism, to describe a system of tension characterised by the coexistence of the secular and the religious, to denote a recognition by secularism of a need to historicise and contextualise itself, or to signal the re-emergence of religion in global public life – to give some well-known examples. My use of the adjective 'postsecular', however, does not imply 'after secular', in the sense of a linear movement away from the differentiation of social life into autonomous spheres, let alone an epochal shift out of what Taylor calls 'The Secular Age', a retreat from secularity or of a return to religion. I use the term 'postsecular consciousness' to characterise *a sensibility that accepts secularity*

---

1   The term 'postsecular' gained currency with the turn in the later writings of German social philosopher Jürgen Habermas and its use has spread to many disciplines. Among a large literature, see J. Habermas, "Notes on Post-Secular Society," *New Perspectives Quarterly* 25, no. 4 (2008): 17–29, and *An Awareness of What is Missing: Faith and Reason in a Post-Secular Age*, translated by C. Cronin (Cambridge: Polity, 2010); see also W. Hudson, "Towards Post-Secular Enlightenment," in *Secularisations and their Debates: Perspectives on the Return of Religion in the Contemporary West*, ed. M. Sharpe and D. Nickelson (Dordrecht: Springer, 2014), ch. 14; P. Losonczi and A. Singh, (eds.), *Discoursing the Post-Secular Essays on the Habermasian Post-Secular Turn* (Berlin: LIT Verlag, 2010); H. de Vries, *Political Theologies Public Religions in a Post-Secular World* (New York: Fordham University Press, 2006); T. Dostert, *Beyond Political Liberalism: Toward a Postsecular Ethics of Public Life* (Notre Dame, IN: Notre Dame University Press, 2006); and the special issue of *Telos* magazine, "Are We Postsecular?," *Telos* 167 (2014).
2   For changing understandings of the mystical, see Davidson, *Christian Mysticism and Australian Poetry*.

in relevant domains, but evidences an openness to what is beyond a strictly secular horizon.

Postsecular consciousness is often more ambivalent about religion than sacral secularity, and less inclined to pursue transcendent purposes through the secular; it may also call the secular itself into question. Whereas, as we saw in Chapter II, sacral secularity could imply high hopes for the secular, the postsecular is associated with a sensibility that is often less persuaded that the secular can achieve maximal goals. However, as in the case of disbelief, there is a good deal of ambiguity where particular individuals are concerned. My terminology throws certain features into relief rather than others. No doubt there is no one essentialist 'postsecular' that can be found across different periods and different intellectuals. On the other hand, there is recurrent evidence of a concern with qualitative dimensions of the natural world and often a sense that these qualitative dimensions are not adequately addressed by the natural sciences, at least in so far as they take a reductionist form. There is also recurrent evidence of a sense of sacral immanence – of something wonderful that can be grasped without resort to the teachings of the churches.

In recent writing some of these issues have been taken up in discussions of changing conceptions of and experiences of the sacred in Australia. Emphasis has been placed on the centrality of the Aboriginal sacred and on postcolonial perspectives.[3] My discussion in this chapter offers another and, in some ways, supplementary optic. I begin my discussion by revisiting the presence of sacral naturalism in nineteenth- and early twentieth-century poets who can be seen as forerunners of changes in sensibility that later became more general. I then discuss writers influenced by vitalism and process philosophy; writers who sought to ground the sacral in the sciences; writers who attempted to recover a spiritual concept of place; and writers who found

---

3   Writers influenced by postcolonialism have attempted to chart transformations of the sacred in the course of the colonial encounter with a new and threatening land, a movement in Australian art and writing around the middle of the nineteenth century toward a conception of the infinite in the representation of place that deepened the sense of the uncanny or unheimlich, the discovery of the horizonality of Australian space as a location of sublime otherness and other substantial changes; see K. Gelder and, J. M. Jacobs, *Uncanny Australia: Sacredness and Identity in a Postcolonial Nation* (Carlton South, Vic.: Melbourne University Press, 1998); B. Ashcroft, F. Devlin-Glass and L. McCredden, *Intimate Horizons: The Post-Colonial Sacred in Australia* (Adelaide: ATF Press, 2009); see also L. McCredden, *Luminous Moments: The Contemporary Sacred* (Adelaide: ATF, 2010), especially 1–14, and Bill Ashcroft's essay, "The Sacred in Australian Culture," in *Sacred Australia: Post-Secular Considerations*, ed. M. Paranjape (Melbourne: Clouds of Magellan, 2009), 21–43.

the sacred in the context of environmental philosophy or psychoanalysis. I conclude with the rise of 'transcultural eclecticism', which at the time of writing is only beginning to be reflected in Australian religious thought.

Sacral Naturalisms

Sacral naturalism refers to a sensibility that finds the sacred in the natural world rather than in history or in social life. Naturalism of this sort has been a marked feature of Australian religious thought, even though experiencing the sacred in nature was not much emphasised in Christian teaching, except perhaps in Franciscan circles, although it was a feature of theosophy.[4] A tendency to find the sacred in nature emerged early in the colonial poet Charles Harpur, who responded to nineteenth-century speculation about purpose in nature, including Robert Chambers' *Vestiges of the Natural History of Creation* (1844), by developing his own sacral evolutionism. Like his friend, poet Henry Kendall (1839–1882),[5] Harpur relocated the sacred in nature and promoted a physico-theology that discovered evidence of a universal mind and teleology in nature, even indications of a perfect plan, writing:

> How vain seems life, how worthless, when we scan
> Its outside only – and we laugh at Man!
> But when we pore into its depths, we see
> An awful import in its mystery:
> For what is deep is holy, and must tend
> To some divinely universal end.[6]

For Harpur, the relation of the human being to God and the universe had to be understood in evolutionary terms. Harpur, however, went further and advanced a religious account of evolution, according to which novel orders might emerge in the universe and supplant humanity itself.[7] Harpur's evolutionary

---

[4] The Franciscan influence is hard to trace outside the work of poets such as Francis Webb. In the late nineteenth century there was a theosophical strand in Australian religious thought that associated the continent with ancient Lemuria; see the novel by G. Firth Scott, *The Last Lemurian: A Westralian Romance* (London: James Bowden, 1898).

[5] Baptised a Presbyterian, Kendall identified Christianity with Wordsworthian pantheism and spoke of God's grand authentic Gospel delivered in nature; see Kendall's "To a Mountain," in *Songs from the Mountains* (Sydney: William Maddock; London; Sampson Low, Marston, Searle and Rivington, 1880).

[6] C. Harpur "Life Without and Within," in *Charles Harpur: Selected Poetry and Prose*, ed. M. Ackland, (Ringwood, Vic.: Penguin, 1986), 113.

[7] C. Harpur, "Note to the poem called Geologia," in *Charles Harpur: Selected Poetry and Prose* 109–110.

idealism did not deny the darker aspects of human life and he blended his idealism with intimations of the tragic fate of Aboriginal people and Calvinist references to the need to redeem the earth from Adam's sin. He tended to replace Christianity with a vision of a sacral cosmos.[8] In his major philosophical poem, "The World and the Soul", Harpur celebrated an Emersonian Over-soul, which retained its perfection in the lower orders of creation, while continually ascending to higher levels within the organism of nature.[9]

A sense of mystery and awe in the presence of nature can also be found in writers in the early twentieth century. The lyric poet John Shaw Neilson (1872–1942), for example, emancipated himself from a Calvinism that he found oppressive, turning to earthly love and a natural world full of imaginal realities.[10] Initially, Neilson tried to reconcile his naturalism with the Christian narratives in which he had been raised by embedding the Resurrection within the cycle of nature,[11] writing:

> O Heart of Spring!
> After the stormy days of Winter's reign
> When the keen winds their last lament are sighing
> The Sun shall raise thee up to life again:
> In thy dim death thou shalt not suffer pain:
> Surely thou dost not fear this quiet dying?
> Whither, oh whither blithely journeying,
> O Heart of Spring!
> O Heart of Spring!
> Youth's emblem, ancient as unchanging light,
> Uncomprehended, unconsumed, still burning:
> Oh that we could, as thee, rise from the night
> To find a world of blossoms lilac-white
> And long-winged swallows unafraid returning ...

---

8   Many Australian poets were mystical in one way or another, among them Mary Fullerton (1898–1946), who was influenced by the Calvinist pantheist poet John Parker. For discussion, see Davidson, *Christian Mysticism and Australian Poetry*.
9   C. Harpur, "The World and the Soul," in *Charles Harpur*, ed. A. Mitchell (Melbourne: Sun Books, 1973), 39–45.
10   J. S. Neilson, "Surely God was a Lover," *Sydney Sun* (9 October 1910), republished in *Heart of Spring* (Sydney: The Bookfellow, 1919), 51.
11   See C. Hanna, *The Folly of Spring: A Study of John Shaw Neilson's Poetry* (St Lucia: University of Queensland Press, 1990); C. Hanna (ed.), *John Shaw Neilson: Poetry, Autobiography and Correspondence* (St. Lucia: University of Queensland Press, 1991); and the discussion in Davidson, *Christian Mysticism and Australian Poetry*, ch. 3. Neilson was well read in high cultural and mystical writings, even though he represented himself as an uneducated workingman.

Whither, oh whither this thy journeying,
O Heart of Spring![12]

Over time, however, Neilson became convinced that his attempts to retain some form of Christianity were mistaken and failed to provide a bridge between nature and the supernatural. Accordingly, he moved away from theism, partly under the influence of the rationalist lecturer J. S. Langley. In place of the idea of God, derived from what he now saw as outdated creeds, Neilson turned to the medieval mystics and to the Symbolist poets.[13] In rhapsodic mood, he posited an unknowable God, accessed through the vibrant images of nature, understood as a system of allegories for a 'Morning World' that had not yet appeared:

God? Did he know him? It was far he flew …
God was not terrible and thunder-blue:
– It was a gentle water bird I knew.[14]

His poem "To the Father of Many" expressed his rejection of distorted religious ideals, while his rapturous vision of a deity of the Spring burst forth in 'The Blue Man and the Barley':

First did I see him in the light
Ere I had wandered into rhyme
Or the old fables dulled the sight
'Twas but a moon till Summer-time
And on the hay-stacks did he climb
On a clear night he was revealed
Kinsman of God I dreamed he was
That blue man in the barley field.[15]

In his poem "The Orange Tree" (ca 1919), Neilson implied that the divine could be rendered in images, even though it was discursively unknowable. Those who plunged into the folly of life, he believed, would find a meaning. Neilson also sought to allow a form of eternal return, if not the immortality of Christian orthodoxy.[16] At the end of his life he regarded himself as of no

---

12 J. S. Neilson, "Heart of Spring," in *Collected Poems of John Shaw Neilson*, ed. R. H. Croll, (Melbourne and Sydney: Lothian Book Publishing Co., 1934), 1.
13 Davidson, *Christian Mysticism and Australian Poetry*, ch. 3.
14 J. S. Neilson, "The Gentle Water Bird," in Hanna, *The Folly of Spring*, 122.
15 J. S. Neilson, "The Blue Man and the Barley," in Hanna, *The Folly of Spring*, 129.
16 For discussion, see J. H. Phillips, *Poet of the Colours: The Life of John Shaw Neilson* (North Sydney: Allen and Unwin, 1988) and C. Hanna (ed.), *John Shaw Neilson* (St.

particular religion, but he continued to find the sacral in nature, rather than in religion or society, although his vision was sometimes tortured.[17]

A different approach to nature, albeit, again, one laden with sacral meaning, can be found in the writings of the Queensland poet and wealthy pastoralist, William Baylebridge (1883–1942). The son of a rigid Methodist father, Baylebridge developed a rich fund of ideas during his extensive travels in Germany (1908–1919).[18] Subsequently, he developed his own sacral naturalist philosophy from a range of sources that included the philosophers Schopenhauer, Nietzsche and Bergson. Like others influenced by Nietzsche, Baylebridge had a view of institutional religion that was severe and uncompromising:

> In Man's constraint our sloths refuse to put them:
> In Mystery's charnel-house we shut them.
> Though, rank with mould, they smell of death,
> We bring the uncleanness forth, and call it faith.[19]

The self-assertion of humanity, he declared, in the language of German philosopher Ludwig Feuerbach (1804–1872), would drive out pseudo-divinities:

> 'Heaven's force expires!' Man's voice, proclaiming
>   Man,
> The annihilation flings. All the shocked gods,
> Thence ranking, to the pit of shadows flee.[20]

Baylebridge recognised, however, that driving out pseudo-divinities did not eliminate the need for projections of anthropological meaning, and in a poem entitled "New Gods and Nearer" he wrote:

> To Heaven resign its own! For Earth begin
> The adoption due, and hail our gods within![21]

Lucia: University of Queensland Press, 1991); see also H. Hewson (ed.), *John Shaw Neilson: A Life in Letters* (Carlton, Vic.: Melbourne University Press, 2001).

17   For the dark side of Neilson, see Hanna, *The Folly of Spring*, Appendix. The Suffering God.

18   See W. Baylebridge, *This Vital Flesh: Collected Works of William Baylebridge*, Memorial ed., vol 1, edited by P.R. Stephensen (Sydney: Angus and Robertson, 1961).

19   W. Baylebridge, "The New Life: New Values, Morality, II Morals Relative," in *This Vital Flesh*, 80.

20   W. Baylebridge, "The New Life: Deity, IV The Death of Pseudo-Divinity," in *This Vital Flesh*, 97.

21   W. Baylebridge, "The New Life: New Values, New Gods and Nearer," in *This Vital Flesh*, 96.

To this extent, his naturalism remained anthropocentric and grounded in the future evolution of humanity.

Baylebridge's alternative to institutional religion, grown effete, was a parareligion linking the human experience of God with a further evolutionary advance to come. In his poem "Deity" he wrote:

> This, of divinity, believe –
> No concept can its other-world achieve.
> That godhead in the man we shadow limned
> The unguessed, the abysmal, deity hath dimmed.
> How shalt thou Man, his truth completed, call?
> God, by his proxy on this destined ball:
> God, written tersely in this animal.[22]

Baylebridge's universe was not secular, and he allowed for a form of spiritual emergence and for the fact that spirit could be apprehended in flesh.[23] Baylebridge's parareligion, however, did not include a role for Christianity. Christianity, he conceded, had achieved a transvaluation of the world, but now another spirit and transvaluation were needed if human beings were to breed a higher humanity and come into a proper relation to God.[24] In a context in which the universe was evolving towards its final unflawed exemplar, the superman or a glorified humanity needed to be bred which would set about fulfilling the purpose of the universe.[25] For Baylebridge, as for Harpur before him, this implied that the universe's animating principle so ordered affairs that man could struggle to become his 'Utmost Self'.

Baylebridge also argued for a national religion that would replace old values with new ones with greater survival power. This national religion, integrating value and order, would relate both to the natural world and to the national character, as Christianity failed to do. It would not employ a set of metaphysical dogmas, but bring human beings into harmony with the world.[26] In place of mystical absorption in the contemplation of the things beyond our knowledge, the national religion would make use of festivals and ceremonies to inspire a civic enthusiasm and be the active soul of corporate existence. In Baylebridge's new order there would be no secular

---

22 W. Baylebridge, "Deity," in *This Vital Flesh*, 138.
23 W. Baylebridge, "Life's Testament" (1914), in *This Vital Flesh*, 20–21.
24 W. Baylebridge, "National Notes," in *This Vital Flesh*, 147.
25 H. M. Green (Henry Mackenzie), *Fourteen Minutes: Short Sketches of Australian Poets and their Work, from Harpur to the Present Day* (Sydney: Angus & Robertson, 1944), 104.
26 W. Baylebridge, "National Notes," in *This Vital Flesh*, 196.

state and no need for an ecclesiastical religion. Instead, religion would be so essential to the state, so bound up with its entire structure, that it would be impossible to think them separately. Given Baylebridge's organicist conception of politics and society, his Nietzschean religion was not without its dangers, although his sacral philosophy had its admirers, among them the poet Judith Wright.

Vitalism

Other writers turned away from mechanist approaches to nature under the influence of vitalist ideas debated in France and Britain. Vitalism in the first half of the twentieth century was associated with the claim that there are living qualities in the natural world that cannot be reduced to inanimate matter or mechanism. It went with a cult of intuition and with a preference for biology and history over physics. Some versions of vitalism primarily manifested in health and public policy concerns.[27] Others celebrated nature as concretely experienced.[28] Experiential vitalism depended on enthusiasm for natural phenomena as they were perceived, and it was compatible with disbelief in the claims of the churches. *Bulletin* Red Page editor and prominent poet, Douglas Stewart (1913–1985), for example, treated religious beliefs as subjects for satire:

> Heaven is a busy place.
> Those in a state of grace
> Continually twanging the harp.
> And Court at eight-thirty sharp.
> Did he do ill or well,
> Shall he be sent to hell
> That scoundrel in the dock?
> The great black Judgement Book
> Says nothing good of him;
> Weeping of seraphim.[29]

---

27 See M. Roe, *Nine Australian Progressives: Vitalism in Bourgeois Social Thought 1890–1960* (St. Lucia: University of Queensland Press, 1984).
28 Less philosophical forms of vitalism flourished among poets such as Ray Mathew (1929–2002) and Kenneth Slessor (1901–1971). Slessor, though militantly secularist, was not free from meta-empirical concerns; see K. Slessor, *Bread and Wine* (Sydney: Angus & Robertson, 1970).
29 D. Stewart, "Heaven is a Busy Place," *The Penguin Book of Australian Verse*, comp. J. Thompson, K. Slessor and R. G. Howarth (Harmondsworth, Middlesex: Penguin, 1958), 178.

Nevertheless, he was not averse to discovering immanent divinity in the natural world, a theme he dealt with in his poetry.

Vitalism was apparent in the work of some novelists, including Vance Palmer (1885–1959). Palmer derived his vitalism from the French philosopher Henri Bergson (1859–1941), but he was also sympathetic to the theosophical thought and cultural radicalism promoted by A. R. Orage (1873–1934) and his London-based journal, *New Age*. Critical of organised religion, Palmer posited a spiritual force in nature. He also connected receptivity to nature and creativity. Palmer believed that Australians had to create their own spiritual identity by developing a mystical faith in the future of the country and taking account of Australia's unique land, fauna and flora.[30]

Palmer's partner, Nettie Palmer (1885–1964), a leading Australian literary critic and translator of the French poet Paul Verlaine, also sympathised with vitalism. Educated at Melbourne University and at Marburg in Germany and in Paris, Nettie Palmer followed debates in France and England. Like Vance, although less hostile to Christianity, she was immersed in both Bergson's vitalist philosophy and the social thought of Bernard Shaw.[31] A utopian and a socialist, and an admirer of Joseph Furphy and of Bernard O'Dowd, Nettie Palmer turned away in stages from her strict Baptist background and developed a questioning outlook, reflecting her immersion in French Symbolist poetry. This outlook was coloured by an indefinite intuitive mysticism. Palmer sought to integrate enlightened rationalism with the unconscious and she repeatedly emphasised the need to do spiritual work.[32]

Perhaps the most vibrant form of vitalism was found in the poetry of Judith Wright (1915–2000). Brought up in the pastoral squirearchy, Wright studied philosophy at the University of Sydney and was unsympathetic throughout her life to church religion and any notion of a transcendent reality. Nonetheless, partly under Walt Whitman's influence, she seems to have accepted some notion of 'soul'. In the same way, she satirised the religion

---

30   V. Palmer, *The Legend of the Nineties* (Melbourne: Melbourne University Press, 1954), 168–9.
31   See N. Palmer, *Nettie Palmer: Her Private Journal 'Fourteen Years', Poems, Reviews and Literary Essays*, edited by V. Smith (St. Lucia: University of Queensland Press, 1988) and V. Smith (ed.), *Letters of Vance and Nettie Palmer 1915–1963* (Canberra: National Library of Australia, 1977); see also V. Smith, *Vance and Nettie Palmer* (New York: Twayne Publishers, 1975) and D. Jordan, *Nettie Palmer: Search for an Aesthetic* (Melbourne: Department of History, University of Melbourne, 1999).
32   Nettie Higgins to Mrs John Higgins, 28 September 1911, Palmer papers (National Library of Australia, MS.1174, folder 471), quoted in D. Walker, *Dream and Disillusion A Search for Australian Cultural Identity* (Canberra: Australian National University Press, 1976), 92.

of the Old Testament in her famous poem "Bullocky" (1946), but remained open to ways in which reoriented Biblical types could illumine experience in a new land. In her mature writings Wright did not so much abandon the sacral as relocate it in the sensual and the passionate. She was also open to an unsayable mystical dimension. Here she was indebted to her philosopher partner Jack McKinney (1891–1966), who was interested in Neoplatonism with its concept of mystical ascent. McKinney wrote extensively about the ways in which language and culture mediated our experience of the world, including a piece entitled 'Approach to the Universal Mystery'.[33] For her part, Wright declared:

> I've never strongly felt the need to posit an 'outside' deity when there's so much to be discovered about the 'inside', or an absolute when the relative's what we live by; except of course for the cosmos, the dance itself. A Creator, A personal God, a separate soul, don't seem necessities to me. Jack's [McKinney] own work implied that we are part of a unity with 'nature' and that human thought is the development of that relationship, which seems to me enough.

Wright's sources included the classical Greek philosopher Heraclitus (535–475), contemporary European theorists such as Carl Jung (1842–1896) and Ernst Cassirer (1874–1945), the American philosopher Susanne Langer (1895–1985), and the British literary critic and anthroposophist Owen Barfield (1898–1997). From Barfield she took the idea that changes in consciousness and changes in our relation to nature were related. Like Barfield, Wright was convinced that there was a link between the decline of our inner and our outer worlds. Against such brokenness, she attempted to rehabilitate feeling as the basis for a new qualitative appropriation of nature and a new anthropology.[34] She also attempted to explore the numinous in the living world. In Wright's work these concerns were integrated with a

---

33 J. McKinney, *The Challenge of Reason* (Brisbane: Mountain Press, 1950) and *The Structure of Modern Thought* (London: Chatto and Windus, 1971); see also M. McKinney and P. Clarke (eds.), *The Equal Heart and Mind: Letters Between Judith Wright and Jack McKinney* (St Lucia: University of Queensland Press, 2004).
34 J. Wright, extract from letter to Shirley Walker, 14th August, 1976, quoted in P. Clarke and M. McKinney (eds.), *With Love & Fury: Selected Letters of Judith Wright* (Canberra: National Library of Australia, 2006), 291; see also B. Bennett, "Judith Wright: An Ecological Vision," in R. Ross (ed.), *International Literature in English: Essays on the Major Writers* (New York: Garland, 1991), 205–21; S. Walker, *Flame and Shadow: A Study of Judith Wright's Poetry* (St Lucia: University of Queensland Press, 1991); and the discussion in Davidson, *Christian Mysticism and Australian Poetry*, ch. 5.

strong sense of local place and the role of Aboriginal histories in it. Her vitalist creed was strikingly down to earth; human beings were a part of a unity with nature and a simple ethic followed from this. 'All that is real is to live, to desire, to be', she wrote.[35] Wright's immanentism implied that a revelation could be received from nature, from the 'living earth', and that a new relation to nature could produce a different humanity.

Process Philosophy

Another, more theoretically ambitious, version of sacral naturalism was associated with process philosophy, a major trend in twentieth-century philosophy hostile to reductionism and mechanism, which had significant, but little-known manifestations in Australia.[36]

Twentieth-century European and American process philosophy advanced a bio-philosophical interpretation of the universe, in which the human being and its experiences were located inside nature. Process philosophers rejected the main doctrines of British empiricism, including the representational theory of mind and Humean accounts of perception, sensation and causation. They argued that an adequate metaphysics could not be based on substances or things. Instead, process philosophers held that substances should be replaced by processes, and that real temporal becoming was a basic feature of reality itself. The two greatest twentieth-century process philosophers were Henri Bergson and the British philosopher and mathematical physicist, A. N. Whitehead (1861–1947).

Process philosophy in Australia was of several sorts. One form of process philosophy, grounded in the natural sciences, was promoted by Samuel Alexander, who left Australia for Oxford at the age of 18 and became the most famous British philosopher of his generation. In his masterwork *Space, Time and Deity*,[37] delivered as the Gifford Lectures (1916–1918), Alexander argued for a process monism, for which space–time was the stuff out of which all existents were made. Alexander's metaphysics assumed a hierarchy of orders or levels of existence with ever higher levels of existence appearing in the course of the process, and a qualitative complex called 'Deity' that was

---

35 J. Wright, "The Moving Image," in *Collected Poems 1942–1985* (Sydney: Angus and Robertson, 1994), 4.
36 Process philosophy receives surprisingly little notice in G. Oppy and N. N. Trakakis eds. *A Companion to Philosophy in Australia and New Zealand* (Melbourne: Monash University Publishing, 2010).
37 S. Alexander, *Space, Time and Deity: Being the Gifford Lectures at Glasgow, 1916–1918*, 2 vols (London: Macmillan, 1920).

still to come. It mainly appealed to those with philosophical and/or scientific training.

Other intellectuals found a form of process philosophy in Marxism, as interpreted by Soviet theorists. Marxist philosophy came to Australia in many different versions, including Soviet and Chinese versions of dialectical materialism, and receptions of the work of Western European Marxists such as György Lukács, Ernst Bloch, Theodor Adorno, Antonio Gramsci and Louis Althusser. Centres of Marxist philosophy emerged after the 1960s at the University of Sydney, where Wal Suchting (1931–1997), in *Marx and Philosophy*,[38] developed an Althusserian Marxism based on scientific practices, and at Flinders University in Adelaide, where Ian Hunt published *Analytical and Dialectical Marxism*,[39] based on a model of dialectical relations. Studies of the relationship between Marxism and religion were produced by Scott Mann, Wayne Hudson, and Roland Boer, among others.[40]

Marxist versions of process philosophy influenced a number of Australian writers and critics. The most interesting process philosopher of this sort was the Marxist cultural critic Jack Lindsay (1900–1990). Born in Melbourne, Jack Lindsay was the eldest son of artist Norman Lindsay and a man of remarkable gifts. Lindsay gained a First in Classics in 1921 at the University of Queensland, where he met the socialist historian Gordon Childe (1852–1957) and was friendly with the nationalist writer and editor, P. R. Stephensen. In 1923–1924, with his father, Kenneth Slessor and Frank Johnson, he produced the literary quarterly *Vision*, one of Australia's first little magazines. From 1926 Lindsay lived in England, while maintaining many connections with Australia.

The young Jack Lindsay embraced the activism implicit in Nietzsche's conception of the Overman (*Übermensch*) and sympathised with his father's Dionysian attempt to overcome the one-sidedness of modernity. In 1928 he wrote and published *Dionysos: Nietzsche Contra Nietzsche*,[41] combining Nietzschean activism and Platonic idealism. Thereafter Lindsay moved in

---

38 W. A. Suchting, *Marx and Philosophy: Three Studies* (Basingstoke: Macmillan, 1986).
39 I. E. Hunt, *Analytical and Dialectical Marxism* (Aldershot: Avebury, 1993).
40 S. Mann, *Heart of a Heartless World: Religion as Ideology* (Montreal: Black Rose, 1998); W. Hudson, *The Marxist Philosophy of Ernst Bloch* (London: Macmillan,1982); and R. Boer, *The Criticism of Heaven and Earth*, 5 vols (Leiden: Brill 2013). Eugene Kamenka prepared the way with his *The Ethical Foundations of Marxism* (London: Routledge and Kegan Paul, 1962) and *The Philosophy of Ludwig Feuerbach* (London: Routledge and Kegan Paul, 1970).
41 J. Lindsay, *Dionysos: Nietzsche Contra Nietzsche: An Essay in Lyrical Philosophy* (London: Fanfrolico Press, 1928).

stages towards a profound concern with worldly affairs, taking the radical prophetic vision of William Blake as the basis for a philosophy of history. Lindsay's world-view combined ethical hostility to philistinism, materialism and commerce with a quest for a rebirth of classical vitality. He was sympathetic both to a Franciscan anarchist social vision and to a high cultural politics of the type advocated by the Hungarian Marxist philosopher and cultural critic György Lukács. When he moved towards a more materialist outlook, he did so without entirely abandoning his earlier idealist commitments.

In 1936 Lindsay converted to a quasi-Hegelian form of Marxism as the only serious contemporary approach to shaping history. Lindsay's Marxism combined an existential philosophy of individual heroic action, derived from Søren Kierkegaard and the German philosopher of existentialism Karl Jaspers (1883–1969),[42] a dialectical philosophy of freedom, of broadly Hegelian provenance, and a form of process philosophy inspired by Soviet interpretations of Engels' *Dialectics of Nature* (1883). Lindsay used Marxist process philosophy to integrate his quasi-religious hopes with a Romantic organicist conception of nature. Specifically, he argued that Engels' concept of the dialectical leap from quantity to quality meant that new ideas and qualities arose from every conflict. Just as every advance in production was in dialectical unity with an advance in culture, so there was a real chance that the initial human harmony with nature would eventually be restored at a higher level in a new order of freedom. In this way, Lindsay was able to combine a sophisticated materialist world outlook with some of the consolations of religion, without retreating from disbelief in religion's literal claims. He was also able, in a stream of books, to defend a classical conception of objective aesthetic qualities and to reconcile it with sociology of knowledge perspectives. Here he may have anticipated some of the work of his friends, cultural critic Raymond Williams and historian Edward Thompson.

Another form of process philosophy, this time indebted to British philosopher and mathematician A. N. Whitehead, appeared in the work of Sydney philosophical poet R. D. FitzGerald (1902–1987). FitzGerald rejected the aestheticism and imported Greek pantheons of Norman Lindsay and

---

42   Jack Lindsay also pioneered a critique of modern science; see, for example, *Origins of Alchemy in Graeco-Roman Egypt* (London: Muller, 1970) and *The Origins of Astrology* (London: Muller, 1971); see also his *Life Rarely Tells: An Autobiography in Three Volumes* (Ringwood, Vic.: Penguin, 1982), 761; B. Smith (ed.), *Culture and History: Essays presented to Jack Lindsay* (Sydney: Hale & Iremonger, 1984).

the poet Hugh McCrae (1876–1958),[43] and turned instead to the concrete physicality of the material world. Interpreting the ordinary in terms of the new physics and Whitehead's process philosophy, in his poem "The Greater Apollo" (1926) FitzGerald set up ordinary life correlates in place of religious categories:

> What is revealed to me and known
> Beyond material things alone?
> It is enough that trees are trees,
> That earth is earth and stone is stone.[44]

The result was a powerful Stoic vision and a willingness to face the transhumanist features of reality for which human beings did not matter:

> For eternity is not space reaching
> on without end to it; not time without end to it,
> nor infinity working round in a circle;
> but a placeless dot enclosing nothing,
> the pre-time pinpoint of impossible beginning,
> enclosed by nothing, not even by emptiness –
> impossible: so wholly at odds with possibilities
> that, always emergent and wresting and interlinking
> they shatter it and return to it, are all of it and part of it.
> It is your hand stretched out to touch your neighbour's,
> and feet running through the dark, directionless like darkness.[45]

FitzGerald's naturalism was unsentimental, but not without a certain disillusioned sacrality.[46]

Whiteheadian process philosophy was also found in the writings of Wilfred Eade Agar (1882–1951), Professor of Zoology at the University of Melbourne and author of a Whiteheadian interpretation of biology, *A Contribution to the Theory of the Living Organism* (1943). Like Whitehead, Agar held that all living organisms were subjects, and that mind, feelings and sentience were real features of reality. 'The main thesis of this book is that all living organisms are subjects … that the characteristic activity of a subject

---

43 R. D. FitzGerald, *The Greater Apollo: Seven Metaphysical Songs* (Sydney, 1927).
44 FitzGerald, *The Greater Apollo*, 169–171.
45 R. D. FitzGerald, "The Face of the Waters," (1944), in *Robert D. FitzGerald*, ed. J. Croft (St Lucia: University of Queensland Press, 1987), 90.
46 *The Elements of Poetry* (St. Lucia: University of Queensland Press, 1963); and *The Greater Apollo*.

is the act of perception,' he wrote.[47] He argued that a world of purposive agents suggested a purposive cosmic agent. Agar used Whitehead's process philosophy as a template for scientific explanations.

His student, the distinguished zoologist Charles Birch (1918–2009), took up his legacy, and used Whiteheadian process philosophy to promote a vision of a sentient, value-laden universe. Educated at the Universities of Melbourne and Adelaide, Birch became Challis Professor of Biology at the University of Sydney. An Anglican and later a Methodist, leading figure in the Student Christian Movement, ecologist, social critic, member of the Club of Rome, lay theologian and winner of the Templeton prize for progress in religion, Birch saw Whiteheadian process philosophy as a key to religious as well as social renewal. A former Vice-Moderator of the Church and Society Group of the World Council of Churches, he promoted Whiteheadian process philosophy in world church circles.

Like the German theologian Dietrich Bonhoeffer (1906–1945), Birch was critical of conventional Christianity and accepted the need for a new Christianity in a world come of age: a Christianity that came to terms with the sciences, modernity and ethical developments since the medieval period. As a lay theologian, Birch was influenced by American Protestant theologians, including the Chicago naturalist theologian Henry Nelson Wieman (1884–1975) and the German existentialist theologian Paul Tillich (1886–1965). Like Wieman, he defended a theological naturalism and rejected the view that the sacred was something separate from and beyond mundane experience. Following Tillich, he construed all theological entities as symbols and spoke of God as 'ultimate concern'. Unlike Tillich, however, and like Whitehead, Birch gave God a powerful causal role in the order of things. Where Tillich held that God was being itself beyond essence and existence, Birch, like Whitehead, made God central to the operation of the physical universe and to the causation of every event. Indeed, his causally active immanent God was the perfect exemplification of the ecological model of life, the source of creativity and novelty in the universe, and experienced by all entities.[48] In developing his process philosophy, Birch also drew on the work of the American process philosopher Charles Hartshorne, for whom God was internally related to creatures and changed in the course of the process. As a result, he arrived at a metaphysical vision for which God and the

---

47   W. E. Agar, *A Contribution to the Theory of the Living Organism* (Melbourne: Melbourne University Press with Oxford University Press, 1943), 7.
48   C. Birch, *Feelings* (Kensington, NSW: University of New South Wales Press, 1995), ch. 5.

universe evolved together in a holistic organic process.[49] Given his scientific eminence and involvement with major American theological naturalists and process theologians, Birch was ahead of many of his Australian audiences and, partly for this reason, he began to publish in the United States in the hope that his ideas would come back to Australia on the rebound.

Birch set out his holistic vision in many accessible books, including *Nature and God*, *On Purpose*, *The Liberation of Life*, *Feelings*, and *Living With the Animals*.[50] In these books he argued that the universe we experience differs from the theory-dependent ontologies of the post-Galilean sciences and that a phenomenological ontology of nature was needed to take account of its concrete reality. Birch was convinced that Whitehead's process philosophy could reconcile such an ontology with actual scientific developments, or would do so in the long run. This was an ambitious claim, especially in the Australian context where big ideas were often treated with suspicion. Like Whitehead, Birch rejected mechanism, any ontology based on substances, and the flight from subjectivity and experience in modern philosophy. Instead, he posited a highly relational, vibrant universe, in which each entity was a feeling, with objective and subjective dimensions, and internally related to the divine.[51] Some form of sentience was at the heart of all entities, and the individual entities of the universe were occasions of experience. At the same time, Birch sought to develop a new concept of God as the cosmic mind, or the within of all things, and contrasted this immanent, experiencing and changing process God with the omnipotent God of classical theism. According to Birch, God did not intervene in the world, but acted on all entities by persuasion or feeling.[52]

Birch's writings had considerable influence in the United States, even though he interpreted Whitehead's metaphysics as an ontology of nature, a view contested by many of Whitehead's more sophisticated followers. Like his friend, the theologian and philosopher David Ray Griffin (b. 1939) at the Center for Process Studies at the Claremont School of Theology in California, Birch promoted the notion of a postmodern world-view,

---

49 Birch, *Feelings*, 116–20. Cf G. Melleuish, "Conceptions of the Sacred in Australian Political Thought," 41–46.
50 C. Birch, *Nature and God* (London: SCM Press, 1965); with J. B. Cobb, *The Liberation of Life: From the Cell to the Community* (Cambridge: Cambridge University Press, 1981); *On Purpose* (Sydney: New South Wales University Press, 1990); *Feelings* (Kensington, NSW: University of New South Wales Press, 1995); and, with Lukas Vischer, *Living With the Animals: The Community of God's Creatures* (Geneva: WCC, 1997).
51 Birch, *Feelings*, ch. 5.
52 Birch, *Feelings*, 89, 111.

which made possible a return to enchantment. With another friend, the distinguished American process theologian John Cobb (b. 1925), he challenged his contemporaries to adopt a higher ethics, based on a radically ecological view of life. Birch championed animal rights and the need for a non-anthropomorphic ethics.[53] His views were influential in Methodist and what later became Uniting Church circles in the context of discussion of 'secularised religion'.[54]

Versions of process philosophy were also important for several feminist philosophers seeking to articulate philosophical cosmologies. The distinguished feminist philosopher Elizabeth Grosz (b. 1952), for example, who played a leading role in the split in the Philosophy Department at the University of Sydney in the 1970s, came into prominence as a defender of a corporeal feminism based on the lived body and sexual difference. Grosz championed corporeal feminism in opposition to French Lacanian psychoanalytical theory. Grosz rejected accounts of the body as a stable material entity and criticised mechanical conceptions of matter. In stages, in response to the work of the French process philosophers Bergson and Gilles Deleuze, she developed her own biologically-based process philosophy.[55]

---

53 C. Birch, *Nature and God; Confronting the Future: Australia and the World: the Next Hundred Years* (Ringwood: Penguin Books, 1975); with John Cobb, *The Liberation of Life*; *On Purpose*; with Lukas Vischer, *Living With the Animals; Biology and the Riddle of Life* (Sydney: New South Wales University Press, 1999); *Science and Soul* (Sydney: University of New South Wales Press, 2007). Birch's legacy was continued for a time by the Australasian Association for Process Thought and its online journal *Concrescence*, in which technical models of process were discussed.

54 For the Methodist dimension, see W. L. Ward, "Aspects of Secularized Religion within the Tradition of New South Wales Methodism since 1930" (Ph D Thesis, University of Wollongong, 1988) and *Men Ahead of Their Time* (Melbourne: Joint Board of Christian Education, 1996). The work of Dean Drayton, a Methodist Whiteheadian who became President of the Uniting Church, also fits this pattern. Drayton, a scientist by training, used Whitehead to promote a less reductionist understanding of nature. He also argued that secularisation could liberate people from religious enculturation, opposed denominationalism, an ordained clergy and individualism, and promoted the priority of the experiential, community groups and dialogue between science and religion. More generally, see B. Mansfield, "From Denomination to Faith Community: Ideas on Mission in the Uniting Church-Dean Drayton 1977–98," in *Making History For God: Essays on Evangelicalism, Revival and Mission*, ed. G. R. Treloar and R. D. Linder (Sydney: Robert Menzies College, 2004), 151–68.

55 Grosz's works include: *Sexual Subversions: Three French Feminists* (Sydney: Allen and Unwin, 1989); *Jacques Lacan: A Feminist Introduction* (London: Routledge, 1990); *Volatile Bodies: Toward a Corporeal Feminism* (Bloomington: Indiana University Press, 1994); *Space, Time, and Perversion* (London: Routledge, 1995); *Becomings: Explorations in Time, Memory and Futures* (Ithaca, NY: Cornell University Press, 1999); *Architecture from the Outside: Essays on Virtual and Real Space* (Cambridge, Mass.: MIT Press, 2001); *The Nick of Time: Politics, Evolution and the Untimely* (Durham, NC: Duke

Like Samuel Alexander half a century before her, Grosz did not retreat from rethinking the nature of space and time, or from other difficult philosophical and scientific issues. From a Jewish background, she sympathised with the feminist mysticism and cult of 'divine bodies' of the French philosopher Luce Irigaray (b. 1930),[56] although she did not develop Irigaray's religious thought. Rather she sought to bring feminism into a new relationship with Darwinism.[57] After decades of feminism influenced by interpretations of French philosophy as 'poststructuralism', which emphasised issues of textuality and discourse, Grosz sought to take account of the sciences and to reconceive the position of women as within nature.

A related, albeit different, relation to process philosophy can be found in the works of the Italian Australian philosopher Rosi Braidotti (b. 1954), Foundation Professor of Women's Studies at the University of Utrecht.[58] Like Grosz, Braidotti mainly worked overseas. Nonetheless, her writings have been closely followed in Australia, partly because she reworked the affirmative approach to desire found in Spinoza, and developed a vitalist process philosophy indebted to Deleuze. Braidotti criticises religion fiercely, but makes what she dubs 'a postsecular turn', based on the claim that human corporeality involved a form of sacrality.[59] Her work covers not only philosophy and feminism, but also philosophy of science and technology, cultural studies and race studies, and she has made contributions to the emerging debates on the posthuman.[60]

Overall, process philosophy was an ambiguous influence on Australian religious thought. On the one hand, it made it possible to move beyond various forms of supernaturalism and to adopt a world-view that privileged internal relations. Those influenced by process philosophy often argued that

---

University Press, 2004); *Time Travels: Feminism, Nature, Power* (Durham, NC: Duke University Press, 2005); *Chaos, Territory, Art: Deleuze and the Framing of the Earth* (New York: Columbia University Press, 2008); and *Becoming Undone: Darwinian Reflections on Life, Politics and Art* (Durham, NC: Duke University Press, 2011).

56 E. Grosz, *Irigaray and the Divine* (Sydney: Local Consumption 1986).
57 Grosz, *Becoming Undone*.
58 Braidotti's works include *Patterns of Dissonance*, translated by Elizabeth Guild (New York: Routledge, 1991); *Nomadic Subjects: Embodiment and Sexual Difference in Contemporary Feminist Theory* (New York: Columbia University Press, 1994); *Metamorphoses: Towards a Materialist Theory of Becoming* (Cambridge: Polity Press, 2002); *Transpositions: On Nomadic Ethics* (Cambridge: Polity Press, 2006); and *The Posthuman* (Cambridge: Polity Press, 2013).
59 R. Braidotti, "In Spite of the Times: The Postsecular Turn in Feminism," *Theory, Culture and Society* 25, no. 6 (2008) 1–24.
60 For discussion, see B. Blaagaard and I. van der Tuin (eds.), *The Subject of Rosi Braidotti: Politics and Concepts* (London: Bloomsbury Academic, 2014).

meaning and value were intrinsic to the universe – claims that connected at some points with theses advanced by vitalist writers. On the other hand, the precise sense in which reality was alleged to be process was often unclear, and attempts to ground particular views in either the natural sciences or in the work of some philosopher made only limited impact on scientists.

Environmental Philosophy

Elements of postsecular consciousness were also associated in Australia with some forms of environmentalism promoted by ecologists and environmental philosophers. Once again, this tendency was indebted to European and American thought, but Australians gained major international presence because of the courage with which they directly addressed crucial issues. The deep ecologist and transpersonalist Warwick Fox (b. 1954), for example, began his career as an ecological theorist by attempting to clarify admixture of systematic ethical and ecosophic concerns in the deep ecology pioneered by the Norwegian philosopher Arne Naess (1912–2009). Drawing on his background in transpersonal psychology, Fox focused on actual experience of nature and on a sense of identity with it. Criticising Naess' reliance on a plurality of ultimate norms, he interpreted Naess' principle of self-realisation to mean that self-realisation could be best achieved through a sense of commonality with the world. Later he developed a general ethical theory applicable to humans, animals, nature and the built environment.[61]

Another environmentalist, alternativist logician Richard Sylvan (originally Routley) (1935–1996), called for a new environmental ethics that was not biased in favour of human beings. Sylvan criticised deep ecology as an amalgam of metaphysical, religious and psychological notions and set out a deep environmental ethics instead.[62] With his wife, Val Routley (later Val Plumwood), Sylvan attacked the human chauvinism of any ethics that assumed that only human beings mattered and attempted to develop a

---

61 W. Fox, *Approaching Deep Ecology: A Response to Richard Sylvan's Critique of Deep Ecology* (Hobart: Centre for Environmental Studies, University of Tasmania, 1986); *Toward a Transpersonal Ecology: Developing New Foundations for Environmentalism* (Boston: Shambhala, 1990); his edited collection *Ethics and the Built Environment* (London: Routledge, 2000; and *A Theory of General Ethics: Human Relationships, Nature and the Built Environment* (Cambridge, MA: MIT Press, 2006).
62 R. Sylvan, *A Critique of Deep Ecology* (Canberra: ANU Department of Philosophy, 1985); also published in *Radical Philosophy* 40 (1985); 1–12 and 41 (1985): 10–22; with D. Bennett, *The Greening of Ethics* (Cambridge: White Horse Press, 1994); and *Transcendental Metaphysics: From Radical to Deep Pluralism* (Cambridge: White Horse Press, 1997).

non-anthropocentric ethics. Sylvan was convinced that Western philosophy had become over-instrumental and failed to account for the nonmundane features of nature as human beings actually experienced it. Against Western philosophy, he insisted on the intrinsic value of the natural world and argued for a non-reductionist ontology of nature. At the end of his life, Sylvan defended green anarchism and was moving towards Eastern philosophies as providing models for a holistic world-view. In his major and still neglected metaphysical treatise, *Transcendental Metaphysics*, Sylvan adopted a radical pluralism according to which there is no single truth of the matter and a complex ontology in which some objects non-exist.[63] However, the possibility of a postsecular ontology was not taken up.

Sylvan's partner of nearly twenty years, Val Plumwood (1939–2008), also made major contributions to environmental philosophy – contributions that implied that the commonsense world-view of most Australian scientists was seriously mistaken. A leading eco-feminist, prominent in the early 1970s in the development of radical ecosophy, Plumwood helped establish the transdiscipline known as ecological humanities. In her major theoretical works, *Feminism and the Master of Nature* (1993) and *Environmental Culture: The Ecological Crisis of Reason* (2002), Plumwood interpreted the environmental crisis as a crisis of dualistic reason and critiqued the Western 'hyperseparation' between the self and the other and between the human being and nature.[64] Consistent with her own love of the forest, and influenced by what she took to be Aboriginal philosophical ecology,[65] Plumwood asserted the claims of nature in what she termed 'the active voice'.[66] At the end of her life she described herself as a philosophical animist.[67] In contrast to postmodern and deep ecological approaches, Plumwood emphasised both the continuities and the divisions between human beings and nature.[68] She agitated for an ecological interspecies ethic of recognition, based on empathy for the other,

---

63   See Sylvan, *Transcendental Metaphysics*.
64   N. Griffin, "Val Plumwood 1939–" in *Fifty Key Thinkers of the Environment*, ed. J. Palmer (London: Routledge, 2001) 285–6.
65   See D. B. Rose, "An Indigenous Philosophical Ecology: Situating the Human," *Australian Journal of Anthropology* 16 (2005): 294–305.
66   V. Plumwood, "Nature in the Active Voice," *Australian Humanities Review* 46 (2009): 113–29.
67   V. Plumwood, "Place, Politics, and Spirituality," in *Pagan Visions for a Sustainable Future*, ed. L. de Angeles, E. R. Orr and T. van Dooren (Woodbury, MN: Llewellyn, 2005), 237 and D.B. Rose,"Val Plumwood's Philosophical Animism: attentive interactions in the sentient world", *Environmental Humanities* 3 (2013): 93–109, especially 97. Retrieved from http://environmentalhumanities.org/arch/vol3/3.5.pdf.
68   N. Griffin, "Val Plumwood 1939-", 283–290.

who should be regarded as fellow agents and narrative subjects.[69] She also advocated a materialist spirituality which located the sacred in the immediate world around us.[70] Her final views were visionary and in her thought nature tended to become a sacred reality invested with rights.

Another feminist environmental philosopher and academic, Freya Mathews (b. 1949), became an international figure in environmental philosophy. Moving in stages away from scientific orthodoxy to a defence of animism, Mathews argues for a view of nature as mindful and communicative, while rejecting religion and any notion of disembodied spirit. In her influential book, *The Ecological Self* (1991), she proposed a non-Cartesian understanding of the human being. Her wider agenda, however, was to argue for a different way of appropriating the universe. The early Mathews argued for a realist interpretation of quantum physics which implied that the universe was holistic and made up of force fields and their variations rather than of things. In later works, such as *For Love of Matter* (2003) and *Reinhabiting Reality* (2005), she rejects what she dubs the de-realisation of the world characteristic of modern philosophy. In place of the metaphysics underlying modernity, with its dualism of mind and matter, Mathews argues that reality has to be understood as subject as well as object and as an expanding plenum, even a cosmic self.[71] The world is not only causal relations, but also a nexus of communication. Mathews embraces radical holism and claims that everything has a sense of the whole of which it was a part. Drawing upon Aboriginal spirituality and her knowledge of Chinese Daoist philosophy, Mathews proposes a panpsychist and non-dualist world-view. She posits a reanimated world, in which everything is unfolding. This universe is a self-realising system and tending to self-increase.[72] Mathews denies that her revival of animism is a regression to a premodern world-view and rejects Australian philosopher John Passmore's defence of anthropocentrism.[73] More broadly, she recommends her animist world-view as the key to cultural and political revival after postmodernism.

---

69 V. Plumwood, *Feminism and the Mastery of Nature* (London: Routledge, 1993) and *Environmental Culture: The Ecological Crisis of Reason* (London: Routledge, 2002); see also D. Hyde, *Eco-logical Lives: The Philosophical Lives of Richard Routley/Sylvan and Val Routley/Plumwood* (Cambridge: White Horse Press, 2014), chs. 6 and 7.
70 N. Griffin, "Val Plumwood 1939–", 287.
71 F. Mathews, *The Ecological Self* (London: Routledge, 1991); see also J. Franklin, *Corrupting the Youth: A History of Philosophy in Australia* (Paddington, NSW: Macleay Press, 2003), 356–7.
72 F. Mathews, *Reinhabiting Reality: Towards a Recovery of Culture* (Albany, NY: SUNY Press, 2005), 3, 8, 25.
73 F. Mathews, *For Love of Matter: A Contemporary Panpsychism* (Albany, NY: SUNY Press, 2003); and *Reinhabiting Reality*. For sympathetic discussion, see K. Rigby,

Another environmentalist, Clive Hamilton (b. 1953), has gained an international readership for his *The Freedom Paradox* (2008) and *Requiem for a Species* (2010). Initially influenced by Carl Jung and Ken Wilber, Hamilton has developed a postsecular ethics inspired by Schopenhauer's aphorism: 'We must learn to understand nature from ourselves, not ourselves from nature'.[74] Like other environmentalists discussed here, Hamilton does not retreat from secularity, but envisages a universe which is, in some respects at least, nonmundane.

Narratives of Place

Other writers arrived at postsecular consciousness by attempting to help Australians take more account of Aboriginal experiences of place as spiritual, as linked with real ancestral beings, and as latent with nonmundane possibilities. As early as 1989, the archaeologist and historian D. J. Mulvaney suggested that a "spiritual concept of place may prove to be Aboriginal society's greatest contribution to multi-cultural Australia." [75] His challenge was taken up by the historian Peter Read (b. 1945). Sensitive to the diverse meanings of 'sacral', Read seeks to help Australians to understand the Aboriginal association between the sacred and place. To do so, he explores places in which spirits are sensed, seen or found.[76] In a trilogy of extraordinary books between 1999 and 2003,[77] he brings a postsecular consciousness to bear on themes and places largely ignored by more positivist historiography. Where secularists imagine a world free of religious illusions, Read believes that for Aborigines the real world is the world of the spiritual, and that this world includes potentially dangerous

---

"Minding (about) Matter: On the Eros and Anguish of Earthly Encounter," *Australian Humanities Review* 38 (2006).

74　C. Hamilton, *The Freedom Paradox: Towards a Post-secular Ethic* (Crows Nest, NSW: Allen and Unwin, 2008); and *Requiem for a Species: Why We Resist the Truth about Climate Change* (London: Earthscan, 2010).

75　D.J. Mulvaney, *Encounters in Place: Outsiders and Aboriginal Australians 1606–1985* (St Lucia: University of Queensland Press, 1989), 224, quoted in Rose, Deborah Bird, *Gulaga: A Report on the Cultural Significance of Mt Dromedary to Aboriginal People, presented to the Forestry Commission of New South Wales and the New South Wales National Parks and Wildlife Service* ([Sydney]: The Service, 1990). The citation is referred to in P. Read, *A Haunted Land No Longer?: Changing Relationships to a Spiritualised Australia* (Sydney: History Council of New South Wales, 2004), History Council Lecture, 4.

76　P. Read, *Haunted Earth* (Sydney: University of New South Wales Press, 2003), 98.

77　P. Read, *A Rape of the Soul So Profound: The Return of the Stolen Generation* (St. Leonards, NSW: Allen & Unwin, 1999); *Belonging: Australians, Place and Aboriginal Ownership* (Oakleigh, Vic.: Cambridge University Press, 2000); and *Haunted Earth*.

place spirits. Read does not retreat from the achievements of secularity, but he brings an exceptional sensitivity to such liminal data. Read relates experiences of the dead, ghosts and spirits and explores ranges of experience celebrated by Chinese Australians rather than by Europeans. He invokes developments in French theory to complex dualisms between fact and interpretation and between past and present, and entertains a third dimension, occupying neither a space in our heads nor an objective reality. He also embraces a postsecular immanentism of the earth. 'We evolved from the earth. We share in its electrochemical structure. Why should we continue to imagine ourselves wholly distinct from it?' he asks.[78]

A different approach to the place, of wider geographic application, was developed by the distinguished Melbourne ethnographer of the Pacific, former Jesuit and historian Greg Dening (1931–2008). Dening's contribution was to marry social anthropology and history in the context of narrative concerns that undid traditional notions of fact and fiction.[79] Heavily influenced by French theoretical texts and inclined to privilege discourse and narrative over classical conceptions of truth, Dening pioneered what came to be known as the Melbourne school of ethnographic history. This school argued that history was performance and that historians should become storytellers, exercising creative imagination. The turn to performance implied sympathy for the claim that reality was intrinsically textual and hermeneutical, and so, to some degree, relative to an interpretive scheme. It also implied an epistemology based on theatricality and participation, as opposed to positivist conceptions of the sciences. Dening's work allowed his readers to participate in worlds as they were lived in the past. Dening himself used such a perspective to maintain a participatory involvement in the liturgy of the Catholic Church, while recognising milestones in his own mind which made it more like theatre than anything literal. Thus, in a moving passage he wrote:

> I am at mass in San Giacomo's in Bellagio. Donna is beside me. We share a faith. How much we share we do not dare to ask ...
>
> In this Italian church, Italian words wash over me. Their ambience is my symboling, not their individual meaning. I baulk at credos in

---

78 Read, *Haunted Earth*, 252.
79 Among Dening's many books, see *The Death of William Gooch: A History's Anthropology* (Carlton, Vic.: Melbourne University Press, 1995); *Mr Bligh's Bad Language: Passion, Power and Theatre on The Bounty* (New York: Cambridge University Press, 1992); *Islands and Beaches: Discourse on a Silent Land, Marquesas, 1774–1880* (Carlton, Vic.: Melbourne University Press, 1980); and *Beach Crossings: Voyaging Across Times, Cultures and Self* (Philadelphia: University of Pennsylvania Press, 2004).

English, but not in Italian. In English, I begin to wonder at my honesty. My mind goes laterally to the ways I believe, not to what I believe. In Italian believing has no words, just a sense that something of what I do is true. In Italian, I know that other believers are the same, for all their differences. I catch the distance between their selves and their believing words – in the distraction of their eyes, in the hunched silence of the old, in the twisting curiosities of the young. Maybe what those Latin traditionalists say is true. The language of religion is best a mysterious language. I doubt, however, that it should be dead.[80]

Drawing on his vast knowledge of Christian tradition, Dening, unusually among recent Australian intellectuals, celebrated a sacrality of time, especially a sacrality of time *in* place. 'We all live in deep time', he wrote.[81] He also extended sacral naturalism to places other than Australia. In doing so, he opened up questions of how experiential particularism could be reconciled with wider schemes of social explanation. Here perhaps he pointed to forms of Australian religious thought still to come.

Responses Influenced by Psychoanalysis

Many Australian intellectuals drawn to some form of sacral naturalism distanced themselves from modern conceptions of the self. Other intellectuals, however, arrived at postsecular consciousness by taking modern, and specifically post-Freudian, conceptions of the self seriously. The Anglican theologian and social critic Bishop Burgmann, for example, whose work was discussed in Chapter II, promoted psychoanalysis as a way of analysing the soul and accessing self-revelation through the unconscious.[82] Burgmann insisted that psychoanalysis was no enemy to religion and philosophy, but rather a distinct gain that tended to broaden both.[83] His stance was shared by some theosophists, by some influenced by the reception of a theory of erotics in Russian and Greek orthodoxy, and by his Morpeth colleague, the Reverend R. S. Lee, who saw psychoanalysis as a means to clearing away the rubbish that clung to Christianity. Lee

---

80   G. Dening, "Soliloquy in San Giacomo," in *Performances* (Melbourne: Melbourne University Publishing, 1996), 267.
81   G. Dening, "Living With and In Deep Time," in *The Historian's Conscience: Australian Historians on the Ethics of History*, ed. S. Macintyre (Melbourne: Melbourne University Press, 2004), 40–8.
82   J. Damousi, *Freud in the Antipodes: A Cultural History of Psychoanalysis in Australia* (Sydney: University of New South Wales Press, 2005), 81–5.
83   E. Burgmann, "In Defence of Freud," *Australian Highway* 11, no. 9 (1929), 151–2.

accepted the psychological character of religious beliefs and the need to understand Christianity as an ego religion, rather than in terms of sin and guilt.[84] Both Burgmann and Lee held that psychoanalysis could help to modernise Christianity without stripping it of either symbols or liturgy.

The most striking applications of psychoanalysis to the diagnosis of Australian spirituality came from those open to the sacred, but critical of the Christianity of the churches. Several Australian writers influenced by Freudian and post-Freudian psychoanalytic theory opened up postsecular perspectives of this sort. Psychoanalysis provides its adherents with a symbolic interpretation of human life that can be deployed to interrogate social and cultural life, as well as a critical perspective from which the inadequacies of historical Christianity can be judged. Many intellectuals sympathetic to psychoanalysis have not been sympathetic to religion. Some, however, while critiquing the churches, have argued that those who deny the sacred are self-deluded and unrealistic. Psychoanalyst and former Catholic priest Neville Symington, for example, construes psychoanalysis as a natural religion, or a system which reveals dynamics of the kind religions allege operating within the psyche itself. Symington sees religion as the guarantor of civilisation in a world prone to self-worship and madness.[85] A major interpreter of the British psychoanalytic theorist Wilfred Bion (1897–1979) and the author of a new theory of narcissism, Symington worked in the Tavistock Clinic in London in the 1970s and 1980s before migrating to Australia in 1986, where he became President of the Australian Psychoanalytic Society (1999–2002). His reconciliation of psychoanalysis with religion implies that the sacral reappears once the human being faces their inner darkness. The message that lies at the heart of mature religion is that constructive emotional action is what gives meaning to our lives.[86] According to Symington, religion and psychoanalysis need each other. Psychoanalysis needed the core values that endow life with meaning, while religion needs to become mature and relevant to modern living.[87]

Psychoanalysis is also one element informing the work of the sociologist and writer John Carroll (b. 1944). Originally a Calvinist and inclined to a tragic view of life, Carroll combines disbelief in the goodness of human

---

84 R. S. Lee, *Freud and Christianity* (London: James Clarke, 1948), 172, 190, 197.
85 N. Symington, *Emotion and Spirit: Questioning the Claims of Psychoanalysis and Religion* (London: Cassell, 1994), 192.
86 Symington, *Emotion and Spirit*, 192.
87 Symington, *Emotion and Spirit*.

nature, a theological sense of transcendence, and an undefined yearning for a richer and metaphysically meaningful culture.[88] Carroll wrote his doctorate on the German anarchist Max Stirner (1806–1856), Nietzsche and Dostoevsky at Cambridge under the literary critic George Steiner. His early work was influenced by Philip Rieff's *Triumph of the Therapeutic*.[89] Sympathetic to nineteenth-century European thought and combining psychological and sociological perspectives, Carroll develops a distinctive diagnosis of cultural changes in the West in a series of interpretative books. Identifying the crisis of belief as the West's major problem, Carroll proclaims disbelief in humanism, secularism and other modern doctrines, while gesturing towards a psychically based sacral outlook for which the sacral emerges in myth.[90] He denounces Western intellectuals for attempting to replace God by man and implies that humanism, in the sense of the belief that human beings can do all things, is the key to the *cul de sac* in which Western culture currently finds itself. 'We live amidst the ruins of the great, five-hundred-year epoch of humanism,' he declares.[91] Accordingly, Carroll laments the decline of religion because over many generations religious practice builds up moral capital in a community, capital that, he argues, will slowly run down in secular times:[92]

> Ego and soul we glimpse in shadow at least, but beyond them there is scant religious language of any gravity that has survived in modernity. Not only are the churches empty, but Christian doctrine is largely bygone.[93]

For Carroll, the West is dying because it lacks a story and is unable to achieve a metaphysical level of meaning. Carroll himself is loyal to a conception of a sacred order or law governing the cosmos. He offers a populist critique of modern élites for failing to teach 'the law' in this sense. Carroll

---

88 See J. Carroll, *Sceptical Sociology* (London: Routledge & Kegan Paul, 1980); *Humanism: The Wreck of Western Culture* (London: Fontana, 1993); *The Wreck of Western Culture: Humanism Revisited* (Carlton North, Vic.: Scribe, 2004); and *The Western Dreaming: The Western World Is Dying for Want of a Story* (Sydney: HarperCollins, 2001).
89 P. Rieff, *The Triumph of the Therapeutic: Uses of Faith After Freud* (New York: Harper Row, 1966); see Carroll's early study, *Puritan, Paranoid, Remissive: A Sociology of Modern Culture* (London: Routledge and Kegan Paul, 1977).
90 See J. Carroll, *Guilt, the Grey Eminence behind Character, History and Culture* (London: Routledge & Kegan Paul, 1985).
91 Carroll, *The Wreck of Western Culture*, 1. For discussion of Carroll's anti-humanism, see G. Melleuish, "Conceptions of the Sacred in Australian Political Thought," 48–51.
92 Carroll, *The Wreck of Western Culture*, 4.
93 J. Carroll, *Ego and Soul: The Modern West in Search of Meaning* (Pymble, NSW: HarperCollins, 1998), 231.

does not, however, develop this theme along traditional religious lines,[94] although he holds that human beings cannot live without structuring myth and that the Christ story needs to be renewed in contemporary terms.[95] His later work is less theistic and influenced by Heidegger.

Psychoanalysis also plays a role in the work of the Jungian literary critic, sometime disciple of James Hillman and insightful commentator on Australian spirituality, David Tacey (b. 1953). More inclined to enchantment than Carroll, Tacey is one of the few Australians to propose elements of an Australian dreaming. Like Hillman, Tacey believes that Jung discovered much that the analytical psychology claiming to follow him tends to repress.[96] Tacey goes beyond Hillman, however, and returns to the theories of Jung, who, he rightly insists, was a dialectical thinker and not to be associated with the New Age.[97] Tacey's faith in psychoanalysis supplements and, to some degree, underwrites his questioning of older religious dogmas and life forms.

Gifted with an eloquent prose style, Tacey historicises Jung's archetypal psychology for the Australian instance and proclaims a paradigm shift from religion to spirituality. In Tacey's view, the spiritual and the religious are separating categories of Australian experience.[98] The Australian experience of spirit is distinctive, almost pre-verbal, and grounded in the ordinary events and experiences of daily life. In a fusion of Jungian, Indigenous and Celtic themes, Tacey advocates a spirituality of the earth and a recovery of the sacramentality of nature, which will enable Australians to overcome their religious woes. He discerns a spiritual revolution in which spirit empties itself into nature.[99] Here he owes much to Veronica Brady and, like her, he acknowledges a mysterious numinous that works towards wholeness at the heart of human creativity. In his later writings, Tacey relates the desacralisation of consciousness to problems of mental health and disease and defends meaning-making as necessary to both our physical and mental wellbeing.[100]

---

94 J. Carroll, *Where Ignorant Armies Clash by Night: On the Retreat of Faith and its Consequences* (Bundoora, Vic: Seminar on the Sociology of Culture, La Trobe University, 1986).
95 J. Carroll, *The Existential Jesus* (Carlton North, Vic.: Scribe Publications, 2007).
96 D. Tacey (ed.), *The Jung Reader* (Hove, East Sussex: Routledge, 2012).
97 D. Tacey, *Jung and the New Age* (Hove, East Sussex: Brunner-Routledge, 2001) and *How to Read Jung* (London: Granta, 2006).
98 D. Tacey, "Spirituality in Australia Today," in *Sacred Australia: Post-Secular Considerations*, ed. M. Paranjape (Melbourne: Clouds of Magellan, 2009), 44–64.
99 D. Tacey, *Edge of the Sacred: Transformation in Australia* (Blackburn North, Vic.: HarperCollins, 1995), 197 and *Australia In Search of A Soul* (North Parramatta, NSW: Eremos Institute and Centre for Ministry, 1997).
100 D. Tacey, *Gods and Diseases: Making Sense of our Physical and Mental Wellbeing* (Sydney: HarperCollins, 2011).

Tacey's archetypal reading of the Australian soul depends on a speculative theory of the evolution of consciousness. According to Tacey consciousness has changed, the traditional image of God has collapsed, and God has to be rediscovered inside the human being. Tacey further argues that a new concept of God is needed as real ordinary presence, which he associates with the mystery and spirit at the core of the universe.[101]

Tacey is critical of the institutional church, which he argues has remained a parental authority dictating an infantilising religion. Australia's churches have mostly discouraged rather than made possible individual experiences of the sacred, he claims,[102] and Christianity is languishing, partly because it has lost touch with the immediacies of everyday living, including our erotic and embodied lives. Its religious language, Tacey maintains, is archaic, its narratives are dualistic, its imagery patriarchal and sexist, and its iconography is literalistic.[103] The Australian churches offer an imported 'heavenism' in place of a real engagement with local experience and landscape. Tacey responds to this situation by discerning a great hunger for spirituality in Australia that can be met by learning from Indigenous spirituality and refocusing spirituality on place and the sacred earth. He believes that Australians need to look to Aboriginal culture rather than to Europe if they are to enter into the psychic field of nature.[104] Tacey implies that Australians suffer from a repressed Aboriginality and that Indigenous Aboriginality is a mirror of what the unconscious life of other Australians can become. He posits a non-Indigenous Aboriginality, which can be the basis for a land-based spirituality adequate to the Australian psyche:

> The Aboriginal sacred experience becomes, whether we like it or not, our own cultural heritage as soon as we send cultural tap-roots down into Aboriginal soil ... the Dreaming, and the wisdom of the ages, comes gradually and subtly toward us.[105]

Tacey uses a generic account of Aboriginality to illuminate both 'Aboriginal spirituality' and the nascent European Australian Indigenous

---

101 D. Tacey, *Re-Enchantment: The New Australian Spirituality* (Sydney: HarperCollins, 2000), 168.
102 Tacey, *Re-Enchantment*, 45.
103 Tacey, *Re-Enchantment*, 29–32.
104 Tacey, *Re-Enchantment*, 93–122.
105 D. Tacey, "Spirit Place," in *Changing Places: Re-Imagining Australia*, ed. J. Cameron (Double Bay, NSW: Longueville Books, 2003), 246–7; and C. San Roque, A. Dowd and D. Tacey (eds.), *Placing Psyche: Exploring Cultural Complexes in Australia* (New Orleans, LA: Spring Journal Books, 2011).

consciousness that he believes is struggling to emerge in a culture dominated by ego-driven identity. On his account, Western European cosmology is reversed in Australia, and this gives rise to a completely different spiritual phenomenology, such that spiritual feeling enters us, as it were, from the feet.[106]

Tacey reads Jung as a tougher and more radical thinker than do many of Jung's more weak-minded admirers. On Tacey's account, Jung can be read as contributing to a new religious vision in cultures in which human beings need religion but have religion in its present form.[107] According to Tacey, Jung is not a conventionally religious thinker, but a prophet open to the exploration of the spirit, who foresees that the spirit becomes darkened because it needs to be reborn.[108] Indeed, for Tacey, Jung is an unrivalled guide at a time when there is a secret unrest at the roots of our being, the spirit of the holy has fallen into the unconscious, and we desperately need to renew our relationship with the sacred.[109] Following Jung, Tacey proposes a non-dualist conception of spirit as invisible. The psyche is a world in which the ego is contained, and not merely the inner consciousness of an individual.[110] He associates spirituality with forces and practices that help us to transcend the alienation of the ego and with being connected to a greater or larger whole, a condition which he claims is normal for human beings and has been abnormally restricted in modernity. Tacey's conception of religion is less clear and related to religious studies discourses of European origin. Religion, he argues, has to make itself more spiritual and churches should change from places of devotional worship to centres of existential spirituality. While religious belief and formal religious affiliation are dying out, Tacey claims that the experience of God and spirituality generally are not.[111] Rather they are transposed into a depth dimension of the immanent so that the proximate, the ordinary and the natural become mysterious. This implies that traditional religions may be dispensable and Tacey is open to forms of postreligion.[112]

---

106 Tacey, *Re-Enchantment*, 94, and "Toward a New Animism: Jung, Hillman and Analytical Psychology" (unpublished paper, 2010); see also D. Tacey, *Edge of the Sacred: Jung, Psyche, Earth* (Einsiedeln: Daimon, 2009).
107 D. Tacey, *The Darkening Spirit: Jung, Spirituality, Religion* (Hove; New York: Routledge, 2013).
108 Tacey, *The Darkening Spirit*, 1–8.
109 Tacey, *The Darkening Spirit*, ch. 1.
110 Tacey, *The Darkening Spirit*, ch. 7.
111 D. Tacey, *The Spirituality Revolution: The Emergence of Contemporary Spirituality* (Hove, East Sussex: Brunner-Routledge, 2003), ch. 1.
112 Tacey, *The Spirituality Revolution*, ch. 8.

Tacey's gnosis hinges on a national Romantic account of landscape. Although Tacey emphasises that spirituality opens us to something that is not human and might transform us, he remains modernist in avoiding both coherent metaphysics and commitment to literal spiritual realities. Instead, he finds existential equivalents drawn from the Australian experience for traditional theological tropes and gestures towards an allegorical interpretation of an eco-theology in which Christ and the Holy Spirit become active parts of a restored qualitative cosmos.[113] Tacey moves towards this cosmosophic vision by endorsing creation theology as articulated by the Australian theologian Denis Edwards and its accompanying conception of 'postmodern science', which he claims offers the prospect of a return of enchantment.

In the Australian context, Tacey stands out as an original and courageous voice. His vision implies the possibility of a more integral and less superficially discursive cultural order. Further, although his texts are accessible, Tacey draws on deep reading in Christian, Islamic and other spiritual traditions in proposing a religious interpretation of the Australian condition and how it might be overcome. In doing so, he raises questions about a possible postsecular consciousness to which other Australians are being drawn in stages as they consider issues of youth suicide and depression, the decline of civil participation, and the abandonment of community, especially rural community, in the pursuit of purely instrumental economic goals.

A related vision can be found in the many books of Catholic priest and archaeologist Eugene Stockton (b. 1934). Like Tacey, Stockton looks to Jung's theory of archetypes for an understanding of the unconscious and posits 'Aboriginal spirituality' and 'Aboriginal religion'. Stockton's approach is indebted to the desert mysticism of the well-known French spiritual writer and priest Charles Foucault (1858–1916), who lived among the Tuareg in the Sahara,[114] and, despite his self-chosen title as 'a bush theologian', he draws many of his ideas from international sources. Specifically, his theology is

---

113 Tacey's method here is indebted to David Ranson's adaption of the correlationalism of the American theologian David Tracey to the Australian context; see D. Ranson, *Across the Great Divide: Bridging Spirituality and Religion Today* (Strathfield, NSW: St. Paul's, 2002).

114 See E. Stockton, *Landmarks: A Spiritual Search in a Southern Land* (Eastwood, NSW: Parish Ministry Publications, 1990); *The Aboriginal Gift: Spirituality for a Nation* (Alexandria, NSW: Millennium Books, 1995); "The Way of A Bush Theologian," in *Evangelisation in an Australian Context*, ed. D. Brennan (Blackburn, Vic.: Collins Dove, 1992), 19–25; and *Wonder: A Way to God* (Strathfield, NSW: St. Paul's, 1998); see also R. Cameron, *Karingal: A Search for Australian Spirituality* (Homebush, NSW: St. Paul's, 1995).

indebted to the theology of Meister Eckhart, to the nondualist theology of Ramon Panikkar, and to Eastern Orthodoxy. He also relies on Perennialist writers, on various New Age authors (Ken Wilber, Rupert Sheldrake), and on theologians inclined to Romantic science (Teilhard de Chardin, Diarmuid O'Murchu). Once again Romantic geography and Celtic Australian nationalism go hand in hand.

Stockton seeks to pioneer an Australian theology, integrating Biblical insights, a reverence for the land and Aboriginal spirituality. Responding to the discourse of the Daly River Indigenous artist and elder, Miriam Rose Ungunmerr-Baumann (b. 1950), about the gift of *dadirri* (deep listening) that Australians were being offered by Aboriginals,[115] he argues that Australians can learn the spiritual meaning of the country from Aboriginal people, if only they will listen. Stockton is a spiritual visionary with an archaeologist's eye and a powerful sense of place.[116] He combines apophaticism with a turn to the sacral in nature and does so within the bounds of Catholic Orthodoxy, generously conceived.

In his main theoretical text, *The Deep Within: Towards An Archetypal Theology* (2011), Stockton advocates archetypal theology as a new discipline, able to recover something of the *theologia* or mystical contemplation that prevailed in the early medieval church. In contrast to the reasoning with concepts of classical Western theology, archetypal theology deals with the 'deep within', and with archetypes as formless bodies of emotion.[117] Stockton links this theology with Biblical types and with the pre-scholastic monastic theology of Western Europe. He posits a collective consciousness independent of individuals, a transcendental ego integral to it, and a non-duality of the deep, transcending subject and object.[118] Stockton is prepared to abandon a reified God who is a being above all other beings and other dualisms of the Latin church. He also accepts religious pluralism and the view that religions are contingent and relative human constructions.[119]

Stockton uses archetypal theology as a way to reposition Christianity for a new age of the world. Through it, he hopes that Australians will see the value of living within the myth as another order of reality. He envisages this as a new consciousness, to which Australians are called, and as involving

---

115 M. R. Ungunmerr, "Dadirri," in Stockton, *The Aboriginal Gift*, 179–84.
116 E. Stockton and J. Merriman (eds.), *Blue Mountains Dreaming: The Aboriginal Heritage* (Lawson, NSW: Blue Mountains Education and Research Trust, 2009).
117 E. Stockton, *The Deep Within: Towards An Archetypal Theology* (Lawson, NSW: Blue Mountains Education and Research Trust, 2011), 6–9.
118 Stockton, *The Deep Within*, 97, 102.
119 Stockton, *The Deep Within*, 3ff.

a spiritual journey of the ego outside itself.[120] Stockton himself envisages a fusion of Christianity and Aboriginal spirituality comparable to the Christian conversion of Ireland, or the merger of Hinduism and animism in Bali. He also discerns an original Aboriginal theologising of Christian themes in Aboriginal Christian art.[121]

Science and the Sacral

Other writers open to postsecular consciousness argue that the sacral has a basis in science itself, a claim made, in more cautious terms, by Australian scientists in the nineteenth century in the context of arguments about the design evident in the physical world. In the twentieth century there were attempts to rehabilitate the sacred by appealing to developments in physics and biology. La Trobe University microbiologist Darryl Reanney (d. 1996), for example, discerned a gap at the centre of Western civilisation resulting from the breakdown of the old faiths, a gap which could only be filled by a renewed sense of the sacred and a shift from mechanism to sacred reverence.[122] In dialogue with New Age figures such as Rupert Sheldrake, Reanney used popular science presentations to open the way for a renewal of enchantment. Reanney was concerned to understand reality as a timeless continuum. He maintained that all matter carries a memory of the perfection which obtained at the beginning of the universe and which it yearns to recover. Similarly, human beings were part of a deep cosmic consciousness and persisted into an after-life that was essential to their being. Reanney discerned deep and nondualist unity behind the diversity of life. He envisaged the new sacred taking the form of an experiential sense of trust and caring, not a new set of beliefs.[123] Reanney also advocated the reintroduction of a cycle of rituals, including a ritual of dying. Nonetheless, he was not a classical theist and he rejected exclusivist religions as 'profaners of the sacred' caught up with their own sense of collective ego.[124]

The physicist, astrobiologist, and winner of the 1995 Templeton Prize for Progress in Religion, Paul Davies (b.1946) also insists that the order

---

120 Stockton, *The Deep Within*, 41.
121 E. Stockton, *Aboriginal Church Paintings: Reflecting Our Faith* (Lawson, NSW: Blue Mountains Education and Research Trust, 2010), Introduction.
122 D. Reanney, *The Death of Forever: A New Future for Human Consciousness* (Melbourne: Longman Cheshire, 1991), 251.
123 Reanney, *The Death of Forever*, 251, and *Music of the Mind: An Adventure into Consciousness* (Melbourne: Hill of Content, 1994).
124 Reanney, *The Death of Forever*, 250.

found in the universe needs an explanation. In his writings, Davies argues that the lawfulness of the universe and that its generation of self-conscious beings cannot be the by product of mindless, purposeless forces.[125] Davies is convinced that physics itself requires metaphysics. The universe, he argues, is not the plaything of a capricious deity, but a coherent, rational, elegant, and harmonious expression of a deep and purposeful meaning.[126] Davies is clear that the being who underpins the rationality of the world does not bear much resemblance to the personal God of the Christian religion.[127] Nonetheless, Davies argues that there is something mysterious about the universe and special about the human place in it. He does not suggest, however, that proof of the meaningfulness of existence will come from anything except science and he leaves the wider philosophical implications of his position unexamined. To this extent, despite anticipations in Brennan, Baylebridge and many others, and also work in theology discussed in the last chapter, the issue of the mystery of the universe remains to be fully explored as a central theme in Australian religious thought.

The strands of religious thought discussed in this chapter sometimes overlapped, but sometimes they did not. Qualitative naturalism, philosophically based reinterpretations of the natural sciences and Aboriginal conceptions of land and place were not as closely related to one another as some writers were inclined to suggest. The geographies invoked were to some extent rhetorical and had little to do with the geographies in which urban Australians lived, with the oceans in which they surfed, or with the Asia in which they travelled. Likewise, French and American cultural influences were often more important than proclamations of nationalist sentiment or geographic uniqueness might suggest. Again, despite pervasive New Age soft-mindedness, Australian intellectuals found it difficult to embrace the horizon of a genuinely global religious thought. Indeed, for the most part they found the challenge of mastering Asian languages, especially Chinese, too difficult. To this extent, there was a certain Romantic refusal

---

125 P. Davies, *God and the New Physics* (New York: Simon and Schuster, 1983); *The Mind of God: Science and the Search for Ultimate Meaning* (London; Sydney: Simon and Schuster, 1992); *The Fifth Miracle: The Search for the Origin of Life* (London: Allen Lane, 1998); and *Information and The Nature of Reality: From Physics to Metaphysics*, ed. with N.H. Gregersed (Cambridge: Cambridge University Press, 2010).
126 P. Davies, "Physics and the Mind of God, The Templeton Prize Address, August 1995," *First Things* (Institute on Religion and Public Life, New York), http://www.firstthings.com/article/1995/08/003-physics-and-the-mind-of-god-the-templeton-prize-address-24.
127 P. Davies, *The Mind Of God: The Scientific Basis for a Rational World* (London: Simon and Schuster, 1992), 191.

of the contemporary in many forms of postsecular consciousness. Those who gestured towards philosophy, like Charles Birch, were less schooled in its history than might have been expected, while those who appealed to science advanced claims most scientists did not accept. In the same way, European Australians who enthused about Aboriginal spirituality rarely spoke Aboriginal languages, at least not well. The importance of postsecular consciousness in Australia lay perhaps less in the alternative it offered than in the release it made possible from the narrowness and lack of empathy found in much of the colonial past.

Transcultural Eclecticism

In the late twentieth and early twenty-first centuries, postsecular attitudes emerged in many areas and Australian religious thought became less certain of its direction, under the influence of what might be called 'transcultural eclecticism'.[128] Australia was open to plural religious influences early, through Chinese immigration, Muslim connections under the Macassan empire, Hindu labourers in the cane fields and Afghan cameleers, but for many decades the reality of pluralism had no impact on religious thought as such. In the course of the twentieth century, however, religious thought came to include engagements with multiple religions and spiritual traditions. Against this background, the sacred was widely associated with place.[129] Others implied that the sacral in Australia has to do with the sacredness of the land rather than religion.[130] The cultural studies scholar Stephen Muecke (b. 1948), however, who cooperated with Broome Aboriginal Paddy Roe in a major exploration of Australian landscape,[131] emphasised that the sacred was basic to the allegedly secular Australian nation and that myths, ritual and magic continued to operate in Australian 'secular' experience. Nevertheless, Muecke defined the sacred in terms derived from the French

---

128 These changes were evident, for example, in the 2006 issue of the literary journal *Meanjin* devoted to 'Faith'. This issue took account inter alia of how the reality of Islam was affecting contemporary attitudes to the secular. It profiled leading Australian writers welcoming the postsecular and re-envisioning the relationship between spirituality, religion and conceptions of God, but not converging on a common outlook; see *Meanjin* 65, no. 4 (2006), especially the contributions of Kevin Hart, Constant Mews, Rachael Kohn and Damon Young.
129 M. Griffith and J. Tulip (eds.), *Signs of Place: Source of the Sacred? 1998 Australian International Religion, Literature and the Arts Conference Proceedings* (Sydney: Centre for Studies in Religion, Literature and the Arts, Australian Catholic University, 1999).
130 See, for example, Gelder and Jacobs, *Uncanny Australia*.
131 K. Benterrak, S. Muecke, P. Roe et al., *Reading the Country: Introduction to Nomadology* (Fremantle, WA: Fremantle Arts Centre Press, 1984).

writer Georges Bataille as only a privileged moment of communal unity.[132] In a series of books he also sought to reassert the sacrality and philosophical seriousness of Aboriginal law. To do so, he rehabilitated the achievements of Aboriginal leader David Unaipon and drew attention to the brilliant interpretations of Ngarinyin elder David Mowaljarlai (1925–1997), whom he represented to the Australian public as an Indigenous philosopher.[133] Here Muecke followed French philosophical ideas, as they were understood in cultural studies circles, and the precedent of an allegedly distinctive 'African philosophy'. Although his work has been criticised as essentialist, in context it was a brave contribution towards a deeper engagement with Aboriginal thought.

Consistent with this, there was a widely noted 'return of the Aboriginal sacred' in cultural discourses,[134] as European Australians increasingly identified to some extent with Aboriginal spirituality as the spirituality of the land. At times Aboriginal identification with their own spirituality as the spirituality of the land was strong enough to rival the parareligious discourse of Anzac Day. Thus, the Aboriginal rights campaigner and poet Hyllus Maris (1933–1986) wrote:

> I am a child of the Dreamtime people
> Part of this land, like the gnarled gum tree
> I am the river, softly singing
> Chanting our songs on my way to the sea
> My spirit is the dust-devils
> Mirages, that dance on the plain
> I'm the snow, the wind and the falling rain
> I'm part of the rocks and the red desert earth
> Red as the blood that flows in my veins
> I am eagle, crow and snake that glides
> Through the rainforest that clings to the
>   mountainside
> I awakened here when the earth was new

---

132 S. Muecke, "The Sacred in History," *Humanities Research* 1 (1999), 27–37; see also S. Muecke, *Ancient and Modern: Time, Culture and Indigenous Philosophy* (Sydney: UNSW Press, 2009).

133 Mowaljarlai produced a profound interpretation of the rock art of the Kimberleys, albeit one that is arguably inflected by his Christian missionary formation; see D. Mowaljarlai and J. Malnic, *Yorro Yorro=Everything Standing Up Alive* (Broome, WA: Magabala Books, 1993).

134 Gelder and Jacobs, *Uncanny Australia*, 82; see also K. Maddock, "Metamorphosing the Sacred in Australia," *Australian Journal of Anthropology* 2 (1991): 213–32.

There was emu, wombat and kangaroo
No other man of a different hue
I am this land.
And this land is me
I am Australia.[135]

But, outside some Uniting Church and Catholic Church circles, there was no unambiguous or substantive redefinition of Australian identity in European Australian religious thought, but rather an opening to multiple realities. In so far as European Australians increasingly recognised the importance and the integrity of what was called 'the Aboriginal sacred', it was not Aboriginal Law that was primarily at stake. In many cases European Australians accepted the sacredness of the land without understanding that sacredness in an Aboriginal sense.

The turn to the land as sacred was also not associated with what European Australians had meant by 'religion' since settlement. In a heavily migrant and, in part, postcolonial and post-Christian Australia, characterised by amazing religious and linguistic diversity,[136] religion became more a matter of consumer choice, with choices changing over time. It also mattered less in intellectual circles.[137] In a world of changing gender roles and new technologies, the Australian churches became less European, and Buddhism and Islam became the fastest growing faiths. On the other hand, many Australians who regarded themselves as of 'no religion' were inclined to regard the land as sacred, to respect Anzac Day, and even to show an interest in meditation. As Australian intellectuals became more cosmopolitan and open-minded, many of them moved away from the exclusive truth approach to the sacred that had made a propensity for disbelief possible in the first place. Likewise, multiculturalism, which had, in part, Christian and Jewish origins,[138] complicated what 'the secular' was taken to be, and the need

---

135   H. Maris, "Spiritual Song of the Aborigine," in L. Mafi-Williams (comp.), *Spirit Song: A Collection of Aboriginal Poetry* (Norwood, SA: Omnibus Books, 1993), 2.
136   For studies that date a post-Christian Australia from 1960, see I. Breward, *A History of the Australian Churches* (Sydney: Allen and Unwin, 1993), 160–87, and R. C. Thompson, *Religion in Australia: A History* (Melbourne: Oxford University Press, 1994), ch. 6; see also D. Hilliard, "The Religious Crisis of the 1960s: The Experience of the Australian Churches," *Journal of Religious History* 21 (1997): 209–27.
137   H. M. Carey, *Believing in Australia: A Cultural History of Religions* (St. Leonards, NSW: Allen and Unwin, 1996, and G. D. Bouma, *Australian Soul: Religion and Spirituality in the 21st Century* (Cambridge: Cambridge University Press, 2006).
138   For the contribution of the Polish Catholic intellectual George (Jerzy) Zubrzycki, see A. Naraniecki, "Zubrzycki and Multicultural Governance in Australia," *Journal*

to work with multiple thick cultural identities was widely accepted. As the Christian sacred receded among intellectuals, postsecular consciousness was less uncommon than in the past.[139]

This did not, of course, mean that older patterns did not continue, among them the preference for an apophatic, deliberately silent, approach to religious mystery, a tendency to fuse the divine and the ordinary in laconic prose or verse,[140] and a preference for immanentism over transcendentalism, despite receptions of both in the nineteenth and twentieth centuries. Many commentators have noted the incarnational nature of much Australian spirituality, often expressed in a preeminence of physical values, in a celebration of sun, desert and surf, and in an acceptance of the flesh and all forms of matter.[141] Others note a descendental temper that emphasises ordinary life, chafes at the highfalutin, and mixes the demotic and hierophany.[142] In the longer term, however, these characteristics may be modified by non-European immigration.

By the twenty-first century Australian intellectuals were less inclined to project the sacred onto history, let alone to endorse an allegedly Biblical concept of history under God. They were also conscious of the vibrancy of religion internationally and of the Islamic communities in Australia, which could not be understood in terms of European ideas about the privatisation of religious faith. Secular intellectuals saw the need for modified cultural space, but had no overarching intellectual system in terms of which to interpret social and cultural change. Those European Australians who identified the sacred with the land tended to generate Romantic visions, as if the land had cultural properties

---

of Intercultural Studies 34 (2013): 246–61. Jewish intellectuals, including Walter Lippman, founder of the Jewish Welfare Society and founding member of the Ethnic Communities Council of Victoria, also played a role.

139 The special issue of *Meanjin* (65, no. 4 (2006)) devoted to 'Faith', took account inter alia of how the reality of Islam was affecting contemporary attitudes to the secular.

140 See Bouma, *Australian Soul*. For the work of the Catholic poet, Bruce Dawe (b. 1930), see D. Haskell, *Attuned to Alien Moonlight: The Poetry of Bruce Dawe* (St. Lucia: University of Queensland Press, 2002), especially ch. 12, and P. Kirkwood, "Two Australian Poets as Theologians: Les Murray and Bruce Dawe." in *Discovering Australian Theology*, ed. P. Malone (Homebush, NSW: St. Paul's Publications, 1988), 195–216.

141 B. Thiering, "From Abraham to Voss: Reflections on an Australian Religious Consciousness," *St. Mark's Review* 86 (1976): 48; see also H. McQueen, *Suburbs of the Sacred* (Ringwood, Vic.: Penguin, 1988), ch. 2.

142 P. Kane, "Chris Wallace-Crabbe, Descendentalist," in *Travelling Without Gods: A Chris Wallace-Crabbe Companion*, ed. C. Atherton (Carlton, Vic.: Melbourne University Press, 2014), 15–32; see also L. McCredden, "The Poet as (Anti-) Theologian: Chris Wallace-Crabbe's Double Vision." in *Travelling Without Gods*, 135–46; B. Dawe, *Sometimes Gladness: Collected Poems 1954–2005* (Melbourne: Pearson Education, 2006), 27.

prior to human interpretations of it, to which Australians should submit. The notion that the natural world was the primary inspiration of religious consciousness was found in the much-praised writings of the Christian novelist Tim Winton (b. 1960). Winton made 'faith' a major theme of his novels and some of his short stories. While critical of the narrow materialism, as he sees it, of Australian culture, he does not envisage easy religion and takes an unsentimental view of both the attractions and the difficulties of belief. Winton emphasises that he is indebted to Ngarinyin thinking and to the work of the Aboriginal religious philosopher David Mowaljarlai in particular, but there are also resonances with earlier strands of believing disbelief in Australia.[143]

Given a greater openness to mysticism, Indigenous traditions and non-Christian religions, some Australian intellectuals, including the Patrick White Prize winner Amanda Lohrey (b. 1947),[144] became spiritual searchers, open to Eastern spiritual traditions. Here the poet Bruce Beaver (1928–2004) was perhaps a forerunner with his hostility to ill-fitting religions, his openness to Islamic mysticism, and his interpretation of the dark night of soul as a galactic mystery.[145] Others became 'hyphenated Christians', drawing on at least one major religious tradition as well as Christianity.[146] Still others embraced a 'progressive Christianity' that accommodated to secular principles,[147] while most of the young took back spiritual authority for their own lives, often deserting the churches.[148] And, while older people remained attached to the sacred, there were also desacralising trends associated with social media and technology.[149] It remains to be seen whether these social and cultural changes will generate new forms of Australian religious thought in the future.

---

143 For the prose vernacular sacred in the work of Tim Winton, see B. Ashcroft, F. Devlin-Glass and L. McCredden, *Intimate Horizons: The Post-Colonial Sacred in Australia*, op.cit. ch. 4. and L. McCredden, and N. O'Reilly, eds. *Tim Winton: Critical Essays* (Perth, University of Western Australia Press, 2014). For his treatment of Christian conversion, see *The Turning* (Sydney: Picador, 2005).

144 Among many novels, see *A Short History of Richard Kline* (Melbourne: Black Inc, 2015).

145 B. Beaver, *The Long Game, and Other Poems* (St. Lucia: University of Queensland Press, 2005).

146 G. Goosen, *Hyphenated Christians: Towards A Better Understanding of Dual Religious Belonging* (Berlin: Peter Lang, 2011) 19. Goosen discusses people who have a first major religion, but draw on a second to a greater or lesser degree.

147 Catholic priest Michael Morwood, for example, argued in many books for a new version of Christianity. He then left the priesthood and became involved with the Progressive Christian Network of Victoria; see his *Tomorrow's Catholic: Understanding God and Jesus in a New Millennium* (Mystic, CT: Twenty-Third Publications, 1997) and other volumes.

148 D. Tacey, "Spirituality in Australia Today", 52.

149 See T. Stanley (ed.) *Religion after Secularization in Australia* (London: Palgrave Macmillan, 2015).

CONCLUSION: REFIGURING THE NATIONAL IMAGINARY

Identifying the existence of a treasure trove of Australian religious thought challenges older stereotypes about Australia and opens up new horizons for research. The six exploratory studies undertaken here have aimed to draw together the work of many scholars as well as my own research and to offer fresh perspectives on a range of issues. They have not covered the whole field. Wider studies of the sacred in Australia and detailed studies of both Aboriginal thought and Aboriginal Christianity are clearly needed. Within these limits, however, a beginning has been made.

My discussion began by arguing that religious thought was comparatively neglected as part of a more general under-representation of religion in Australian historical writing. I then suggested that a wider concept of religious thought is needed to take account of the religious thought that emerged in Australia, one that encompasses both forms of thought falling within religion in an organisational sense and forms of thought falling outside it. I then tracked various 'shapes of disbelief' in many different kinds of intellectuals and across multiple sites and contexts, noting significant differences between the early colonial period, the later nineteenth century and the twentieth century, including both esoteric discernments and confessional verdicts. I then considered sacral secularity, or the tendency to associate the secular with sacral characteristics. Here my discussion challenged the tendency in much of the historiography to confuse secularity with secularism. The secular in Australia was not always discontinuous with the religious and was often Protestant Christian. I then discussed the significance of religious liberalism in Australia and showed that religious liberals were concerned with both the modernisation of Christianity and often with social reform as well. I emphasised the transnational character of this liberalism, which often provided a range of intellectual perspectives in advance of attitudes in Australian society more generally. I then considered interactions between religious thought and philosophy in Australia, relations that have been played down in some of the historiography. Once again, the terrain is richer than many historians have suggested, and a number of intellectuals assayed the religion–philosophy interface in creative ways.

I then turned to the development of theology, which has been neglected in Australian historical writing. My discussion showed that the cultural capital associated with Christianity was significant. It emphasised the extensive presence of theological resources, the quality of theological discussion, and the gradual emergence of independent theology, as confidence grew and as more attention was paid to local contexts and to the Asia-Pacific. Finally, I dealt with the emergence of postsecular consciousness, in the form of various sacral naturalisms, and then as part of a more diffuse transcultural eclecticism. My discussion concentrated on writers influenced by vitalism and process philosophy; writers who sought to ground the sacral in the sciences; writers who attempted to recover a spiritual concept of place; writers who found the sacred in the context of environmental philosophy; and writers who approached the sacred influenced by psychoanalysis.

Cumulatively, these studies show that Australian religious thought was wider than confessional thought and often more interesting than some historians have assumed. They provide evidence of intellectual seriousness over a range of areas and suggest that religious thought had an influence at times on the development of the Australian national moral community. They also imply that attempts to think about Australian thought as either 'religious' or 'secular' may be too schematic. These studies also suggest that Australian religious thought has been more mystical and also more socially engaged than some of the older studies imply, just as it was more transnational, even when it concerned itself with issues of local geography, land and place. However, these are only a beginning. More work needs to be done on the situation in different parts of the country, most obviously in Western Australia, Queensland, the Northern Territory and Tasmania, on changes from one period to another, on the many different streams of Christian thought and on non-Christian religious thought. Obviously, more detailed studies may qualify the patterns I have found.

The question of whether Australian religious thought is distinctive in certain respects cannot be adequately answered on the basis of these studies. However, there are recurrent tendencies that may not be found in quite the same combinations in other settler societies. For example, there is a tendency in much Australian religious thought to avoid positive religious affirmations, which sometimes goes with an inarticulate sense of a numinous 'no thing'. Much Australian religious thought also tends towards what might be called religious republicanism or 'spiritual democracy'. This tendency was evidenced as early as the convict period in a critical attitude to 'church religion'. There is also a recurrent emphasis on the need for individuals to judge matters for themselves. Then there is a widespread acceptance in Australian religious thought of what might be called 'moralism': a tendency to identify 'true religion' with kindness, work for others and practical help. This tendency may be found more strongly among Australian intellectuals than among American or Canadian or South African intellectuals. There is also a tendency in much of Australian religious thought towards an untheorised pragmatism, a willingness to accept inconsistencies and tensions, a capacity to proceed without agreement on first principles, which is arguably less common internationally. Finally, Australian religious thought often inclines to 'immanentism', to locating the nonmundane in the world at hand and in ordinary life, and this tendency can be found both among intellectuals with explicit religious beliefs and among those whose religious thought is more implicit.

These tendencies are not inconsistent with the fact that Australian religious thought has been profoundly shaped by Christianity and by the presence of Aboriginal law. They suggest, however, that 'the utterly transcendent' has not been as central to Australian religious thought as it has been central to religious thought in some other societies. The call of 'the utterly transcendent' may have been felt by deeply committed evangelicals, by Carmelites, by Calvinists and by Jews, among many others, but a focus on 'the utterly transcendent' has not been the main concern in the religious thought of most Australian intellectuals. Nor have most Australian intellectuals been primarily concerned with detailed disputes over religious doctrine, partly because Christianity has been largely received as a spiritual and moral influence rather than as a powerful conceptual framework. No great work was written in Australia attacking Christianity or in its defence, and, despite decades of disfiguring sectarianism, nothing substantive was written by adherents of one church about another. Instead, Australian religious thought has often been about ultimate concern, especially as it pertains to treating others fairly, to achieving just social outcomes, and to recognising intrinsic value in the natural world.

Better acknowledging the nature, extent and quality of Australian religious thought has implications that may go to refiguring the national imaginary. Firstly, there is probably a need to extend existing understandings of the religiously related cultural capital available to Australian intellectuals. And doing so means accepting the role of the churches and church-based institutions, both as locations for intellectual life and as reference points for many who moved away from them. Secondly, the extent of Australian religious thought underlines the fact that non-material motivations were important in Australia, and this undermines older stereotypes of a practical utilitarian people, unmoved by ideas. Thirdly, the extent of religious thought in Australia qualifies, to some extent, older narratives about an unintellectual and culturally deprived Australia and draws attention to instances of transnational agency, including the transnational experiences of both clergy and women writers. Fourthly, religious thought in Australia was not without significance in a range of policy areas, most obviously education and social welfare, although further research might well find a similar salience in local government and international affairs. Fifthly, religious thought might feature more prominently in studies of Australian political thought and in accounts of Australian literary and artistic achievement. Likewise, more work could be done on the ways in which economic and legal thought were shaped by transpositions of Christian ideals. All these considerations point to the need for further research into what is clearly an extensive and important area of Australian intellectual history.

INDEX

Aarons, Eric 58
Aboriginal Christianity xx, 188–90, 235
Aboriginal cultural forms 52, 184–91, 224, 234
Aboriginal ecology 216
Aboriginal law 231–2
  Eurocentric interpretations xx
  responses to 183–91
Aboriginal legends 52
'Aboriginal religion' xx, 151, 184–91, 226
Aboriginal religions 150–1, 198
Aboriginal sense of place 218
Aboriginal spirituality 86, 184–91, 217, 218–9, 224, 226, 227–8, 231–2, 234
Aboriginal theology 189–90
Aboriginal thought 235
Aboriginality, non-Indigenous 224
Adam, David Stow 119
Adams, Francis 72
Adorno, Theodor 208
adult education 80–1
Advaita Vedanta 58, 103
Agar, Wilfred Eade 210–1
The Age (Melbourne) 31–2
agnosticism 3 n7, 4, 6, 12–17, 23
  see also epistemological agnosticism
Alexander, Samuel 25, 162, 207–8
Alexandrian Fathers 83
Althusser, Louis 208
Anabaptist tradition 173
analytical philosophy 163, 164
anarchists 23–4
  bookshops xii
Anderson, Francis 80, 84, 118–21, 134–5
Anderson, John 24–6, 45, 127, 128, 137
Andrews, Jack 104
Anglicanism, and Christian socialism 81

New South Wales x n6
  origins 89
  Sydney 175
  see also Church of England
Anglo-Catholics 42–3
  ecclesiology 177–8
  theologians 87
Angus, Samuel 122–9
animal rights 26, 213
animism 216, 217
Anselm 163
anthropologists 86, 184–6, 187
Anthroposophy 37
anticlericalism xvi, xvii, 9–11, 78, 79, 151–2, 177
  of Miles Franklin 40
anti-imperialism xviii
Anzac Day, Anglo-Catholic origins 67
apophaticism 39, 48, 155, 227
Archibald, John Feltham 17
Armstrong, David 138, 164
Árnason, Jóhann 167
Arnold, Matthew 6, 12, 72
Arthur, Governor ix
Asia, missionary involvement in 192
Asian Christianity, engagement with 192–3
Asian philosophies 168
atheism 3 n7, 4, 23–5
  see also existential atheism
atheists 23, 127
The Atlas (newspaper) xvi n39, 78
Atonement, rejection of 9, 11, 96, 112
Australasian Association for Process Thought 213 n53
Australasian Journal of Psychology and Philosophy 119
Australasian Secular Association 21, 22, 26
Australian Catholic Record 172
Australian Catholic University 152, 153
Australian Christian Lobby xii

Australian Church, Melbourne 29, 81, 102, 115–8
Australian Constitution, recognition of deity 67
  and religious freedom 23
  separation of church and state 90, 100
Australian eJournal of Theology 172
Australian history, and religion ix–xvii
Australian Labor Party xi, 73
Australian materialism 138–9
Australian Natives' Association 104
Australian Psychoanalytic Society 221
Australian Quarterly Journal of Theology, Literature and Science 11
'Australian theology' 190, 227–8
Badham, Charles 32
Baillie, John 124
Banfield, Edmund James 55
Banks, Robert 177
Barfield, Owen 206
Barth, Karl 158, 172, 177
Bataille, Georges 153, 231
Baur, F.C. 4, 89, 123
Baylebridge, William 19, 202–4
Beauvoir, Simone de 149
Beaver, Bruce 55 n186, 234
belief 1–2, 3
beliefs, as regulator of practical life 12, 16
Bellamy, Edward 105
Belloc, Hilaire 82
Bentham, Jeremy 77
Benthamites ix, 76, 132
Berdyaev, Nikolai 168
Bergson, Henri 145, 152–3, 205, 207, 213
Besant, Annie 34, 35
Bible, challenges to 4–5, 6–7, 115
Biblical scholarship 129–30, 170, 172, 175, 178, 183, 193

– 239 –

Bilimoria, Purushottima   57, 150
biology, and religion   228
  Whiteheadian interpretation   210–1
Bion, Wilfred   221
Birch, Charles   211–3
Blacket, John   11–12
Blake, William   209
Blanchot, Maurice   154–7
Bland, F.A.   87
Blavatsky, Madame   34
Bloch, Ernst   xxii, 51, 208
Board, Peter   80
Boer, Roland   208
Boismenu, Alain Marie Guynot de   46
Bonaventure   181
Bonhoeffer, Dietrich   50, 211
Bonnefoy, Yves   153
Boomerang (newspaper)   73
Bosanquet, Bernard   136
Bourke, Richard   x, 64, 76, 78
Boutroux, Émile   140, 145
Boyd, Martin   43
Bradlaugh, Charles   21, 22, 100
Bradley, F.H.   136
Brady, Veronica   49–51, 223
Braidotti, Rosa   214
Brandes, Georg   16
Brennan, Christopher   19, 32–4
Brennan, Patricia   182
Brentano, Franz   167
Brewer, J.S.   90–1
Bright, Charles   118
British idealism *see* idealism, British
British Society for Psychical Research   32
broadcasting, as religious opportunity   88
Brotherhood of Saint Laurence   81
Broughton, William   x n6, 63, 78, 89
Browning, Robert   23
Brunner, Emil   172
Buber, Martin   54
Buckley, Vincent   44–50
Budden, Chris   191
Buddhism   55, 103
  and Alfred Deakin   29
  and C.W. Leadbeater   35
  and Colin Johnson   52

  and Rosa Praed   37
Buddhist Society of New South Wales   55
Bulletin (Sydney)   xvii, 17
Bultmann, Rudolf   129
Bunsen, Josiah   108
Burgmann, Ernest   82–6, 87, 89, 220–1
Butler, Bishop, *Analogy of Religion*   6
Byles, Marie   55
Caird, Edward   118, 127, 134, 137, 144
Caird, John   112, 134, 144
Calvinism   30, 47, 64, 69, 109, 112, 173, 174, 190, 221
  rejection of   95, 98, 124, 134, 200
Cambridge, Ada   12–16
Cameron, Peter   124 n139
Campbell, John McLeod   112
Campbell, R.J.   111, 118
Campbell, Richard   155 n76, 163–4
Campion Society, Melbourne   82, 150
capitalism, criticism of   83, 102
  support for   xiv
Caputo, John   158
Carey, Samuel Pearce   173
Carmichael, Henry   76–7, 132
Carnley, Peter   172, 178
Carroll, John   221–3
Cassirer, Carl   206
Catholic bishops, as reformers   65–6
Catholic doctrine, modernisation   178–9
Catholic intellectuals   44–5
Catholic priests, government payment   x
Catholic religious orders   xv n34, 171
Catholic scholasticism   147–8, 149, 163
Catholic social thought   82
Catholic theologians   178–82
The Catholic Worker (journal)   82, 150
Centre for Public and Contextual Theology, Canberra   90
Chalmers, Thomas   70–1

Channing, William Ellery   68, 94, 98–9
Charles Strong Lecture and Trust   118
Charlesworth, Max   146–52, 160–1
Charlton, James   57–8
Chesterton, G.K.   82
Childe, Gordon   208
Chrétien, Jean-Louis   157
Christian doctrines, humanist revision   127
  rejection of   101, 124–5
Christian Science   40, 41–2
Christian socialism   81, 83, 90–1, 96, 117
Christianity, and Aboriginal governance   xv
  Australian attitude to   1
  and comparative religion   6–7, 11
  decline of   224
  forms in Australia   3
  history of   120–1, 130
  as liberation movement   85
  modernisation of   221, 235
  reform of   130–1
  in service to humanity   134, 237
  as social activism   107
  and state   111
  as way of life   125–6, 127
  see also evangelical Christianity; practical Christianity
Christians, and Aboriginal welfare   xiv
Christologies   181
Chryssavgis, John   194
church, as civil institution   ix, 113
Church Act (1836)   x, 64, 76, 78
church and state   xiv
  Anglican conceptions   63–4
  Catholic conceptions   65–6
  Protestant conceptions   65
  separation of   ix, xv
  see also Australian Constitution; Church Act (1836); society and religion
Church Fathers, theology of   108
  see also Alexandrian Fathers; Greek Church Fathers

Index

'church in society'
    ecclesiology 88–90
Church of England, as
    established religion ix,
    xiv, 63
    see also Anglicanism
churches, and church-based
    institutions 237
    approaches to
        membership 108
    book societies xii
churchism, criticism of xvii,
    224, 236
    rejection of 3, 9–10, 12,
        13, 38–9, 59, 71, 75, 96,
        99, 100, 109
Churchward, Lloyd xvii
citizenship, preparation
    for 80, 87, 88
    and self-realisation 107,
        119
    statist conceptions 92
    see also religious citizenship
civic Protestantism x–xi, 65,
    78, 110–1
civics education 80, 97
civil administration, and
    Church of England ix, x
civil theology 80
civilisation, philosophy
    of 120–1
Cixous, Hélène 153
Clapperton, Jane Hume 96
Clark, Andrew Inglis 98–101
Clark, Manning xix
Clarke, Marcus 7–9
    *For the Term of His Natural
        Life* 9
Clarke, William
    Branwhite 6
Classicism 32
clergymen, as scientists 5
clericalism, rejection of *see*
    anticlericalism
Coady, Tony 150
Cobb, John 213
Coffey, David 181
Cole, E.W. 4–5
Colenso, John 6
Collingwood Workingmen's
    Club 104
Colloquium (journal) 172
colonial chaplains 173
The Commonweal
    (journal) 105
communalism,
    Durkheimian 46

Communism 53, 58–9, 74
    criticism of 80, 82
Communist bookshops xii
Communist Party, and
    historians xviii
Communist press xvii
comparative religion 113
compulsory education 107
Concrescence (journal) 213
    n53
confessional approaches, to
    religious history xviii
confessional disbelief 42–52,
    59
Confoy, Maryanne 172
Congregationalists 110–1,
    118
conscription, opposition
    to xiii, 102
contextual theology 183–94
convicts, hostility to
    clergy xvi
transportation, religious
    aspects ix–x
Conway, Ronald 49
Coomaraswamy, Ananda 45,
    55
cosmic evolution, philosophy
    of 134
cosmic parareligion 20–1
Costello, Timothy 173
Cowen, Shimon Dovid 54
Cowper, William 173
Cox, Harvey 89
creation theology 180, 226
creeds, freedom from 3, 9,
    10–11, 95, 103, 115, 124
Criminology Society,
    Melbourne 117
Croce, Benedetto 145
Cullman, Oscar 175–6
cultural anthropology, 19th
    century 6
cultural changes, responses
    to 195–6, 232–4
D'Arcy, Eric 148
Danglow, Jacob 53
Daoist philosophy 56, 217
Darwinism 4, 5, 6, 29, 115,
    214
    challenges to 31, 97
Davies, Paul 228–9
Davis, Andrew Jackson 21
Davis, Jack 51
Dawe, Bruce 233 n140
Dawson, Christopher 82
Day, Dorothy 82

de Beauvoir *see* Beauvoir,
    Simone de
Deakin, Alfred 27–30, 67,
    103, 116, 117
Deakin University 150
deep ecology 215
Deissmann, Adolf 122
deist controversy, 18th
    century 8
deist ideas xvi
Deleuze, Gilles 153, 213,
    214
Democratic Labor Party xi–
    xii
Deniehy, Daniel 68
Dening, Greg 219–20
Derrida, Jacques 153, 154
desire, affirmative approach
    to 214
Deutscher, Max 167
Dicker, Gordon 195
disbelief xxiii, 1–60, 198,
    235
distinctiveness, of Australian
    religious thought 236
divinity of Christ, denial
    of 11, 95–6
doctrinal disputes 237
    see also heresy; religious
        controversies
Dodd, C.H. 175
Doniela, William 167
Dostoevsky, Fyodor 162, 222
doubt, rise of 3, 4, 6
Dowling, Henry 173
Drayton, Dean 213 n54
Dumbrell, William 177
Dupuche, John 193
Durkheim, Émile 184
Dyer, Keith 193
Eastern Hill Unitarian
    Church, Melbourne 101
Eccles, Sir John 48
ecclesiology 173–8
    see also 'church in society'
        ecclesiology
Eckhart, Meister 83, 155,
    227
ecological humanities 216
ecological view of life 213
economic thought and
    theory 5
    and Christian ideals 238
    and theology 193
    see also capitalism
ecumenists 172
Eddy, Mary Baker 40

– 241 –

education, and moral
   improvement   110
Education Act (New South
   Wales) (1870)   78
educational reform   132
Edwards, Denis   172, 180–1,
   226
Eggleston, Frederic
   William   91
Elcho Island revival,
   1976   188
Eliade, Mircea   49, 184 n52
Eliot, George   31
Elkin, A.P.   86–7, 89, 185
Emerson, Ralph Waldo   29,
   68
Emilsen, William   178
Emmanuel College, University
   of Queensland   163
Empire (Sydney)   32
Engels, Friedrich, *Dialectics of
   Nature*   209
Enlightenment, conception of
   the public   79
   and religion   xiii
environmental
   philosophy   xxiv, 215–8,
   236
epistemological
   agnosticism   109
Ern Malley hoax   46
Erskine, Thomas   112
Essays and Reviews   4
Esson, Louis   101
ethnicity, and
   Christianity   xii
ethnographers   185, 219
ethnographic history,
   Melbourne   219
Eucharist   177–8
Eucken, Rudolf   140–1, 152
eugenics   84
Evangelical Anglicans   x,
   63, 82–3
   hostility to Roman
      Catholicism   42–3
evangelical Christianity   x,
   xiii, 173–7
Evatt, Elizabeth   182
Evatt, H.V.   80 n74
evolutionary idealism   199–
   200
evolutionism   34
exclusion of religion   66
existential atheism   160
existentialism   149, 162,
   209

Fabianism   90
Fagenblat, Michael   159–60
Family First Party   xi–xii
Farrer, Austin   163
federal theology   174, 176
Federation, and Christian
   nationalism   67
feelings   210–2
Fehér, Ferenc   167
Fellowship of Australian
   Writers   75
feminism   117, 130
   and Christian Science   40,
      41
   and Darwinism   214
   theology   129, 182–3
   see also women's suffrage
feminist philosophers   213–
   4, 216–7
feminist reformers   80
feminist writers   36–7
Feuerbach, Ludwig   202
Finniss, B.T.   6–7
Fiorenza, Elisabeth
   Schüssler   182
First Church of Christ,
   Scientist, Melbourne   41
Fisher, Anthony   139
FitzGerald, R.D.   209–10
Fitzpatrick, Brian   xvii
Fletcher, Scott   135
Fletcher, William Roby   118
Flinders University   208
Forrest, Peter   164–5
Foucault, Charles   226
Foucault, Michel   153
Fox, Patricia   172
Fox, Warwick   215
Frame, Tom   90
Franciscan influence   44,
   199, 209
Franklin, Miles   40–1
Frazer, James   184
Free Religious Fellowship,
   Melbourne   101, 102, 117
freedom, philosophy   209
Freemasonry   67
freethinkers   23, 45
   Melbourne   7
freethought   3, 4, 17, 21,
   95, 102
Freethought Association   21,
   25
French philosophy   149–50,
   152–6, 158
French Protestantism   124
Fullerton, Mary   200 n8

Furphy, Joseph   41, 96,
   104–6, 118, 205
Garland, D.J.   67
Garrigou-Lagrange,
   Réginald   148
Gascoigne, Robert   195
Geering, Lloyd   124 n139
German philosophers,
   translation of   143
German philosophy   30, 129,
   133, 140, 166–8, 202
Gibson, Alexander
   Boyce   146, 149, 161–2
Gibson, Lucy   145
Gibson, Ralph Siward   146
Gibson, William Ralph
   Boyce   88, 135, 140–6, 149,
   152, 161, 166
Gilbert, Kevin   52
Gill, Athol   173
Gillen, Frances James   185
Gilmore, Hugh   90
Gilmore, Mary   75–6
gnosticism   32, 34, 37–8, 45,
   122–3
godless society, Australia
   as   xii–xiii
Goldstein, Vida   41
Goldsworthy, Graeme   177
Gollan, Robin   xvii
Gondarra, Djiniyini   188–9
Gore, Charles   83, 87, 107–8,
   116, 119
government funding, of
   religious institutions   x, xv
Gramsci, Antonio   208
Gray, Robert   55–6
Greek Church Fathers   177
   see also Alexandrian Fathers
Greek Orthodox
   tradition   166
   see also Orthodox theology
Green, T.H.   80, 87, 91, 92,
   119, 134, 135
Gresham, W.H.   xiv
Gribben, Robert   172
Griffin, David Ray   212
Griffin, Marion Mahony   37
Griffin, Walter Burley   37
Grosz, Elizabeth   213–4
Guénon, René   45, 55
Habel, Norman   172, 191
Habermas, Jürgen   197 n1
Hacker, William Philip   82
Haire, James   172, 178, 192–3
Hall, Gerard   195
Hamilton, Clive   218

Index

Hamilton, Sir William 108–9, 133
Hammond, T.C. 42, 174
Hancock, Keith 87
Hanson, Richard Davies 4
Harbinger of Light (journal) 21
Harford, Lesbia 59 n199
Harnack, Adolf von 113, 126
Harpur, Charles 68–9, 103, 199–200
Hart, Kevin 152–61
Hartley, Frank 90
Hartshorne, Charles 162, 211
Harward, Nancy 37
Harwood, Gwen 43
Hearn, William Edward 5–6
Hebert, Gabriel 178
Hegelianism, Scottish 107, 112, 118, 119, 121, 134
Heidegger, Martin 129, 143, 154, 160
Hellenism 32
Heller, Ágnes 167
Henderson, Kenneth 88
Henry, Michel 157
Heraclitus 206
heresy charges 130
  and Charles Strong 115, 117
  and Lloyd Geering 124 n139
  and Peter Cameron 124 n139
  and Samuel Angus 122, 124
heterodoxy xvii, xxiii, 4
Hewett, Dorothy 58
Higgins, Henry Bournes 23, 116
Higgins, Nettie *see* Palmer, Nettie
higher criticism, German 4, 6 n17, 13, 16, 115, 126
higher education, Christian institutions xvi
Higinbotham, George 9–11, 79–80, 115, 117
Hill, Charles 179
Hillman, James 223
Hinduism 57
historians, and religious thought xvii–xix
historical criticism *see* higher criticism

history, as performance 219
  philosophy of 209
Hölderlin, Friedrich 33
holistic vision 212, 215, 217
Holland, Henry Scott 87
Holmes, Oliver Wendell 100
Holyoake, George 31
home church movement 177
Honner, John 172
Hooker, Richard 89, 174
Hudson, Wayne 208
Hügel, Baron von 124
humanism 3, 71, 72, 135
  rejection of 222
  see also secular humanism
humanity, faith in 120
Hume, David 8
Hume Clapperton, Jane *see* Clapperton, Jane Hume
Humphry Ward, Mrs, *Robert Elsmere* 4
Hunt, Anne 180
Hunt, Ian 208
Husserl, Edmund 143
Hutchings, Patrick 150, 162
idealism 33, 120, 137, 162
  British 134, 136
  Scottish 107, 108, 134, 135–6, 166
  see also evolutionary idealism; personal idealism; Platonic idealism; social idealism
idealistic pragmatism 91
Illingworth, J.R. 83, 107
immanence 38, 39, 44, 48, 56, 107, 114, 198
  in the *saeculum* 87
immanentism 206–7, 218, 237
immigration 230
imperialism 63–4, 65
incarnational theology 87, 88, 89
Indigenous intellectuals 51–3, 188–91
  see also Aboriginal thought
Indigenous spirituality *see* Aboriginal spirituality
individualism 131, 236–7
  see also radical individualism
industrial relations xi, 23
Inge, Dean 123
institutional religion *see* churchism

intellectual history xxi
international cooperation 107, 121
Irenaeus 181
Irigaray, Luce 153, 214
'irreligious Australia' xvi, xvii, xviii, xxiii
Isaacs, Sir Isaac 53
Islam 54–5
  and the secular 233 n139
James, William 29, 34, 142
Jaspers, Karl 209
Jefferis, James 110–1
Jensen, Peter 176–7
Jesuit scholarship 82, 148, 150, 170, 179
Jesus' life, and Christianity 114
Jewish intellectuals 53–4, 159–60
Johnson, Colin 52
Johnson, Frank 208
Johnson, Richard x, 173
Jones, Henry 135–6, 140
Jowett, Benjamin 4, 8
Judaism 53–4, 160
Jung, Carl 206, 218, 223, 225
Kant, Immanuel 102
Kaye, Bruce 89–90
Kelly, Anthony 155, 180
Kendall, Henry 199
Kennedy, Gerard 81
Kevans, Denis 53
Kierkegaard, Søren 16, 162, 209
Kingsley, Charles 81
Kitchen, Merrill 172
Kleutgen, Josef 147
Knox, David Broughton 174–6
labour movement, and Catholic Church xi
labour radicalism 73
Laird, John 128
laity, authority of 9–11
Lake, Kirsopp 123–4, 128
land, cultural properties 233–4
  as sacred 187, 232
  and spiritual meaning 187, 189–92
Land Tenure Reform League xiv
landscape, cultural exploration of 230
Lane, William 73–5

– 243 –

Lang, John Dunmore 69–71, 76, 78
Langer, Susanne 206
Langley, J.S. 201
Langtry, Bruce 165
Lascaris, Manoly 38
Latham, Sir John 23
Laurie, Henry 135, 136
Lawson, Henry 71–2, 75
Lawson, Louisa 59 n199
Lawton, Bill 195
Le Couteur, P.R. 166–7
Le Doeuff, Michèle 153
Leadbeater, Charles Webster 35–6
League of Nations 89, 121
Lee, Dorothy 183
Lee, R.S. 87, 220–1
legal thought, and Christian ideals 238
Leibowitz, Yeshayahu 160
lending libraries xii
Lessing, Gotthold Ephraim 9, 105
Levinas, Emmanuel 143, 153, 159
Liberal Catholic Church, Sydney 32, 36, 45
liberal Christian, Charles Strong as 111–8
liberal theologies, Melbourne 8–9
liberalism 29, 90, 91
  see also neoliberalism; religious liberalism
liberation theology 85, 192
The Liberator (journal) 22
Lightfoot, J.S. 8
Lilburne, Geoffrey 190
Lillie, John 77
Lindsay, A.B. 162
Lindsay, Elaine 182
Lindsay, Jack 208–9
Lindsay, Norman 19–20, 208, 209
linguistic philosophy 148
Lippman, Walter 233 n138
literary societies xii
literature, colonial access to xii
Loader, Bill 193
Locke, John, *Essay Concerning Human Understanding* 6
Loeve, Yehuda Arieh 54
Lohrey, Amanda 57–8, 234
Lonergan, Bernard 179
Lorenzen, Thorwald 173

Lowe, Robert 78
Lukács, György 208, 209
Lux Mundi 87, 88
Lyceum Movement, Melbourne 21, 75, 102
Lyons Group xii
MacCallum, Mungo 32, 80, 136, 137
MacIntyre, Alasdair 165
Mackie, John L. 26
MacKinlay, Elizabeth 196
Macmurray, John 162
Maconochie, Alexander 132
Macquarie, Lachlan x
Macquarrie, John 163
Mafi-Williams, Lorraine 52
Magdalene (journal) 182
Maher, Frank 82
Maimonides 160
Major, Henry D.A. 123
Mallarmé 32
Malpas, Jeff 168
Mann, Scott 208
Mann, Tom 105 n58
The Manor, Clifton Gardens, Sydney 36
Mansel, Henry 12
Marion, Jean-Luc 156–7
Maris, Hyllus 231–2
Maritain, Jacques 45, 46
Márkus, György 167
Márkus, Maria 167
Marsden, Samuel 63, 173
Marshall, T.H. 92
Marson, Charles 90
Martineau, James 10, 29, 94, 99, 112
Marxism, as religion 80–1
Marxist philosophy 208, 209
Mascall, Eric 163
materialism 164
  see also Australian materialism
materialist spirituality 217
Mathew, Ray 204 n28
Mathews, Freya 56, 217
Maurice, F.D. 8, 81, 90, 91
Maurin, Peter 82
May, John D'Arcy 172
Mayo, Elton 84, 85 n99
McAuley, James 45–6
McCabe, Joseph 23
McCaughey, Davis 178
McCoy, Sir Frederick 6
McCrae, Hugh 210
McIntyre, John 172

McKinney, Jack 206
McQuillan, Paul 195
meaning-making 223
mechanics' institutes xii, 105
Melbourne Anarchist Club 23
Melbourne Peace Society 117
The Melbourne Review (journal) 97
Ménégoz, Eugène 124
Merton, Thomas 50
metaphysics 216, 229
  philosophy as 162
  see also realist metaphysics
migrant culture 232
Mill, John Stuart, *A System of Logic* 108
Miller, Barry 163
Miller, Crawford 172
Miller, Morris 167
Millikan, David 195
missionary activities xxii, 192
Mitchell, William 11–12, 136, 137 n15
Modern Thought (journal) 97, 99
modernisation, of Christianity 221, 235
modernist, Charles Strong as 111–8
modernists 122–30
modernity, Christian response to 84–5
Moorhouse, James 7–9, 11
Moorhouse lectures 8
moral improvement, and secularism 22
moralism 237
Moran, Cardinal, and *Rerum Novarum* (1891) 66
Morling, G.H. 173
Morpeth circle 87–9
Morpeth Review 83, 87
Morris, William 105
Morwood, Michael 234 n147
Moule, C.F.D. 175
Mounier, Emmanuel 44–5
Movement for the Ordination of Women 183 n50
Mowaljarlai, David 231, 234
Moyes, John 81
Mudrooroo *see* Johnson, Colin
Muecke, Stephen 230–1
Müller, Max 111

Index

multiculturalism 232–3
Mulvaney, D.J. 218
Murdoch, Walter 80
Murray, John Courtney 150
Murray, Les 47–8
Muscio, Bernard 121, 137 n15
Muslims 54–5
mysticism 29, 33, 155, 226, 234
Naess, Arne 215
nation-building, and Christian ideals xiv
national religion, Christianity as xiv–xv
 proposal for 203–4
natural theology 11, 110, 113, 172
natural world, and religious consciousness 234
naturalism 143–4
 see also sacral naturalisms; spiritual naturalism
nature, ontologies of 212, 216
Ne Temere decree, 1908 xiii
Neander, August 108
negative theology 154, 157, 158, 160
Neilson, John Shaw 200–2
neoliberalism, 20th century 131
Neoplatonism 206
New Age writers 227, 228
New Australia, Paraguay 73, 74, 75
New Testament studies 175–6, 183
New Thought movement 42, 102
Newman, John Henry 108
Nietzsche, Friedrich 16, 18–19, 20, 129, 202, 222
Nietzschean activism 208
non-material motivations 237–8
Noonuccal, Oodgeroo *see* Oodgeroo Noonuccal
Normal Institution, Sydney 76
Norwood Baptist Church, Adelaide 118
O'Collins, Gerald 182
O'Dowd, Bernard 96, 101, 102–4, 116, 118, 205
Olcott, Colonel 34, 35
O'Murchu, Diarmuid 227

Oodgeroo Noonuccal 51–2
Oppy, Graham 165–6
Orage, A.R. 205
original sin, rejection of 96
Ormerod, Neil 172, 182
Orthodox theology 193–4, 227
 see also Greek Orthodox tradition
Otto, Rudolf 49
Pacifica: Australasian Theological Studies 172
pacificism 117
 see also conscription, opposition to
paganism 19, 21, 34
Palágyi, Melchior 145
Palapathwala, Ruwan 195
Paley, William 108
 View of the Evidences of Christianity 6
Palmer, Nettie 101, 205
Palmer, Vance 205
Panikkar, Ramon 227
pantheist ideas xvi
parareligious rituals 103
Parker, Theodore 11
Parkes, Henry 23, 68, 79
Particular Baptists 98, 173
Partridge, Percy 26
Passmore, John 26, 227
Paterson, Banjo 72
Patočka, Jan 167
Pearson, Charles Henry 90–1, 115
penal reform 132
Pentecostal theology 193
personal idealism 107, 119, 125, 134, 135, 140–6
personality, and freedom, philosophy of 142
 value of 107, 119, 127
phenomenology 142–3, 146, 149–50, 156–7, 167
 theological 152–61
philosophy, of
 religion 132–69
 and religious thought xxiv, 166, 168–9, 235
 –religion distinction 139, 145
phrenology 27
Phronema (journal) 194
physicalism 164
physics, and religion 228–9
Pickard, Stephen 192

Place, U.T. 138
place, narratives of 218–20
Plantinga, Alvin 165
Platonic idealism 208
Platonism 83–4, 108, 123
 rejection of 164
Plumwood, Val 215–7
pluralism 146–52, 227, 230–4
 see also radical pluralism
poetry 33
poets, and spirituality 3 n9
Polding, John Bede 65–6
political liberalism *see* liberalism
political thought, and religious thought xvii, 238
politicians, and Christian social thought 92 n133
politics, Christian involvement xi–xii
Ponge, Francis 55
Popper, Sir Karl 48
Porter, Muriel 182
Portus, G.V. 80–1
post-Christian 232–3
postcolonial theology 192
postcolonialism 198 n3, 232–3
posthuman debates 214
'postmodern science' 226
postmodernism 154, 192
'the postsecular' 197–8
postsecular consciousness xxiv, 196–234, 236
practical Christianity 65
practical theology 195, 196
Praed, Rosa 36–7
pragmatism 34, 237
 see also idealistic pragmatism
Preece, Gordon 195
Presbyterian Church, New South Wales 124
Presbyterianism 70, 112
Prichard, Katharine Susannah 58
Priestley, Joseph 94
Primitive Methodist Church, Adelaide 96
Princeton Seminary 122, 174
Pringle-Pattison, Seth 135, 141
process philosophy xxiv, 164, 207–15, 236

– 245 –

Protestant theologians,
  German 113, 114
Protestantism x
  diversity of xiii
  and political identity xv
  see also civic Protestantism;
    French Protestantism
Pseudo-Dionysus 155–6
psychoanalysis xxiv, 220–8,
  236
  and humanism 84
psychology, as resource for
  clergy 84–5
public education, Catholic
  rejection 79–80
  and religion 76–81
public theology 81–90
Quaife, Barzillai 133
quantum physics 164
  interpretations of 217
Radcliffe-Brown, A.R. 184
radical Christians 90
radical ecosophy 216
radical individualism 13–
  15, 19
radical pluralism 24, 216
Rahner, Karl 179–82
rationalism 18, 176
Rationalist Society 23
rationalist utilitarianism 26
rationalists 23, 76, 101, 105
Read, Peter 218–9
realism 167, 217
  Scottish 133, 137
realist metaphysics 24–5,
  46
realists 174
Reanney, Darryl 228
Red Bishop see Burgmann,
  Ernest
Redding, Paul 168
Reid, Thomas 133
religion, constructions
  of xix–xx
  criticism of xvii–xviii
  decline of 222
  Durkheimian conception
    of 86
  and education 76–81
  in historical writing xix,
    235
  –philosophy
    distinction 139, 145
  and psychoanalysis 221
  scientific study of 113
  as social reality 86–9
  and spirituality 223–6

and state see state, and
  religion
religious agencies, service
  delivery xvi
religious belief, Australian
  attitudes to 59–60
religious citizenship 87–9,
  116, 127, 136
religious controversies, press
  coverage xii, xvi n39
religious education 109
  state funding xv
  in state schools 23
religious freedom, and the
  Constitution 23
religious liberalism xxiii–
  xxiv, 93–131, 235
religious schools xvi
  rejection of state support
    for 100
religious socialism 72
religious thought, definition
  of xix
  neglect of xvii–xix
  wider context of 235
Rentoul, J.L. 115
republicanism 68–72, 115,
  236
Reznikoff, Charles 55
Richard of St Victor 181
Richardson, Henry
  Handel 16–17, 19
Richardson, Walter 16–17
Ridley College,
  Melbourne 163
Rieff, Philip, Triumph of the
  Therapeutic 222
Ritschl, Albrecht 113
Robinson, Bishop 89
Robinson, D.W.B. 175–6
Roe, Paddy 230
Roman Catholicism,
  Anglican hostility to 42–3
Romanticism 33, 42, 46,
  233
Rose, Deborah Bird 187
Rosmini 65–6
Ross, Lloyd 87
Routley, Richard see Sylvan,
  Richard
Routley, Val see Plumwood,
  Val
Royce, Josiah 29
Rush, Ormond 178
Russian philosophy 168
Ryan, Patrick Joseph 147
Sabatier, Auguste 123, 144

Sabbatarianism, opposition
  to 117
sacral naturalisms xxiv,
  199–204, 207–15, 220, 236
sacral secularity xxiii, 61–93,
  198
'the saeculum' 65–6
Santamaria, B.A. 48–9
Sartre, Jean-Paul 149
scepticism 4
Schiller, F.C. 34, 140
Schleiermacher,
  Friedrich 111
Schneerson, Menachem
  M. 54
scholastic philosophy 147–8
schools of arts xii
Schopenhauer, Arthur 8,
  218
Schuon, Frithjof 55
Schweitzer, Albert 113, 128
Schweizer, Eduard 173
science, and
  philosophy 214–5
  and the sacral xxiv,
    228–30, 236
  and theology 193
science and technology, and
  humanism 84
sciences, and
  Christianity 5–6
scientific reductionism 138
scientists, and criticism of
  religion xvii
SCM see Student Christian
  Movement
Scots Church,
  Melbourne 111, 115
Scott, Ernest 35
Scott, Rose 41
Scottish Hegelianism see
  Hegelianism, Scottish
Scottish idealism see idealism,
  Scottish
Scottish realism see realism,
  Scottish
Scotus, Duns 44
Second British
  Empire 63–4
Second Vatican Council 45,
  46, 49, 82, 147, 149, 178
sectarianism xiii, 2
'the secular', in
  Australia 61–8
  non-religious
    conceptions 66
secular humanism 131

Index

secularism 4, 21–3, 61–2
  rejection of 222
secularity, and
  secularism 235
self, conceptions of 220
self-realisation, through
  commonality 215
sentience 210–2
Serle, Geoffrey xvii
sermons, and colonial
  literature xii
sexuality, theology of 193
Shand, Alexander 142
Shaw, Bernard 205
Sheldrake, Rupert 227, 228
Sherlock, Charles 172, 195
Sherrington, Sir Charles 48
Shestov, Lev 168
Sikhs 58
Sinclaire, Frederick 101
Singer, Peter 26, 139
Sisterhood of International
  Peace 117
Slessor, Kenneth 204 n28, 208
Smart, J. 138
Smith, William
  Robertson 112
social cohesion, and
  religion 86, 88
social conservatism 126
social gospel tradition 173
social idealism 30, 80
Social Improvement Friendly
  Help and Children's Aid
  Society, Melbourne 117
social issues, responses
  to 195–6
social justice, promotion
  of 66, 111
social reform 107, 117–8, 131, 134, 136
  religious impact xi, xiv, 238
  role of state 97
  and spiritualism 27
socialism 102
  and the New
    Testament 105
  as religion 102
Socialist (journal) 102
society and religion,
  harmonisation 109–10
Society for the Study of
  Christian Sociology 118
sociology, developments
  in 113

Sophia (journal) 150, 162
soul, notion of 205
South Australian Fabian
  Society 90
Southwell, Charles 21
Spence, Catherine Helen 80, 95–7
Spence, William
  Guthrie 72
Spencer, Herbert 6, 12, 23, 32, 33, 140
Spencer, Walter
  Baldwin 184–5
Spinoza, Baruch 214
spiritual democracy 236
spiritual naturalism 36
spiritual values 3
spiritualism 17, 21, 26–7, 100–1, 102, 105
spiritualists 26–30
spirituality, and Australian
  poets 3 n9
  Brady's redefinition 50–1
  shift from religion 223–6
Spurgeon, C.H. 173
Srzednicki, Jan T.J. 167
St Andrew's Theological
  College, Sydney 122, 172
St Mark's National
  Theological Centre,
  Canberra 89, 196
St Mark's Review 172
Stanley, Dean Arthur 108
Stanner, W.E.H. 185–6
state, and religion 197, 203–4
  exclusion of religion
    from 66
  see also Christianity, and
    state; church and state
Stead, Christina 19
Steiner, Rudolf 37
Stephens, Alfred George 17–18
Stephensen, P.R. 19, 208
Stewart, Douglas 204–5
Stewart, Harold 46, 55
Stewart, John McKellar 18, 152–3, 166
Stirner, Max 222
Stockton, Eugene 226–8
Stone, Julius 53
Stout, G.F. 142
Stow, Randolph 56
Strauss, David 4, 13, 89, 123
Strehlow, C.F.T. 184

Strong, Charles 29, 41, 81, 98, 102, 105, 111–8, 134–5
Strong, Jane 118
Student Christian
  Movement 80, 92 n133
Suchting, Wal 208
supernaturalism, rejection
  of 9, 23, 25, 31, 106, 109, 116, 125, 128–9, 130, 131, 164
Sutherland, Alexander 97–8
Swedenborg, Emanuel 16, 29
Swinburne, Richard 165
Sydney Theosophical
  Lodge 36
Sykes, Alfred Depledge 118
Sylvan, Richard 215–6
Symbolism 32–3
Syme, David 30–2
Syme, Ebenezer 30–1
Symes, Joseph 21–2
Symington, Neville 221
Tacey, David 223–6
Tavistock Clinic,
  London 221
Taylor, Charles, *A Secular
  Age* 62, 197
Teilhard de Chardin,
  Pierre 227
Temple, William 81, 83, 107–8, 124
Tennant, Kylie 41 n137
Tennyson, Alfred Lord 12
Terry, W.H. 102
theiology – theology
  distinction 154
theism 162, 164–5
  challenges to 131, 163
theologians, Australian 172
  visits to Australia 172
theological colleges 171
theological journals 172
theological
  modernism 106–21
theological phenomenology *see*
  phenomenology, theological
theology, development
  of xxiv, 170–96, 236
Theosophical Society 29, 102
theosophy 32, 34–7, 100–1, 106, 220
Thiering, Barbara 50, 129–30
'thisness' of things 44
Thompson, Edward 209
Thoreau, Henry David 13
Thornhill, John 172, 179

– 247 –

Tillich, Paul 89, 211
Tindal, Matthew xvi
Tocsin (journal) 104
Toland, John xvi
Torres Strait Islanders, cultural practices 186
trade unionism, as religion 71–2
Trakakis, Nick 166
transcendence 56, 237
Transcendental Thomism 179–82
transcendentalism 29, 33, 103
transcultural eclecticism 230–3
transnational influence xxi–xxii, 93, 108, 117, 119, 123, 128, 140, 146–7, 153, 159, 235, 238
The Trinity 178–82
  rejection of 9, 11
Troeltsch, Ernst 88
'true religion' xiii, 11, 63, 69, 77, 94, 109, 125
Tucker, Horace 117
Tulip, Marie 182
Turner, Archibald 90
Turner, Ian xvii
Tyndale, William 174
Ullathorne, Bernard 66
Unaipon, David 52, 231
unbelief xxiii, 1–2, 21, 59
Underhill, Evelyn 124
Unemployed Workers Movement 83
Ungunmerr-Baumann, Miriam Rose 227
Unitarianism 9, 10, 11, 68, 94–106
United Aboriginal and Indigenous Christian Congress 191
Uniting Church of Australia 178
  and social issues 118
universities, democratisation of 107
  and theology 171
  see also names of universities, e.g. Deakin University
University of Melbourne, Philosophy Dept 148–9, 161–2, 165
University of Sydney 32, 119 n115, 208, 213
University of Tasmania 100

utilitarianism 132–3, 139, 238
  critique of 91
  see also rationalist utilitarianism
utopianism 72–6, 117–8
Vattimo, Gianni 158
Vaughan, R.W.B. 66
Vedanta *see* Advaita Vedanta
Veiling, Terry 195
Victorian Association of Spiritualists 28
Victorian Rationalist Association 102
Victorian Socialist Party 102, 104, 105 n58
Village Settlement Movement 117–118
Vision (journal) 208
vitalism xxiv, 204–7, 236
Voegelin, Eric 46
von Harnack, Adolf *see* Harnack, Adolf von
von Hügel, Baron *see* Hügel, Baron von
Wainwright, Elaine 183
Walker, Alan 89
Walker, Thomas 26
Walt Whitman movement 103
war memorials 67
Ward, Russel xvii, xviii
Warfield, Benjamin 122, 174
Waten, Judah 58
Watts, G. Stuart 80 n76, 128–9
WEA *see* Workers' Educational Association
Webb, C.C.J. 84
Webb, Francis 44, 199 n4
Wedgwood, J.I. 36
Weil, Simone 153
Weininger, Otto 16
wellbeing, and meaning-making 223
West, cultural decline 222
West, John 64 n16, 91
Westcott, B.F. 8
Westminster Confession, proposed reform 115
White, Erin 182
White, Patrick 38–41
Whitehead, A.N. 207, 209, 210
Whitman, Walt 205
Wieman, Henry Nelson 211

Wigner, Eugene 48
Wilber, Ken 218, 227
will, Schopenhauer's philosophy 8
Williams, Hartley 11
Williams, Raymond 209
Wilmot, Frank 101
Wilton, Charles 11
Winton, Tim 234
Wise, Bernard 91
Wittgenstein, Ludwig 148
Women's Christian Temperance Union xi
women's liberation *see* feminism
women's organisations, Christian involvement xi
Women's Peace Army 41
women's suffrage 97
Women's Suffrage League xi
Wood, D'Arcy 178
Wood, George Arnold 119 n115
Woodbury, Austin 148
Woods, John Crawford 96
Woolley, John 108–10
The Worker (newspaper) 73
workers' education 80, 107
Workers' Educational Association xii, 80, 107, 121, 128
Wright, Judith 204, 205–7
Young Women's Christian Association xi
Zen, and Harold Stewart 55
Zionism 53, 54
Zubrzycki, George 232 n138

Milton Keynes UK
Ingram Content Group UK Ltd.
UKHW021823100424
440890UK00007B/85